JOURNAL FOR THE STUDY OF THE NEW TESTAMENT
SUPPLEMENT SERIES
67

Executive Editor
Stanley E. Porter

JSOT Press
Sheffield

The Portrait
of Philip in Acts

A Study of Roles and Relations

F. Scott Spencer

Journal for the Study of the New Testament
Supplement Series 67

To Janet
who understands

Published by JSOT Press
JSOT Press is an imprint of
Sheffield Academic Press Ltd
The University of Sheffield
343 Fulwood Road
Sheffield S10 3BP
England

Typeset by Sheffield Academic Press
and
Printed on acid-free paper in Great Britain
by Billing & Sons Ltd
Worcester

British Library Cataloguing in Publication Data

Spencer, F. Scott
    Portrait of Philip in Acts: Study of Roles and
    Relations. —(JSNT Supplement
    Series, ISSN 0143-5108; No. 67)
    I. Title II. Series
    226.6

ISBN 1-85075-340-7

CONTENTS

PREFACE

This volume represents a substantial revision of a doctoral thesis submitted in 1989 to the Department of Theology in the University of Durham, England. Drafts of material in Chapters 2, 4 and 6 were aired at the British New Testament Conference (Durham, England, 1987) and the annual meetings of the Southeastern Commission for the Study of Religion (Charlotte, North Carolina, 1990) and the North Carolina Religious Studies Association (Winston-Salem, North Carolina, 1990).

My study in England (1984–88) was facilitated by an Overseas Research Scholarship, a Theology Scholarship and Resident Tutorship at the College of St Hild and St Bede, Durham, and a Tyndale Research Grant at Tyndale House, Cambridge.

I am indebted to several people for their various contributions to my work, although I naturally assume full responsibility for the final product. Special thanks goes to James D.G. Dunn, Lightfoot Professor of Divinity, for first suggesting the focus on 'Philip' and then carefully supervising the research and writing of my doctoral thesis. I also remember fondly his and Meta's gracious hospitality on numerous occasions.

I am also grateful to my examiners, Professor I. Howard Marshall and Dr Andrew N. Chester, for their constructive comments, and to Professor C.K. Barrett for two stimulating discussions in his home and his many valuable contributions to Lukan scholarship reflected in the bibliography.

During the past three years of maintaining a busy teaching schedule alongside revising this book for publication, I have appreciated the encouragement of my colleagues at Wingate College.

The staff at Sheffield Academic Press are to be commended for their expert handling of the entire project. I am especially grateful to Dr David Hill, the former Executive Editor of the JSNT Supplement Series, for accepting this study in the series and offering much insight and encouragement throughout the revision process. Mr Andrew Kirk also merits my thanks for his skillful oversight of the final stages of publication.

Finally, words cannot adequately express the debt I owe my wife, best friend and colleague, Dr Janet M. Spencer, for her unfailing support and understanding even while pursuing her own scholarly career. And I must not forget our daughters, Lauren Michael, who was born in England as this book was just beginning to take shape, and Meredith Leigh, who was born just after this book's completion. They thus frame this work and keep it in proper perspective.

ABBREVIATIONS

AB	Anchor Bible
AbrN	*Abr-Nahrain*
AGJU	Arbeiten zur Geschichte des antiken Judentums und des Urchristentums
AnBib	Analecta biblica
ANRW	*Aufstieg und Niedergang der römischen Welt*
AOAT	Alter Orient und Altes Testament
ATR	*Anglican Theological Review*
ATANT	Abhandlungen zur Theologie des Alten und Neuen Testaments
BAGD	W. Bauer, W.F. Arndt, F.W. Gingrich, and F.W. Danker, *Greek-English Lexicon of the New Testament*
BARev	*Biblical Archaeology Review*
BBB	Bonner biblische Beiträge
BETL	Bibliotheca ephemeridum theologicarum lovaniensium
Bib	*Biblica*
BJRL	*Bulletin of the John Rylands University Library of Manchester*
BNTC	Black's New Testament Commentaries
BTB	*Biblical Theology Bulletin*
BurH	*Buried History*
BWANT	Beiträge zur Wissenschaft vom Alten und Neuen Testament
BZ	*Biblische Zeitschrift*
BZAW	Beihefte zur *ZAW*
BZNW	Beihefte zur *ZNW*
CBQ	*Catholic Biblical Quarterly*
CTL	Crown Theological Library
EBib	Etudes bibliques
EKKNT	Evangelisch-Katholischer Kommentar zum Neuen Testament
EvQ	*Evangelical Quarterly*
EvT	*Evangelische Theologie*
ExpTim	*Expository Times*
EWNT	H. Balz and G. Schneider (eds.), *Exegetisches Wörterbuch zum Neuen Testament*
FB	Forschung zur Bibel
FRLANT	Forschungen zur Religion und Literatur des Alten und Neuen Testaments
GTA	Göttinger theologische Arbeiten

HNT	Handbuch zum Neuen Testament
HSM	Harvard Semitic Monographs
HTKNT	Herders theologischer Kommentar zum Neuen Testament
HTR	*Harvard Theological Review*
HUCA	*Hebrew Union College Annual*
IBS	*Irish Biblical Studies*
IDB	G.A. Buttrick (ed.), *Interpreter's Dictionary of the Bible*
IDBSup	*IDB*, Supplementary Volume
Int	*Interpretation*
JAC	*Jahrbuch für Antike und Christentum*
JB	Jerusalem Bible
JBL	*Journal of Biblical Literature*
JJS	*Journal of Jewish Studies*
JQR	*Jewish Quarterly Review*
JSJ	*Journal for the Study of Judaism in the Persian, Hellenistic and Roman Period*
JSNT	*Journal for the Study of the New Testament*
JSNTSup	*Journal for the Study of the New Testament*, Supplement Series
JSOT	*Journal for the Study of the Old Testament*
JSS	*Journal of Semitic Studies*
LCL	Loeb Classical Library
LEC	Library of Early Christianity
LD	Lectio divina
MNTC	Moffatt NT Commentary
NCB	New Century Bible
Neot	*Neotestamentica*
NHS	Nag Hammadi Studies
NICNT	New International Commentary on the New Testament
NIDNTT	C. Brown (ed.), *The New International Dictionary of New Testament Theology*
NIGTC	New International Greek Testament Commentary
NIV	*New International Version*
NovT	*Novum Testamentum*
NovTSup	*Novum Testamentum* Supplements
NRT	*La nouvelle revue théologique*
NRSV	New Revised Standard Version
NTD	Das Neue Testament Deutsch
NTAbh	Neutestamentliche Abhandlungen
NTL	New Testament Library
NTS	*New Testament Studies*
OBT	Overtures to Biblical Theology
PerRelSt	*Perspectives in Religious Studies*
RB	*Revue biblique*
REB	Revised English Bible
RelSRev	*Religious Studies Review*

ResQ	*Restoration Quarterly*
RHPR	*Revue d' historie et de philosophie religieuses*
RSV	*Revised Standard Version*
SANT	Studien zum Alten und Neuen Testament
SBLDS	SBL Dissertation Series
SBLMS	SBL Monograph Series
SBLSP	SBL Seminar Papers
SBS	Stuttgarter Bibelstudien
SBT	Studies in Biblical Theology
SJLA	Studies in Judaism in Late Antiquity
SNT	Studien zum Neuen Testament
SNTSMS	Society of New Testament Studies Monograph Series
SPB	Studia postbiblica
TDNT	G. Kittel and G. Friedrich (eds.), *Theological Dictionary of the New Testament*
THKNT	Theologischer Handkommentar zum Neuen Testament
TLZ	*Theologischer Literaturzeitung*
TNTC	Tyndale New Testament Commentaries
TQ	*Theologische Quartalschrift*
TRev	*Theologische Revue*
TU	Texte und Untersuchungen
TynBul	*Tyndale Bulletin*
TZ	*Theologische Zeitschrift*
VC	*Vigiliae christianae*
WMANT	Wissenschaftliche Monographien zum Alten und Neuen Testament
WTJ	*Westminster Theological Journal*
WUNT	Wissenschaftliche Untersuchungen zum Neuen Testament
ZAW	*Zeitschrift für die alttestamentliche Wissenschaft*
ZDPV	*Zeitschrift des deutschen Palästina-Vereins*
ZNW	*Zeitschrift für die neutestamentliche Wissenschaft*
ZTK	*Zeitschrift für Theologie und Kirche*

Chapter 1

INTRODUCTION

1. *Purpose and Rationale*

The purpose of this study is to analyze the literary portrait of Philip in the book of Acts. Its concern is not so much with burrowing beneath the text to uncover the 'historical' Philip as it is with carefully examining the final form of Acts to discover the role(s) which the 'character' Philip plays in the narrative. This is not to say that all historical study will be abandoned (see the discussion of method below) or that the 'literary' and 'historical' Philips must be sharply distinguished from one another as bearing little or no resemblance. The point is simply to set clear parameters for investigation, and, as we shall see, an analysis of Philip's characterization in Acts will raise more than enough issues to occupy our attention.

One major reason why there are plenty of matters to deal with is that Philip has been virtually ignored in New Testament scholarship. Current monographs devoted to the study of Philip are in very short supply (I have not actually discovered any worth mentioning). Various articles may be found related to the Philip material in Acts, but for the most part these are concerned with special topics other than Philip himself, such as the origins of Simonian Gnosticism[1] or the relationship between water-baptism and Spirit-reception.[2] The

1. E.g. E. Haenchen, 'Simon Magus in der Apostelgeschichte', in *Gnosis und Neues Testament* (ed. K.-W. Tröger; Studien aus Religionswissenschaft und Theologie; Berlin: Evangelische, 1973); G. Lüdemann, 'The Acts of the Apostles and the Beginning of Simonian Gnosis', *NTS* 33 (1987), pp. 420-26; R. Bergmeier, 'Die Gestalt des Simon Magus in Act 8 und in der simonianischen Gnosis—Aporien einer Gesamtdeutung', *ZNW* 77 (1986), pp. 267-75.
2. E.g. O.C. Edwards, Jr, 'The Exegesis of Acts 8:4-25 and its Implications for Confirmation and Glossolalia: A Review Article of Haenchen's Commentary', *ATR* (Supp. Ser.) 2 (1973), pp. 100-12; M. Gourgues, 'Esprit des commencements et

study of key personalities has been a hallmark of recent *Actaforschung*, but the spotlight has fallen principally upon Peter and Paul (predictably) and Stephen,[1] while Philip has been left in the shadows.

Of course, it may be argued that Philip has been largely bypassed in Lukan scholarship because he is simply not a character of great significance. But even a cursory look at Acts would suggest otherwise. Philip appears as a principal actor in a pivotal chapter (Acts 8) charting the gospel's first advance beyond the Jewish capital of Jerusalem, and he proves to be a successful missionary/evangelist within a narrative which clearly prizes such achievement. Philip also is associated on some level with all three Lukan heroes mentioned above: Stephen (Acts 6.5), Peter (8.5-25) and Paul (21.8); if a man is judged by the company he keeps, then Philip seems to deserve more respect. Finally, since the account of Philip's ministry incorporates a number of leading Lukan themes—such as outreach to the Samaritans, confrontation with magic, the beginnings of the Gentile mission, supernatural guidance and the practice of hospitality—one would suspect Philip's role within the total Lukan story to be more than peripheral.

Taken together, these notable components of the portrait of Philip in Acts would seem to certify his honored place within the narrative. But other elements of this portrait may be construed as denigrating his status or stigmatizing his competence in some fashion; for example, (1) his more mundane functions of waiting on tables (Acts 6.5) and providing hospitality (21.8) in contrast to his more 'spiritual' and

---

esprit des prolongements dans les *Actes*: Note sur la "Pentecôste des Samaritains" (*Act*. VIII,5-25)', *RB* 93 (1986), pp. 376-85.

1. See the surveys of research in E. Richard, 'Luke—Writer, Theologian, Historian: Research and Orientation of the 1970's', *BTB* 13 (1983), p. 7; and F. Bovon, *Luke the Theologian: Thirty-Three Years of Research (1950–83)* (PTMS, 12; Allison Park, PA: Pickwick, 1987), pp. 344-59. Special recent studies related to Peter, Paul and Stephen include W. Dietrich, *Das Petrusbild der lukanischen Schriften* (Stuttgart: Kohlhammer, 1972); J. Jervell, *The Unknown Paul: Essays on Luke–Acts and Early Christian History* (Minneapolis: Augsburg, 1984); J. Roloff, 'Das Paulus-Darstellung des Lukas: Ihre geschichtlichen Voraussetzungen und ihr theologisches Ziel', *EvT* 39 (1979), pp. 310-31; G. Stanton, 'Stephen in Lucan Perspective', in *Studia Biblica 1978*. III. *Papers on Paul and Other New Testament Authors* (JSNTSup, 3; Sheffield: JSOT Press, 1980), pp. 345-60; J. Kilgallen, *The Stephen Speech: A Literary and Redactional Study of Acts 7.2-53* (AnBib, 67; Rome: Biblical Institute, 1976).

spectacular pursuits of proclamation and miracle-working, and (2) his apparent failures to expose the chicanery of Simon Magus and to impart the Spirit to his Samaritan converts (both duties are reserved for Peter, 8.14-24).

To what extent, if any, these aspects may be judged as truly damaging to Philip's reputation in Acts can only be determined after thorough literary analysis. But in any event, they should not prompt us from the start to cast Philip aside as a lowly figure of little consequence in Luke's presentation. If in fact Philip does emerge within Acts as the target of some deliberate 'smear' campaign, then he is certainly a character of some standing treated seriously, even if critically. After all, there is no need to bother with downgrading someone who has little or no stature in the first place.

In short, the juxtaposition of commendable and (potentially) questionable facets of Philip's ministry in Acts suggests that his role in the narrative is both complex and significant. He is more of a 'round' and 'dynamic' character (as opposed to a 'flat' and 'static' one), a multidimensional figure who exhibits 'a variety of potentially conflicting traits' and whose 'basic profile changes over the course of the narrative'.[1] As such a figure, Philip invites careful analysis and deserves to be brought out of the shadows and given his day in the sun in Lukan scholarship.

While modern research has reflected scant interest in Philip's literary role within Acts, it is interesting to note that various scholars, sensing something of Philip's historical importance within first-century Christianity, have speculated on his involvement in the composition of certain New Testament books. Indeed, Philip the evangelist seems to be a favorite nominee for author/source of a number of anonymous New Testament documents whose origins remain largely a mystery. Alternately, Philip has been proposed as (1) a man of 'both originality and enterprise' responsible for composing the first 13 chapters of the Gospel of Mark ('the original Mark');[2] (2) a major source for the special material in Luke's Gospel, including the infancy stories, the Sermon on the Plain and the travel narrative in the central

---

1. M.A. Powell, *What Is Narrative Criticism?* (Minneapolis, MN: Fortress Press, 1990), p. 55, dependent on E.M. Forster, *Aspects of the Novel* (ed. O. Stallybrass; Harmondsworth: Penguin Books, 1974), pp. 73-81.

2. E. Trocmé, *The Formation of the Gospel according to Mark* (London: SPCK, 1975), pp. 253-59.

section;[1] (3) a major source (along with his daughters) for presumed Samaritan traditions underlying the Fourth Gospel;[2] and (4) the Paulinist author of the letter to the Hebrews, supposedly written from Caesarea to Jewish Christians in Jerusalem.[3]

After enumerating a similar (though longer) list of hypothetical roles which scholars have assigned to Stephen the martyr (Philip's 'Hellenist' associate), G. Stanton understandably quips: 'One is tempted to say in desperation: will the real Stephen please stand up!'[4] He also exposes a common weakness in these various investigations of Stephen: they fail to examine adequately the complex portrait of Stephen within the Lukan narrative before moving on to more dubious matters of Stephen's alleged relationship to other New Testament books and traditions in which his name never appears.[5] Likewise, I would suggest, insufficient attention has been paid to the portrait of Philip in Acts before advancing speculative theories concerning his wider contribution to Christian origins. Ultimately, any sound assessment of Philip's historical role within early Christianity must be coordinated with a thorough study of his literary role in Acts, especially since Luke's presentation remains both the earliest and fullest account of Philip available to us.[6]

2. *Structure and Method*

A study of the portrait of Philip in Acts could be structured either sequentially or geographically. In the first case, we would begin with the first reference to Philip in Acts 6.5 and then proceed in order

---

1. B. Reicke, *The Roots of the Synoptic Gospels* (Philadelphia: Fortress Press, 1986), pp. 169-73, 187-88.

2. A.M. Johnson, Jr, 'Philip the Evangelist and the Gospel of John', *AbrN* 16 (1975–76), pp. 49-72.

3. W.M. Ramsay, *Luke the Physician and Other Studies in the History of Religion* (Grand Rapids: Baker, repr. 1956 [1908]), pp. 303-305.

4. Stanton, 'Stephen', p. 345.

5. Stanton particularly laments the frequent disjointing of the Stephen speech and narrative ('Stephen', pp. 346-47).

6. For a similar emphasis on the priority of careful literary analysis over historical reconstruction with respect to the Gospel texts and the figure of Jesus, see S. Freyne, *Galilee, Jesus and the Gospels: Literary Approaches and Historical Investigations* (Philadelphia: Fortress Press, 1988), p. 3; and G. Stanton, *The Gospels and Jesus* (Oxford: Oxford University Press, 1989), pp. 2-3, 12-13, 139.

through the rest of the Philip material up through the final scene in 21.8-14. This approach has the advantage of tracing the portrait of Philip step-by-step as it unfolds in Acts. In the second instance, we would focus on the significance of Philip's ministry in key locations: Jerusalem (Acts 6.1-7), Samaria (8.4-25), the coastal plain (8.26-40) and Caesarea (21.8-9). At least since the work of Conzelmann, scholars have been alert to the importance of geographical elements within Luke's narrative.[1]

The structure which I will follow, however, in examining the Lukan *Philippusbild*, while appreciative of both sequential and geographical factors, deals principally with *relational* aspects of Philip's characterization. Specifically, I will explore Philip's relations, on the one hand, with notable individuals or groups he evangelizes (Samaritans, Simon Magus, Ethiopian eunuch) and, on the other hand, with important fellow-ministers in the early church (Peter and Paul). Such an approach capitalizes on Luke's well-known interest in the boundary-breaking outreach of select missionaries to diverse segments of humankind. It also takes seriously a basic premise of both literary and sociological analysis, which regards the individual—within a story or society—as part of a network of relationships which profoundly shapes and defines his or her identity.

Chapter 2 examines Philip's missionary breakthrough to the Samaritans, as reported in Acts 8.5-13. Although I will consider this incident from a variety of angles, the dominant concern will be to determine its significance as the climax of a series of episodes within Luke–Acts involving the Samaritan people or territory.

Chapter 3 continues to deal with Philip's Samaritan mission but focuses more narrowly upon his encounter with a single, notorious Samaritan: Simon Magus. Here special attention will be paid to Philip's role as a combatant of magical power (like Paul) and a model of true greatness (in contrast to Simon).

Chapter 4 turns to consider the episode at the end of Acts 8 featuring Philip's witness to the Ethiopian eunuch. Again a variety of aspects will be investigated against the backdrop of Luke's entire narrative, but particular emphasis will be placed on discerning the eunuch's peculiar social identity and the nature of Philip's achievement in evangelizing such a figure.

1. H. Conzelmann, *The Theology of Luke* (London: SCM Press, 2nd edn, 1982), pp. 18-94.

Chapters 5 and 6 aim to determine Philip's stature as a Christian minister in relation to the two dominant heroes in Acts, Peter and Paul. In the first case, Philip will be compared with Peter in the context of their overlapping ministries to the early Jerusalem community (Acts 6.1-7), the Samaritans (8.5-25) and 'God-fearing' Gentile officials (8.26-40; 10.1-11.18). Lastly, the study of Philip's association with Paul will concentrate principally upon their brief meeting in Philip's Caesarean home (21.8-14), but it will also attempt to unravel the implications of Philip's earlier flight from Jerusalem on account of Paul's (Saul's) violent campaign against the church (8.1-5; 9.1-2).

Each chapter will take up various methodological matters appropriate to the particular literary unit under investigation. But there are certain broad interpretive perspectives which have influenced the entire study and merit brief discussion presently in relation to recent trends in Lukan scholarship.

Post-war study of Luke–Acts was dominated for a number of years by a *redaktionsgeschichtlich* approach pioneered by such notable German scholars as Hans Conzelmann and Ernst Haenchen.[1] Particular attention was paid to Luke as a creative editor (redactor) who had shaped the various sources at his disposal into an extended account supporting his peculiar theological bias (*Tendenz*). Accordingly, it was thought that Luke's theology could best be discovered by examining the ways in which Luke altered his received material. Since it was assumed that Luke was directly dependent upon Mark in composing his Gospel, deviations of the Lukan text from Mark in parallel passages were regarded as especially revealing of Luke's theological interests. Concerning the book of Acts, certain 'breaks and seams' in the text were pinpointed as supposed indicators of editorial activity and deliberate modification of underlying traditions. Among the conclusions emerging from such analysis was the view that Luke was

---

1. See H. Conzelmann, *Theology of Luke*; *Die Apostelgeschichte* (HNT; Tübingen: Mohr [Paul Siebeck], 2nd edn, 1972); 'Luke's Place in the Development of Early Christianity', in *Studies in Luke–Acts: Essays Presented in Honor of Paul Schubert* (ed. L.E. Keck and J.L. Martyn; London: SPCK, repr. 1976 [1966]), pp. 298-316; and E. Haenchen, *The Acts of the Apostles: A Commentary* (Oxford: Basil Blackwell, 1971); 'The Book of Acts as Source Material for the History of Early Christianity', in Keck and Martyn (eds.), *Studies in Luke–Acts*, pp. 258-78. Both scholars, of course, built on the form-critical work of M. Dibelius (cf. *Studies in the Acts of the Apostles* [ed. H. Greeven; London: SCM Press, 1956]).

preoccupied with 'early catholic' concerns of ecclesiastical institutionalization, appropriate to an age when the parousia was no longer expected to be imminent.

More recent German Lukan scholarship, while not always endorsing a thoroughgoing 'early catholic' assessment of Lukan theology, is still heavily dependent upon Conzelmann and Haenchen in its basic methodology. Standard tradition-historical and redaction-critical questions still set the prevailing agenda. Even in *Actaforschung*, where source analysis is (admittedly) extremely problematic, attempts to uncover Luke's purpose by separating tradition from redaction continue to characterize most commentaries and special studies.[1] Likewise, segments of contemporary British, French and American scholarship reflect a continuing commitment to historically oriented, redaction-critical investigation of Luke–Acts, although again it must be emphasized that specific interpretive conclusions now often run counter to the opinions of Conzelmann and Haenchen.[2]

During the last 15 years or so, however, numerous voices have been raised, especially on the American scene, calling for a new approach to the study of Luke–Acts.[3] While most of these scholars continue to

1. See the useful survey of German commentaries on Acts from 1980 to 1985 in F. Hahn, 'Der gegenwärtige Stand der Erforschung der Apostelgeschichte: Kommentare und Aufsatzbände 1980–1985', *TRev* 82 (1986), pp. 177-90. A. Weiser (*Die Apostelgeschichte* [2 vols.; Ökumenischer Taschenbuchkommentar zum NT 5/1, 2; Gütersloh: Gerd Mohn; Würzburg: Echter, 1981–85]) and G. Lüdemann (*Das frühe Christentum nach den Traditionen der Apostelgeschichte: Ein Kommentar* [Göttingen: Vandenhoeck & Ruprecht, 1987]) give particular attention to detailed identification of traditional and redactional elements within each unit of Acts.

2. E.g. I.H. Marshall, *The Gospel of Luke: A Commentary on the Greek Text* (NIGTC; Exeter: Paternoster Press, 1978); J. Dupont, *Nouvelles études sur les Actes des Apôtres* (LD, 118; Paris: Cerf, 1984); J.A. Fitzmyer, *The Gospel according to Luke* (2 vols.; AB, 28; Garden City, NY: Doubleday, 1981–85). See the survey of recent scholarship in the new edition of W.W. Gasque, *A History of the Interpretation of the Acts of the Apostles* (Peabody, MA: Hendrickson, 1989), pp. 345-59, including the striking assessment of typical reactions to Conzelmann: 'One conclusion that unites nearly all recent study on Luke–Acts is that Conzelmann's classic formulation of the purpose of the Lukan writings. . . was incorrect' (p. 346).

3. C.H. Talbert (review of *The Gospel according to Luke [X-XXIV]*, by J.A. Fitzmyer, *CBQ* 48 [1986], p. 337) marks 1974 as a watershed in Lukan studies. In that year P.S. Minear delivered his ground-breaking lectures (later published

appreciate redaction criticism as a legitimate tool of research, they have also become increasingly aware of the limitations of its typical application to Lukan studies. In particular, four problems have been exposed.[1]

1. A zealous practice of redaction criticism runs the risk of reading too much into divergences between a text and its alleged source(s). In Luke's case, deviations from Mark do not necessarily reflect tendentious editorial changes. The possibility must not be minimized that such differences represent simple stylistic variations or even the influence of independent Lukan traditions.

2. In determining Luke's theological purpose(s), consideration of traditional material which Luke has taken over *unchanged* may be just as vital as concentrating upon supposed revisions of sources. When Luke incorporated various traditions (including Markan) into his literary work, he made them his own and accorded them a significant function within his overall narrative.[2]

3. While the standard 'two-source' theory predicated upon Markan priority still represents the dominant approach to Gospel origins, its status as an 'assured result' of New Testament criticism is no longer as secure as it once was. Important questions have been raised, refinements have been suggested, and other viable paradigms have been advanced.[3] As a result, interpretive schemes tied too closely to any single source hypothesis are increasingly proving less convincing.

4. The lack of contemporary 'synoptic' parallels to the book of Acts makes the hunt for precise sources a highly speculative venture.

---

as *To Heal and to Reveal: The Prophetic Vocation according to Luke* [New York: Seabury, 1976]), and the Luke–Acts Seminar of the SBL began (see findings in two volumes edited by Talbert: *Perspectives on Luke–Acts* [Danville, VA: Association of Baptist Professors of Religion; Edinburgh: T. & T. Clark, 1978]; and *Luke–Acts: New Perspectives from the Society of Biblical Literature* [New York: Crossroad, 1984]).

1. See C.H. Talbert, 'Shifting Sands: The Recent Study of the Gospel of Luke', *Int* 30 (1976), pp. 392-95.

2. Cf. C.M. Tuckett, *Reading the New Testament: Methods of Interpretation* (London: SPCK, 1987), p. 122; R.C. Tannehill, *The Narrative Unity of Luke–Acts: A Literary Interpretation* (2 vols.; Philadelphia: Fortress Press, 1986–90), I, p. 6; I.H. Marshall, *Luke: Historian and Theologian* (Grand Rapids: Zondervan, 1970), pp. 19-20, 218.

3. See, e.g., M.D. Goulder, *Luke: A New Paradigm* (2 vols.; JSNTSup, 30; Sheffield: JSOT Press, 1989).

Accordingly, efforts to determine at what points and to what extent Luke has edited received traditions are prone to be equally dubious. Guesses may be made on the basis of presumed dislocations (breaks and seams) in the text, but detecting these dislocations remains a considerably subjective enterprise, lacking sufficient controlling criteria.[1] Moreover, excessive concern with supposed *breaks* in the narrative may cause one to slight the importance of numerous transparent *links* within the story as indicators of Luke's theology.

In the face of these observations, Lukan scholars are increasingly opting for an analytical approach which focuses upon Luke–Acts as a unified literary whole whose message is discovered principally through the study of interlocking narrative patterns and themes in the final form of the text. Luke–Acts is being viewed not so much as a 'window' into traditions and histories lying behind it as a 'mirror' reflecting the dimensions of its own 'narrative world'.[2] Or put another way, concern for positioning the Lukan material within a diachronic stream of tradition history is giving way to mounting interest in more synchronic analyses of the numerous literary connections binding together the entire work.[3] Comparing Luke with the other Gospels may still prove useful in isolating what is distinctively Lukan, but the ultimate interpretive context is taken to be Luke's own presentation. The best commentary on Luke and Acts is Luke–Acts.[4]

In charting these recent literary-critical developments in Lukan (and other Gospel) study, S.D. Moore distinguishes between 'composition criticism' and 'narrative criticism'. The former, illustrated by R.F. O'Toole's *The Unity of Luke's Theology*, represents 'a holistic variation of redaction criticism in which the work itself (in this case, Luke–Acts), viewed rigorously and persistently in its entirety, becomes the primary context for interpreting any part of it'. Still, the

---

1. Regarding the continued attempts by commentators on Acts to distinguish tradition and redaction, Hahn comments: 'Hier wird weiterzuarbeiten sein; vor allem ist eine brauchbare Kriteriologie immer noch ein Desiderat' ('Gegenwärtige Stand', col. 190; see also cols. 180-81).

2. Cf. Powell, *What Is Narrative Criticism?*, p. 8.

3. However, the recent work of M.C. Parsons (*The Departure of Jesus in Luke–Acts: The Ascension Narratives in Context* [JSNTSup, 21; Sheffield: JSOT Press, 1987]) represents a creative combination of diachronic and synchronic approaches.

4. The emphasis on the unity of Luke and Acts through the hyphenated title 'Luke–Acts' is scarcely a new phenomenon, dating back to the pioneering work of H.J. Cadbury (*The Making of Luke-Acts* [London: Macmillan, 1927], pp. 8-11).

interpretive agenda remains principally theological, aiming 'to para-phrase Luke's. . . christological, ecclesiological, soteriological, and ethical message, so far as it can be deduced from the narrative format'. 'Narrative criticism', on the other hand, represented by R.C. Tannehill's two volumes on *The Narrative Unity of Luke–Acts,* also takes an avowedly holistic approach to the text but focuses much more on elements such as plot, point of view, character and conflict within Luke's narrative, utilizing techniques common to secular literary criticism. An interest in Luke's *story* predominates over his theology.[1]

The present work on Luke's portrait of Philip owes much to the recent shift in Lukan studies but should not be restrictively tied to any one method. As stated above, I intend to concentrate on analyzing the Philip material in its narrative context of Luke–Acts—a clearly 'holistic' approach with primary attention to the final form of the Lukan text. More specifically, this study is akin to O'Toole's 'composition' analysis in certain respects. I maintain an interest in classic theological issues, especially those pertaining to church and ministry, the Spirit and salvation, as these relate to Philip's presenta-tion in Acts; my chief partners in dialogue remain traditional Lukan scholars rather than modern literary critics; and I consistently follow the older convention of referring to the writer of Luke–Acts simply as 'Luke', without distinguishing between real author, implied author and narrator.[2]

On the other hand, at various points this study is more like Tannehill's 'narrative-critical' investigation. For example, in dealing with Philip's mission to the Samaritans, his clash with Simon the magician and his accommodation of Paul in Caesarea, I pay special

---

1. S.D. Moore, *Literary Criticism and the Gospels: The Theoretical Challenge* (New Haven: Yale University Press, 1989), pp. 4-7.

2. I make no assumptions, however, regarding the historical identity of 'Luke' other than that he (she?) was part of the 'we'-group who travelled with Paul to Philip's home (see Chapter 6 below). The lack of distinction between real and implied author poses no great problem, since, as Powell avers with respect to the Gospels, 'no two of these works have the same author and there is no reason to believe that the real authors did not fully accept the ideas expressed in their books' (*What Is Narrative Criticism?*, p. 5; cf. p. 97 on the implied author as a possible 'index' to the real author). J.M. Dawsey's theory (espoused in *The Lukan Voice: Confusion and Irony in the Gospel of Luke* [Macon, GA: Mercer University Press, 1986]) that the Gospel of Luke features an unreliable narrator has not proved convincing to most narrative critics (see Tannehill, *Narrative Unity,* I, pp. 7-8).

attention to the significance of these episodes as components of a series of related scenes which unfold over the course of Luke's narrative. Moreover, the overriding concern with Philip's 'roles and relations' corresponds directly to Tannehill's analysis of the portrait of Jesus in Luke's Gospel:

> I have chosen to focus on major roles in the narrative, understood in the context of the comprehensive purpose which is being realized throughout the narrative. I will be standing on the borderline between character and plot, understanding characters in terms of role, which is character in action and interaction within the unfolding plot.[1]

> The central chapters of this work are organized by narrative roles. They concern Jesus as he interacts with groups which appear repeatedly in the narrative.[2]

While such a focus on the 'narrative world' of Luke–Acts dominates this study, I try not to lose sight of important dimensions of the 'social-historical world' of Luke's time, which can profitably illuminate our reading of his text. I agree with Stanton that 'since the "story world" of the evangelists is not a timeless world, but one set in a particular first century religious and cultural setting, historical studies are still essential'.[3] Increasingly, we are encountering combinations of literary and historical analysis, such as S. Freyne's recent work on *Galilee, Jesus and the Gospels*,[4] and frank admissions by narrative critics that their method does not preclude historical investigation. In his helpful survey of narrative criticism, M.A. Powell corrects the common misconception that such analysis is inherently 'nonhistorical':

> In reality, nothing in the assumptions or presuppositions of narrative criticism calls into question the legitimacy of historical investigation. . . Narrative criticism demands that the modern reader have the historical information that the text assumes of its implied reader. . . In a basic sense, this comprises practical information that is common knowledge in the world of the story: how much a denarius is worth, what a centurion does, and so forth. It may also include recognition of social and political realities that lie behind the story.[5]

---

1. Tannehill, *Narrative Unity*, I, p. 1.
2. Tannehill, *Narrative Unity*, I, p. 5.
3. Stanton, *Gospels*, p. 29.
4. Subtitled, *Literary Approaches and Historical Investigations*.
5. Powell, *What Is Narrative Criticism?*, p. 96; cf. D. Rhoads and D. Michie,

Similarly, Tannehill declares in introducing his volume on Acts that

> an understanding of first century society and of historical events within it
> may be important for understanding Acts as a narrative. . . I believe that
> study of first-century Mediterranean literature and society may illuminate
> unspoken assumptions behind the narrative and may also suggest specific
> reasons for emphases in the text.

Tannehill admits that his ensuing narrative commentary on Acts makes only 'limited and tentative' use of historical analysis, but he encourages others to pursue the matter further.[1]

Given the narrower focus on a single Lukan character, I am able to enhance the analysis of Philip's roles and relations in Acts with pertinent historical investigations. In particular, I have been stimulated by recent sociological approaches to New Testament interpretation to examine issues related to group identities and boundaries, social status, leadership models and authority structures in the light of first-century Jewish and Greco-Roman society.[2] Especially important to ascertaining the significance of the Lukan Philip is a social-historical assessment of such groups as Samaritans, magicians, Ethiopians, eunuchs, 'God-fearers', itinerant charismatics and resident ministers—all of whom represent people Philip either encounters or exemplifies in Acts. Much can be learned about these people from Luke's own commentary throughout his narrative, but much is also silently assumed of a first-century audience. By exploring other writings from the period, we may hope to uncover common societal perceptions which Luke and

---

Mark as Story: An Introduction to the Narrative of a Gospel (Philadelphia: Fortress Press, 1982), pp. 79-80.

1. Tannehill, *Narrative Unity*, II, p. 5.

2. The key questions which sociological analysis addresses to the New Testament are conveniently enumerated in H.C. Kee, *Knowing the Truth: A Sociological Approach to New Testament Interpretation* (Minneapolis, MN: Fortress Press, 1989), pp. 65-69. For particular applications of sociological insights to Lukan studies, see H.C. Kee, *Good News to the Ends of the Earth: The Theology of Acts* (London: SCM Press; Philadelphia: TPI, 1990); P.F. Esler, *Community and Gospel in Luke–Acts: The Social and Political Motivations of Lucan Theology* (SNTSMS, 57; Cambridge: Cambridge University Press, 1987); H. Moxnes, *The Economy of the Kingdom: Social Conflicts and Economic Relations in Luke's Gospel* (OBT; Philadelphia: Fortress Press, 1988). A first step toward combining sociological and narrative analysis is taken in D.B. Gowler, 'Characterization in Luke: A Socio-Narratological Approach', *BTB* 19 (1989), pp. 54-62 (with primary reference to the portrait of the Pharisees).

his readers either shared or deviated from. In any event, our understanding of Philip's social roles and relations in Acts will be deepened.

Finally, while I eschew most source analysis and reconstruction as conventionally practiced in older Lukan scholarship, I do examine Luke's apparent use of the Septuagint[1] in shaping the Philip narratives (particularly the accounts of Philip's selection as one of the seven table-servants and his outreach to the Ethiopian eunuch). At this point, I especially build upon the creative work of a number of scholars who have scrutinized Luke's adaptation of the scriptural stories surrounding Moses and Elijah.[2]

Freyne has voiced the opinion of many scholars today that 'no one perspective can exhaust the possibilities of our texts, or adequately uncover their varied fields of reference'.[3] I have certainly found this to be true of the texts in Acts related to Philip and have elected to employ a variety of analytical methods in the interest of providing as complete and illuminating a description of the portrait of Philip as possible.

---

1. Cf. the judgment of D. Tiede: 'Luke's narrative is a scriptural commentary. The Scriptures it interprets are the Scriptures of Israel' (*Luke* [Augsburg Commentary on the NT; Minneapolis, MN: Augsburg, 1988], p. 26).

2. See the recent appraisal of such studies in C.A. Evans, 'Luke's Use of the Elijah/Elisha Narratives and the Ethic of Election', *JBL* 106 (1987), pp. 75-83.

3. Freyne, *Galilee*, p. 3.

Chapter 2

PHILIP AND THE SAMARITANS

1. *Introduction*

The first and last references to Philip in Acts are notably brief and distinctive in the roles which they assign him: (1) table-servant to the church in Jerusalem (Acts 6.5) and (2) host to Paul in Caesarea (21.8-9). While these references might be regarded as incidental and scarcely worth investigating, this study will take them seriously and probe them carefully below. But on any reckoning, the core of the Philip material in Acts appears in ch. 8, highlighting the role of missionary/evangelist. Other secondary parts which Philip plays must be related to this primary role.

Acts 8 features Philip's encounters with two parties: the Samaritans and the Ethiopian eunuch. This chapter takes up the first of these encounters, beginning with a broad overview of 8.4-25 and then narrowing to consider the specific activities and setting of Philip's Samaritan mission in the context of Luke's two-volume work.

2. *A Literary Overview of Acts 8.4-25*

Luke clearly cordons off Acts 8.4-25 as a single literary unit by a favorite *inclusio* technique[1] involving vv. 4-5 and 25.

> οἱ μὲν οὖν διασπαρέντες διῆλθον εὐαγγελιζόμενοι τὸν λόγον. Φίλιππος δὲ κατελθὼν εἰς [τὴν] πόλιν τῆς Σαμαρείας ἐκήρυσσεν αὐτοῖς τὸν Χριστόν (8.4-5).

> οἱ μὲν οὖν διαμαρτυράμενοι καὶ λαλήσαντες τὸν λόγον τοῦ

---

1. See C.H. Talbert (*Reading Luke: A Literary and Theological Commentary on the Third Gospel* [New York: Crossroad, 1984], pp. 54, 111, 147, 185, 188, 226) for examples of the technique of 'inclusion', as he calls it, in Luke's Gospel.

κυρίου ὑπέστρεφον εἰς Ἱεροσόλυμα, πολλάς τε κώμας τῶν Σαμαριτῶν εὐηγγελίζοντο (8.25).

Common elements include: (1) commencing with μὲν οὖν, a frequent transitional and summary device in Acts;[1] (2) reference to 'proclaiming (εὐαγγελίζομαι) the word (τὸν λόγον)', echoing a key theme within the intervening narrative (cf. εὐαγγελίζομαι, v. 12; λόγος, vv. 14, 21); and (3) localization in Samaritan territory (cf. v. 14).

Within Acts 8.4-25 appear two distinct scenes involving different actors. The first (vv. 4-13, of which vv. 4-5 forms the introduction) features the Samaritan mission of Philip the evangelist, a representative of those scattered from Jerusalem after the persecution of Stephen (cf. 8.1). The second (vv. 14-25, of which v. 25 forms the conclusion) focuses on the Samaritan mission of the Jerusalem apostles, Peter and John, while Philip completely disappears from view. Some have thought that Philip is meant to be included with Peter and John among the witnesses mentioned in v. 25,[2] but the fact that these witnesses return to Jerusalem after their Samaritan tour seems to rule Philip out, given his recent expulsion from the Holy City (8.1-5).

A closer analysis of the two scenes further reveals their internal unity. Scene one is solidified by juxtaposing the activities of Philip and Simon Magus among the Samaritans through the repetition of key words such as προσέχω (vv. 6, 10, 11), ἐξίστημι (vv. 9, 11, 13), πόλις (vv. 5, 8, 9), δύναμις (vv. 10, 13) and μεγάλη (vv. 7, 10, 13). Scene two is held together by an altercation between the Jerusalem apostles, chiefly Peter, and Simon Magus, dealing principally with the matter of rightly receiving the Spirit (λαμβάνειν πνεῦμα ἅγιον, vv. 15, 17, 19) and the word (λόγος, vv. 14, 21).

Despite this clear demarcation of scenes, the *inclusio* pattern noted

---

1. See, e.g., Acts 1.6; 2.41; 5.41; 9.31; 11.19; 12.5; 13.4; 15.3, 30; 16.5; 23.31. In these passages μὲν οὖν may mark either the beginning of a new section, the close of a previous section or both (functioning as a hinge). Acts 8.4 may be viewed as the conclusion to the Stephen story as well as the introduction to the report of Philip's mission. Cf. E. Richard, *Acts 6.1–8.4: The Author's Method of Composition* (SBLDS, 41; Missoula, MT: Scholars Press, 1978), p. 227; S.H. Levinsohn, *Textual Connections in Acts* (SBLMS, 31; Atlanta: Scholars Press, 1987), pp. 141-50.

2. E.g. K. Lake and H.J. Cadbury, *The Beginnings of Christianity: The Acts of the Apostles*. IV. *English Translation and Commentary* (London: Macmillan, 1933), p. 95; I.H. Marshall, *The Acts of the Apostles* (TNTC; Leicester: Inter-Varsity Press, 1980), p. 160.

above encourages a search for interlocking components between the scenes. We find, in the first place, that the same audience remains in view in both sections, specifically, those citizens of Samaria who embraced Philip's message (vv. 5-7, 12, 14) and were baptized in Jesus' name (vv. 12, 16). Also, one particular Samaritan, Simon Magus, appears prominently in each of the two scenes as one obsessed with visual manifestations of power (θεωρέω/ὁράω, vv. 13, 18; δύναμις/ἐξουσία, vv. 10, 13, 19). Indeed, throughout the Samaritan story, Luke consistently alternates in focus between Simon the antagonist and the Christian missionary protagonist.[1]

Philip	vv. 6-8
Simon	vv. 9-11
Philip	v. 12
Simon	v. 13
Peter (and John)	vv. 14-17
Simon	vv. 18-19
Peter	vv. 20-23
Simon	v. 24

It should be noted, however, that the Philip/Simon (vv. 6-13) and Peter/Simon (vv. 14-24) sequences are presented in different ways. The former is a purely third-person description following no chronological order (vv. 9-11 represents a 'flashback' to Simon's exploits before Philip's arrival), while the latter is organized around a dialogue-encounter mainly in the second person.

Since the recipients of Philip's ministry carry over into Acts 8.14-25, it should not be thought that Philip's disappearance at this stage means that he is utterly forgotten. Indeed, the fact that Philip's converts receive a supplementary benefit (the Spirit) and, in the case of Simon, a stiff reprimand from a visiting missionary cannot help but reflect back on Philip's achievements in some fashion. Exactly how the events of 8.14-25 color the portrait of Philip will occupy our attention in subsequent chapters, but at this point we simply observe that Philip's reputation represents another unifying concern in 8.4-25.

Generally scholars have recognized the heavy Lukan shaping of Acts 8.4-25 and perceived a certain coherence, at least on the surface, in its structure. But in probing behind the present form of the text to uncover the sources which Luke utilized, many have detected a

---

1. Richard notes a similar 'salient alternating pattern' involving Stephen and Saul in Acts 7.53–8.3 (*Acts 6.1–8.4*, p. 229).

number of seams which supposedly betray a patching together of discrete traditions. Resulting from such analyses are nagging doubts about Luke's compositional skills and prevailing opinions that any supposed unity in 8.4-25 is more illusory than real. D.-A. Koch speaks bluntly of the 'uneinheitlichen Gesamteindrucks, der sich in Act 8.5-25 bietet'.[1]

Among the breaks in the narrative commonly exposed by source and redaction critics are the following: (1) the awkward *Rückblende* in vv. 9-11 interrupting the natural flow from v. 8 to v. 12; (2) the lone explicit connection between Philip and Simon Magus in v. 13; and (3) the post-baptismal account of Spirit-reception in vv. 14-17, which creates an anomalous theological situation in the interest of exalting apostolic authority and severs the original link between vv. 13 and 18. Broadly speaking, explanations for these phenomena in Luke's account tend to propose either (1) that vv. 14-17 constitutes a redactional bridge joining two originally independent traditions—one disclosing the rivalry between Philip and Simon and the other reporting the conflict between Peter and Simon—within a common Samaritan setting,[2] or (2) that only one of the missionary encounters with Simon has a traditional basis, the other being a Lukan construction with possible dependence on some isolated reports about both Philip's and Simon's activities in Samaria.[3]

Without evaluating all the details of the various tradition-historical theories surrounding Acts 8.4-25, some general observations are offered. First, the speculative nature of these reconstructions of

---

1. D.-A. Koch, 'Geistbesitz, Geistverleihung und Wundermacht: Erwägungen zur Tradition und zur lukanischen Redaktion in Act 8.5-25', *ZNW* 77 (1986), p. 68; cf. pp. 72-73.

2. See O. Bauernfeind, *Kommentar und Studien zur Apostelgeschichte* (WUNT, 22; Tübingen: Mohr [Paul Siebeck], 1980), pp. 124-25; E. Trocmé, *Le 'Livre des Actes' et l'histoire* (Paris: Presses Universitaires de France, 1957), pp. 181-83.

3. For the view that only the Philip–Simon encounter derives from a traditional report, see Haenchen, *Acts*, pp. 305-308; J. Roloff, *Die Apostelgeschichte* (NTD, 5; Göttingen: Vandenhoeck & Ruprecht, 1981), pp. 131-33. The theory is that behind Acts 8.18-24 was an earlier story about Simon's desire to purchase *Philip's* miraculous powers, not Peter's ability to impart the Spirit. Among those who judge only the Peter–Simon altercation to be pre-Lukan, see K. Löning, 'Lukas—Theologe der von Gott geführten Heilsgeschichte', in *Gestalt und Anspruch des Neuen Testaments* (ed. J. Schreiner and G. Dautzenberg; Würzburg: Echter, 1969), pp. 205-209; Weiser, *Apostelgeschichte*, I, pp. 199-201.

Luke's writing process must be appreciated. C.K. Barrett wisely prefaces his remarks regarding the composition of 8.4-25 with these cautionary words:

> What sources did Luke use? How did he combine them? What was their historical value, and how far was any historical value they may originally have possessed preserved and how far destroyed in the editorial process? These are not questions that can be answered with confidence, and those who discuss them should remember that they are usually guessing, even when their guesses are guided by observation and probability.[1]

We are severely hampered by the lack of contemporary material with which to compare and contrast Luke's presentation in Acts 8. Ostensibly relevant traditions, such as those in the *Acts of Peter* or those related to Simonian Gnosis, manifest only minimal correspondence with the data in Acts 8 and are too late to provide any definitive clues as to particular reports Luke might have utilized.

Secondly, what appears to one reader as a *historical break* in the text might strike another as a *literary link*. For example, the observation that Acts 8.18 picks up Simon's visual interest in miraculous displays from v. 13 need not suggest some continuous underlying story into which Luke has spliced his own material. The recurrent emphasis on Simon's 'seeing' may just as plausibly reflect a Lukan literary device whereby one part of a narrative echoes another, thus creating a unified stylistic effect.

Thirdly, we should consider R. Pesch's appraisal of Acts 8.4-25 'als eine—freilich von Lukas bearbeitete—ursprüngliche Überlieferungseinheit'.[2] Pesch recognizes the coherence of the Lukan account and argues that its present form can best be accounted for as an adaptation of an equally coherent, similarly structured traditional report of the Samaritan mission.[3] Of course, Pesch's source hypothesis remains just

---

1. C.K. Barrett, 'Light on the Holy Spirit from Simon Magus (Acts 8,4-25)', in *Les Actes des Apôtres: Traditions, rédaction, théologie* (ed. J. Kremer; BETL, 48; Paris-Gembloux: Duculot; Louvain: Louvain University Press, 1979), p. 283; cf. G. Stählin, *Die Apostelgeschichte* (NTD, 5; Göttingen: Vandenhoeck & Ruprecht, 1966), p. 116.

2. R. Pesch, *Die Apostelgeschichte* (2 vols.; EKKNT, 5/1, 2; Zürich: Benziger; Neukirchen–Vluyn: Neukirchener Verlag, 1986), I, p. 271.

3. After a thorough assessment of scholarly opinion, Pesch concludes:

> Angesichts der unlösbaren Aporien literarkritischer (und darauf gestützter traditionsgeschichtlicher) Hypothesen ist also der Versuch geboten, 8,4-25 als einheitlichen, von

as much an educated guess as its competitors, but it does illustrate that, as it stands, the text of 8.4-25 scarcely bears indisputable marks of a multi-layered foundation. If we insist on peering through Luke's story in search of what lies behind it, we may only be able, given the story's careful design, to envisage an original model which more resembles than deviates from the final version.

Whatever the exact tradition history of Acts 8.4-25, prime consideration must be given to the evidence that Luke has deftly shaped his account into a cohesive literary whole. In addition to structural matters, the preponderant Lukan imprint is also displayed in numerous terms and themes characteristic of Luke–Acts: for example, ὁμοθυμαδόν (v. 6), χάρις (v. 8), dual ministry of proclamation and miracle-working (vv. 4-8, 12-13), Christian superiority over magic (vv. 6-13), the activity of the Spirit (vv. 15-20), financial matters (vv. 18-20), repentance (v. 22) and prayer (vv. 15, 22, 24)—all of which will be discussed in the course of this study. Therefore, in seeking to understand Luke's purposes in portraying Philip's Samaritan ministry, we must give priority attention to the place of 8.4-25 within the overall Lukan narrative, not to some alleged reconstruction of redactional activity. It is still important to investigate external materials—such as those pertaining to ancient Samaritan history and culture—but chiefly in order to illuminate Luke's thought-world, not to circumscribe his sources.

From this bird's-eye view of Acts 8.4-25 I turn to the specific characterization of Philip's work in Samaria. For the sake of analysis, this examination will be carried out in three stages. The present chapter is limited to Philip's ministry among the Samaritans at large. His interaction with Simon Magus in particular as well as his relationship with the Jerusalem apostles (especially Peter) will be treated in subsequent chapters. Despite this division of topics, however, care will be taken at each stage not to lose sight of the narrative unity governing Luke's account.

Lukas bearbeiteten Erzählzusammenhang zu verstehen. Dieser Erzählzusammenhang wird durch die Themen Samaria-Mission und Auseinandersetzung mit dem in Samaria wirken den Magier Simon zusammengehalten (*Apostelgeschichte*, I, p. 272).

3. *Philip's Ministry in Samaria*

Throughout the report of the Samaritan mission in Acts 8.4-25, Philip's ministry receives direct attention only in vv. 4-8 and 12-13, and then only in summary form. The content of his preaching is encapsulated in a few brief statements by the narrator, unaccompanied by any extended discourse such as we find with other key characters in Acts. There are no developed stories unfolding individual miraculous incidents, only the bare mention that certain types of miracles occurred. Except for Simon, the Samaritan beneficiaries of Philip's labors are undistinguished, lumped together as 'the crowds' and 'many who . . . ' (vv. 6-7). In short, the depiction of Philip's activity in Samaria reads like a concise overview.[1]

We should not be deceived, however, into thinking that Philip's role in the Samaritan episode is negligible just because it is succinctly described. As already suggested, the disclosure of Philip's missionary breakthrough in Samaria occupies a foundational position in Acts 8.4-25 on which the entire story builds. Also, the fact that a more detailed Philip story immediately follows in 8.26-40 demonstrates that Luke takes more than a passing interest in Philip's pursuits. Thus, the sketch of Philip's outreach to the Samaritans merits close examination.

a. *Introduction (Acts 8.4-5)*
Acts 8.4-5 clearly connects backward to 8.1b and forward to 11.19-20 through the common usage of διασπείρω (the only three instances of the verb in the New Testament) and other linking terms.

> That day a severe persecution (διωγμός) began against the church in Jerusalem; and all except the apostles were scattered (διεσπάρησαν) throughout the countryside of Judea and Samaria (8.1b).

> Now those who were scattered (οἱ μὲν οὖν διασπαρέντες) went from place to place (διῆλθον), proclaiming (εὐαγγελιζόμενοι) the word (τὸν λόγον). Philip went down to the city of Samaria and proclaimed the Messiah to them (8.4-5).

> Now those who were scattered (οἱ μὲν οὖν διασπαρέντες) because of the persecution (τῆς θλίψεως) that took place over Stephen traveled (διῆλθον) as far as Phoenicia. . . and they spoke the word (τὸν λόγον)

---

1. Cf. Barrett: 'when the actions ascribed to Philip are examined they appear to be confined to the purest generalities' ('Light on the Holy Spirit', p. 285).

2. *Philip and the Samaritans* 33

to no one except Jews. But among them were some. . . who, on coming to Antioch, spoke to the Hellenists also, proclaiming (εὐαγγελιζόμενοι) the Lord Jesus (11.19-20).

Since Harnack, the close parallels between Acts 8.4 and 11.19-20 have pointed to an underlying 'Antioch' source into which Luke has interpolated various blocks of material, including the Philip cycle in 8.5-40.[1] Once again, however, the iterative pattern may be viewed as characteristic of Luke's style, a means of interlocking various parts of his narrative.[2] The pervasive Lukan language (e.g. μὲν οὖν, διέρχομαι, εὐαγγελίζομαι, λόγος) confirms this perspective.

The backward link of Acts 8.4-5 to 8.1b establishes a larger context for understanding the Philip material at a number of points.

1. A bridge is provided between the Philip and Stephen stories, a not surprising phenomenon in light of the pairing of the two characters in their first appearances in Acts (the list of table-servants, 6.5).

2. Philip's ministry emerges as a direct result of persecution in Jerusalem, thereby slotting into the prominent Lukan 'theme of human opposition which does not stop the mission but contributes to its spread'[3] (Lk. 4.16-37; Acts 13.44-48; 18.6; 28.25-28).

3. In Acts 8.1 the region of Samaria is associated with Judea as a first point of departure beyond Jerusalem, a connection echoed in 1.8 and 9.31. Thus, Philip's Samaritan mission is linked geographically with his work along the coastal plain of Judea

---

1. A. Harnack (*The Acts of the Apostles* [CTL, 27; London: Williams & Norgate; New York: Putnam's Sons, 1911], pp. 131-88) grouped together Acts 6.1–8.4, 11.19-30, 12.25, and chs. 13–15 as Antiochene traditions and associated the Philip material in 8.5-40 with the narratives in 3.1–5.16, 9.29–11.18, and 12.1-24, which featured Peter and a Jerusalem–Caesarea setting. Harnack thought it probable that Philip himself, possibly along with his daughters, was Luke's source for this Philip–Peter unit. See the survey of opinion on the 'Antioch' source in J. Dupont, *The Sources of Acts: The Present Position* (London: Darton, Longman & Todd, 1964), pp. 35-39, 62-72.

2. On Luke's penchant for holding his story together by repetitive phrases, sometimes at wide intervals, see Cadbury, 'Four Features of Lucan Style', in Keck and Martyn (eds.), *Studies in Luke–Acts*, pp. 88-97.

3. Tannehill, *Narrative Unity*, I, p. 30.

(8.26-40) and with Peter's ministry in the same area (9.32–10.48).

4. Finally, the nexus between Acts 8.1 and 8.4-5 sets apart the itinerant evangelist, Philip, from the company of apostles who remain in Jerusalem. This distinction goes back to 6.1-7 and becomes a critical factor in 8.14-25. Moreover, it eliminates any prospect of identifying Philip the evangelist with his apostolic namesake (Lk. 6.14; Acts 1.13).[1]

The forward link of Acts 8.4-5 to 11.19-20 reinforces the relationship between Philip's mission and the persecution provoked by Stephen. It also connects Philip's work more broadly with territories beyond Judea and people ('Ελληνισταί) besides Palestinian Jews.

Within Acts 8.4-5, two significant verbs, διασπείρω and διέρχομαι, characterize the movements of Philip and the other fugitives from Jerusalem. Although rare in the New Testament, διασπείρω and its cognate, διασπορά, are widely circulated in the LXX where they most commonly refer to the dispersion of Jews from Israel to the lands of Gentile nations (ἔθνη).[2] The context is typically one of disobedience and punishment, that is, Israel's disobedience to God's law and God's resultant act of judgment in scattering his people. This course of events has its primeval pattern in the Babel episode (διασπείρω, Gen. 11.4, 8, 9), its legal basis in the warnings of the Pentateuch (Lev. 26.33; Deut. 4.27; 28.64; 32.26) and its climax in Israel's exile lamented by the prophets (Jer. 13.24; 15.7; 18.17; Bar. 2.4, 13, 29; 3.8; Ezek. 5.12; 12.14, 15; 22.15; cf. *Pss. Sol.* 9.1-2). When διασπείρω/διασπορά is used in a positive connection, the accent falls on the Lord's gracious restoration of his scattered flock to the promised land, often as a sign of eschatological blessing (Isa. 11.12; 56.8; Jer. 39[32].37; Ezek. 11.17; 34.12; Zeph. 3.10; Ps. 146[147].2; Jdt. 5.19).

Luke's usage of διασπείρω coincides with the LXX in applying the term to the dispersion of Jews from Jerusalem into foreign territories. This sense certainly fits Acts 11.19-20, where the fugitives associated with Stephen settle in Phoenicia, Cyprus and Antioch. In the case of

---

1. Contra E.F.F. Bishop, 'Which Philip?', *ATR* 28 (1946), pp. 154-59.

2. Cf. K.L. Schmidt, 'διασπορά', *TDNT*, II, p. 99; G. Schneider, *Die Apostelgeschichte* (2 vols.; HTKNT, 5/1, 2; Freiburg: Herder, 1980–82), I, p. 479 n. 65.

Philip, while he physically stays within Israel's borders, his interaction with the Samaritan nation (ἔθνος, 8.10) and an Ethiopian traveller (8.26-39) locates him socially on the fringes of Judaism (if not beyond) and justifies his identity as one of the διασπαρέντες.

Despite sharing a common referent, however, Lukan and LXX usages of διασπείρω differ markedly in their overall perspectives. Far from envisaging the flight from Jerusalem as retribution against a rebellious people, Luke regards it as fulfilling Christ's charge to the disciples to bear witness—'beginning from Jerusalem'—about God's salvation to the nations (Lk. 24.47; Acts 1.8). By and large, in forecasting the redemption of the nations, the Old Testament pictures a 'centripetal' movement of Gentiles to Zion at the end of the age, complementing the ingathering of dispersed Israelites from the four winds (e.g. Isa. 2.2-4; 49.6; 56.6-8; Mic. 4.1-3; Zech. 2.10-12; 8.1-8, 20-23).[1] Luke, on the other hand, while happy to report the conversion of many pilgrims to Jerusalem 'from every nation under heaven' (Acts 2.5, 41),[2] also supports a 'centrifugal' mission in which the gospel is carried from Jerusalem and spread to every land.[3] Philip and the other διασπαρέντες inaugurate such a mission. It is interesting that among these missionaries are 'men of Cyprus and Cyrene' (Acts 11.20) who apparently migrated to Jerusalem in the first place (before

1. On this 'centripetal' movement, 'the eschatological pilgrimage of the Gentiles to the Mountain of God', see J. Jeremias, *Jesus' Promise to the Nations* (Philadelphia: Fortress Press, repr. 1982 [1958]), pp. 55-61. In Isa. 49.6, part of which Luke applies to Paul's mission in Acts 13.47, there is an emphasis upon Israel's being 'a light to the nations' so that God's salvation might reach 'to the end of the earth', but in the LXX this is conjoined with the return of Israel from the dispersion (καὶ τὴν διασπορὰν τοῦ Ισραηλ ἐπιστρέψαι).

2. Of course, these were Diaspora Jews who had gathered in Jerusalem (Acts 2.5), thus symbolizing the restoration of Israel. But included among these pilgrims were proselytes as well (2.10), and the larger Pentecostal narrative certainly portends the ingathering of the Gentile nation in its emphasis upon 'every nation under heaven' (2.5), the Spirit's outpouring 'upon all flesh' (2.17; cf. v. 39) and the opportunity for salvation for 'whoever calls on the name of the Lord' (2.21).

3. F. Hahn (*Mission in the New Testament* [SBT, 7; London: SCM Press, 1965], pp. 21-25) suggests that, while Palestinian Jews did not aggressively seek after proselytes, Hellenistic Jews in the Diaspora were more mission-minded—like Luke. However, this supposed distinction of Diaspora Judaism has been convincingly challenged in such studies as A.T. Kraabel, 'Six Questionable Assumptions', *JJS* 33 (1982), pp. 449-60; and J. Nolland, 'Proselytism or Politics in Horace *Satires* I,4,138-43?', *VC* 33 (1979), pp. 347-55.

their conversion to Christianity?) from the Diaspora. However, according to Luke's story, rather than finding the kingdom of God established forever in the Holy City, as the Old Testament suggests, they find their messiah violently rejected by the Jewish authorities and themselves forced to disperse again, this time preaching the gospel of Christ as they go.

διέρχομαι is a characteristic Lukan verb of motion,[1] appearing in a variety of 'coming and going' situations, but most frequently in the context of missionary activity.[2] It may denote the specific passage from one place to another ('And when he wished to cross over [διελθεῖν] to Achaia. . . ' [Acts 18.27]) or a more general 'passing through' or 'travelling about' a region. This latter sense suits the absolute use of διέρχομαι in 8.4 and 11.19 and reinforces the notion of a 'scattered' (διασπείρω) mission. Philip's ministry in particular follows the pattern of a wandering evangelist, as demonstrated in the parallel expressions, διῆλθον εὐαγγελιζόμενοι (8.4)/διερχόμενος εὐηγγελίζετο (8.40), which frame the Philip cycle. In addition to 11.19, the closest parallels involving διέρχομαι to Philip's roving mission include: (1) the first mission of the Twelve ('they. . . went through [διήρχοντο] the villages, bringing the good news' [Lk. 9.6 differs from Mk 6.12]); (2) Peter's 'inspection' tour along the Palestinian coast ('as Peter went here and there [διερχόμενον] among all the believers. . . ' [Acts 9.32]); (3) Jesus' ministry as summarized by Peter ('he went about [διῆλθεν] doing good' [Acts 10.38]; and (4) Paul's missionary journeys ('he. . . went from place to place [διερχόμενος καθεξῆς] through the region' [Acts 18.23; cf. 13.6, 14; 14.24; 15.41; 16.6; 19.1, 21; 20.2, 25]). Thus, Philip's itinerant ministry mirrors that of all the main figures in Luke–Acts.

b. *Proclamation (Acts 8.4-5, 12)*
Since Philip is among those scattered from Jerusalem after Stephen's martyrdom, his ministry may be broadly characterized as 'proclaiming the word' (Acts 8.4). More specifically, however, his proclamation in Samaria is encapsulated in two terse phrases:

---

1. 31 of 42 occurrences in the New Testament appear in Luke–Acts.
2. Lake and Cadbury, *Beginnings of Christianity*, IV, p. 108.

ἐκήρυσσεν αὐτοῖς τὸν Χριστόν (8.5)

εὐαγγελιζομένῳ περὶ τῆς βασιλείας τοῦ θεοῦ καὶ τοῦ ὀνόματος Ἰησοῦ Χριστοῦ (8.12)

The two verbs, κηρύσσω and εὐαγγελίζομαι, comprise part of a rich Lukan vocabulary designating that central component of Christian ministry, the act of preaching.[1] They can take the same objects (e.g. 'kingdom of God', 'Christ', 'Jesus'), and frequently, as in Acts 8.5, 12, they appear close together as alternative expressions for the same proclamation event (cf. Lk. 4.18-19; 4.43-44; 8.1; 9.2, 6; Acts 10.36-37). Thus, Luke typically utilizes κηρύσσω and εὐαγγελίζομαι as stylistic variants with no appreciable semantic distinction.[2]

While Luke shares a predilection for κηρύσσω with Matthew and Mark, the employment of εὐαγγελίζομαι is virtually unique among the Synoptics (Mt. 11.5 [par. Lk. 7.22] is the only exception). Conversely, the cognate noun, εὐαγγέλιον, which is relatively common in Matthew and Mark, surfaces in Luke–Acts only in Acts 15.7 and 20.24 (compared to 25 uses of the verb). Luke scatters his use of εὐαγγελίζομαι throughout both volumes in characterizing the ministries of angels, John the Baptist, Jesus, the Twelve, Paul and other missionaries. However, the heaviest concentration occurs in the larger Philip narrative in Acts 8.4-40, where it appears five times in the space of 37 verses.[3] These five references are couched in various constructions: twice with an accusative denoting the content of the proclamation (vv. 4, 35), once with a prepositional (περὶ) phrase also disclosing what is being preached (v. 12) and twice with an accusative indicating the audience being addressed (vv. 25, 40).[4] In terms of its distribution in Acts 8, εὐαγγελίζομαι emerges at key structural points in the story (in connection with different subjects)—beginning (the dispersed ones, v. 4), transition (Peter and John, v. 25) and end (Philip, v. 40); it also denotes the nature of Philip's work within each of the two main scenes (vv. 12, 35). On any reckoning, the ministry

1. Related terms include: ἀναγγέλλω, διδάσκω, διαγγέλλω, λαλέω, καταγγέλλω, πείθω; cf. Conzelmann, *Theology*, pp. 218-25; Fitzmyer, *Luke*, I, pp. 145-49.
2. Tannehill, *Narrative Unity*, I, p. 78.
3. The next greatest concentration is four occurrences in a section pertaining to Paul's first missionary journey (Acts 13.32–14.21).
4. See Marshall, *Luke: Historian*, p. 160.

of the word designated by εὐαγγελίζομαι represents a central theme of the Philip story.

Concerning the substance of Philip's proclamation, I consider first the centrality of 'Christ' (v. 5). Used here with the definite article, Christ should no doubt be understood in the titular sense of 'the Christ' or 'the messiah'. This conforms generally with distinctive Lukan usage in which Χριστός is rarely employed as a proper name[1] and predominantly refers to the anointed messianic ruler of Jewish expectation.[2] Luke makes it plain that the awaited Christ has at last been revealed in the person of Jesus of Nazareth. From his birth (Lk. 2.11, 26) and throughout his earthly ministry (Lk. 4.41; 9.20), Jesus fulfilled the messianic role, but it was especially through Jesus' death, resurrection and ascension that 'God made him both Lord and messiah' (Acts 2.36). While the notion of a *crucified* Christ certainly ran against the tide of traditional Jewish thought (cf. Lk. 23.35, 39), Luke repeatedly appeals to scriptural prophecy in stressing the necessity (δεῖ) of a suffering messiah (Lk. 24.26, 44-46; Acts 3.18; 17.2-3; 26.22-23).[3]

Most instances in Acts where Christ is the focus of missionary proclamation explicitly identify Christ with Jesus in the immediate context and presuppose, naturally enough, a Jewish audience (e.g. 5.42; 2.31-32, 36; 3.20; 9.22; 17.2-3; 18.5, 28).[4] Philip's preaching of Christ *simpliciter* in 8.5 without a direct tie-in to Jesus is unusual for Acts (although see 26.23), but the larger context of Philip's message in ch. 8 establishes clear links with 'the name of Jesus Christ' (v. 12)

1.   When used as a proper name in Luke–Acts, 'Christ' always appears in combination with 'Jesus' and mostly in formulaic constructions involving ἐν τῷ ὀνόματι (e.g. Acts 2.38; 3.6; 4.10; 10.48; 16.18).

2.   See Cadbury, 'The Titles of Jesus in Acts', in Lake and Cadbury (eds.), *Beginnings of Christianity*. V. *Additional Notes to the Commentary*, pp. 357-59; J.C. O'Neill, *The Theology of Acts in its Historical Setting* (London: SPCK, 1961), pp. 119-29; S.S. Smalley, 'The Christology of Acts Again', in *Christ and Spirit in the New Testament: In Honour of Charles Francis Digby Moule* (ed. B. Lindars and S.S. Smalley; Cambridge: Cambridge University Press, 1973), pp. 79-93; D.L. Jones, 'The Title *Christos* in Luke–Acts', *CBQ* 32 (1970), pp. 69-76.

3.   On the 'Scripturally-grounded "musts"' related to Jesus' passion in Luke–Acts, see C.H. Cosgrove, 'Divine ΔΕΙ in Luke–Acts: Investigations into the Lukan Understanding of God's Providence', *NovT* 26 (1984), pp. 173-76; cf. also Smalley, 'Christology of Acts Again', pp. 88-92.

4.   O'Neill, *Theology of Acts*, p. 120.

and 'the good news of Jesus' (v. 35). The Samaritan setting for this Christ-centered message is noteworthy, since it discloses Luke's understanding that the Samaritans, whatever their social and religious idiosyncrasies, still shared a general messianic consciousness with other Jewish groups.

Secondly, Philip proclaims 'the kingdom of God' (Acts 8.12). The notion of God's kingdom as the subject of Christian preaching emerges at critical junctures within the Lukan narrative.[1] Concluding the first major Gospel section dealing with Jesus' public ministry is the narrator's report:

> But he said to them, 'I must proclaim the good news of the kingdom of God (εὐαγγελίσασθαί με δεῖ τὴν βασιλείαν τοῦ θεοῦ) to the other cities also; for I was sent (ἀπεστάλην) for this purpose'. So he continued proclaiming (κηρύσσων) the message in the synagogues of Judea (Lk. 4.43-44).

The 'also' (καί) intimates that Jesus' mission in the cities of Nazareth and Capernaum (4.16-41) was likewise characterized by proclaiming the kingdom of God. In particular, the verbs εὐαγγελίζομαι, κηρύσσω and ἀποστέλλω are all echoed in the Isaiah citation which Jesus claims to fulfill in the synagogue at Nazareth (Isa. 61.1; 58.6; Lk. 4.18-21). In Luke's eyes, apparently, bringing good news to the poor, proclaiming release to the captives, and so on elucidates what it means to preach the kingdom of God and delineates the basic program of Jesus' entire mission.[2] The emphasis on Jesus' heralding of God's kingdom as divinely mandated ('I must proclaim. . . I was sent for this purpose') confirms how central this task is to Jesus' vocation.

Another Lukan summary statement regarding Jesus' itinerant mission repeats the kerygmatic focus on the kingdom of God (Lk. 8.1), and only Luke among the evangelists reports that Jesus spoke to the crowds about the kingdom of God before the miraculous feeding incident (9.11). Flanking this episode in Luke 9 are references which

1. O. Merk ('Das Reich Gottes in den lukanischen Schriften', in *Jesus und Paulus: Festschrift für Werner Georg Kummel zum 70. Geburtstag* [Göttingen: Vandenhoeck & Ruprecht, 1975], pp. 204-206) observes that about one fourth of all references to βασιλεία τοῦ θεοῦ in Luke–Acts occur in a context of proclamation and that as a rule these references are unique to Luke; cf. also M. Völkel, 'Zur Deutung des "Reiches Gottes" bei Lukas', *ZNW* 65 (1974), pp. 62-70.
2. On the relationship between Lk. 4.43-44 and the Nazareth pericope in 4.16-30, see Tannehill, *Narrative Unity*, I, pp. 77-79, 81-83; Völkel, 'Deutung', pp. 63-67.

indicate that Jesus not only proclaimed the kingdom of God himself, but also commissioned his disciples to do the same (v. 2 differs from Mk 6.12; v. 60).

In Acts the priority of a kingdom-preaching ministry is sustained by statements at the beginning and end of the narrative (1.3; 28.23, 31).[1] In the former case, the risen Jesus is 'speaking about the kingdom of God' to his followers, thus continuing his earthly mission. The closing verses of Acts report Paul's proclamation of the kingdom of God, thus illustrating how the missionaries of the early church effectively carry on Jesus' work.[2] In the body of Acts, further evidence arises of Paul's testimony regarding the kingdom of God, especially connected with his Ephesian ministry (19.8; 20.25; cf. 14.22). But surprisingly, the only other reference to proclaiming the kingdom of God is that associated with Philip's ministry in 8.12. In light of Lk. 9.2, it is particularly strange that the Twelve (including Peter) are not *explicitly* depicted in Acts as preachers of God's kingdom. This may have something to do with their persistent misunderstanding of the kingdom, implied in Acts 1.6, as too narrowly restricted to Israel's national interests.

As to the substance of the kingdom-message proclaimed by Philip and Paul, Luke supplies few details. What information is provided, however, all points to Jesus. Philip's proclamation of God's kingdom is placed alongside his witness to 'the name of Jesus Christ' (Acts 8.12), and, likewise, Paul's is conjoined with convincing the Jews 'about Jesus' (28.23) and teaching 'about the Lord Jesus Christ' (28.31).[3] Thus, 'there is little doubt that Luke uses βασιλεία as a shorthand way of referring to the entire Christian proclamation—and that includes reference to the life of Jesus'.[4] The Jesus who is the

---

1. R. Maddox, *The Purpose of Luke–Acts* (FRLANT, 126; Göttingen: Vandenhoeck & Ruprecht, 1982), p. 133.

2. Stanton remarks that with their emphasis on proclaiming the kingdom of God 'the closing verses of Acts. . . are almost as important for Luke's theology as the closing verses of Matthew for Matthean theology' (*Jesus of Nazareth in New Testament Preaching* [SNTSMS, 27; Cambridge: Cambridge University Press, 1974], p. 17).

3. Merk, 'Reich Gottes', pp. 205-206; Schnackenburg, *God's Rule and Kingdom*, p. 261.

4. Stanton, *Jesus of Nazareth*, pp. 17-18. There seems to be little basis for the view of Lake and Cadbury that the kingdom of God in Acts refers to 'the Christian Church' (*Beginnings of Christianity*, IV, p. 4).

'kingdom-preacher par excellence'[1] in Luke's Gospel becomes the focus of the church's kingdom-proclamation in the book of Acts.[2]

As to the vexed question of whether the announced kingdom is a present reality or future hope, the primary stress in Acts seems to fall on the former, since the good news of the Christian message obviously includes the promise of immediate benefits such as forgiveness of sins and the gift of the Spirit (Acts 2.38; 10.43; cf. Lk. 24.47).[3] The possibly future-oriented exhortation to 'enter the kingdom of God' in Acts 14.22 is a lone exception in Luke's account of the early church's kerygma.[4]

The recipients of the message of God's kingdom include especially 'the poor, the maimed, the lame, the blind' (those invited to the great banquet, Lk. 14.13, 21; cf. 14.12-24; 6.20; 7.22; 18.22-25), tax collectors (Lk. 7.28-29), children (Lk. 18.15-17), those forced to leave home (Lk. 18.28-30) and even a convicted criminal (Lk. 23.42-43)—in other words, the outcasts and disadvantaged of Jewish society.[5] Even more radical is Luke's forecast that Israel as a people will generally spurn the opportunity to enter God's kingdom, leaving the door wide open to respondents from Gentile nations (Lk. 4.25-27; 13.28-30). In Acts 1 the risen Jesus, while speaking of the kingdom of God (v. 3), responds to the disciples' query regarding Israel's possession of the kingdom (v. 6) with a slight rebuff (v. 7) and clear redirection of their attention to the worldwide kingdom destined to be established through their Spirit-inspired testimony (v. 8). This universal perspective on God's kingdom becomes most realized in the ministry of Paul. At Ephesus he commences his kingdom-preaching in the synagogue (Acts 19.8), but in the face of mounting opposition he transfers to a private hall where he lectures daily for two years. As a result, 'all the

---

1. Fitzmyer, *Luke*, I, p. 154.

2. Cf. Merk: 'Der Verkünder im Evangelium des Lukas aber ist in den kerygmatischen Texten der Apg zum Verkündigten geworden' ('Reich Gottes', p. 219).

3. See Maddox, *Purpose of Luke–Acts*, pp. 132-37.

4. Contra Haenchen, who erroneously thinks that 'the kingdom of God' proclaimed in Acts 8.12, 28.23, 31 has the same futuristic sense as in 14.22, simply because in these places 'it is mentioned along with the events of Jesus' (*Acts*, p. 723). Maddox contends that even in Acts 14.22 Luke intended a present, non-eschatological understanding of 'entering the kingdom of God' (*Purpose of Luke–Acts*, pp. 136-37).

5. See H.C. Kee, *Miracle in the Early Christian World: A Study in Sociohistorical Method* (New Haven: Yale University Press, 1983), pp. 200-202.

residents of Asia, both Jews and Greeks, hear the word of the Lord' (19.9-10). Later, in recapitulating his Ephesian ministry, Paul emphasizes again this outreach 'both to Jews and to Greeks' (20.21) and characterizes his overall mission as 'preaching the kingdom' (20.25).[1] At the end of Acts, Paul's kingdom-preaching begins once more with the Jews (28.23), this time at Rome, but following their disbelief he announces that the 'salvation of God has been sent to the Gentiles' and widens his kingdom-centered mission to embrace 'all' visitors at his hired dwelling over a two-year period (28.28-31).

In short, Luke makes it plain that proclaiming the kingdom of God extends beyond the boundaries of Judaism; the blessings of Christ's salvation are offered to all people. Obviously, then, Philip's declaration of the kingdom of God to a Samaritan populace after being driven from Jerusalem fits well the general Lukan pattern.

Finally, we examine the significance of Philip's preaching about 'the name of Jesus Christ'. In simple terms, the ancient tendency to associate a person's name with his character and achievements[2] suggests that preaching the name of Jesus Christ was essentially synonymous with bearing testimony to his nature and ministry. A more comprehensive understanding of Luke's meaning in Acts 8.12 may be gained by comparing the many and varied references to the name of Jesus throughout Luke–Acts (especially Acts), even though the particular construction—εὐαγγελιζομένῳ περὶ . . . τοῦ ὀνόματος Ἰησοῦ Χριστοῦ—is unique in Luke's writing.

1.   Jesus Christ is the exclusive name whereby human beings experience salvation (Acts 4.12). All are invited to call upon his name in order to be saved (Acts 2.21; 9.14, 21) and to be baptized in his name as evidence of repentance and faith (Acts 2.38; 8.16; 10.48; 19.5; 22.16).

2.   The benefits of salvation are imparted in the name of Jesus, including forgiveness of sins (Lk. 24.47; Acts 10.43), physical healing (Acts 3.6, 16; 4.7, 10, 30) and release from demonic enslavement (Lk. 9.49; 10.17; Acts 16.18; 19.13, 17). The 'in the name' formula may imply something of Jesus' authorization to his disciples to perform salutary works, but predominantly it signifies 'the living power of

---

1.   See F. Pereira, *Ephesus: Climax of Universalism in Luke–Acts: A Redaction-Critical Study of Paul's Ephesian Ministry (Acts 18.23–20.1)* (Jesuit Theological Forum Studies, 1; Anand, India: Gujarat Sahitya Prakash, 1983), pp. 118-26.

2.   H. Bietenhard, 'ὄνομα, ὀνομάζω, κτλ.', *TDNT*, V, p. 243.

Jesus at work in the church'.[1] Put another way, the efficacy of Jesus' name illustrates his continuing dynamic presence with his people.[2]

3. The Jerusalem apostles and Paul are credited with speaking or teaching in Jesus' name. Such references typically occur in a persecution context befitting Luke's general emphasis on suffering for the sake of Jesus' name. For example, Luke reports that, after the apostles were flogged and charged by the Sanhedrin 'not to speak in the name of Jesus. . . they rejoiced that they were considered worthy to suffer dishonor for the sake of the name' (Acts 5.40-41; cf. Lk. 21.12, 17; Acts 4.17-18; 5.28; 9.15-16, 27, 29; 21.13; 26.9-10). The notion of speaking 'in Jesus' name' may again suggest the backing of Jesus' authority (the disciples = Jesus' ambassadors), but this does not exhaust its meaning. Proclamation 'in Jesus' name' is closely associated in Acts with expounding the good news about Jesus and his ministry. When the Jewish authorities object to the apostles' speaking in Jesus' name, the protest is not against their claims to be Jesus' emissaries as much as their bold announcement that—through his name— Jesus himself was still alive and dynamically present to heal and to save (Acts 3.16; 4.7-12). Describing Saul's witness in Damascus, Barnabas says that the former persecutor 'had spoken boldly in the name of Jesus' (9.27); earlier, however, the narrator reports concerning the same event simply that Saul 'proclaimed Jesus' (9.20). Clearly, in the book of Acts, preaching in Jesus' name is tantamount to declaring the Christian gospel.[3]

This last item relates most closely to Philip's preaching about the name of Jesus Christ. Although he proclaims good news περὶ. . . τοῦ ὀνόματος Jesus Christ, this is scarcely to be distinguished in any substantive way from the more common ἐν τῷ ὀνόματι references. In both cases, the accent falls on testifying to the gospel of Christ. In another instance, Luke employs to the same effect a variant expression

---

1. Marshall, *Luke: Historian*, p. 179.
2. See Conzelmann, *Theology*, pp. 177-78.
3. On this connection between Jesus' name and gospel-preaching, see especially J.A. Ziesler, 'The Name of Jesus in the Acts of the Apostles', *NTS* 25 (1977–79), pp. 28-41; however, I do not follow Ziesler in concluding that this emphasis is wholly exclusive of any tendency to associate Jesus' name with 'a presently active Jesus' (p. 38). In particular, the references to Jesus' name in conjunction with the healing incident at the temple seem to incorporate both the idea of Jesus' powerful presence and the message of salvation in Jesus proclaimed by the apostles (Acts 3.6, 16; 4.10, 12, 17, 18).

to preaching 'in the name of Jesus'. Saul is commissioned by the risen Lord 'to bring my name' (βαστάσαι τὸ ὄνομά μου) before the world (9.15), a task which appears identical to his ensuing ministry of preaching Jesus/in the name of Jesus in Damascus (9.20, 27).

Although Philip is not explicitly forbidden to preach in Jesus' name nor reported as suffering for the sake of Jesus' name, it is interesting that his Samaritan mission—which includes the proclamation of Jesus' name—is a direct outgrowth of Saul's persecution (cf. Acts 8.1-5). Later in the Acts narrative Saul confesses that his antagonism to the church had been part of a violent campaign 'against the name of Jesus of Nazareth' (26.9-11). In a sense, then, from the larger Lukan perspective, Philip should be numbered among those who suffered for their devotion to Jesus' name and who persisted in declaring that name in spite of opposition.

Again, while Philip's miracles are not explicitly performed 'in the name of Jesus', the particular mighty acts of exorcising unclean spirits and healing the lame (Acts 8.7) are among those which Luke characteristically attributes to the power of Jesus' name. And finally, the reference to the Samaritans' baptism 'in the name of the Lord Jesus' (8.16) corresponds directly to other Lukan uses of the name of Jesus in relation to baptismal practice.

c. *Miracle-Working (Acts 8.6-7, 13)*

The display of miracle-working alongside the ministry of proclamation, the combination of word and deed, is a common phenomenon in Luke's story of Jesus and the early church.[1] In the important synagogue scene in Nazareth, Jesus draws on Isaianic prophecy in characterizing his ministry as preaching good news to the poor and miraculously restoring sight to the blind (Lk. 4.18-19; cf. 7.22). The discussion which then ensues between Jesus and the assembly calls attention both to Jesus' 'gracious words' (4.22) and—more extensively—to his wonder-working activity (4.23-27). The next episode, set in Capernaum, likewise features the authority of Jesus' teaching and his power to work miracles (exorcisms in this case, 4.31-37).

---

1. See L. O'Reilly, *Word and Sign in the Acts of the Apostles: A Study in Lucan Theology* (Analecta Gregoriana, 243; Rome: Editrice Pontifica Università Gregoriana, 1987); P.J. Achtemeier, 'The Lukan Perspective on the Miracles of Jesus: A Preliminary Sketch', in Talbert (ed.), *Perspectives on Luke–Acts*, pp. 156-57; Jervell, *Unknown Paul*, pp. 86-87.

Following the scene in which Jesus cures a leper is a summary note that 'many crowds would gather to hear him and to be cured of their diseases' (Lk. 5.15 differs from Mk 1.45; cf. Lk. 6.17). Not surprisingly, then, the following pericope opens with the announcement that, while Jesus was teaching, 'the power of the Lord was with him to heal' (5.17 differs from Mk 2.1-2).

This twofold ministry of word and miracle is, as we would expect, also carried out by Jesus' followers. In their inaugural mission the Twelve scatter, 'bringing the good news and curing diseases everywhere' (Lk. 9.6; cf. 9.1-2; 10.9). In Acts the primitive Jerusalem community gathers for prayer, beseeching the Lord to empower them 'to speak your word with all boldness, while you stretch out your hand to heal, and signs and wonders are performed' (4.29-30). This request is soon realized in the ministries of the Jerusalem apostles and Stephen (5.12-13, 40-42; 6.8-10). In the second half of Acts, Paul's work is similarly depicted as a blend of potent word and miraculous sign (e.g. 13.4-12; 14.3, 7-10; 19.10-12; 20.7-12).

Obviously, Luke esteems the performance of miracles as a critical component of the evangelical missions of Christ and his church. As H.C. Kee has concluded, 'For Luke miracle functions, not only to heighten the drama of the narrative, but also to show that at every significant point in the transitions of Christianity from its Jewish origins in Jerusalem. . . the hand of God is evident in the form of public miraculous confirmation'.[1] Philip's missionary breakthrough to the Samaritans, attended by mighty works, represents a clear case in point.

As to the nature of the miracles which Philip performs, we observe the familiar Lukan juxtaposition of exorcisms and healings (Acts 8.7; cf. Lk. 4.33-40; 6.17-18; 8.26-55; 9.1; 10.9, 17; 13.32; Acts 5.16; 19.11-12). In the former case, the only detail provided is that the unclean spirits depart from their victims, 'crying with a loud voice' (βοῶντα φωνῇ μεγάλῃ). This manifestation is most reminiscent of Jesus' liberation of a demon-possessed man at Capernaum (ἀνέκραξεν φωνῇ μεγάλῃ; Lk. 4.33 differs from Mk 4.24). As for Philip's acts of healing, those involving the paralyzed (παραλελυμένοι) and lame (χωλοί) also parallel other incidents in Luke–Acts. Paralytics are raised up by Jesus and Peter (Lk. 5.17-26; Acts 9.32-35), and the

1. Kee, *Miracle*, p. 220; cf. J.A. Hardon, 'The Miracle Narratives in the Acts of the Apostles', *CBQ* 16 (1954), p. 311.

lame are made to walk by Jesus (as a special proof of his messianic vocation, Lk. 7.22) and by Peter and Paul (in major miracle stories prompting audience amazement, Acts 3.1-10; 14.8-18).

While Philip's miraculous deeds are generally typical of Luke's presentation, nonetheless their brief mention stands in contrast to the more extended miracle accounts associated with other characters. Of course, this may simply reflect the fact that Luke had no detailed reports of Philip's miracles at his disposal. Whatever the underlying cause, the net effect on a narrative level of the cursory account is that Philip's wonder-working ministry in Samaria appears somewhat less spectacular than the mighty demonstrations of Jesus, Peter and Paul. Counterbalancing, however, any diminished respect for Philip's achievements is the double emphasis in Acts 8.7 on the 'many' (πολλοί) afflicted persons who benefit from his powerful ministry, resulting in 'great joy' (πολλὴ χαρά) throughout the city (8.8).

Apart from identifying the particular types of miracles which Philip performs in Samaria, Luke also tags Philip's mighty works more generally as σημεῖα καὶ δυνάμεις μεγάλας (Acts 8.13; cf. τὰ σημεῖα, 8.6). The significance of this language is related in part to Simon's reputation as the 'Great Power' (8.10), which I will investigate fully in the next chapter. Also, however, the import of σημεῖον and δύναμις must be assessed against the background of their several occurrences throughout Acts, often in conjunction with a third term, τέρας. In Peter's speech at Pentecost, he announces that the last days forecast by Joel have begun, as evidenced in the Spirit's outpouring soon to be accompanied by prophetic utterances, dreams, visions, wonders (τέρατα) and signs (σημεῖα, an addition to the LXX source) (Acts 2.17-19). Such phenomena represent a continuation of the new age, inaugurated by 'Jesus of Nazareth, a man attested... by God with deeds of power, wonders, and signs' (δυνάμεσι καὶ τέρασι καὶ σημείοις, 2.22). The use of a plural form of δύναμις to designate Jesus' 'deeds of power' echoes two references in Luke's Gospel (10.13; 19.37); in Acts a similar usage applies only to Philip (8.13) and to a single instance in Paul's ministry (19.11). Interestingly, these references to Philip's and Paul's δυνάμεις are both attended by intensive modifiers: 'great' (μεγάλας) in the first case, and 'extraordinary' (τυχούσας) in the second.[1]

---

1. J.D.G. Dunn notes this parallel between Acts 8.13 and 19.11 and views the emphasis on *great* signs and wonders as evidence of Luke's general attitude that 'the

The σημεῖα καὶ τέρατα anticipated in Peter's speech are indeed quickly manifested in the ministry of the Jerusalem apostles (Acts 2.43). In particular, lively interest is aroused over the 'notable sign' (γνωστὸν σημεῖον, 4.16; cf. 4.22) of healing a man crippled from birth. Even though this incident sparks bitter opposition to the apostles' work, their ministry of signs and wonders continues and even expands dramatically (4.29-30; 5.12-16). In addition to the Twelve, Stephen, Paul and Barnabas are also credited with working signs and wonders in the Acts account (6.8; 14.3; 15.12). The Stephen example is most instructive, given his association with Philip in the group of seven table-servants. As with Philip, Stephen's miracles are characterized as 'great' (μεγάλη), and though not specifically labelled as δυνάμεις, they result from his being 'full of. . . power (δυνάμεως)'. The Stephen speech draws attention to the signs and wonders performed by Moses in Egypt and the Sinai desert (7.36). These acts effectively vindicated Moses, whom the Israelites had rejected, as God's chosen prophet, ruler and liberator (7.35-37).[1] Accordingly, in Luke's view, Moses functions as a prototype (7.37; cf. 3.22) of the rejected messianic prophet (Jesus) and his persecuted servants (such as Stephen and Philip),[2] whose ministries are divinely authenticated through the working of miracles; and the Exodus experience prefigures the dynamic eschatological age of salvation ushered in by Christ.[3] More uniquely related to Philip's signs and mighty works— which elicit amazement from Simon the magician (Acts 8.13)—is the possible typological association with Moses' wondrous deeds which

more eye-catching the miracle the greater the propaganda value' (*Jesus and the Spirit: A Study of the Religious and Charismatic Experience of Jesus and the First Christians as Reflected in the New Testament* [London: SCM Press, 1975], p. 167).

1. The function of Moses' signs and wonders to authenticate his prophetic vocation is clearly brought out in Exod. 4.1-9; Deut. 34.10-12; and Josephus, *Ant.* 2.274-87. Cf. O'Reilly, *Word and Sign*, pp. 170-78; G. Macrae, 'Miracle in *The Antiquities* of Josephus', in *Miracles: Cambridge Studies in their Philosophy and History* (ed. C.F.D. Moule; London: Mowbray, 1965), pp. 296-98.

2. On Luke's characterization of Jesus and early Christian missionaries as rejected 'prophets like Moses', see below, Chapter 3 section 3a.

3. Cf. K. Rengstorf, 'σημεῖον, σημαίνω, κτλ.', *TDNT*, VII, p. 241; G.W.H. Lampe, 'Miracles in the Acts of the Apostles', in Moule (ed.), *Miracles*, pp. 170-71.

overwhelm the magicians of Pharaoh.[1]

From this brief survey of the evidence, it is clear that Luke consistently regards signs and wonders as convincing demonstrations of authentic ministry. While such a viewpoint is reflected occasionally elsewhere in the New Testament (Rom. 15.17-19; 2 Cor. 12.12; Heb. 2.4), another perspective looks more warily at signs and wonders as part of the deceptive stock-in-trade of false prophets. For example, the only references to σημεῖα καὶ τέρατα in Matthew and Mark apply to the end-time activities of dangerous pseudo-messiahs (Mt. 24.24; Mk 13.22—no Lukan par.; cf. 2 Thess. 1.9-10).[2] Nevertheless, despite Luke's positive assessment of signs and wonders, he is scarcely blind to the machinations of false, wonder-working prophets. Witness the marked distinction between Philip the evangelist, whose mission is legitimated in part by the performance of salutary miracles, and Simon Magus, whose wonder-working is ultimately exposed as wickedly motivated (Acts 8.18-24; cf. 13.4-12; 16.16-18; 19.11-20).[3]

d. *Response (Acts 8.6-8, 12)*

Broadly considered, the Samaritans' reaction to the preaching and miracle-working ministry of Philip is quite favorable, leading to mass acceptance of the Christian message and baptism (Acts 8.12); in other words, Philip's Samaritan mission is a glowing success. More specifically, the following dimensions of the Samaritans' reception may be explored.

1. In accordance with Philip's ministry of word and sign, the Samaritans' response is described as both *hearing and seeing* (ἀκούειν... καὶ βλέπειν, Acts 8.6). This dual focus of aural and visual perception is common in Luke's writing. John's disciples are instructed to report to their master 'what [they] have seen and heard' of Jesus' aid to the diseased and destitute (Lk. 7.22). The manifestations of the Spirit's advent at Pentecost are phenomena which the crowds 'see and hear' (Acts 2.33). Again, the Jerusalem apostles as well as Paul ground their witness in those things which they 'have seen and heard' concerning Christ (Acts 4.20; 22.14-15). Most closely

---

1. See below, Chapter 3 section 3b, for a working out of this Philip–Moses connection.

2. Cf. Moule, 'The Vocabulary of Miracle', in Moule (ed.), *Miracles*, p. 235.

3. Cf. Talbert, *Reading Luke*, p. 246. Again, this matter will be pursued in more detail in Chapter 3.

related, however, to the Samaritans' response to Philip's work is the case of the lowly shepherds who, after hearing the angels' joyous news of Christ's birth and seeing for themselves the confirming 'sign' (σημεῖον) of the infant in the manger, return to their flocks 'glorifying and praising God for all they had heard and seen' (Lk. 2.10-20). It is striking that both Samaritans and shepherds would have ranked among the despised classes of Jewish society and that their openness to God's revelation in Christ stands in contrast to the prevailing posture of many Jews, whose 'ears are hard of hearing' and whose eyes are closed to seeing the message of salvation (Acts 28.27-28; cf. Lk. 8.10).

Although hearing and seeing are frequently paired together in Luke–Acts, it should not be assumed that the two responses are always equally valued. For example, the larger context of Acts 8.4-13 gives clear priority to hearing the word as the basis of the Samaritans' faith and baptism.[1] Before any miracles are reported, Philip's preaching is highlighted along with the fact that the crowds 'listened eagerly to what was said' by him (8.6a).[2] When the Samaritans' belief is mentioned, it is directly connected to Philip's 'proclaiming the good news about the kingdom of God' (8.12). The only indication of the Samaritans' attraction to Philip's miracles is the βλέπειν-reference in 8.6. Nothing is said of their being amazed (ἐξίστημι) over Philip's exploits as they previously had been over Simon's magic (8.9).[3]

This accent on faith's coming principally by hearing the word appears to be the dominant strain in Acts (connected with the importance of the missionary speeches), although miracles still frequently play a vital supporting role (as in 8.6-8; cf. 3.1-26; 13.4-12; 16.25-34; 19.8-20) and even occasionally provide the sole spur to faith (9.35, 42). In the Gospel of Luke, however, seeing Jesus' miraculous deeds marks a response of equal, if not superior, importance to hearing his

---

1. J. Roloff, *Das Kerygma und der irdische Jesus: Historische Motive in den Jesus-Erzählungen der Evangelien* (Göttingen: Vandenhoeck & Ruprecht, 1970), pp. 193-94 n. 306.

2. Jervell is mistaken when he states that 'Philip's mission to Samaria. . . *begins* [my emphasis] with a miraculous event' (*Unknown Paul*, p. 81).

3. D. Georgi ignores this fundamental distinction between the Samaritans' respective responses to Philip and Simon and, consequently, is led to the erroneous judgment that in Philip's ministry 'miracle activity takes the spotlight from proclamation' (*The Opponents of Paul in Second Corinthians* [Philadelphia: Fortress Press, 1986], p. 168).

message. J. Roloff notes in particular the different balances between
(1) 'seeing and hearing' the products of Jesus' ministry in Lk. 7.22
(reversed order—'hear and see'—in Matthean parallel [11.4]), where,
in the context of 7.1-22, the emphasis falls upon seeing Jesus' miraculous works; and (2) 'hearing and seeing' what Philip says and does in
Acts 8.6, where, as noted above, hearing the gospel message receives
'top billing' in the surrounding passage.[1] The major (but not exclusive) focus in Luke's Gospel on recognizing the *demonstration* of
God's power in Jesus shifts in the book of Acts to believing the *declaration* of the Christian gospel.[2]

2.   In reporting the Samaritans' response to Philip's word, Luke
employs characteristic terminology:

προσεῖχον δὲ οἱ ὄχλοι τοῖς λεγομένοις ὑπὸ τοῦ φιλίππου
ὁμοθυμαδόν (8.6a)

ὅτε δὲ ἐπίστευσαν τῷ φιλίππῳ εὐαγγελιζομένῳ. . . (8.12a)

ὁμοθυμαδόν appears repeatedly in Acts (only once in the rest of the
New Testament) in reference to the unified worship of the primitive
Jerusalem church (Acts 1.14; 2.46; 4.24), the harmonious decision of
the 'Apostolic Council' (15.25) and the cohesive reactions of various
audiences to Christian preaching, like that of the Samaritans who
welcomed Philip's testimony 'with one accord'. Interestingly, outside
the Samaritan context, ὁμοθυμαδόν-responses to Christian missionaries are typically negative. The Jews at Corinth 'made a united attack
upon Paul' (18.12), and the citizens of Ephesus 'rushed together' to
seize Paul's companions (19.29). Stephen's fate was sealed when his
hearers 'covered their ears and. . . all rushed together upon him'
(7.57). From Luke's perspective, then, the gospel cuts two ways:
prompting mass acceptance by some (e.g. Samaritans) and rejection by
others.[3]

προσέχω refers not only to the Samaritans' attentiveness to Philip,
but also to their prior attraction to Simon Magus (Acts 8.10, 11). This

1.   Roloff, *Kerygma*, pp. 192-96; cf. the discussion in F. Neirynck, 'The Miracle
Stories in the Acts of the Apostles: An Introduction', in Kremer (ed.), *Les Actes des
Apôtres*, pp. 203-204.

2.   In Acts 4.20 and 22.14-15, 'seeing and hearing' are mentioned in the same
order as in Lk. 7.22, but the emphasis is still clearly on the apostles' and Paul's
speaking/bearing witness to what they have already 'seen and heard' of Jesus.

3.   See Kee, *Good News*, pp. 87-88.

correspondence has sparked J.D.G. Dunn's appraisal that the Samaritans' 'reaction to Philip was for the same reasons and of the same quality and depth as their reaction to Simon'; in other words, it revealed 'very little discernment and depth' and was the product more of 'mass emotion' and 'herd-instinct' than a solid faith-commitment.[1] In short, the Samaritans were not yet true believers. What Dunn fails to recognize, however, is that Luke actually makes a clear distinction between the Samaritans' earlier response to Simon and their present response to Philip. I have already instanced their less enthralled preoccupation with Philip's miracles. But more than this, the respective προσέχω-expressions are not the same. With respect to Philip, the Samaritans' 'listened eagerly *to what was said*' (προσεῖχον... τοῖς λεγομένοις, v. 6); in Simon's case, they 'listened eagerly *to him*' (προσεῖχον δὲ αὐτῷ, v. 11; cf. v. 10). It was not Philip himself, but Philip's message about Christ, which arrested the Samaritans' attention; by contrast, the Samaritans' attachment to Simon was more of a personality fixation, an enchantment with a cult figure. The closest Lukan parallel to the Samaritans' 'eager listening' to Philip's preaching is not their former devotion to Simon but rather the opening of Lydia's heart 'to listen eagerly to what was said by Paul' (προσέχειν τοῖς λαλουμένοις ὑπὸ τοῦ Παύλου, Acts 16.14).[2]

The Samaritans' adherence to Philip's gospel is reinforced in the πιστεύω-phrase in Acts 8.12. However, Dunn also interprets this verse as suggesting the Samaritans' superficial response to Philip's mission. He builds his case on the use of πιστεύω with the dative, which supposedly signifies a mere 'assent of the mind' to Philip's proclamation and not a heartfelt commitment to God's word.[3] It can certainly be debated, however, whether Luke cared anything for the modern theological distinction between 'trust' (*fiducia*) and 'assent' (*adsensus*). But even assuming that he did, it is doubtful how much we

---

1. J.D.G. Dunn, *Baptism in the Holy Spirit: A Re-examination of the New Testament Teaching on the Gift of the Spirit in Relation to Pentecostalism Today* (Philadelphia: Westminster Press, 1970), pp. 64-65.

2. I fail to see why Dunn dismisses the Lydia example as 'hardly to be compared' with the Samaritans' case (*Baptism*, p. 64). Both Acts 8.6 and 16.14 stress 'listening eagerly to what was said' by Christian missionaries, the only difference being the variant terms for 'what was said' (λεγομένοις/λαλουμένοις). There is, of course, no doubt about the genuineness of Lydia's response.

3. Dunn, *Baptism*, p. 65; '"They Believed Philip Preaching" (Acts 8.12): A Reply', *IBS* 1 (1979), pp. 181-82.

can press the meaning of 'intellectual assent' into the linguistic
construction of Acts 8.12. The uses of πιστεύω with the dative τῷ
κυρίῳ (Acts 5.14; 18.8) and τῷ θεῷ (16.34) clearly denote genuine
faith. Just because the dative clause in 8.12 focuses on what was
preached about Christ rather than on Christ personally seems to be an
insignificant distinction (especially since 8.5 has already established
that Philip proclaimed Christ in Samaria). Believing the preached
word of the gospel, even though not regularly conveyed in a dative
construction, is a familiar Lukan description of valid Christian faith
(e.g. Acts 4.4; 15.7; 18.27; cf. 13.48-49).[1]

Publicly demonstrating their reception of the Christian gospel, the
Samaritans, as is customary in Acts, submit to baptism in the name of
Jesus. Surprisingly, however, this baptism is not accompanied by the
outpouring of the Spirit which passages like Acts 2.38 would lead us
to expect. This familiar conundrum in Luke's story surrounding the
relationship between water-baptism and Spirit-reception will be carefully explored in a later chapter.[2]

3. A natural by-product of Philip's benevolent ministry is the
Samaritans' experience of πολλὴ χαρά ('great joy', Acts 8.8). In
Acts 15.3 the Samaritan believers again respond with 'great joy'
(χαρὰν μεγάλην), this time over the news of Paul's Gentile mission.
Presumably, the Samaritans' rejoicing in 8.8 relates both to Philip's
message and his mighty works. Likewise, elsewhere in Luke–Acts, the
ministries of both word and miracle inspire a joyful response. The
angel announces to the shepherds 'good news of great joy for all the
people' (Lk. 2.10). Philip's other convert, the Ethiopian eunuch, also
exults (χαίρω, 8.39) over the evangelist's witness to Jesus, as does a
group of Gentiles upon hearing God's word heralded by Paul and
Barnabas in Pisidian Antioch (13.48). Joy is not the deepest level of
response to the preached word, requiring as it does the complement of
sincere faith and commitment (cf. Lk. 8.13-15), but it still represents
for Luke an important indicator of basic receptivity to the gospel.

Illustrating the response of joyful praise to the working of miracles,
we may cite the outcome of Jesus' healing of the crippled woman,
when 'the entire crowd was rejoicing at all the wonderful things that
he was doing' (Lk. 13.17; cf. 19.37), and the spirited demonstration in

---

1. Cf. E.A. Russell, '"They Believed Philip Preaching" (Acts 8.12)', *IBS* 1
(1979), pp. 169-76; Marshall, *Acts*, p. 156.
2. See below, Chapter 5 section 3.

the temple precincts of the lame man restored to health (Acts 3.8-9).

e. *Conclusion*

Although not described in elaborate fashion, the Samaritan ministry of Philip the evangelist in Acts 8.4-13 clearly reflects the principal hallmarks of authentic mission activity disclosed throughout Luke–Acts. Philip proclaims the good news, focusing upon the kingdom of God established in (the name of) Jesus Christ. This message is complemented and confirmed by the performance of miraculous signs, healings and exorcisms in particular; and, ultimately, this dynamic, double-barrelled ministry of word and deed elicits from the Samaritan throng true Christian commitment, marked by faith, joy and baptism.

Such a pattern of outreach to marginalized persons beyond the pale of Jerusalem-centered Judaism emerges again and again in Luke's narrative, characterizing the vocations of all the leading figures, notably, Jesus, Peter and Paul. By association, then, the Lukan Philip must be accorded his own ranking as a distinguished missionary/ evangelist within early Christian mission history.

4. *Philip, Samaria/Samaritans and Luke–Acts*

Although I have isolated and analyzed several key parts of Philip's Samaritan ministry, what is probably the most important aspect of this ministry from Luke's perspective remains to be examined. The *Samaritan setting* of Philip's work recalls a well-known geographic/ ethnic emphasis in Luke–Acts; indeed, the Philip story in Acts 8 stands out as the climax of a series of Lukan reports featuring Samaria/ Samaritans. On three occasions in Luke's *Sondergut* the Samaritans feature prominently in relation to Jesus' ministry (Lk. 9.51-56; 10.25-37; 17.11-19), and in the programmatic statement of Acts 1.8 the region of Samaria marks a critical intermediate stage in the gospel's advance to the ends of the earth. In addition to these transparent references to Samaria/Samaritans prior to Acts 8, the Stephen speech in Acts 7 may reflect the use of Samaritan tradition, as various scholars have recently maintained (see below).

Studies of the role of Samaria/Samaritans in Luke–Acts have typically treated the evidence systematically and ignored the important *sequential* element in the unfolding of Luke's plotted story.[1] As

1. E.g. J. Jervell, *Luke and the People of God: A New Look at Luke–Acts*

Tannehill has pointed out, however, from the start Luke announces his intention to present his material 'in order' (καθεξῆς, Lk. 1.3), which, on the basis of what follows, seems to mean 'an order appropriate to narrative' rather than a strictly historical or chronological sequence.[1] Therefore, to understand fully the significance of Philip's Samaritan mission from Luke's point of view, it is necessary not simply to compare the other Samaritan stories but also to chart carefully the narrative progression of this material up to its denouement in Acts 8.

Moreover, in seeking to evaluate Philip's achievement in evangelizing the Samaritans in Acts 8, we will need to delineate, as precisely as possible, Luke's understanding of the Samaritans' peculiar ethnicoreligious identity within the social world of first-century Judaism. To this end, we must certainly follow closely the literary clues in Luke's text but also keep an eye open to illuminating comparative material on the Samaritan people, especially that provided by Josephus.

a. *Jesus' Rejection by a Samaritan Village (Luke 9.51-56)*
The three pericopae in Luke's Gospel dealing with Jesus and the Samaritans are loosely held together as parts of the so-called 'travel narrative' or 'central section' of the book (9.51–19.44). The first scene in 9.51-56, depicting an altercation between Jesus and the inhabitants of a Samaritan village, introduces this extended narrative. Characteristic attitudes of both Jesus and his disciples toward the Samaritans are plainly revealed, thus providing a useful gauge for evaluating Philip's outreach to the same group in Acts 8.

A key transition in Jesus' itinerary is signalled in Lk. 9.51b: 'he set his face to go to Jerusalem'. Prior to this point in the story, Jesus' public ministry has been localized in the region of Galilee (4.14–9.50). Now his career moves inexorably to its culmination in Jerusalem, where the events of death, resurrection and ascension will unfold.[2] Unlike the other Synoptics which chart Jesus' movement

(Minneapolis, MN: Augsburg, 1972), pp. 113-32; M.S. Enslin, 'Luke and the Samaritans', *HTR* 36 (1943), pp. 277-97; *idem*, 'Samaritan Ministry and Mission', *HUCA* 51 (1980), pp. 29-38.

1. Tannehill, *Narrative Unity*, I, pp. 9-12; cf. R.J. Dillon, 'Previewing Luke's Project from his Prologue (Luke 1:1-4)', *CBQ* 43 (1981), pp. 217-23; M. Völkel, 'Exegetische Erwägungen zum Verständnis des Begriffs ΚΑΘΕΞΗΣ im lukanischen Prolog', *NTS* 20 (1973–74), pp. 289-95.

2. M. Miyoshi regards ἀνάλημψις in Lk. 9.51 as referring primarily to Jesus'

directly from Galilee to trans-Jordanian country (Mt. 19.1-2; Mk 10.1), Luke plots Jesus' course southward into Samaria. Jesus sends an advance party to prepare for his stay in an unnamed Samaritan village (9.52). Such action goes against the stark mandate issued to Jesus' disciples in Matthew to 'enter no town of the Samaritans' (10.5b), but it coincides with Jesus' stopover at Sychar recounted in John 4. However, Luke and John portray the reaction to Jesus' foray into Samaritan territory very differently. The Johannine Jesus finds a warm and enthusiastic reception in Sychar (Jn 4.39-42), whereas in Luke 9 the Samaritans flatly refuse to host Jesus, 'because his face was set toward Jerusalem' (v. 53). Clearly assumed here is the historic tension between Jerusalem-honoring Jews and the Samaritans who venerated Mt Gerizim as the only true place of worship.[1]

As a further sign that little love was lost between Samaritans and Jerusalem-oriented Jews, James and John counter the Samaritans' rebuff with a scheme to destroy their village with heavenly fire (9.54). While the appended phrase, 'as Elijah did', is not attested in the best manuscripts, it no doubt correctly identifies the source of inspiration for the two disciples' dramatic plea (cf. 2 Kgs 1.9-14; Sir. 48.3).[2] Jesus, however, will have no part of such violent retribution. He delivers a general rebuke to James and John (9.55), punctuated according to some ancient witnesses by the explanatory statements, 'You do not know what manner of spirit you are of; for the Son of Man came not to destroy the lives of human beings but to save them'. J.M. Ross has argued that, despite the omission of these statements in the Alexandrian uncials, there are sufficient grounds for accepting them as part of Luke's original text.[3] Whether or not Ross has made

---

ascension (cf. ἀναλαμβάνω, Acts 1.2, 11, 22) but also encompassing the events of Jesus' passion and resurrection prior to his 'taking up' (*Der Anfang des Reiseberichts Lk 9.51–10.24: Eine redaktionsgeschichtliche Untersuchung* [AnBib, 60; Rome: Biblical Institute, 1974], pp. 8-9). Cf. also Parsons, *Departure*, pp. 107-111, 129-33.

1. Cf. Jervell, *Luke*, pp. 113-17.

2. The ἀνάλημψις-reference in Lk. 9.51 is likely also an allusion to Elijah's 'assumption' into heaven (cf. 4 Kgdms 2.9, 10, 11; Sir. 48.9; 1 Macc. 2.58). On the influence of the Elijah story on Lk. 9.51-56, see T.L. Brodie, 'The Departure for Jerusalem (Luke 9,51-56) as a Rhetorical Imitation of Elijah's Departure for the Jordan (2 Kgs 1,1-2,6)', *Bib* 70 (1989), pp. 96-109; Miyoshi, *Anfang*, pp. 8-9, 13; Evans, 'Luke's Use of the Elijah/Elisha Narratives', pp. 80-82.

3. (1) It is easier to explain the omission of the disputed words than their inclusion

his case, the disputed expansions in Lk. 9.55-56 accurately capture the salvific tenor of the Lukan Jesus' ministry (cf. Lk. 19.10).

The scene in Lk. 9.51-56 fits well with external reports of Samaritan–Jewish conflict in the first century CE. Josephus, for example, relates an episode from the time of Coponius (6-9 CE) in which a band of Samaritans littered (and defiled) the Jerusalem temple with human bones during Passover (*Ant.* 18.29-30). More pertinent, however, to the incident in Luke 9 is Josephus's account of Samaritan–Jewish hostilities during the governorship of Cumanus (48–52 CE). As a company of Galilean pilgrims made their way to Jerusalem, one of them was murdered in the north Samaritan border town of Gema. This naturally provoked retaliation. A large contingent of Galileans mobilized for war against the Samaritans, and representatives were dispatched to Cumanus, demanding retribution against the perpetrators of the murder. Cumanus, however, played down the crisis and attended to other affairs. Meanwhile, when news of the Gema incident reached Jerusalem, a mob army quickly formed under the leadership of Eleazar and Alexander; although it was still feast-time, they marched to a Samaritan site near Shechem and duly 'massacred the inhabitants without distinction of age and burned the villages'. Both Roman and Jewish authorities eventually intervened in an attempt to quell the uprising. Some of the Jewish brigands were executed, but others continued to wreak havoc all over Samaria. Finally the matter was taken to Caesar who, on the urging of Herod Agrippa, condemned the Samaritans for their murderous act, executed three of their leading citizens and banished Cumanus for his incompetent handling of the ordeal (*War* 2.232-45; cf. *Ant.* 15.118-36).

The Galilean pilgrimage to Jerusalem through Samaria, the Samaritans' cool reception and the consequent Jewish reprisals—all of these elements are strikingly echoed in Lk. 9.51-56. By contrast, however, the Lukan Jesus displays a remarkably moderating spirit in the face of a potentially explosive situation fuelled by ethno-religious hatred.[1]

---

by later versions; (2) other stories of Jesus following a similar literary form usually end with a saying of Jesus; (3) the content of the disputed words fits the general tenor of the genuine sayings of Jesus (J.M. Ross, 'The Rejected Words in Luke 9.54-56', *ExpTim* 84 [1972–73], pp. 85-88).

1. On the comparison between Lk. 9.51-56 and the Gema incident, see J.M. Ford, *My Enemy is my Guest: Jesus and Violence in Luke* (Maryknoll, NY:

Concerning the function of Lk. 9.51-56 in the wider context of the Gospel narrative, prime consideration must be given to the parallel with 4.16-30, acknowledged by many scholars.[1] As Jesus' trek from Galilee to Jerusalem commences with rejection in a Samaritan village, so his earlier ministry within Galilee began with dismissal from his hometown of Nazareth. And both incidents conclude with reports of Jesus' moving on (πορεύομαι, 4.30; 9.56) to another locale. While most commentators simply note this basic correspondence between the Samaritans' and Nazarenes' rejections of Jesus and leave it at that, J.T. Sanders has recently explored what he feels are two critical differences between these episodes. First, Luke provides the Samaritans with 'a reasonable excuse' for their refusal to entertain Jesus—namely, his Jerusalem destination—whereas the Nazarenes are accorded no such alibi. Secondly, while 'in Nazareth Jesus threw it in the teeth of his Jewish congregation that God's grace had always gone to Gentiles and not to Israelites' (Lk. 4.24-27), thereby inciting the crowd to kill him, in the case of the inhospitable Samaritan village, 'Jesus turns the other cheek... To put the matter as bluntly and plainly as possible, no charge is made against the Samaritans who reject Jesus'.[2]

Does Luke in fact mitigate the gravity of the Samaritans' rejection of Jesus, as Sanders thinks? In response to his first point, it can scarcely be maintained that Luke somehow justifies the Samaritans' snubbing of Jesus because he was bound for a city (Jerusalem) which they especially despised. Later in the travel narrative, a Samaritan leper appears unperturbed that Jesus is still 'on the way to Jerusalem' (17.11); he cries out for Jesus' help and falls at Jesus' feet in grateful praise (17.15-18). Moreover, in Luke's eyes, Jesus' journey to Jerusalem is much more than a mere token of 'his Jewish behaviour' which the Samaritans would understandably find offensive. As is well known, in Luke's geographical plan Jerusalem is the place of the

Orbis, 1984), pp. 84-91; D. Flusser, 'Lukas 9:51-56—Ein hebräisches Fragment', in *The New Testament Age: Essays in Honor of Bo Reicke* (2 vols.; ed. W.C. Weinrich; Macon, GA: Mercer University Press, 1984), I, pp. 166-67.

   1. E.g. Tannehill, *Narrative Unity,* I, p. 230; Enslin, 'Samaritan Ministry', pp. 30-33; Miyoshi, *Anfang,* pp. 16-18; D. Tiede, *Prophecy and History in Luke–Acts* (Philadelphia: Fortress Press, 1980), p. 55.

   2. J.T. Sanders, *The Jews in Luke–Acts* (London: SCM Press, 1987), p. 144; cf. pp. 180-81.

messiah's initial revelation (Lk. 1–2) and ultimate vindication (Acts 1–2). It is where he is 'taken up' (Lk. 9.51; Acts 1.2, 11), the inevitable goal of his entire mission. Thus, for the Samaritans to spurn Jesus because of his Jerusalem-orientation would represent more than predictable socioreligious prejudice in Luke's view: it would also signify blatant repudiation of Jesus' messiahship.[1]

Regarding Sanders's second point, there is an apparent difference in intensity between the Nazarene and Samaritan responses to Jesus (the former seek to kill Jesus; the latter merely decline to accommodate him) coupled with a different level of interaction on Jesus' part with his opponents (he directly confronts the Nazarenes; he never encounters the Samaritans personally). Still, it is not true that the Samaritans are let off scot-free, while the poor Nazarenes are severely judged. To be sure, Jesus resists a violent and vindictive, Elijah-style reply to the Samaritans' action and leaves the door open for subsequent repentance and salvation, but he does not condone their present behavior nor linger to plead for reconciliation. Rather he turns away from the unfriendly Samaritan village and redirects his mission to other places potentially more receptive (9.56; 10.1-20).

Some have thought that ἑτέραν κώμην in 9.56 designates another Samaritan village and that Luke localizes the mission of the seventy (-two) in ch. 10—and indeed all the events in the central section—in Samaritan territory.[2] But this is far from certain. The geographical data in the travel report is too sparse and disconnected to provide an exact itinerary.[3] Generally speaking, from 9.51 onward the narrative simply directs Jesus' movement toward Jerusalem (cf. 13.22; 17.11; 19.11, 28) without undue regard for mapping a precise course. There are the two pericopae which feature Samaritans in a positive light (10.25-37; 17.11-19) and the enigmatic note in 17.11 that Jesus 'was going through the region between (διὰ μέσον) Samaria and Galilee',[4]

1. Cf. Jervell, *Luke*, pp. 123-24.
2. E.g. C.C. McCown, 'The Geography of Luke's Central Section', *JBL* 57 (1938), pp. 56-66; E. Lohse, 'Missionarisches Handeln Jesu nach dem Evangelium des Lukas', *TZ* 10 (1954), pp. 1-13; Enslin, 'Samaritan Ministry', pp. 29-38.
3. Cf. Fitzmyer, *Luke*, I, pp. 165-66, 824-26.
4. The precise significance of the geographical note in Lk. 17.11 has been a matter of considerable discussion. See, e.g., J. Blinzler, 'Die literarische Eigenart des sogenannten Reiseberichts im Lukas-Evangelium', in *Synoptische Studien* (ed. J. Schmid and A. Vögtle; Munich: Zink, 1953), pp. 46-50; Sanders, *Jews*,

but these are hardly sufficient grounds for positing a Samaritan setting for the entire travel narrative. As for the location of the places visited by Jesus and his followers immediately after the Samaritans' rejection, we can only speculate, but it would be a surprising turn of events in Luke's story for Jesus so soon to court deliberately the disfavor of other Samaritan centers.[1] Moreover, the mention of Chorazin, Bethsaida and Capernaum in 10.13-15, while not settling the matter, seems to suggest the region around the Sea of Galilee as the principal target area.

Whatever the locale, the number of participants in this itinerant mission seems to intimate the gospel's projected extension to all peoples. Talbert traces the textual variation between seventy and seventy-two messengers back to the Hebrew and Greek texts of Genesis 10, which enumerate seventy (MT) and seventy-two (LXX) nations comprising the post-diluvian world. He thus concludes that 'whatever the original reading. . . the point is the same. The number seventy or seventy-two symbolizes all the nations of the world: the mission is a universal one'.[2] It is also possible that the seventy/seventy-two discrepancy goes back to the number of Spirit-inspired elder-prophets appointed to assist Moses in Numbers 11 (the question turns on whether the pair, Eldad and Medad, are added to the original seventy; cf. 11.26-30). If this is part of the background to Luke 10, however, once again the notion of a worldwide gospel mission may still be suggested, since for Luke the chief purpose of Spirit-empowered proclamation by Jesus' assistants is to bear witness to the ends of the earth (Lk. 24.47-49; Acts 1.8).[3] Accepting that the sending of the

pp. 144-45; Conzelmann, *Theology*, pp. 68-73. M. Hengel cuts across the debate with a sober conclusion:

> In Luke 17.11, the geographical information over which scholars have argued so much and which tends to be over-interpreted remains utterly obscure. We do not know what the author had in mind here. For 'Luke's only concern is to explain the presence of a Samaritan among the Jews' (17.16) (*Between Jesus and Paul: Studies in the Earliest History of Christianity* [London: SCM Press, 1983], p. 100).

1. G. Sellin, 'Komposition, Quellen und Funktion des lukanischen Reiseberichts (Lk. ix 51-xix 28)', *NovT* 20 (1978), pp. 115-16.

2. Talbert, *Reading Luke*, p. 115. Cf. W. Manson, *The Gospel of Luke* (MNTC; London: Hodder & Stoughton, 1930), p. 123.

3. In arguing that the seventy(-two) messengers in Lk. 10 primarily recall the elder-prophets in Num. 11, S. Garrett downplays any allusion to the seventy(-two) nations of Gen. 10 (*The Demise of the Devil: Magic and the Demonic in Luke's*

seventy(-two) in Luke 10 does prefigure the expansion of mission boundaries to include Gentiles, then the Samaritans' preceding rejection of Jesus in 9.51-56 functions as a catalyst of this expansion. Rejection by one group prompts a turn to more receptive peoples.

This pattern is precisely what we find in the Nazareth episode. Jesus senses that, despite their admiring words, his own people do not fully grasp the import of his prophetic mission and will ultimately find him unacceptable (Lk. 4.22-24). He then implicitly associates his ministry with events involving Elijah and Elisha which demonstrate that God's prophets have often found truer acceptance outside the land of Israel among needy foreigners (4.25-27). This is clearly not a case of invoking Elijah as a precedent for harsh reprisals against the Nazarenes, as James and John are inclined to do against the Samaritans.[1] Jesus is no more disposed in Nazareth than in Samaria toward annihilating those who oppose him or barring the door to future conversion.[2] Even when the Nazarenes forcefully attempt to kill him, he quietly escapes without incident (4.28-30). What the appeal to Elijah and Elisha does suggest is the future widening of the Christian mission beyond the limits of recalcitrant Jews, like those in Jesus' hometown, to incorporate Gentiles who will gladly welcome the gospel.[3]

In short, the Samaritans in Lk. 9.51-56, although patently at odds with Jerusalem-honoring Jews, are nonetheless closely identified with them—at least those Jews in Nazareth—as jointly antagonistic to Jesus' mission. While the way is not irrevocably blocked to their own repen-

---

Writings [Philadelphia: Fortress Press, 1989], pp. 47-48). I see no reason, however, why both options could not be mutually relevant to Luke's interests.

1. Tannehill notes that in Luke 'the Elijah stories are being used critically. Elijah is not only prototype but also antitype, and the contrast receives strong accent in Luke 9' (*Narrative Unity*, I, p. 230). A similar critical treatment is to be seen with respect to Elisha in the next scene (Lk. 9.61-62; cf. 1 Kgs 19.19-21).

2. L.C. Crockett goes too far in concluding that Lk. 4.25-27 foreshadows 'Jewish–Gentile *reconciliation*' [his emphasis], but he is correct in observing that this passage is 'certainly not' designed to disclose God's final rejection of Israel ('Luke 4.25-27 and Jewish–Gentile Relations in Luke–Acts', *JBL* 88 [1969], p. 183).

3. Cf. J.B. Tyson, 'The Gentile Mission and the Authority of Scripture in Acts', *NTS* 33 (1987), p. 622; Tannehill, *Narrative Unity*, I, pp. 70-72. R. Brawley's recent attempt to overturn the standard view that Lk. 4.25-27 foreshadows the Gentile mission in Acts (*Luke–Acts and the Jews: Conflict, Apology, and Conciliation* [SBLMS, 33; Atlanta: Scholars Press, 1987], pp. 6-11) is not convincing (cf. my review, *WTJ* 52 [1990], pp. 156-58).

tance and salvation, the obstinacy of these Samaritans and Nazarenes has in fact paved the way for extended outreach to the more receptive Gentiles.

In addition to the leading role which Jesus plays in Lk. 9.51-56, a secondary role is assumed by the disciples, especially James and John. The sending of messengers (ἄγγελοι) ahead of Jesus to prepare (ἐτοιμάζω) for his arrival is a common phenomenon in Luke's Gospel (10.1; 19.29-30; 22.8), especially reminiscent of the forerunning ministry of John the Baptist (1.17, 76; 3.4; 7.27).[1] The identity of the messengers whom Jesus dispatches in 9.52 is not disclosed, but it is possible that James and John should be included in their number. The report that James and John 'saw' the Samaritans' rejection intimates that they had been present in the village and experienced the rebuff at first hand. In any event, these two disciples are singled out as pleading for fiery judgment against the stubborn Samaritans.

Besides recalling the example of Elijah, this drastic request may be related in the disciples' thinking to the prediction (of John the Baptist) that Jesus would 'baptize with fire' and 'burn the chaff with unquenchable fire' (Lk. 3.16-17).[2] What James and John fail to realize, however, is that such activity points to a final judgment against unrepentant rebels (cf. Lk. 10.12-15, 'on that day' [v. 12]) and does not license swift retribution in the present age. This misunderstanding of Jesus' mission is a typical handicap of the disciples in the latter half of Luke 9. The insensitive reaction of James and John to the Samaritans should thus be correlated with the disciples' confusion over Jesus' transfiguration (9.32-36), faithless inability to heal an afflicted child (9.37-43), misguided bickering over who was the greatest (9.46-48) and exclusion of any minister outside their circle (9.49-50).[3]

---

1. See Miyoshi, *Anfang*, pp. 25-26. The comparison between Lk. 9.52 and 7.27 is especially strong:

καὶ ἀπέστειλεν ἀγγέλους πρὸ προσώπου αὐτοῦ (9.52)

ἰδοὺ ἀποστέλλω τὸν ἄγγελόν μου πρὸ προσώπου σου (7.27)

2. Cf. Fitzmyer, *Luke*, I, pp. 827, 664.

3. By focusing so exclusively on Lk. 9.51-56 as the beginning of a new section, scholars tend to overlook the contacts between this passage and the preceding material in Lk. 9. Among those, however, who acknowledge these contacts are Marshall, *Gospel of Luke*, pp. 400-402; and J. Kodell, 'Luke and the Children: The Beginning and the End of the Great Interpolation (Luke 9:46-56; 18:9-23)', *CBQ* 49 (1987), pp. 419-23.

This sketch of the disciples' strident dealings with the Samaritans affords an interesting contrast to Philip's more congenial interaction in Acts 8. Specific implications of such a contrast will be enumerated below.

b. *Two Model Samaritans (Luke 10.25-37; 17.11-19)*

In view of the Samaritans' clear-cut rejection of Jesus in Lk. 9.51-56, it is surprising to find that later in the travel narrative two Samaritans—the 'good', compassionate traveller in the classic parable (10.30-35) and the 'grateful', faith-possessing leper in the familiar miracle story (17.11-19)—are singled out as paragons of Christian discipleship. Moreover, in both accounts the Samaritan figure is now contrasted with Jews whose conduct continues to prove deficient in some way. Obviously, then, the parallelism between Jewish and Samaritan callousness to Jesus' mission, established in the opening scene of the travel narrative, soon begins to pull apart, and first steps are taken toward the Samaritans' mass acceptance of Christ under Philip's ministry. At this stage, however, given the limited focus on two isolated Samaritans, there can be no talk as yet of any wholesale change in Samaritan disposition toward Jesus.

To fill out this general picture of the Samaritans' developing role in Luke's narrative, the two stories featuring model Samaritans must be analyzed in more detail. The Parable of the Good Samaritan revolves around dramatically opposing responses to a severely wounded traveller lying helpless on the road. On the one hand, two Jewish religious officials negligently 'pass by on the other side' (10.31-32); but on the other hand, a Samaritan goes out of his way to assist the victim and nurse him back to health (10.33-35). Though not explicitly stated, the well-known animosity between Samaritans and Jerusalem-centered Jews undoubtedly forms a critical part of the parable's background, creating a 'shock effect' on its audience.[1] From the perspective of the inquisitive lawyer addressed by Jesus (10.25-30, 36-37),[2] the honored

---

1. The 'surprise' element in the Samaritan's ministry is noted by R.W. Funk, 'The Good Samaritan as Metaphor', *Semeia* 2 (1974), p. 80; J.D.M. Derrett, *Law in the New Testament* (London: Darton, Longman & Todd, 1970), pp. 220-21.

2. On the role of lawyers in Luke, see A.J. Saldarini, *Pharisees, Scribes and Sadducees in Palestinian Society: A Sociological Approach* (Wilmington, DE: Michael Glazier), pp. 182-84. The basic conclusion is that 'in the author's world lawyers. . . functioned as authoritative experts in social and religious law and

clerics most expected to fulfill the law of neighborly love fail miserably in their duty, whereas the despised Samaritan startlingly pursues the righteous course of action. Small wonder that the jolted lawyer cannot bring himself to identify the true neighbor directly; in place of the ignominious 'Samaritan' label, he uses the circumlocution, 'the one who showed him mercy' (10.37).[1]

The fact that the victim in the parable was journeying '*from Jerusalem* to Jericho' (and thus was presumably a Jew) when misfortune befell him makes the Samaritan's ministry all the more remarkable. Josephus supplies a typical assessment of Samaritan attitudes toward the Jews:

> they alter their attitude according to circumstance and, when they see the Jews prospering, call them their kinsmen, on the ground that they are descended from Joseph and are related to them through their origin from him, but, when they see the Jews in trouble, they say that they have nothing whatever in common with them nor do these have any claim of friendship or race, and they declare themselves to be aliens of another race (*Ant.* 9.29).

Although clearly polemical and one-sided, this passage accurately captures something of the fluctuating nature of Samaritan–Jewish relations in the first century CE.[2] It would certainly have been the norm for Samaritans to keep their distance 'when they saw the Jews in trouble'. How radical, then, for the Lukan Jesus to spotlight a Samaritan who sacrificially aids a stricken Jew, even committing himself to future assistance, if necessary ('when I come back. . . ', 10.35).[3]

The apparent literary influence of 2 Chron. 28.5-15 on the Parable of the Good Samaritan[4] also brings into view the striking reversal of

custom, officials and guardians of community norms' (p. 183).

1. J. Jeremias, *Jerusalem in the Time of Jesus: An Investigation into Economic and Social Conditions during the New Testament Period* (Philadelphia: Fortress Press, 1969), pp. 354-55 n. 8; B. van Elderen, 'Another Look at the Parable of the Good Samaritan', in *Saved By Hope: Essays in Honor of Richard C. Oudersluys* (ed. J.I. Cook; Grand Rapids: Eerdmans, 1978), pp. 115-16.

2. Cf. R.J. Coggins, *Samaritans and Jews: The Origins of Samaritanism Reconsidered* (Growing Points in Theology; Oxford: Basil Blackwell, 1975), p. 94; and further discussion of Samaritan–Jewish relations below.

3. Cf. Ford, *My Enemy*, p. 92.

4. See the detailed discussion in F.S. Spencer, '2 Chronicles 28:5-15 and the Parable of the Good Samaritan', *WTJ* 46 (1984), pp. 317-49.

standard societal patterns. The context of the Chronicler's story was Israel's (= Samaria's) devastating military defeat of her kinsfolk in Judah. However, as Israel's triumphant army returned to Samaria with the spoils of war—including thousands of Judean captives—Oded the prophet met them and rebuked their harsh treatment of the Judean people. Consequently, a Samarian delegation 'took the captives, and with the booty they clothed all that were naked among them; they clothed them, gave them sandals, provided them with food and drink, and anointed them; and carrying all the feeble among them on donkeys, they brought them to their kindred at Jericho...' (2 Chron. 28.15). Thus, the very Samarians who had attacked their Judean neighbors turned aboutface and became the agents of healing and restoration. Likewise, the Samaritan in the Lukan parable—though not the cause of the Jewish traveller's misfortune—flouts the customary response of cold-heartedness toward a bitter enemy and displays sympathetic charity instead.

This exceptional nature of the Samaritan's activity in Luke 10 provides the key point of contrast with the Samaritan incident in 9.51-56. In the earlier scene only Jesus overturns conventional attitudes; otherwise, Samaritans and Jerusalem-bound Jews (James and John) remain entrenched in their prejudice toward one another. In the parable, however, a lone Samaritan—sharply distinguished from Jewish cultic personnel—now breaks with tradition and conforms to Jesus' avowed standard and personal example of neighborly love.[1] By so identifying with Jesus' way of life and by bearing, as it were, the marks of Christian discipleship, the 'Good Samaritan' is proof positive that individual Samaritans may abandon their initially recalcitrant position toward Jesus and be 'converted'. Accordingly, Jesus' staunch refusal to annihilate the Samaritans in 9.55 is thoroughly vindicated.[2]

In the story of the cleansing of the ten lepers, another Samaritan stands out from his Jewish counterparts as a sincere respondent to Jesus' mission. In this case, the accent falls on the proper acknowl-

---

1. Van Elderen notes how Jesus' activity in Lk. 18.35-43 especially corresponds with the Good Samaritan's behavior. Near Jericho Jesus heals a blind beggar who is crying out for mercy and, in the process, stands out as a model of compassion over against an insensitive crowd seeking to silence the afflicted man ('Another Look', pp. 117-18).

2. Cf. D. Gewalt, 'Der "Barmherzige Samariter" zu Lukas 10,25-37', *EvT* 38 (1978), p. 408.

edgment of Jesus' miraculous power rather than on following his teaching and example. As the story begins, the lepers cry out in unison: 'Jesus, Master (ἐπιστάτα), have mercy on us!' (17.13). ἐπιστάτα is a uniquely Lukan title for Jesus (substituted for διδάσκολος in the Synoptic parallels), normally uttered by Jesus' disciples (Lk. 5.5; 8.24, 45; 9.33, 49). In the present instance, it seems to reflect some recognition of Jesus' authority by all ten lepers.[1] But as the story progresses, it becomes evident that only the Samaritan experiences a true change of heart as well as physical healing. He alone really 'sees' (ἰδών, v. 15) what has happened to him and 'turns back' (ἐπιστρέφω, vv. 15, 18) to worship Jesus. A series of rhetorical questions posed by Jesus underscores the significance of this 'returning' (17-18). In Luke's writing, ἐπιστρέφω customarily signifies genuine repentance and conversion (Lk. 1.16, 17; 22.32; Acts 3.19; 9.35; 11.21; 15.19; 26.18, 20; 28.27). No doubt the experience of the Samaritan leper should be interpreted along these lines, especially since his response to Jesus is ultimately characterized in terms of 'faith' (Lk. 17.19).[2]

Apart from exposing the Samaritan's discipleship, the narrative in Lk. 17.11-19 also highlights his peculiar ethnic identity. His grateful return to Jesus is particularly amazing, seeing that 'he was a Samaritan' (v. 16b) or, alternatively, a 'foreigner' (ἀλλογενής, v. 18). Although a New Testament *hapax*, ἀλλογενής (lit. 'belonging to another race') was used in the famous temple inscription warning non-Jews against trespassing into the inner courts[3] and appears frequently in the LXX to designate those 'aliens' or 'strangers' set apart from the people of Israel (e.g. Exod. 12.43; 27.33; Joel 3[4].17; Jer. 28 [51].51; Ezek. 44.7, 9; 1 Esd. 8.69-93; 9.7-36; 1 Macc. 3.36, 45; Jdt. 9.2). Thus, from the perspective of early Judaism, an ἀλλογενής was a Gentile outsider.

Is not J. Bowman right to conclude, then, that for Luke the

---

1. On the significance of the ἐπιστάτα-title in this context, see O. Glombitza, 'Der dankbare Samariter. Luk. xvii 11-19', *NovT* 11 (1969), pp. 241-43, 245.

2. On the 'Christian' status of the grateful Samaritan, see Glombitza, 'Dankbare Samariter', pp. 243-46; H.D. Betz, 'The Cleansing of the Ten Lepers (Luke 17:11-19)', *JBL* 90 (1971), pp. 315-16, 318-21.

3. J.H. Moulton and G. Milligan, *The Vocabulary of the Greek Testament* (London: Hodder & Stoughton, 1930), p. 23; cf. R.J. Coggins, 'The Samaritans and Acts', *NTS* 28 (1982), p. 431.

Samaritans 'represent an essential part of the gentile world'?[1] Certainly the ἀλλογενής label wrecks Jervell's case that the Samaritans in Luke–Acts are stationed wholly within the Israelite camp (although, admittedly, 'they are Jews who have gone astray').[2] Jervell recognizes Luke's use of a related term, ἀλλόφυλος, in reference to non-Jews in Acts 10.28, but thinks that ἀλλογενής is somehow 'weaker' in connoting the idea of separateness from Israel.[3] However, twice in the LXX ἀλλογενής and ἀλλόφυλος appear together in synonymous parallelism (Isa. 61.5; Zech. 9.6), and there is no conspicuous evidence suggesting any subtle distinction between the terms in Lukan usage.[4]

Also pointing to a Samaritan–Gentile connection is the probable literary link between the Samaritan leper in Luke, cleansed by Jesus, and the Syrian leper, Naaman, healed by Elisha in 2 Kings 5.[5] Both sufferers are cured when they obey the prophetic command to 'go' (πορεύομαι, Lk. 17.14; 4 Kgdms 5.10) and perform some ritual, and both respond to their healing by 'returning' (ἐπιστρέφω, 4 Kgdms 5.15; cf. v. 14) to their benefactors and praising God. Luke, of course, specifically cites the Naaman incident in 4.27 as an illustration of Jesus' (and the early church's) projected missionary turn to the Gentiles. Jesus' ministry to the Naaman-like Samaritan ἀλλογενής in 17.11-19 may then represent a first-fruit of this Gentile harvest which

---

1. J. Bowman, *The Samaritan Problem: Studies in the Relationship of Samaritans, Judaism, and Early Christianity* (PTMS, 4; Pittsburgh: Pickwick, 1975), pp. 69-70. Also associating the Samaritans with Gentiles in Luke–Acts are Jeremias ('Σαμάρεια, Σαμαρίτης, Σαμαρῖτις', *TDNT*, VII, pp. 91-93) and Enslin ('Samaritan Mission', pp. 29-30).

2. Jervell, *Luke*, p. 117; cf. pp. 113-32.

3. Jervell, *Luke*, pp. 117, 131 n. 41; cf. J.A. Montgomery, *The Samaritans: The Earliest Jewish Sect: Their History, Theology and Literature* (New York: Ktav, repr. 1968 [1907]), p. 160 n. 20.

4. In *War* 5.193, when referring to the temple inscription prohibiting entry to foreigners, Josephus uses ἀλλόφυλος in place of ἀλλογενής; cf. Moulton and Milligan, *Vocabulary*, p. 23.

5. On the influence of the Naaman incident on Lk. 17.11-19, see W. Bruners, *Der Reinigung der zehn Aussätzigen und die Heilung des Samariters Lk 17,11-19: Ein Beitrag zur lukanischen Interpretation der Reinigung von Aussätzigen* (FB, 23; Stuttgart: Katholisches Bibelwerk, 1977), pp. 287-306; Enslin, 'Luke and the Samaritans', pp. 295-96; R.E. Brown, 'Jesus and Elijah', *Perspective* 12 (1971), pp. 90-91.

comes to fruition in Acts.[1] If so, a notable shift has occurred in the role of the Samaritans within Luke's narrative. In 9.51-56 the Samaritans mirrored the Jews in Nazareth as fellow-rejectors of Jesus' mission who, by their rejection, opened the door for evangelizing the Gentiles. Now in 17.11-19 a Samaritan switches sides, so to speak, and himself takes on the part of one of those anticipated Gentile converts.

Still, acknowledging the grateful Samaritan's 'Gentile' identity does not provide a complete ethnic profile of this fascinating character. For despite his 'foreign' status, the Samaritan leper still attends to Mosaic purity regulations (along with his nine Jewish companions),[2] just as the good Samaritan in the parable fulfilled the love-command in Leviticus 19. This persisting 'Jewish' characterization alongside the ἀλλογενής-reference in 17.18 suggests that the Samaritans should properly be classified in Luke's presentation as a kind of median social group, a *tertium genus*, neither fully Jewish nor fully Gentile, but manifesting partial affinity with both peoples.[3] At this point, J.T. Sanders correctly associates the Samaritans in Luke–Acts with other 'twilight' figures on the periphery of Judaism, such as tax collectors, 'sinners' and 'God-fearers'.[4] However, proselytes should probably not be included in this marginal realm (since they are total converts to Judaism) nor should the Samaritans be so completely identified with other borderline groups as to ignore prevailing distinctions between them in Luke's portrayal.[5] (For example, the Samaritans initially

---

1. Cf. the observation of G.B. Caird: 'For Luke the most attractive part of the story was that the Samaritan, by his eager appreciation, showed up his Jewish fellow-sufferers, and gave a foretaste of the opening of the kingdom to the Gentiles' (*The Gospel of St Luke* [Pelican NT Commentaries; Harmondsworth: Penguin Books, 1963], p. 195).

2. Even though we should probably envisage the Samaritan as heading off to his own temple and priest while the nine Jews go to Jerusalem (Marshall thinks the plural ἱερεῖς indicates that 'each man would go to the appropriate priest' [*Gospel of Luke*, p. 651]), all ten lepers share a common respect for Pentateuchal legislation.

3. Cf. Hengel, *Between Jesus and Paul*, p. 122; Coggins, 'Samaritans and Acts', pp. 431-32; G. Bouwman, 'Samaria im lukanischen Doppelwerk', in *Theologe aus dem Norden* (ed. A. Fuchs; Studien zum NT und Seiner Umwelt A/2; Linz, 1976), p. 119.

4. Sanders, *Jews*, pp. 132-53.

5. Contra J.T. Sanders:

> it matters not a whit whether the person who anoints Jesus or the leper who is healed or the one who prays for redemption in the Temple is an outcast, a Samaritan, or a

reject Jesus, while the religious outcasts and 'God-fearers' consistently prove receptive.)

This ambiguous status of the Samaritans in Luke–Acts correlates with other perceptions of this group in early Jewish literature.[1] Recall Josephus' opinion, cited above, that the Samaritans could appear one moment as Jewish 'kinsmen' and the next as 'aliens of another race' (*Ant.* 9.291). In a similar vein, he portrays the Samaritans elsewhere as 'apostates from the Jewish nation' who still 'profess themselves Jews' in expedient situations (*Ant.* 11.340-41). Josephus also, however, frequently identifies the Samaritans with the pagan 'Cutheans' (cf. 2 Kgs 17.24) imported to settle northern Israel after the Assyrian conquest (*War* 1.63; *Ant.* 9.288-90; 10.184; 11.19, 20, 88, 302; 13.225) and in one place labels them 'the Sidonians in Shechem' who campaigned to rename the Gerizim temple in honor of Zeus (*Ant.* 12.257-64).[2]

The Mishnah likewise contains references to the Samaritans as

proselyte or God-fearer. Their response to Jesus or their exemplary piety is of one piece, and the differences exist only for verisimilitude and for narrative interest (*Jews*, p. 147).

1. Recent historical studies have tended to view the relationship between Samaritans and Jews in the ancient world as complex and ambiguous. While recognizing the tensions which prevailed between these two socioreligious groups, there is a growing reluctance among scholars to speak of any clear-cut, permanent schism. Samaritanism is now being explored more as one first-century Jewish option among many ('a variety of Judaism') and as a diverse phenomenon in its own right ('varieties of Samaritanism'). See especially the two survey articles by J.D. Purvis: 'The Samaritans and Judaism', in *Early Judaism and its Modern Interpreters* (ed. R.A. Kraft and G.W.E. Nickelsburg; Philadelphia: Fortress Press; Atlanta: Scholars Press, 1986), pp. 81-98; and 'The Samaritan Problem: A Case Study in Jewish Sectarianism in the Roman Era', in *Traditions in Transformation: Turning Points in Biblical Faith* (ed. B. Halpern and J.D. Levinson; Winona Lake, IN: Eisenbrauns, 1981), pp. 323-50. Also helpful are F. Dexinger, 'Limits of Tolerance in Judaism: The Samaritan Example', in *Jewish and Christian Self-Definition*. II. *Aspects of Judaism in the Graeco-Roman Period* (ed. E.P. Sanders, A.I. Baumgartner and A. Mendelson; London: SCM Press, 1981), pp. 88-114; R. Pummer, 'The Present State of Samaritan Studies', *JSS* 21 (1976), pp. 39-61; *JSS* 22 (1977), pp. 27-47; and the collection of studies in A.D. Crown (ed.), *The Samaritans* (Tübingen: Mohr [Paul Siebeck], 1989).

2. On Josephus's sentiment toward the Samaritans, see Coggins, *Samaritans and Jews*, pp. 93-99; R. Pummer, 'Genesis 34 in Jewish Writings of the Hellenistic and Roman Periods', *HTR* 75 (1982), pp. 183-86.

'Kutim' (= 'Cutheans') as well as other comments impugning their heritage. R. Eliezer, for example, notes in one place the Samaritans' 'doubtful stock' (*m. Qidd.* 4.3) and in another compares anyone who eats their bread 'to one who eats the flesh of swine' (*m. Seb.* 8.10). Similarly, the Samaritans are aligned with Gentiles disallowed from making sin-offerings and paying temple taxes (*m. Seq.* 1.5). However, other passages clearly incorporate the Samaritans into the people of Israel, as in the stipulation that the Common Grace must be recited when at least three Israelites dine together—including when one participant is a Samaritan (*m. Ber.* 7.1; cf. 8.8; *m. Dem.* 3.4; *m. Ned.* 3.10). On the whole, this mixed evaluation of the Samaritans in the Mishnah is not far from the opening statements of *Masseket Kutim*, the later Talmudic tractate given over to the Samaritan question: 'The usages of the Samaritans are in part like those of the Gentiles, in part like those of Israel, but mostly like Israel'.[1]

c. *Christ's Commission to Witness in Samaria (Acts 1.8)*
The next stage in Luke's presentation of Samaria/Samaritans comes with Christ's charging his followers in Acts 1.8 to be his witnesses throughout Samaria. This commission, which obviously sets the stage for the Samaritan mission in Acts 8, also relates back and moves beyond the Gospel story at a number of points. Once again Jesus sends his disciples into Samaritan territory, as in Lk. 9.52, and once again the Elijah motif emerges. The commissioning occurs just before Christ is 'taken up' into heaven (like Elijah) and includes the promise of a special Spirit-endowment, just as Elisha received from the ascending Elijah (4 Kgdms 2.9-15). At last James and John can look forward to wielding the power of Elijah in Samaria, but unto salvation rather than destruction. In comparison with the situation in Luke 17, where a lone Samaritan seeks out and then returns to Jesus,

---

1. Translation in Montgomery, *Samaritans*, p. 197. On the 'ambivalent attitude' towards the Samaritans conveyed in early rabbinic literature, see the thorough study of L. Schiffmann, 'The Samaritans in Tannaitic Halakhah', *JQR* 75 (1985), pp. 323-50. Schiffmann marks the Bar Kokhba revolt as the time when attitudes began to harden and 'the status of the Samaritans began to change in the eyes of the Tannaim from that of semi-Jews to that of non-Jews' (p. 350). See also Jeremias, *Jerusalem*, pp. 354-58; Montgomery, *Samaritans*, pp. 165-203; G. Alon, *Jews, Judaism and the Classical World: Studies in Jewish History in the Times of the Second Temple and Talmud* (Jerusalem: Magnes, 1977), pp. 354-73.

in Acts 1.8 Christ now authorizes an active mission *to* Samaria designed to reach *all* the region (ἐν πάσῃ. . . Σαμαρείᾳ). The significance of Samaria—the land of the Samaritans[1]—again relates to its intermediate position between Jewish and Gentile realms, in this case, between Judea—the land of the Jews[2]—and the ends of the earth. It is true that Samaria is linked most closely with Judea in Acts 1.8, no doubt because of the geographical proximity of the two regions and their intertwined political histories. But 'Judea and Samaria' still appear to be distinct entities in Luke's mind and should not simply be lumped together as parts of the land of Israel. For in addition to its Judea-connection (also 8.1; 9.31), Samaria is also paired with Phoenicia as supportive of Paul's Gentile mission in contrast to certain Jewish-Christian segments of Judea (15.1-3).

d. *Shechem in the Stephen Speech (Acts 7.15-16)*
In the last 25 years the Stephen speech in Acts 7 has been diligently mined for underlying Samaritan traditions.[3] From this effort has arisen a variety of hypotheses concerning the historical origins of Stephen and the speech attributed to him. A. Spiro contends that Stephen actually was a Samaritan, following a tradition preserved by the fourteenth-century Samaritan chronicler, Abul Fath.[4] M.H.

1. In the first century a mixed population of Jews, Gentiles and Samaritans inhabited the region of Samaria, but Luke is not interested in such demographic particulars. As Hengel states, 'basically so far as Luke's terminology goes, we can say that he always uses the word Σαμάρεια to refer to the territory of the Samaritans, that ethnic religious group whose members are not proper Jews but even less can be counted among the Gentiles' (*Between Jesus and Paul*, p. 122).
   2. 'Judea' can refer in Luke–Acts to the entire land of Israel (Lk. 1.5; 7.17; 23.5; Acts 10.37), but for the most part, as in the present case, it designates that part inhabited by the Jews. Cf. Pesch, *Apostelgeschichte*, I, p. 70; Schneider, *Apostelgeschichte*, I, p. 203.
   3. Although suggested by E.H. Plumptre as early as 1878 ('The Samaritan Element in the Gospels and Acts', *The Expositor* 7 [1878], pp. 34-39), the real impetus for investigating Samaritan traditions within the Stephen speech came with the published summary of A. Spiro's work as an appendix to J. Munck's commentary on Acts ('Stephen's Samaritan Background', in *The Acts of the Apostles* [rev. W.F. Albright and C.S. Mann; AB, 31; Garden City, NY: Doubleday, 1967], pp. 285-300).
   4. Spiro, 'Stephen's Samaritan Background', pp. 285-300. Among those who follow Spiro in assuming Stephen's Samaritan identity are J.D. Purvis ('The Fourth Gospel and the Samaritans', *NovT* 17 [1975], pp. 176-77), A.M. Johnson, Jr

Scharlemann thinks that Stephen was an idiosyncratic Jew 'strongly influenced by an acquaintance with Samaritan concepts and expectations', possibly obtained at a place like Ephraim.[1] C.H.H. Scobie suggests that Stephen and his circle were 'representatives of some type of Palestinian sectarian Judaism (Northern? Galilean?), with little use for the Jerusalem cult, and possibly with certain contacts with and sympathies for Samaritanism', and along with R. Scroggs views the discourse in Acts 7 as the product (in large measure) of the Samaritan mission conducted by the Stephen–Philip group.[2] O. Cullmann identifies Stephen and his followers with the Hellenists of Acts 6.1 and regards them as 'heterodox' Jews with theological links to both the Samaritan and the Qumran communities.[3] Finally, and most eccentrically, L. Gaston speculates that Stephen was originally a member of a pre-Christian, Samaritan baptist sect known as the Nasarenes, whose ideas later influenced the Ebionites.[4]

The aim of this study is not to settle the debate regarding the pre-Lukan history of Stephen and his speech, but to ascertain whether or not Acts 7 *in its present form* reflects Samaritan coloring and, if so, to determine the impact of this coloring upon Luke's overall presentation.[5] The ultimate goal, of course, is to correlate possible Samaritan

('Philip the Evangelist', pp. 51-57) and Bouwman ('Samaria', pp. 133-39).

1. M.H. Scharlemann, *Stephen: A Singular Saint* (AnBib, 34; Rome: Pontifical Biblical Institute, 1968), p. 53.

2. C.H.H. Scobie, 'The Origins and Development of Samaritan Christianity', *NTS* 19 (1972–73), pp. 398-99; R. Scroggs, 'The Earliest Hellenistic Christianity', in *Religions in Antiquity: Essays in Memory of Erwin Ramsdell Goodenough* (ed. J. Neusner; Leiden: Brill, 1968), pp. 200-201.

3. O. Cullmann, *The Johannine Circle* (London: SCM Press, 1976), pp. 39-53; 'Von Jesus zum Stephanuskreise und zum Johannesevangelium', in *Jesus und Paulus*, pp. 44-56.

4. L. Gaston, *No Stone on Another: Studies in the Significance of the Fall of Jerusalem in the Synoptic Gospels* (NovTSup, 23; Leiden: Brill, 1970), pp. 154-61.

5. This treatment of the Stephen speech from a Lukan perspective follows the basic supposition expressed by Barrett: 'whether or not Stephen. . . uttered the words attributed to [him] we may be confident that Luke approved of the opinions he ascribed. . . to [this] noted Christian [leader]' ('Old Testament History according to Stephen and Paul', in *Studien zum Text und zur Ethik des Neuen Testaments: Festschrift zum 80. Geburtstag von Heinrich Greeven* [ed. W. Schrage; Berlin: de Gruyter, 1986], p. 57 n. 1). Among those studies which have confirmed the integral place of the Stephen speech within Luke's narrative, see J. Bihler, *Die Stephanusgeschichte im Zusammenhang der Apostelgeschichte* (Munich: Hueber,

elements within Stephen's speech in Acts 7 with the adjoining portrayal of Philip's Samaritan mission in Acts 8.

From the start we must be alert to at least two major difficulties plaguing the hunt for Samaritanisms in the Stephen speech. First, there is the familiar religious-historical problem of dating. With the exception of the Samaritan Pentateuch (hereafter SP), finalized by the first century BCE, all extant Samaritan literature dates from no earlier than the fourth century CE.[1] Thus, the evidence with which to compare Samaritan thought and a first-century piece like the Stephen speech is slim indeed. Secondly, we face the problem of distinctiveness. To prove a specifically Samaritan tendency within Acts 7, elements of unique Samaritan character—not shared by other Jewish traditions—must be isolated. This 'dissimilarity' criterion greatly weakens claims of Samaritan influence based on textual affinities between Acts 7 and the SP against the MT and LXX.[2] For instance, the peculiar chronology of the Abraham narrative shared by the SP and Acts 7.4 also appears in Philo (*Mig. Abr.* 177), who was scarcely dependent on Samaritan ideas, and the correspondence between the SP and Acts 7.37 in the prophet-like-Moses text from Deuteronomy 18 is paralleled in the Qumran literature (4QTest 175; 4QBibPara 158).[3] Moreover, modern text-critical studies in light of the Dead Sea Scrolls have shown the SP to be but one representative of an expansionist Palestinian (non-Masoretic) text-type which developed during the Persian and Hellenistic eras. This means that SP variants from the MT and LXX are not necessarily Samaritan glosses, but may reflect readings shared by a number of other texts (Hebrew or Greek) within the

1963); Richard, *Acts 6.1–8.4*; Stanton, 'Stephen'; J. Via, 'An Interpretation of Acts 7.35-37 from the Perspective of Major Themes in Luke–Acts', *PerRelSt* 6 (1979), pp. 190-207.

1. Cf. R. Bergmeier, 'Zur Frühdatierung samaritanischer Theologumena', *JSJ* 5 (1974), pp. 121-53; R. Pummer, *The Samaritans* (Iconography of Religions, 13.5; Leiden: Brill, 1987), pp. 6-8.

2. The relevant passages are Acts 7.4 compared with Gen. 11.32; 7.5 with Deut. 2.5; 7.32 with Exod. 3.6; and 7.37 with Deut. 18.15. See M. Wilcox, *The Semitisms of Acts* (Oxford: Clarendon Press, 1965), pp. 27-30, 33-34; Scobie, 'Origins', pp. 391-94.

3. Cf. Barrett, 'Old Testament History', pp. 61, 63-64; E. Richard, 'Acts 7: An Investigation of the Samaritan Evidence', *CBQ* 39 (1977), pp. 196-97, 202-206; G. Schneider, 'Stephanus, die Hellenisten und Samaria', in Kremer (ed.), *Les Actes des Apôtres*, pp. 226-27.

same 'family'. Only those tendentious Samaritan additions peculiar to the final SP recension in the second/first century BCE can lay claim to an unmistakeably Samaritan provenance.[1]

Given these observations, much of the 'cumulative'[2] evidence marshalled to demonstrate the Samaritan character of the Stephen speech proves suspect. But all is not lost. We are not completely in the dark regarding distinctive, first-century Samaritan beliefs. In particular, one foundational tenet is known which set early Samaritanism at odds with the rest of Judaism: 'the sanctity (and necessity) of Shechem/Gerizim as the divinely ordained center of Israel's cultic life'.[3]

The rebuilding of Shechem as the new religious and cultural headquarters of Samaritan society and the construction of a temple on nearby Mt Gerizim date back to the late fourth century BCE.[4] At first this action need not have caused a serious rift with Jerusalem-based Judaism, since other Jewish worship centers were tolerated outside the Holy City. The Tobiads, for example, had their own temple and cult in Transjordania, as did the Egyptian Jews in Leontopolis led by the high priest exiled from Jerusalem, Onias IV.[5] Eventually, however, as tensions between Jews and Samaritans heightened, the respective temples on Mt Zion and Mt Gerizim began to be viewed as rival places of Yahweh-worship. 'In the presence of Ptolemy himself', so Josephus reports, a dispute erupted between the two parties concerning the legitimacy of their sanctuaries, 'the Jews asserting that it was

---

1. Cf. J.D. Purvis, *The Samaritan Pentateuch and the Origin of the Samaritan Sect* (HSM, 2; Cambridge, MA: Harvard University Press, 1968), pp. 69-87; R. Pummer, 'The Samaritan Pentateuch and the New Testament', *NTS* 22 (1975–76), pp. 441-43.

2. Several scholars admit to being impressed and ultimately persuaded by this 'cumulative' effect of possible Samaritan threads within the Stephen speech, e.g., Scharlemann (lists 15 possible points of contact between the Stephen speech and Samaritanism, *Stephen*, pp. 50-51), Scroggs ('Earliest Hellenistic Christianity', pp. 192-93) and Scobie ('Origins', p. 396). Richard rightly criticizes this stance on the grounds that 'weak arguments, no matter how numerous, prove very little' ('Acts 7', p. 194).

3. Purvis, 'Samaritans and Judaism', p. 89.

4. Cf. Purvis, *Samaritan Pentateuch*, pp. 105-109; G.E. Wright, 'The Samaritans at Shechem', *HTR* 55 (1962), pp. 357-66.

5. Cf. H. Koester, *History, Culture, and Religion of the Hellenistic Age.* I. *Introduction to the New Testament* (Philadelphia: Fortress Press, 1982), pp. 247-48.

the temple at Jerusalem which had been built in accordance with the laws of Moses, and the Samaritans that it was the temple on Mt Gerizim' (*Ant.* 13.74-79; cf. 12.6-10).

Certainly by the Hasmonean period, the temple issue was a bitter dividing point between Jews and Samaritans, sometimes precipitating violent action. In 128 BCE John Hyrcanus razed the temple on Mt Gerizim, and by the end of the century he had brutally destroyed the cities of Samaria and Shechem and brought the entire Samarian province under his authority. Around the same time, the Samaritans edited their peculiar version of the Pentateuch, incorporating an important addition to the Exodus Decalogue (the so-called 'Samaritan Tenth Commandment'), extolling Mt Gerizim/Shechem as the only true place of worship ordained by God.

> And when the Lord your God brings you into the land of the Canaanites which you are entering to take possession of it [Deut. 11.29], you shall set up these stones. . . And when you have passed over the Jordan, you shall set up these stones, concerning which I command you this day, on Mt Gerizim. And there you shall build an altar to the Lord your God [Deut. 27.2-6]. . . That mountain is beyond the Jordan. . . beside the oak of Moreh in front of Shechem [Deut. 11.30].[1]

The Deuteronomy citations utilized in this expansion diverge markedly from the MT. The 'Mt Gerizim' reference from Deut. 27.4 constitutes a change from the MT's 'Mt Ebal', and the location of Moreh near Shechem is a pure addition to Deut. 11.30. Such alterations are consistent with the SP's repeated tendency to read 'the place which the Lord your God has chosen (*bahar*)'—meaning Shechem—instead of 'the place which the Lord your God will choose (*yibhar*)' (MT)—meaning Jerusalem.[2]

That this jealousy for the primacy of their respective holy sites continued to characterize Jewish and Samaritan convictions in the first century CE is confirmed by the Josephus accounts of provocations at

---

1. Citation from J. Bowman, *Samaritan Documents Relating to their History, Religion and Life* (Pittsburgh Original Texts and Translations, 2; Pittsburgh: Pickwick, 1977), pp. 23-24; on the Samaritan Decalogue, see pp. 9-25; M. Gaster, *The Samaritans: Their History, Doctrines and Literature* (Schweich Lectures; London: Oxford University Press, 1925), pp. 185-90.

2. Cf. Pummer, *Samaritans*, p. 6; Purvis, 'Samaritan Problem', pp. 335-36; E. Tov, 'Proto-Samaritan Texts and the Samaritan Pentateuch', in Crown (ed.), *The Samaritans*, pp. 403-404.

Jerusalem and Gema mentioned above and by the frank assessment of the Samaritan woman in the Fourth Gospel: 'Our ancestors worshiped on this mountain (Gerizim), but you say that the place where people must worship is in Jerusalem' (Jn 4.20).

Granting the currency of a unique Samaritan devotion to Mt Gerizim/Shechem in Luke's day, is there any evidence that the Stephen speech reflects an awareness of such a belief? Scobie has advanced the thesis that in fact 'the theme of Shechem as the site of the one true sanctuary. . . gives the historical section of Acts 7 a remarkable and hitherto unnoticed underlying unity'.[1] He finds a pro-Shechem tendency associated with three of Israel's heroes featured in the discourse: Abraham, Joseph and Moses. However, in the first and last of these examples, Scobie's case appears weak.

In describing Abraham's divine encounters (7.2-8), an allusion to Exod. 3.12 intrudes which originally concerned God's dealings with Moses.

when you [Moses] have brought the people out of Egypt, you shall worship God on this mountain (λατρεύσετε τῷ θεῷ ἐν τῷ ὄρει τούτῳ) (Exod. 3.12).

and after that they shall come out and worship me in this place (λατρεύσουσίν μοι ἐν τῷ τόπῳ τούτῳ) (Acts 7.7b).

The shift in Acts 7 from Moses to Abraham and from 'this mountain' to 'this place' suggests to Scobie a further allusion to God's promise to Abraham revealed at 'the place (τόπος) at Shechem' that his descendants would possess the land of Canaan (Gen. 12.6-7). Through this conflation of Old Testament texts, the Stephen speech supposedly exalts Shechem as the chief Abrahamic center of worship.[2]

While a Shechem allusion is possible here, it is not likely. Too great a burden falls on the lone lexical parallel (τόπος) between Acts 7.7b and Gen. 12.6.[3] Moreover, in the Lukan context, 'this place' seems to

---

1. C.H.H. Scobie, 'The Use of Material in the Speeches of Acts III and VII', *NTS* 25 (1978–79), p. 409. The criticisms which have been directed against Scobie's work focus predominantly on his earlier investigation ('Origins'). But 'Use of Material' marks a considerable advance, taking into account objections which had been raised against the previous article and offering a more nuanced, sophisticated analysis. Curiously, little attention has been paid to this update of Scobie's position.

2. Scobie, 'Use of Material', pp. 406-407.

3. G. Stemberger, 'Die Stephanusrede (Apg 7) und die jüdische Tradition', in *Jesus in der Verkündigung der Kirche* (ed. A. Fuchs; Studien zum NT und seiner

refer to the temple at *Jerusalem* (οὗτος τόπος, Acts 6.13, 14; 21.28 [twice]), not Shechem,[1] although the Stephen speech does not promote the Jerusalem shrine as the only or even primary τόπος where God manifests himself (7.33, 49). Finally, while the Abraham section of Acts 7 partially echoes Gen. 12.1-7, the principal source for vv. 6-7 (which include the allusion to Exod. 3.12) is Gen. 15.13-14, not Gen. 12.6-7.[2]

From the lengthy Moses segment of Stephen's speech, Scobie focuses on the portable tabernacle in the wilderness (Acts 7.44). Constructed by Moses according to the divine pattern, this 'tent of testimony' became, in Stephen's opinion, the center of Israel's worship from the conquest under Joshua through the Davidic age, until it was tragically displaced by the idolatrous temple of Solomon 'made with human hands' (7.45-48). Scobie contends that this pro-tabernacle/anti-temple position reflects Samaritan tradition ennobling Shechem/Mt Gerizim. More specifically, he thinks that the reference to bringing the tabernacle into Canaan (7.45) would trigger memories of the ancient ceremony on Mt Ebal and Mt Gerizim (Josh. 8.30-35; cf. Deut. 27.4-12) and that the hostile stance toward Solomon's Jerusalem temple coincides with the Samaritans' exclusive devotion to the Gerizim temple.[3]

But nothing in Acts 7.45 explicitly points to the Ebal/Gerizim ritual or to worship at all. If a worship setting is to be recalled, why not Gilgal, where circumcision and passover rites were enacted soon after entering the promised land (Joshua 4–5)? Most critically, it must be appreciated that Stephen's anti-temple remarks encompass *all* man-made houses of worship, including the Gerizim temple. Aware of this problem, Scobie theorizes that the speech's radical spiritualizing of worship stems from Christian redaction of a Samaritan source. But unless one is already predisposed toward an underlying Samaritan source, no clear clues emerge from the speech as it stands to suggest

Umwelt A/1; Linz, 1976), p. 159.

    1. K. Haacker, 'Samaritan, Samaria', *NIDNTT*, III, p. 464; G. Schneider, 'Stephanus', p. 228.

    2. Richard, *Acts 6.1–8.4*, pp. 49-54; N.A. Dahl, 'The Story of Abraham in Luke–Acts', in Keck and Martyn (eds.), *Studies in Luke–Acts*, p. 143; J. Dupont, 'La Structure oratoire du discours d'Etienne (Actes 7)', *Bib* 66 (1985), pp. 163-67.

    3. Scobie, 'Use of Material', pp. 408-409 (building in part on traditions in *Samaritan Chronicle II*).

any layering of different cultic viewpoints. In any event, our concern is with the final Lukan form of Acts 7, where the accent falls on the transcendent universality of God's presence.[1]

When it comes to the Joseph material in Acts 7, Scobie's analysis proves more persuasive.[2] The only explicit references to Shechem appear in 7.15-16 in an unusual context:

> so Jacob went down to Egypt. He himself died there as well as our ancestors, and their bodies were brought back to Shechem and laid in the tomb that Abraham had bought for a sum of silver from the sons of Hamor in Shechem.

The subject of μετετέθησαν and ἐτέθησαν in 7.16 is ambiguous, but likely relates back to all who had died in Egypt according to v. 15, Jacob as well as his family ('our ancestors').[3] These venerable patriarchs are said to be buried at Shechem in a tomb purchased by Abraham from the Hamorites. Such a report runs counter to other burial legends surrounding Israel's historic heroes. Gen. 50.13, for example, locates Jacob's tomb in the cave of Machpelah in Hebron bought by Abraham from Ephron the Hittite (cf. Genesis 23). Gen. 33.19 reports, however, that Jacob purchased the piece of ground in Shechem from the sons of Hamor, and Josh. 24.32 discloses that the bones of Joseph were brought up from Egypt and buried in this plot. The Old Testament is silent regarding the burial place of Jacob's other sons, but extracanonical accounts mention the Machpelah site in Hebron (*Jub.* 46.9; *T. Reub.* 7.2; *T. Levi* 19.5; *T. Judah* 26.4; Jos. *Ant.* 2.199; *War* 4.532).

In seeking to relate Acts 7.15-16 to these mixed traditions, harmonization[4] seems impossible in view of the black-and-white differences in detail, and the verdict that Acts reflects an unwitting confusion of

---

1. Cf. D.D. Sylva, 'The Meaning and Function of Acts 7.46-50', *JBL* 106 (1987), pp. 261-75.

2. Scobie, 'Use of Material', pp. 407-408.

3. Scobie, 'Use of Material', p. 407; contra Barrett ('Old Testament History', p. 62) and Jeremias (*Heiligengräber in Jesu Umwelt (Mt. 23,29; Lk 11.47): Eine Untersuchung zur Volksreligion der Zeit Jesu* [Göttingen: Vandenhoeck & Ruprecht, 1958], p. 37), who regard only οἱ πατέρες ἡμῶν in 7.15 as the subject of the verbs in 7.16.

4. As attempted by W.H. Mare, 'Acts 7: Jewish or Samaritan in Character?', *WTJ* 34 (1971–72), pp. 10, 19-20.

the evidence[1] seems unlikely, given Luke's typically deft handling of a wide range of Old Testament material.[2] Therefore, some conscious Lukan purpose apparently lay behind the distinctive connection of Abraham, Jacob and all twelve sons with a piece of property in Shechem; and no doubt this purpose had something to do with the Samaritans, given Shechem's notorious reputation in early Judaism as the hub of Samaritan life and Luke's general interest in the Samaritan people. Scobie and others have surmised that Acts 7.15-16 was in fact dependent on a local Samaritan tradition.[3] This is a plausible assumption, but it must be admitted that the only external support for such a tradition derives from Christian witnesses of the third century and later.[4]

Accepting that Acts 7.15-16 exploits the Samaritan connection with Shechem, we have another piece to fit into the puzzle of Luke's overall portrayal of the Samaritans. Once again Luke swims against the tide of prevailing Jewish opinion on the Samaritan question. For not only does Shechem's exaltation as Israel's hallowed cemetery not give Hebron its due, it also contravenes an anti-Samaritan strain within Hellenistic Jewish literature vilifying Shechem and its inhabitants. In what is commonly recognized as the earliest unequivocal reference to the Samaritans, ben Sira speaks opprobriously about 'the foolish people that dwell in Shechem' who comprise 'no nation

1. S. Lowy, *The Principles of Samaritan Bible Exegesis* (SPB, 28; Leiden: Brill, 1977), p. 53.
2. Stemberger, 'Stephanusrede', p. 164.
3. Scobie, 'Use of Material', pp. 407-408; Jeremias, *Heiligengräber*, pp. 36-38; H.G. Kippenberg, *Garizim und Synagoge: Traditionsgeschichtliche Untersuchungen zur samaritanischen Religion der aramäische Periode* (Religionsgeschichtliche Versuche und Vorarbeiten, 30; Berlin: de Gruyter, 1971), pp. 111-12. Interestingly, a critic such as Stemberger, who generally opposes a Samaritan backdrop for the Stephen speech, recognizes the utilization of Samaritan tradition in this case ('Stephanusrede', pp. 162-65, 173). Richard stops short of tracing Acts 7.16 to a specifically Samaritan tradition, but he does assert that the author of the Stephen speech deviates at this point from his customary Old Testament source and 'is in fact emphasizing an old tradition which presented Shechem as the burial place of the patriarchs' (*Acts 6.1–8.4*, pp. 323-24 n. 184), knowing full well the polemical effect of Shechem's association with Samaritan territory ('The Polemical Character of the Joseph Episode in Acts 7', *JBL* 98 [1979], pp. 259-60).
4. The patristic witnesses include Julius Africanus, Jerome and George Syncellus. See the references and discussion in Kippenberg, *Garizim*, pp. 111-12; and Barrett, 'Old Testament History', pp. 62-63.

(ἔθνος)' (Sir. 50.25-26; cf. Deut. 32.21).[1] Intertestamental treatments of Genesis 34 regularly portray the Shechemite defilers of Israel's daughter (Dinah) in an unfavorable light, at times even omitting all reference to their circumcision (*T. Levi* 5-7; Jdt. 9.2-4; cf. 5.16; *Jub.* 30; Theodotus; Josephus, *Ant.* 1.337-40). There is some doubt as to the intended targets of these anti-Shechemite references, but the Samaritans, with their historic attachment to Shechem, seem the most likely candidates.[2] Certainly calling Shechem 'a city of imbeciles' (*T. Levi* 7.2) strikes one as an obvious anti-Samaritan slur along the lines of the Sirach text cited above. Moreover, it hardly commends Shechem as a suitable final resting place for Israel's fathers, as Luke understands it.

Criticism of the Samaritans' veneration of Shechem may also be glimpsed in Pseudo-Philo's *Biblical Antiquities*. Cadbury detects within this work

> a varied and interesting anti-Samaritan technique. It abbreviates or relocates the episodes which the Bible had placed in Shechem and other northern localities, or it reports them in speeches rather than in narrative, and thus escapes the necessity of any geographical location.[3]

Interestingly, far from truncating and minimizing the biblical presentation of Shechem, Luke elaborates and accentuates it.

Further insight into the Shechem-reference in Acts 7.16 may be gained by examining its function in the entire Stephen speech. In the opening Abraham section (7.2-8), which sets the tone for the rest of the discourse,[4] the patriarch's tenuous connection to the promised land

---

1. Cf. Coggins, *Samaritans and Jews*, pp. 82-86; Purvis, *Samaritan Pentateuch*, pp. 119-29.

2. Kippenberg regards the story in Gen. 34 as the 'Magna Charta jüdischer Gewalttätigkeit gegen die Sichemiter' (*Garizim*, p. 90; cf. pp. 87-90 for a larger discussion of anti-Samaritan polemic behind Jewish interpretation of Gen. 34). Also see Coggins, *Samaritans and Jews*, pp. 88-94; J.J. Collins, 'The Epic of Theodotus and the Hellenism of the Hasmoneans', *HTR* 73 (1980), pp. 91-104. For an alternative position which raises doubts about anti-Samaritan bias in early Jewish literature, see R. Pummer's studies: 'Antisamaritanische Polemik in jüdischen Schriften aus der intertestamentarischen Zeit', *BZ* 26 (1982), pp. 224-42, and 'Genesis 34 in Jewish Writings'.

3. H.C. Cadbury, *The Book of Acts in History* (London: A. & C. Black, 1955), pp. 105-106.

4. This foundational function of Acts 7.2-8 has been thoroughly explored by Dahl ('Story of Abraham', pp. 42-48), although he regards 'promise and fulfillment' as

is emphasized. He received his initial revelation of God 'in Mesopotamia, before he lived in Haran' (7.2).[1] He eventually migrated to Canaan and was assured that his posterity would possess 'this country' and worship God there (7.4-7); 'yet [God] did not give him any of it, not even a foot's length' (7.5a) and announced that before settling in the land Abraham's 'descendants would be resident aliens (πάροικον) in a country belonging to others' (7.6). Once established, this motif of the *Relativierung des heiligen Landes*[2] runs throughout the balance of the speech in conjunction with the equally prominent theme of Israel's rejection of her prophets.[3] Joseph was rejected by 'the patriarchs', his brothers, and sold into slavery in Egypt, but throughout his afflictions in a foreign land, 'God was with him' (7.9-10). Moses heard God's call to deliver his people from Egyptian bondage, but his countrymen spurned his leadership, forcing him to flee and become a 'resident alien (πάροικος)' in Midian (7.29; cf. v. 35). Even here, however, Moses found himself on 'holy ground' attended by God's presence (7.30-33). After the exodus, God continued to direct Moses through the wilderness, and the Israelites continued to resist his ministry (7.38-42). True worship centered around a movable 'tent of testimony', built to divine specifications, but Israel eventually opted for a fixed, human-made sanctuary ill-fitting the omnipresent 'Most High' God (7.44-50). Finally, at the climax of the speech, Stephen drives home the relevance of this historical survey: as ancient Israel had repeatedly resisted God's messengers, so

the main unifying theme of the Stephen speech.

1. W.D. Davies notes that the reference to 'before he lived in Haran' 'adds force to the extra-territorial nature of the revelation' (*The Gospel and the Land: Early Christianity and Jewish Territorial Doctrine* [Berkeley: University of California Press, 1974], p. 270).

2. Stemberger, 'Stephanusrede', pp. 164-65, 173. See also Davies, *Gospel and the Land*, pp. 267-74; Kilgallen, *Stephen Speech*, pp. 17-21.

3. See Stanton, 'Stephen', pp. 353-57; Kilgallen, *Stephen Speech*, pp. 108-113; Via, 'Interpretation of Acts 7.35-37', pp. 191-96; R. Tannehill, 'Israel in Luke–Acts: A Tragic Story', *JBL* 104 (1985), pp. 79-81. For a historical viewpoint that identifies a 'deuteronomistic' tradition underlying the Stephen speech which correlated the Jews' rejection of Jesus with their perennial rejection of the prophets, see O. Steck, *Israel und das gewaltsame Geschick der Propheten: Untersuchungen zur Überlieferung des deuteronomistischen Geschichtsbildes im Alten Testament, Spätjudentum und Urchristentum* (WMANT, 23; Neukirchen–Vluyn: Neukirchener Verlag, 1967), pp. 265-67; G. Schneider, 'Stephanus', pp. 230-37.

her descendants—Stephen's opponents—have recently betrayed and murdered the Righteous One, Jesus (7.51-52).

As part of this thematic agenda in Acts 7, Shechem represents another piece of foreign territory—symbolically, if not geographically, outside the Holy Land—where Israel's leaders were welcomed,[1] and the foreign Shechemites (Hamorites) who supplied the grave for these leaders stand in contrast to the obstinate Israelites who drove the prophets to their grave! It may in fact be more pathos than polemic underlying this perspective: tragically, even in death Israel's fathers found a home only among the alien Shechemites.[2] In any case, the reception of God's messengers by Shechem/Shechemites appears to be prototypical of the reception of Christ and his gospel by Samaria/ Samaritans and antitypical of the rejection of Christ by Jerusalem/ Jews.

In light of this conclusion, the developing story of Samaria/ Samaritans in Luke–Acts may be updated as follows:

1. The parallelism between Jewish (Nazarene) and Samaritan repudiations of Jesus' mission in Lk. 4.16-30 and 9.51-56 has been further broken apart.

2. While in one sense affirming an Israelite heritage for the Samaritans perpetuated in the patriarchal tomb in Shechem, the Stephen speech primarily depicts the Samaritans as citizens of a strange land (cf. ἀλλογενής, Lk. 17.18) who proved more receptive to God's prophets than their Judean counterparts.

3. Historical precedent is established for Christ's worldwide mission announced in Acts 1.8. As God has never been statically bound to one locale and as his messengers have always ventured beyond the promised land into foreign territories— like Shechem—so the Spirit of Christ, dynamic and unfettered, will empower Christ's witnesses to carry the gospel beyond Jerusalem and Judea to all nations—including Samaria.

---

1. Cf. Richard, 'Polemical Character', pp. 259-60; Dahl, 'Story of Abraham', pp. 143, 155 n. 24.

2. Cadbury's contention that the Shechem reference in Acts 7.16 represents 'the most biting form of anti-Jewish polemic' (*Book of Acts*, p. 105) appears exaggerated in light of the note of forgiveness toward the hostile Jews sounded at the close of the Stephen narrative ('Lord, do not hold this sin against them', Acts 7.60; cf. Lk. 23.34).

e. *Philip's Samaritan Mission in Lukan Perspective*

The step-by-step analysis of the Samaritan profile which emerges in Luke's narrative up through Acts 7 has set the stage for exploring Philip's climactic Samaritan mission in Acts 8. Numerous points of contact exist between the Philip incident and the preceding Samaritan story.

1. Thus far Luke's portrayal of Samaria/Samaritans has been fruitfully compared and contrasted with contemporary reports in Josephus's *Antiquities*. Once again an interesting parallel may be drawn.[1] Josephus's account of Alexander's conquest of the Holy Land concludes with this snippet:

> When Alexander died, his empire was partitioned among his successors (the Diadochi); as for the temple on Mount Garizein, it remained. And, whenever anyone was accused by the people of Jerusalem of eating unclean food or violating the Sabbath or committing any other such sin, he would flee to the Shechemites, saying that he had been unjustly expelled (*Ant.* 11.346-47).

The historical reliability of this passage is admittedly uncertain. The association of the Samaritans with antinomian renegades from Jerusalem fits too closely with Josephus's stigmatizing of the Samaritans as 'apostates from the Jewish nation' (*Ant.* 11.340) and does not square with the Samaritans' reputation for strict adherence to the Mosaic law.[2] Nevertheless, there likely were some examples continuing into Josephus's day of Jews ostracized from Jerusalem (for whatever reason) who found temporary refuge among the Samaritans, if only because Samaria was nearby and the Samaritans would have doubtless had some sympathy for anyone at odds with Jerusalem.

In any event, it is striking how the scenario in Acts 6–8 coincides with Josephus's report. When persecution breaks out over Stephen's alleged invective against law and temple (6.11-14), some Jewish Christians escape from Jerusalem to Samaria (8.1); notable among

---

1. Cf. Scroggs, 'Earliest Hellenistic Christianity', p. 197; Bouwman, 'Samaria', pp. 137-38.

2. The viewpoint that the ancient Samaritans freely compromised their religious beliefs and practices under the pressures of Hellenization (based largely on the incident in the era of Antiochus IV reported in Josephus, *Ant.* 12.257-64) has been proven unfounded in recent studies. See Hengel, *Judaism and Hellenism: Studies in their Encounter in Palestine during the Early Hellenistic Period* (2 vols.; London: SCM Press, 1974), I, pp. 293-94; Pummer, 'Genesis 34', pp. 184-86.

these is Philip the evangelist who receives a warm welcome from the Samaritan people (8.5-13). However, while recounting similar events pertaining to Jewish–Samaritan relations, Luke and Josephus once again stand at opposite poles in their implicit commentary on these events. Far from effectively censuring the Samaritans for harboring fugitives from Jewish law, as Josephus does, Luke regards the Jerusalem authorities who oppose Stephen and force Philip's exodus to Samaria as 'stiff-necked people, uncircumcised in heart and ears. . . forever opposing the Holy Spirit. . . ones that received the law as ordained by angels and yet. . . have not kept it' (7.51, 53). Conversely, the Samaritans who 'listened eagerly' to Philip are commended as those who 'accepted the word of God' (8.14).

2. A well-known feature of Luke's writings is the wide-ranging tendency to parallel the activities of the earthly Jesus in Luke's Gospel with those of his disciples in Acts.[1] In this way, the early church is presented as continuing the work which Jesus began. Several links have already been noted between Luke's characterization of Jesus' and Philip's respective ministries. But certainly the most dramatic illustration of this correspondence pertains to their common interaction with the Samaritans.

Not to be missed is the contrastive as well as comparative dimension of this parallel. As noted above, *en route* to Jerusalem Jesus was denied lodging in a Samaritan village (Lk. 9.51-56), thus matching his experience in Nazareth where the Jews 'put him out of the city' and sought to kill him (Lk. 4.29). While Philip's expulsion from Jerusalem by hostile Jews corresponds with Jesus' Nazareth-ordeal, his interaction with the Samaritans contrasts dramatically with Jesus' encounter. For Philip, now moving *away from Jerusalem*, successfully enters a Samaritan city—indeed '*the* [main] city of Samaria'[2]—and receives a grand reception for his proclamation of Christ. Clearly the partnership initially established between Jews and Samaritans in their rejection of Jesus' mission, which already showed signs of breaking

---

1. Cf. the studies by R.F. O'Toole, *The Unity of Luke's Theology: An Analysis of Luke–Acts* (Good News Studies, 9; Wilmington, DE: Michael Glazier, 1984), pp. 62-94; 'Parallels between Jesus and his Disciples in Luke–Acts', *BZ* 27 (1983), pp. 195-212.

2. B.M. Metzger, *A Textual Commentary on the Greek New Testament* (London: UBS, 1975), pp. 355-56. The inclusion of the definite article follows the best manuscript evidence: 𝔓[74], Sinaiticus, Alexandrinus and Vaticanus.

apart later in Luke's Gospel, is thoroughly shattered in Acts 8. As for Philip, by returning to a people who had formerly wanted nothing to do with Jesus and winning them over to his message, he pursues a model ministry of reconciliation, seeking and saving that which was lost (cf. Lk. 15.11-32; 19.10).

3. Like the two model Samaritans in Luke's Gospel, Philip's Samaritan audience responds positively to Christ. In comparison with the grateful Samaritan in Luke 17, the affinity extends to various details. When the Samaritan leper 'sees' that he has been miraculously healed by Jesus, he responds with exuberant praise, thereby attesting his personal 'faith' (πίστις). Likewise, the Samaritans in Acts 8 'see' the miraculous signs of healing performed by Philip, burst forth with 'great joy' and 'believe' (πιστεύω) the Christian message (vv. 6-8, 12).

While the nature of Samaritan response to Christ is similar in Luke 10, 17 and Acts 8, the extent of that response differs considerably. The parable of the Samaritan helper and the story of the Samaritan leper feature only two isolated Samaritans in border areas around Samaria (near Jericho?/'between Samaria and Galilee'), whereas in Acts 8 'many' in the heart of Samaritan country receive supernatural healings and exorcisms, and the 'crowds' embrace the gospel. The only exceptional Samaritan now is Simon Magus, who stands out from the crowd as the sole example of spurious devotion to Christ.

4. Philip's Samaritan encounter may be viewed not only in relation to Jesus' actions and attitudes, but also the apostles'. Philip's willingness to proclaim the gospel and work beneficent wonders among the Samaritans stands in obvious contrast to James and John's rash request that the Samaritans be destroyed (Lk. 9.54). It is interesting, too, that Philip the evangelist—who is outside the circle of the Twelve and yet exorcises unclean spirits and proclaims Jesus' name in Samaria—fits the general description of the maverick reprimanded by John in Lk. 9.49: 'Master, we saw someone casting out demons in your name, and we tried to stop him, because he does not follow with us'. Jesus sharply rebukes this exclusivist attitude (9.50), just as he does the following plea for the Samaritans' annihilation (9.55). In a sense, then, at the end of Luke 9 Jesus legitimates independent Samaritan missions—like Philip's—despite apostolic protest.

Fulfilling Christ's commission in Acts 1.8, Peter and John eventually make their way to Samaria where they exercise a dynamic ministry (8.1-25). (John's assistance in calling down the 'fire' of the Spirit, not of judgment, upon the Samaritans marks a decided change in his attitude.) But it is still Philip the evangelist, not an apostle, who inaugurates the Samaritan mission in Acts and indeed takes the first missionary step beyond Jerusalem.

In short, alongside Luke's tendency to exalt the Jerusalem apostles, he allows them to be 'upstaged' in some respects by an independent evangelist like Philip. A fuller assessment of the relationship between Philip and the apostles (especially Peter) will be the focus of Chapter 5.

5.   While Philip's Samaritan mission generally fulfills the Lukan plan for extending the gospel to the region (χώρα) of Samaria (cf. Acts 8.1, 14), more specifically the locus of Philip's work is 'the city (πόλις) of Samaria' (8.5a). Exactly which city is meant is difficult to determine, not least because the ancient city called 'Samaria' no longer existed as such in Luke's day, having been rebuilt as a Hellenistic *polis* and renamed by Herod as Sebaste. Hengel is probably correct that εἰς τὴν πόλιν τῆς Σαμαρείας simply reflects the setting of Philip's ministry within 'a Samaritan "capital" the name of which Luke either no longer knew or left out as being unimportant'.[1]

At any rate, the allusion to a principal Samaritan center recalls the mention of Shechem in the preceding chapter.[2] As noted above, the Shechem reference in the context of Acts 7 typifies foreign—in this case, Samaritan—soil where God's prophets of old were welcomed after suffering rejection from their own people. In Acts 8 the point is reinforced and brought up to date with the situation in the early church. Philip the evangelist, a contemporary prophet of the kingdom of God, is driven out of the Jewish capital and takes his message to the Samaritan capital where he finds an enthusiastic reception.[3]

6.   Philip's achievement in evangelizing the Samaritans must be measured, at least in part, in terms of the social boundaries which he crosses. Through Acts 7, as we have seen, the Samaritans in Luke's

---

1.   Hengel, *Between Jesus and Paul*, p. 126.

2.   Historically, Shechem as such was also not in existence in Luke's day, having been rebuilt in 72 CE as Flavius Neapolis. But the link between the references to a major Samaritan city in Acts 8.5 and the biblical city of Shechem in 7.16 would still have been obvious to Luke's readers.

3.   Cf. Richard's comments: 'Shechem here [Acts 7.16] prepares for the spread of the good news outside of Jerusalem to Samaria' ('Polemical Character', pp. 259-60).

narrative occupy a kind of middle ground between Jews and Gentiles. They share part of Israel's religious heritage but at the same time appear at variance with Jerusalem-oriented Judaism and even occasionally as pure outsiders (ἀλλογενεῖς). In Acts 8 the reference to the ἔθνος of Samaria (v. 9) seems to suggest a race of people distinct from the Jews and constituent of the Gentile nations destined to hear the gospel (cf. Lk. 2.32; 24.47; Acts 2.5; 10.35; 13.47). Moreover, since Philip goes to Samaria to escape Jewish belligerence in Jerusalem, the story seems to be moving away from Judaism and in the direction of the Gentiles, following the pattern established as early as the Nazareth pericope (Lk. 4.24-27). Nevertheless, the persisting connection of Samaria with Judea in 8.1 and 9.31, the emphasis on Philip's preaching 'the messiah' and the lack of uproar in the Jerusalem church over the Samaritans' baptism and reception of the Spirit (like that erupting over Cornelius) preclude a complete Samaritan–Gentile equation in Acts 8.

So once again the Samaritans slot into a median social category in Luke's presentation. The most we can say, then, at this stage about the extent of Philip's mission is that it traverses the boundaries of Jerusalem-based Judaism but falls short of a clear-cut incursion into the Gentile world.

7. Finally, as Jesus' sending of messengers into a Samaritan village in Lk. 9.52 contradicts Mt. 10.5b, so does Philip's mission to the city of Samaria in Acts 8.5.[1] Whereas in Matthew, the disciples receive Jesus' mandate—εἰς πόλιν Σαμαριτῶν μὴ εἰσέλθητε—in Acts, Philip the evangelist κατελθὼν εἰς τὴν πόλιν τῆς Σαμαρείας. Moreover, the ministry which the Matthean disciples are directed to carry out among the lost sheep of Israel—preach the kingdom, heal the sick, cast out demons (Mt. 10.7-8)—is precisely what Philip does among the Samaritans (cf. Acts 8.5-8, 12-13).

It is possible that Luke was defending the legitimacy of Samaritan Christianity against advocates of a restrictive mission policy like that reflected in Mt. 10.5b. (This position should not be equated with Matthew's overall viewpoint, since by the end of his Gospel a universal Christian mission is envisaged [28.16-20; cf. 4.12-16; 8.10-12; 15.21-28].) If such were the case, a calculated, apologetic aim may

---

1. Cf. Bauernfeind, *Kommentar*, p. 122; M. Hengel, *Acts and the History of Earliest Christianity* (London: SCM Press, 1979); reprinted in Hengel, *Earliest Christianity* (London: SCM Press, 1986), p. 78.

underlie Luke's association of Philip's Samaritan mission with the authority of (1) the earthly Jesus (both his teaching and example, Lk. 9.51-56; 10.25-37; 17.11-19), (2) the resurrected Christ (Acts 1.8), (3) Israel's venerated patriarchs (Acts 7.15-16) and (4) Christ's apostles (Acts 8.14-25).

5. Conclusion

This chapter demonstrates that the report of Philip's Samaritan mission in Acts 8 is an integral part of Luke's narrative network, with particularly strong links to the Gospel story of Jesus. The ministries of the Lukan Jesus and Philip are remarkably similar in substance and setting. Both figures proclaim the good news of God's kingdom and work miracles of healing and liberation, and they both defy cultural norms by reaching out beyond their Jewish compatriots to the Samaritan people. Moreover, experiences of persecution provide the impetus in each case for extending the boundaries of mission.

Jesus sets the tone for the Samaritan mission by rebuking James and John's fire-and-brimstone proposal and recounting his parable of the Samaritan helper, and he takes the first step by cleansing/converting the lone Samaritan leper. Philip then continues the work which Jesus began, but more than that, he greatly expands upon it by ministering to and baptizing the Samaritan masses. Of course, in Luke's view, Philip's success could only be credited to his Christ-centered message and Spirit-supplied power (cf. Acts 6.5; 8.29, 39; and further discussion below).

In his 'imitation' of Jesus, the Lukan Philip is a noteworthy example of someone who never knew or followed Jesus in the flesh and yet bears the marks of a true Christian disciple. While Peter's Christ-like demeanor in Acts may be viewed as a by-product of his Gospel contact with the earthly Jesus, Philip's Jesus-style activity flows exclusively from his relationship with the risen Christ. Thus, the Philip story in Acts 8.4-13 reveals not only the narrative unity of Luke–Acts, but also the theological unity of the historical Jesus–exalted Christ.

Chapter 3

PHILIP AND SIMON MAGUS

1. *Introduction*

The material pertaining to Simon Magus in Acts 8 has generated considerable discussion in recent years. For the most part, however, scholars have mined Acts 8 for insights into the mysterious, 'historical' Simon and the relationship of this figure to the Gnostic heretic denounced by the early church fathers.[1] Seldom has sufficient attention been paid to the *Lukan* portrayal of Simon Magus, especially his interaction with Philip the evangelist. In this chapter the Philip–Simon encounter will be explored with the aim of further elucidating Philip's role in Luke's narrative.

On the surface it may appear that Philip and Simon have very little to do with each other in the Samaritan incident. They only intersect explicitly in Acts 8.13, and then the story quickly moves on to the clash between Simon and *Peter* (vv. 18-24). But a closer examination of Acts 8.5-24, recalling some previous observations, reveals a more intertwined depiction of Philip and Simon. In particular, v. 13 should not be read as an isolated statement but as the climax of an extended comparison between Philip and Simon beginning at v. 5.[2]

   1.   They both minister in the same Samaritan city (πόλις, vv. 5, 8, 9).

---

   1. For helpful surveys of scholarship on the Simon Magus question, see W.A. Meeks, 'Simon Magus in Recent Research', *RelSRev* 3 (1977), pp. 137-42; E. Grässer, 'Acta-Forschung seit 1960 (Fortsetzung)', *TRu* 42 (1977), pp. 25-34; K. Rudolph, 'Simon—Magus oder Gnosticus? Zur Stand der Debatte', *TRu* 42 (1977), pp. 279-359.
   2. This Philip–Simon parallelism is observed in K. Beyschlag, *Simon Magus und die christliche Gnosis* (WUNT, 16; Tübingen: Mohr [Paul Siebeck], 1974), pp. 100-101; Roloff, *Apostelgeschichte*, pp. 131-32.

2. They both work wondrous deeds (signs/magic, vv. 6-7, 9, 11) and proclaim messages (λέγω, vv. 6, 9).
3. They both attract the Samaritans' attention in great numbers (crowds/least to the greatest, vv. 6-7, 9-10).[1]
4. The Samaritans' response to both is described as 'listening eagerly' (προσέχω, vv. 6, 10, 11).
5. Simon is acclaimed as the δύναμις μεγάλη (v. 10) and evokes amazement (ἐξίστημι, vv. 9, 11) from the Samaritans; Philip works δυνάμεις μεγάλας among the Samaritans and thus elicits Simon's amazement (ἐξίστημι, v. 13).

In effect, Luke sets up a competitive match between Philip and Simon for the affections of the Samaritan people. How, then, does Philip fare in this competition? What does the encounter in 8.13 suggest regarding the outcome of this rivalry? And in addition to those characteristics which Philip shares with Simon, are there other qualities which distinguish the evangelist and give him precedence over the Samaritan magician?

As for the scene in Acts 8.18-24, although Philip himself is out of the picture, his relationship to Simon Magus still comes into question. For the same Simon who is baptized and dogs Philip's steps in 8.13 is now exposed by Peter as a power-monger deserving of God's judgment, one who has 'no part or share' in the Christian community (8.20-23). The question can scarcely be dodged: in what way does this 'apostasy' of Simon reflect on the integrity of Philip's Samaritan mission? And is it significant that a visiting apostle from Jerusalem comes in to chasten one of Philip's apparent converts? In short, does the disclosure of Simon's deceit effectively stigmatize Philip's ministry in any sense?

Before addressing these matters, a brief discussion of method is required. Focusing principally on its Lukan context, the Philip–Simon encounter must be interpreted first of all as part of a series of confrontations between missionaries and magicians in Acts, and the duplicitous Simon must be evaluated in conjunction with other Lukan 'apostates'. Secondarily, attention may be directed to relevant traditions outside Luke–Acts for purposes of comparison and contrast. Of

---

1. Bauernfeind suggests that the mention of 'both men and women' responding to Philip's ministry in 8.12 is an indication of the breadth of Philip's influence comparable to Simon's attraction of 'the least to the greatest' (*Kommentar*, p. 125).

potential importance in this regard are several patristic appraisals of Simon and his followers.

Caution must be exercised, however, in using these extra-Lukan Simonian traditions[1] to illuminate material in Acts. Since Acts 8 remains the earliest source of information regarding Simon, we must be wary of reading later characterizations of Simon back into Luke's account. Especially problematic is the judgment of some scholars that Luke was attacking a Gnostic heresy—similar to that combatted by Justin Martyr, Irenaeus and Hippolytus[2]—which venerated Simon as the Highest God and mythological Redeemer, attended by his consort, Helena/Ennoia (the First Idea). These scholars admit that a Gnostic profile of Simon is hardly self-evident in Acts 8, but they insist, for various reasons, that anti-Gnostic polemic still lies behind the text. Haenchen and Lüdemann, for example, theorize that Luke deliberately and falsely cast Simon in the role of a Samaritan magician as a means of discrediting the popular Gnostic hero.[3] However, while early Christian apologists were known to downgrade their opponents by branding them magicians and sorcerers and while Luke was clearly critical of Simon's claims and behavior, it by no means follows necessarily that Luke has distorted Simon's Gnostic identity. Later in Acts, another μάγος (Elymas) is severely judged (13.5-12) and Ephesian magic books are incinerated (19.18-19), but there are no hints that these incidents were aimed at Gnostic targets.[4] Moreover, when Luke undermines certain mythological and philosophical systems, he seems to do so directly (Acts 14.11-18; 17.16-31), without masking his opponents as tricksters.[5]

---

1. For a collection and general discussion of the various Simonian traditions, see R.P. Casey, 'Simon Magus', in Lake and Cadbury (eds.), *Beginnings of Christianity*, V, pp. 151-63; E. Meyer, *Ursprung und Anfänge des Christentums* (3 vols.; Stuttgart: Cotta'sche, 1924), III, pp. 277-302; Beyschlag, *Simon Magus*, pp. 7-78.

2. Justin, *Apol.* 1.26; Irenaeus, *Adv. Haer.* 1.23; Hippolytus, *Ref.* 6.9-20; cf. also Epiphanius, *Haer.* 21.

3. Haenchen, *Acts*, p. 307; *idem*, *Gott und Mensch: Gesammelte Aufsätze* (Tübingen: Mohr [Paul Siebeck], 1965), p. 297; G. Lüdemann, *Untersuchungen zur simonianischen Gnosis* (GTA, 1; Göttingen: Vandenhoeck & Ruprecht, 1975), p. 42; *idem*, 'Acts', p. 423.

4. Cf. Bergmeier, 'Gestalt des Simon Magus', p. 270.

5. For a more extended critique of Haenchen's and Lüdemann's theories, see K. Beyschlag, 'Zur Simon-Magus-Frage', *ZTK* 68 (1971), pp. 395-415;

C.H. Talbert is no closer to the mark in supposing that Luke purposefully hides Simon's true Gnostic colors in order to preserve the harmony and orthodoxy of the apostolic age and thus undercut any Gnostic claim to the heritage of primitive, authentic Christianity.[1] Apart from the objections which could be levelled against Talbert's thoroughgoing 'early catholic' and anti-Gnostic interpretation of Luke–Acts, his perspective on Simon in Acts 8 founders on the fact that, even without Gnostic qualities, this figure is still a rebellious troublemaker disrupting the early church's Samaritan mission. Luke does not cast Simon as a *Gnostic* heretic; but as a baptized believer who blasphemes, as it were, the gift of the Holy Spirit, Simon surely appears as some kind of heretic. By openly exposing Simon's 'apostasy' during the earliest stages of the Christian mission, Luke clearly does not portray the apostolic era as idyllic or error-free (as Talbert supposes) and seems disinclined to cover up any aspect of Simon's identity, Gnostic or otherwise.[2]

In conclusion, Luke's characterization of Simon Magus seems to have nothing to do with Gnosticism.[3] Hence, those patristic reports of Simon as the Gnostic arch-villain prove largely irrelevant for our purposes. However, other early Christian accounts—such as those in the Pseudo-Clementine literature and Origen—which treat Simon as a popular Samaritan magician, as does Acts 8, may spark some insights

---

R. Bergmeier, 'Quellen vorchristlicher Gnosis?', in *Tradition und Glaube: Das frühe Christentum in seiner Umwelt* (ed. G. Jeremias, H.-W. Kuhn and H. Stegemann; Göttingen: Vandenhoeck & Ruprecht, 1971), pp. 200-20; R.McL. Wilson, 'Simon and Gnostic Origins', in Kremer (ed.), *Les Actes des Apôtres*, pp. 485-91; E. Yamauchi, *Pre-Christian Gnosticism: A Survey of the Proposed Evidences* (London: Tyndale Press, 1973), pp. 58-65.

1. C.H. Talbert, *Luke and the Gnostics: An Examination of the Lucan Purpose* (Nashville: Abingdon Press, 1966), pp. 83-97.

2. Cf. W.C. van Unnik, 'Apostelgeschichte und die Häresien', in *Sparsa Collecta: The Collected Essays of W.C. van Unnik* (NovTSup, 29; Leiden: Brill, 1973), I, pp. 402-409.

3. C.K. Barrett leaves open the possibility that Luke 'pillories gnostic leaders in the person of Simon Magus' but hastens to add 'a more important observation . . . that Luke studiously avoids gnostic thought and language' (*Luke the Historian in Recent Study* [London: Epworth, 1961], p. 62). In a later study, Barrett flatly states, 'there is nothing in Acts 8 to suggest that Simon was a gnostic' and 'for Luke Simon was not a gnostic but a μάγος' ('Light on the Holy Spirit', p. 286).

into Luke's presentation (still bearing in mind, of course, that Acts 8 predates these other Simonian traditions).

2. Philip and Simon the 'Great Power'

Acts 8.9-11 emphasizes Simon's reputation as a great and powerful figure in Samaria. Simon reportedly proclaimed εἶναί τινα ἑαυτὸν μέγαν (8.9) and inspired the Samaritan people *en masse* to believe and confess the same. 'From the least to the greatest (ἕως μεγάλου)' they extolled Simon as ἡ δύναμις τοῦ θεοῦ ἡ καλουμένη μεγάλη (8.10). In its Lukan context, this description apparently signifies Simon's fame as a 'divine man', a supernatural being in human form.[1] In Lk. 22.69 'the power of God' denotes God himself, as illustrated by comparison with Acts 7.55-56:

$$\text{ἐκ δεξιῶν τῆς δυνάμεως τοῦ θεοῦ (Lk. 22.69)}$$
$$\text{ἐκ δεξιῶν τοῦ θεοῦ (Acts 7.55-56)}$$

In the Synoptic parallels, 'the Power' *simpliciter* designates the person of God (Mt. 26.64; Mk 14.62), suggesting that τοῦ θεοῦ in Lk. 22.69 and Acts 8.10 represents an explanatory Lukan addition.[2] So the Samaritans in Acts esteem Simon as 'the Power *which is God* called Great' or, more succinctly, the 'Great Power'. That 'Great Power' should be viewed as Simon's formal title is demonstrated by several analogies in Luke–Acts of a double-name couched in a καλέω-construction (e.g. Συμεὼν ὁ καλούμενος Νίγερ, Acts 13.1; cf. Lk. 6.15; 8.21; Acts 1.23; 15.37).

The likelihood that ἡ δύναμις μεγάλη points to Simon's divine pretensions is strengthened by the observation that notions of 'greatness' and 'power', taken separately or together, were commonly associated with ancient deities. Given the wide range of religious-historical options[3] and the relative vagueness of attributes like 'great' and 'powerful', it is virtually impossible to pinpoint any single source behind Simon's identification as the 'Great Power'. Yet, in view of the

---

1. Cf. Roloff, *Apostelgeschichte*, pp. 134, 137-38; Beyschlag, *Simon Magus*, pp. 102-106.

2. Cf. Bergmeier, 'Frühdatierung', p. 148; Conzelmann, *Apostelgeschichte*, pp. 60-61.

3. See Beyschlag, *Simon Magus*, pp. 106-20; Lüdemann, *Untersuchungen*, pp. 42-49; Rudolph, 'Simon—Magus', pp. 320-28.

setting of Acts 8, it is interesting to note that some recent studies have demonstrated a possible *Samaritan* background to the 'Great Power' concept. H.G. Kippenberg has observed that the Samaritan Targum periodically renders the Hebrew 'God' in Aramaic as 'the Power' or 'Powerful One', and certain early Samaritan liturgical traditions (from the *Durran* and *Memar Marqah*) specifically stress the 'greatness' of this 'Powerful One'. Such divine appellations especially befit the God of Israel who acted mightily on behalf of his people, notably in delivering them from Egyptian enslavement.[1] Building on Kippenberg's work, J.E. Fossum argues,

> The divine name of the Great Power, which appears in the oldest account of Simon [Acts 8], is. . . a Samaritan name of YHWH. It is true that the epithet 'great' was frequently applied to gods in Hellenistic times, and that also the 'power' of the gods was praised as 'great', but 'the Great Power' is an authentically Samaritan divine name, and the encomium of 'the Power' or even 'the Great Power' as 'great' is a Samaritan characteristic.[2]

By frankly disclosing Simon's veneration by the Samaritans as the embodiment of divine energy, the 'Great Power', Luke causes Philip's greatness to stand out by comparison. For not only does Philip match Simon's feats in Samaria, the Christian evangelist also dramatically surpasses and overwhelms the renowned Magus. Indeed, the juxtaposition of Philip's and Simon's Samaritan exploits demonstrates not merely that both figures worked miracles and attracted multitudes, but also that both vied for the devotion of the same Samaritan throng and that Philip emerged as the undisputed champion. The story in Acts 8 makes plain that Simon had been on the scene in Samaria prior to Philip's arrival (v. 9) and had forged his enormous popularity over a 'long time' (v. 11). Philip's Samaritan mission, then, takes on the character of a direct supplanting of Simon's long-standing position. Moreover, the terse narrative in 8.5-8 gives the impression that this

---

1. Kippenberg, *Garizim*, pp. 329-48.

2. J.E. Fossum, *The Name of God and the Angel of the Lord: Samaritan and Jewish Concepts of Intermediation and the Origin of Gnosticism* (WUNT, 36; Tübingen: Mohr [Paul Siebeck], 1985), pp. 171-72; cf. Coggins, 'Samaritans and Acts', pp. 430-31. Kippenberg and Fossum both proceed to theorize that Samaritanism must have been the *Mutterboden* from which Simonian Gnosis sprang. Such a speculative assessment of Gnostic origins, however, goes beyond our simple concern to demonstrate a *possible* point of contact between Luke's presentation of Simon Magus and external Samaritan traditions.

capture of Samaritan hearts was swift and total and accomplished without a struggle.[1]

Of course, the crowning sign of Philip's victory is the remarkable capitulation of Simon himself in Acts 8.13. Even he (καὶ αὐτός)—the self-confessed and much-adored δύναμις μεγάλη—cannot help but be amazed by Philip's patently superior δυνάμεις μεγάλας; as a result, he believes the Christian message, is baptized and becomes Philip's devoted follower (προσκαρτερῶν τῷ φιλίππῳ).[2]

Not only does Philip best Simon in Acts 8 in terms of the sheer power of his ministry; he also outclasses the Samaritan magician in terms of motivation. The picture of Simon gleaned from Luke's report is of a thoroughly self-absorbed trickster willing to defraud others for his own gain. To the extent that he has a message, Simon proclaims himself and his own grandeur (8.9b). His miraculous displays, although not specified, are generally portrayed as sensational works of μαγεία designed purely to court the crowd's favor (8.9-11). He even endeavors to traffic in the gift of the Spirit, presumably to exploit further a thrill-seeking public (8.18-24). By contrast, while Philip in no sense falls behind Simon as a channel of spiritual power, his aim is not to impress or manipulate others for his own aggrandizement. As noted above, the priority of Philip's Samaritan ministry is neither wonder-working nor self-proclamation, but the preaching of good news about Christ and the kingdom of God. He desires not that the Samaritans worship him but that they honor the name of Jesus Christ. Philip performs miracles, to be sure, but these serve to release the afflicted from the bondage of disease and demonization (8.7) and to undergird his liberating gospel message.[3] They are not devices to evoke mere amazement. In fact, Luke studiously avoids ἐξίστημι in recounting the Samaritans' response to Philip's efforts.

The upshot of the Philip–Simon contest in Acts 8 is that Philip, the messenger of Christ, decisively proves himself greater than the great

---

1. G. Schneider observes that while Simon's popularity had been acquired over an extended period, Philip 'sehr schnell zum Erfolg kam' (*Apostelgeschichte*, I, p. 490 n. 60).

2. προσκαρτερέω is used several times in Acts to denote Christian devotion to various aspects of worship and fellowship (Acts 1.14; 2.42, 46; 6.4). Most comparable, however, to Simon's attachment to a person (Philip) in 8.13 is the reference in 10.7 to Cornelius's slaves 'who served him'.

3. Cf. Garrett, *Demise of the Devil*, pp. 63-65.

magician Simon. The evangelist's power is stronger and his motives purer. Such aspects of Philip's greatness merit further attention against the backdrop of Luke's entire narrative.

a. *The Struggle for Power*
The supremacy of Christian power (δύναμις) and authority (ἐξουσία)[1] over all competitive forces is a consistent theme running throughout Luke–Acts. Jesus, conceived by the 'power of the Most High' (δύναμις ὑψίστου, Lk. 1.35), commences his public ministry in 'the power of the Spirit' (4.14) which had just been proven in a triumphant encounter with the devil (4.1-13). As he fulfills his vocation, Jesus inevitably builds a reputation among astonished audiences as one who teaches 'with authority' (ἐν ἐξουσίᾳ) and 'with authority and power (ἐν ἐξουσίᾳ καὶ δυνάμει). . . commands the unclean spirits and out they come!' (4.32, 36). Moreover, he imparts this prowess to his disciples, enabling them to exercise 'authority. . . over all the power of the enemy' (10.19; cf. 9.1). Like the other Synoptic writers, Luke envisages the climax of Jesus' work as his exaltation to 'the right hand of the power of God' (22.69; Mt. 26.64; Mk 14.62), from where he will return to earth 'with power and great glory', shaking 'the powers of the heavens' in his train (21.26-27; Mt. 24.29-30; Mk 13.25-26). Unique to Luke, however, is the emphasis that Jesus will pour out the Spirit from his exalted seat, thereby imbuing his followers with divine δύναμις for the purpose of effective witness, supported by mighty works (24.49; Acts 1.8; 2.33; 4.33).

As a Spirit-empowered evangelist, exorcist and worker of δυνάμεις μεγάλας, the Lukan Philip takes his place alongside Jesus and the apostles as a dynamic subjugator of the powers of darkness. But in confronting specifically magical power associated with a magus-figure, Philip aligns most directly with Paul in Acts. In fact, at the beginning of each of the three so-called missionary journeys, Paul clashes victoriously with practitioners of magical arts.[2]

---

1. ἐξουσία is used in Acts 8.19 of the 'power' which Simon requests to impart the Spirit. The term is synonymous with δύναμις in 8.10 and throughout Luke–Acts.

2. For a discussion of these parallel incidents from the Pauline mission in relation to Philip's encounter with Simon, see G. Klein, 'Der Synkretismus als theologisches Problem in der ältesten christlichen Apologetik', *ZTK* 64 (1967), pp. 50-77; E.S. Fiorenza, 'Miracles, Mission and Apologetics: An Introduction', in *Aspects of*

1. Setting out from Antioch, Paul and Barnabas first arrive on the island of Cyprus where they encounter 'a certain magician (μάγον), a Jewish false prophet, named Bar-Jesus' (Acts 13.6). The use of μάγος in 13.6, 8 to designate Bar-Jesus clearly associates him with Simon in Acts 8, who was well-known in Samaria as μαγεύων—one who does the work of a μάγος (v. 9; cf. μαγεία, v. 11).[1] In 13.10, 'Luke has Paul let fly a long string of deeply incriminating charges'.[2] Bar-Jesus (= Elymas) is labelled 'son of the devil', 'enemy of all unrighteousness, full of all deceit and villainy', and perverter of 'the straight paths of the Lord' (τὰς ὁδοὺς [τοῦ] κυρίου τὰς εὐθείας). Culminating in Paul's sentence of divine judgment (13.11), this confrontation most readily recalls Peter's threat of severe punishment following his exposure of Simon's 'wicked' and 'iniquitous' heart, 'not right (εὐθεῖα) before God' (8.20-23). However, a link may still be established with Philip's interplay with Simon. Both Philip and Paul encounter magicians in the course of proclaiming the word to receptive hearers (8.4-6; 13.7), and both emerge victorious in showdowns with the established local sorcerer. Though this last point is less obvious in the Elymas incident, A.D. Nock offers a pertinent hypothesis:

> There may be in it [the scene in Acts 13.6-12] some suggestion of the outdoing of the magician at his own game: blinding is one of the things which his [Elymas's] type claimed to be able to do, and a demonstration of power before a personage in authority [Sergius Paulus] is also characteristic.[3]

2. At Philippi, the first major venue of the second missionary journey, Paul and Silas are met by 'a slave girl who had a spirit of divination (πνεῦμα πύθωνα) and brought her owners a great deal of money by fortune-telling (μαντευομένη)' (Acts 16.16). This portrayal of the girl as a 'pythoness' suggests a supernatural ability to

---

Religious Propaganda in Judaism and Early Christianity (ed. E.S. Fiorenza; Notre Dame, IN: University of Notre Dame Press, 1976), pp. 8-20; Garrett, *Demise of the Devil*, pp. 61-99.

1. Cf. G. Delling, 'μάγος, μαγεία, μαγεύω', *TDNT*, IV, p. 359. Except for the 'magi' in Matthew, the occurrences of μάγος and cognates in the New Testament are restricted to the Simon and Elymas episodes in Acts.

2. Garrett, *Demise of the Devil*, p. 86.

3. A.D. Nock, 'Paul and the Magus', in Lake and Cadbury (eds.), *Beginnings of Christianity*, V, pp. 185-86.

speak as a 'ventriloquist' (πύθων = ἐγγαστρίμυθος) for the gods,[1] and the use of μαντεύομαι intimates that this power was employed for clairvoyant purposes, such as soothsaying and necromancy. Thus, she may be compared with a figure like the witch of Endor consulted by King Saul in the familiar Old Testament story.[2]

At first glance, the Philippian sorceress in Acts 16 appears to support Paul's efforts. She begins to follow the missionary party around, declaring them 'slaves of the Most High God who proclaim to you a way of salvation' (16.17). But Paul sees through this response as a taunting charade. So, becoming irritated with the situation, he exorcises the evil spirit within the girl. The result, however, is not only the liberation of the possessed girl but also the indignation of her employers whose business was being jeopardized (16.18-24).

The issue of financial profit for magical services ties in with Simon's greed so sternly opposed by Peter in Acts 8, but the picture of the sorceress tagging along with the Christian missionary especially parallels Simon's attachment to Philip. Moreover, the contrast between the phony discipleship of the slave girl and the exemplary reception of Paul's message by another businesswoman in Philippi— Lydia—corresponds to an apparent deficiency in Simon's response relative to the Samaritan crowd who 'listened eagerly' to Philip's word (προσέχω, 16.14; 8.6).

3. Virtually the whole of Paul's final missionary journey is taken up with the three-year stay in Ephesus. After Paul performs some spectacular feats (Acts 19.11-12), a group of wandering Jewish exorcists, the seven sons of Sceva, decide to exploit for themselves the evidently powerful name of Jesus. But their scheme meets with terrible disaster, proving that Jesus' authority is not to be presumptuously usurped (19.13-16). The effects of the exorcists' humiliation reverberate throughout Ephesian society. Many professing believers come forward and renounce similar occultic practices, demonstrating their repentance by burning their costly magic manuals (19.17-19).

But further conflict is in store for Paul in Ephesus, again on the economic front. The lucrative enterprise dealing in shrines of the

---

1. See Plutarch, *Def. Orac.* 9.414E; W. Foerster, 'πύθων', *TDNT*, VI, pp. 918-20; Haenchen, *Acts*, p. 495 n. 4.

2. 1 Kgdms 28.8: καὶ [Σαουλ] εἶπεν αὐτῇ Μάντευσαι δή μοι ἐν τῷ ἐγγαστριμύθῳ. Cf. F.F. Bruce, *The Acts of the Apostles: The Greek Text with Introduction and Commentary* (Chicago: Inter-Varsity Press, 1952), p. 315.

goddess Artemis is being decimated in the wake of Paul's conversion of 'a considerable number of people (ἱκανὸν ὄχλον)' away from pagan worship (Acts 19.26). The significance of Paul's achievement lies in stripping the power of the 'Great' Artemis of the Ephesians (μεγάλη, 19.27, 28, 34, 35; μεγαλειότης, 19.27), revered by 'all Asia and the world' (19.27).

Apart from matching again the Peter–Simon segment in Acts 8 in terms of censuring magicians who tamper with the things of Christ, the Ephesus episode in Acts 19 also strikingly parallels the report of Philip's Samaritan mission. Just as Paul—proclaiming the kingdom of God (19.8), working 'extraordinary miracles' (δυνάμεις, 19.11) and promoting 'the name of the Lord Jesus' (19.17)—turns a number of Ephesian magic-devotees to faith in Christ, so Philip, conducting a similar ministry (8.5-8, 12-13), diverts the attention of the Samaritan masses away from Simon Magus to Christ.[1] And just as Paul undercuts the appeal of the Great Goddess Artemis, venerated by all, so Philip deflates the Great Divine-Power, Simon Magus, adored by the whole Samaritan nation, from the least to the greatest.

These three Pauline episodes echo the main emphases of the Philip–Simon narrative in Acts 8. The stress on sharp, punitive measures taken against wonder-working magicians[2] and on the bankrupting of their fraudulent enterprises[3] both call to mind similar concerns in the exchange between Simon and Peter (8.18-24). But the basic conquest of magical power through dynamic preaching and superior miracle-working matches Paul's ministry most closely with Philip's. By featuring a similar subduing of magicians as the starting point of both the mission of the Stephen circle scattered from Jerusalem and each principal phase of the Pauline mission, Luke has established within his narrative an essential harmony between these two mission movements and their leading figures, Philip and Paul.

b. *Miracle and Motivation*
The evaluation of wonder-workers and magicians in the ancient world went beyond tallying who had the most power, who performed the

---

1. Garrett also notes that both Philip and Paul encounter sorcerers (Simon/sons of Sceva) after fleeing from hostile Jews (Acts 8.1-13; 19.8-20) (*Demise of the Devil*, p. 91).
2. Cf. Kee, *Miracle*, pp. 211-18.
3. Cf. Barrett, 'Light on the Holy Spirit', pp. 288-91.

greatest feats. There was also deep concern over the motivation behind miraculous activity—was it altruistic or exploitative?—and the source of supernatural authority—was it divine or demonic? In short, the character of miracle-workers was closely scrutinized.[1]

Philostratus, in recounting the spectacular career of the first-century itinerant philosopher, Apollonius of Tyana, takes great pains to distance Apollonius from the many money-grubbing 'wizards' and 'old hags' who peddled their 'quackeries' among gullible, 'simple-minded' folk 'addicted to magical art' (*Apol.* 6.39).[2] Apollonius certainly worked wonders, but only for the noblest purposes, as Philostratus makes clear in relating Apollonius's *apologia* against charges of wizardry:

> And yet I have been much esteemed in the several cities which asked for my aid, whatever the objects were for which they asked it, and they were such as these: that their sick might be healed of their diseases, that both their initiations and their sacrifices might be rendered more holy, that insolence and pride might be extirpated, and the laws strengthened. And . . . the only reward which I obtained in all this was that men were made much better than they were before. . . (*Apol.* 8.7)

Later, however, toward the end of the third century, when a Roman governor named Hierocles began to compare and even exalt Apollonius of Tyana in relation to Jesus of Nazareth, the Christian author Eusebius aimed to set the record straight. Not surprisingly, Eusebius attacked the very character of Apollonius's works which Philostratus had defended. Regarding a particularly famous miracle attributed to Apollonius, Eusebius contended 'that fraud and make-

---

1. The tendency to scrutinize the claims of miracle workers and magicians is especially evident in the second to fourth centuries CE among both Christians and pagans. For surveys and appraisals of the evidence, see Kee, *Miracle*, pp. 252-79; idem, *Medicine, Miracle and Magic in New Testament Times* (SNTSMS, 55; Cambridge: Cambridge University Press, 1986), pp. 12-25; S. Benko, *Pagan Rome and the Early Christians* (London: Batsford, 1985), pp. 103-139; H. Remus, *Pagan–Christian Conflict over Miracle in the Second Century* (Patristic Monograph Series, 10; Cambridge, MA: Philadelphia Patristic Foundation, 1983), pp. 52-72; G.W.H. Lampe, 'Miracles and Early Christian Apologetic', in Moule (ed.), *Miracles*, pp. 205-18; W.R. Schoedel and B.J. Malina, 'Miracle or Magic?', *RelSRev* 12 (1986), pp. 31-39.

2. Citations of Apollonius are from Philostratus, *The Life of Apollonius of Tyana* (2 vols.; ed. and trans. F.C. Conybeare; LCL; Cambridge, MA: Harvard University Press; London: Heinemann, 1912).

believe was in this case everything, and that if ever anything reeked of wizardry this did' (*Treat. of Eus.* 23).[1] Moreover, this instance was typical, in Eusebius's view, of a 'whole series of miracles wrought by him [Apollonius]. . . accomplished through a ministry of demons' (*Treat. of Eus.* 31).

This heated debate among pagans and Christians over the legitimacy and integrity of alleged miracle-workers is also attested in the writings of Lucian and Origen. The second-century pagan satirist, Lucian of Samosata, wrote an entire tract exposing the chicanery of a popular, wonder-working prophet named Alexander and in another work criticized the 'charlatanism and notoriety-seeking' of the Cynic philosopher, Peregrinus (known more, however, for his piety and inspired teaching than his miracle-working). For a brief period, Peregrinus professed the Christian faith and took advantage of fellow-believers, thus confirming Lucian's opinion regarding the Christian community that 'if any charlatan and trickster, able to profit by occasions, comes among them, he quickly acquires sudden wealth by imposing upon simple folk' (*Pas. of Per.* 13).[2]

Celsus also cast aspersions on the Christian movement and, more explicitly than Lucian, directed his attack against the wonder-working reputation of Christian ministers. We know of Celsus's viewpoint only from the polemical treatise which Origen wrote against him. Celsus is quoted as correlating even the works of Jesus 'with the works of sorcerers who profess to do wonderful miracles, and the accomplishments of those who are taught by the Egyptians, who for a few obols make known their sacred lore in the middle of the market-place'. Origen challenges this calumny by appealing forcefully to the unimpeachable rectitude of Jesus' behavior in contrast to the evil conduct of greedy magicians:[3]

> in fact no sorcerer uses his tricks to call the spectators to moral reformation. . . Nor do they even want to have anything to do with reforming men, seeing that they themselves are filled with the most shameful and infamous sins. Is it not likely that one who used the miracles that he

1. Citations of *The Treatise of Eusebius* are from the LCL (incorporated into Philostratus, *Life of Apollonius*, II, pp. 485-605).

2. Citations of *The Passing of Peregrinus* are from Lucian (8 vols.; ed. and trans. A.M. Harmon, K. Kilburn and M.D. MacLeod; LCL; Cambridge, MA: Harvard University Press; London: Heinemann, 1913–67).

3. Cf. Lampe, 'Miracles and Early Christian Apologetic', pp. 212-13.

performed to call those who saw the happenings to moral reformation, would have shown himself as an example of the best life, not only to his genuine disciples but also to the rest? Jesus did this in order that . . . [those] who have been taught as much by his doctrine as by his moral life and miracles the right way to live, might do every action by referring to the pleasure of the supreme God. If the life of Jesus was of this character, how could anyone reasonably compare him with the behaviour of sorcerers? (*Con. Cel.* 1.68; cf. 2.49).[1]

A final example of the early church's insistence on the moral uprightness of her miracle-workers over against fraudulent magicians may be adduced in the following appraisal of the apostle Thomas:

he goes about the towns and villages, and if he has anything he gives it all to the poor, and he teaches a new God and heals the sick and drives out demons and does many other wonderful things; and we think he is a magician. But his works of compassion, and the healings which are wrought by him are without reward, and moreover his simplicity and kindness and the quality of his faith, show that he is righteous or an apostle of the new God whom he preaches (*Acts of Thomas* 20).[2]

Though stemming from an earlier period, Luke–Acts manifests a very similar concern for separating authentic miracle-workers from deceitful magicians. As noted above, Philip distinguishes himself from Simon Magus by using his power to alleviate human suffering rather than merely to elicit public admiration and by proclaiming Christ's name and God's kingdom instead of boosting his own reputation. This last item, commending self-effacement and denouncing self-advancement, is quite important to Luke. He recalls that the movement launched by Theudas, who (like Simon) 'claim[ed] to be somebody', ended in utter failure, as he and his supporters ἐγένοντο εἰς οὐδέν (Acts 5.36).[3] Likewise, Luke reports that the popular Judas the Galilean 'perished' (ἀπώλετο) and his followers dispersed (5.37). The story is told of Herod that, while basking in his audience's acclaim—'The voice of a god, and not of a mortal!'—he was promptly stricken dead 'because he had not given the glory to God' (12.22-23). Finally,

---

1. Citations of *Contra Celsum* are from Origen, *Contra Celsum* (ed. and trans. H. Chadwick; Cambridge: Cambridge University Press, 1953).
2. Citation is from E. Hennecke and W. Schneemelcher (eds.), *New Testament Apocrypha* (2 vols.; Philadelphia: Westminster Press, 1963–66), II.
3. On the correspondence between Theudas and Simon in Acts, see Bauernfeind, *Kommentar*, p. 125; Stählin, *Apostelgeschichte*, p. 120; Beyschlag, *Simon Magus*, p. 102.

as Christianity pervades Ephesus we learn that the city's businessmen fear (justifiably) 'that the temple of the great goddess will be scorned, and she will be deprived of her majesty' (19.27). As all other self-promoters and claimants of divinity come to ruin in Acts, so Simon, the legendary 'Great Power', forfeits his devotees and faces impending destruction (εἰς ἀπώλειαν, 8.20).

By contrast, the messengers of Christ shun the limelight in Luke's narrative. Jesus himself sets the standard that 'the least among all of you is the greatest' (Lk. 9.48), particularly the one who (like Jesus) serves others at the table (Lk. 22.24-27). Moreover, the Lukan Jesus (against Matthew) echoes the humble response found in Mark: 'Why do you call me good? No one is good but God alone' (Lk. 18.19; Mk 10.18). In Acts both Peter and Paul remonstrate with excitable crowds who want to deify them, vigorously claiming their mere humanity (Acts 3.11-12; 10.25-26; 14.11-18),[1] and Peter particularly underscores that miracles owe nothing to him and everything to the name of Jesus (Acts 3.12, 16; 4.7, 10).

Philip does not affirm his humility in so many words, but his overall characterization points in this direction. Philip embarks on his Samaritan mission as an erstwhile table-servant to poor widows (Acts 6.1-6) and recent victim of persecution and dislocation (8.1-4). However awkward it may appear both logically and historically (as many have supposed) for such a figure to become a successful evangelist, Luke's literary purpose is clear: Philip the least—friend of the poor, table-waiter, himself oppressed and homeless—becomes the greatest, overwhelming the 'great' Simon Magus revered by even the 'greatest' Samaritans (cf. 8.10).[2]

Furthermore, Philip proves to be an exemplary herald of God's kingdom. As noted previously, for Luke the kingdom of God belongs in a special way to the poor and infirm, the homeless and destitute (e.g. Lk. 6.20; 14.13-21; 18.22-24). Additionally, the kingdom comes as the Father's gracious gift, inspiring responses of divestment (selling possessions/almsgiving) and investment in heavenly treasure (Lk.

---

1. An exception may be noted in Acts 28.6: the Maltans call Paul a god, and he makes no explicit denial. However, neither does he affirm the acclamation (in fact, no responsive comment of Paul is recorded). At any rate, in the overall account of Paul's voyage to Rome as a bound prisoner, Luke repeatedly brings out Paul's attitude of humble dependence on God (27.21-26, 35; 28.15).

2. See the full discussion of Philip's role as table-waiter in Chapter 5 section 2.

12.32-34).[1] Whether charity officer in Jerusalem or liberator of the possessed, paralyzed and lame in Samaria, Philip shows the signs of a true servant of God's kingdom. On the other hand, Simon's attempt to buy what can only be divinely bestowed and his preoccupation with personal greatness mark him as woefully out of step with kingdom concerns. If the least in the kingdom is greater than the greatest born of woman (John the Baptist, Lk. 7.28), how much greater is the humble kingdom-servant (Philip) than one who feigns greatness and flouts God's rule (Simon).

c. *Conclusion*

Whether Luke aimed to challenge the problem of syncretistic compromise within the church of his day,[2] or to counter the polemicizing of Christianity as a magic-based religion, or to achieve some other purpose, he obviously depicted the early Christian missionaries as successful over yet separated from the activities of contemporary 'divine-men'.[3] In Luke's estimation, Christ's servants were not only eminent miracle-workers, but also men and women of model character, working solely for the glory of God and the good of others. Philip the evangelist stands out in his encounter with Simon Magus as a prominent representative of such ministers.

It is important to pause momentarily and take due account of this thorough Lukan shaping of Acts 8.5-13 to highlight Philip's genuine greatness. We are thus alerted to the possibility that any supposed downgrading of Philip in the following scene is more apparent than real.

3. *Philip, Simon and the 'Prophet like Moses'*

In the previous chapter, the correspondence was noted between Moses' 'wonders and signs' (Acts 7.36) and Philip's 'signs and great miracles' (8.6, 13), and the suggestion was made that the Lukan Philip may be cast as a 'prophet like Moses' whose Magus encounter recalls Moses' clash with Pharaoh's magicians. In the present section, this Philip–Moses connection will be developed more fully in the context of

---

1. Cf. Kee, *Miracle*, p. 201.
2. Klein, 'Synkretismus'.
3. Barrett, 'Light on the Holy Spirit', p. 291.

Luke–Acts and certain external traditions pertaining to the Mosaic prophet and Simon Magus.

a. *Philip and the 'Prophet like Moses' in Luke–Acts*

The only direct New Testament citations of the 'prophet like Moses' text in Deuteronomy 18 appear in Acts 3.22 and 7.37. Since these references cluster in the early chapters of Acts dealing with the fledgling Jerusalem church, scholars have often assumed that Luke has simply transmitted the 'prophet like Moses' concept from primitive christological tradition.[1] While this view is possible, it is not a necessary corollary that the 'prophet like Moses' was peripheral to or uncharacteristic of *Lukan* concerns. If Luke was not the first explicitly to identify the Deuteronomic 'prophet like Moses' with Jesus, he certainly made this perspective his own by incorporating it into his writings. Moreover, recent studies have demonstrated plausibly that, beyond his citation of Deut. 18.15, 18, Luke was widely influenced by a 'prophet like Moses' pattern in characterizing Jesus and his disciples.

P.S. Minear acknowledges Luke's association of Jesus with a variety of Old Testament figures (Abraham, David, Elijah, Jonah, etc.) but contends that 'in Luke's mind the most strategic. . . is the link to Moses'.[2] The attraction of the Mosaic story lies in its rich store of appropriate, poignant images:

> The portraits in Luke's gallery of Jesus as prophet, revealer, teacher, servant, judge, ruler, Son of God, covenant-maker, deliverer, have too many points of contact with the portrait of Moses to be accidental. . . For Luke no analogy to the redemptive work of Jesus could be more evocative or more far-reaching than this comparison to Moses.[3]

More specifically, Minear calls attention to the Moses-like activity of the Lukan Jesus in ascending to the mountain to commune with God before descending to announce 'the promises and imperatives of the new dispensation' in the so-called 'Sermon on the Plain' (Lk. 6.12–

---

1. E.g. O. Cullmann, *The Christology of the New Testament* (London: SCM Press, 2nd edn, 1963), p. 37; J.A.T. Robinson, *Twelve New Testament Studies* (SBT, 34; London: SCM Press, 1962), pp. 150-51; J.D.G. Dunn, *Christology in the Making: An Inquiry into the Character of Earliest Christianity* (London: SCM Press, 1980), p. 138; Jeremias, 'Μωϋσῆς', *TDNT*, IV, pp. 868-69.

2. Minear, *To Heal*, p. 105.

3. Minear, *To Heal*, p. 109.

7.1).[1] In addition, Minear notes that the Acts citations of Deuteronomy 18 appear in contexts which transparently connect Jesus' recent rejection and vindication among his own people with the similar experiences of Moses in ancient Israel (cf. Acts 3.13-15, 17-23; 7.23-27, 35, 39-41).[2]

The most exhaustive exploration of the 'prophet like Moses' model in Luke–Acts has been undertaken by D.P. Moessner.[3] He argues that the entire central section of Luke (9.51–19.44) has been constructed to chart 'the journey of the prophet Jesus whose calling and fate both recapitulate and consummate the career of Moses in Deuteronomy. We have here nothing less than the prophet like Moses (Deut. 18.15-19) in a New Exodus unfolding with a dramatic tension all its own.'[4] In Moessner's view, this narrative pattern is strikingly adumbrated in 9.1-50, especially in the watershed transfiguration scene where Luke uniquely emphasizes Jesus' Moses-like, mountain-top revelation 'in glory' (ἐν δόξῃ, 9.31; cf. v. 32; Deut. 5.24) and specifies that the discussion between Jesus, Moses and Elijah centered on 'his [Jesus'] departure ['exodus'], which he was about to accomplish at Jerusalem'

---

1. Minear, *To Heal*, p. 116.

2. Minear, *To Heal*, pp. 105-11, 117-21.

3. See *Lord of the Banquet: The Literary and Theological Significance of the Lukan Travel Narrative* (Minneapolis, MN: Fortress Press, 1989), which pulls together in book form what otherwise appears in a series of published articles from 1982–86 (see bibliography).

4. D.P. Moessner, 'Luke 9:1-50: Luke's Preview of the Journey of the Prophet like Moses of Deuteronomy', *JBL* 102 (1983), p. 582. The theory that the central section of Luke is patterned after the Moses-material in Deut. 1–26 was earlier set forth in brief by C.F. Evans ('The Central Section of St Luke's Gospel', in *Studies in the Gospels: Essays in Memory of R.H. Lightfoot* [ed. D.E. Nineham; Oxford: Basil Blackwell, 1955]; cf. more recently *Saint Luke* [TPI New Testament Commentaries; Philadelphia: TPI; London: SCM Press, 1990], pp. 34-36, 433ff.). In addition to Moessner, a number of other scholars have taken up and developed Evans's thesis in various ways. See, e.g., J. Drury, *Tradition and Design in Luke's Gospel: A Study in Early Christian Historiography* (London: Darton, Longman & Todd, 1976), pp. 138-64; M.D. Goulder, *The Evangelists' Calendar: A Lectionary Explanation of the Development of Scripture* (London: SPCK, 1978), pp. 95-101; J.A. Sanders, 'The Ethic of Election in Luke's Great Banquet Parable', in *Essays in Old Testament Ethics (J. Philip Hyatt. In Memoriam)* (ed. J.L. Crenshaw and J.T. Willis; New York: Ktav, 1974), pp. 255, 264-66; Tiede, *Prophecy and History*, pp. 39-63.

(9.31).[1] Moessner further detects the 'prophet like Moses' framework behind Luke's characterization of three major Christian witnesses in Acts: Peter, Stephen and Paul.[2] They, like Jesus, Moses and other prophets in the Deuteronomistic tradition, appeal to the nation of Israel and suffer rejection. Stephen, for example, whose speech focuses heavily on Moses—especially his revelations of God and repudiations by Israel (Acts 7.17-44)—himself enjoys a vision of God's glory (6.15; 7.55-56) which, in tandem with his preaching, provokes a (predictably) violent response by a 'stiff-necked people' (7.51–8.1).[3]

While disagreement is bound to exist over precise points of comparison, the basic thesis seems established that to a great extent Luke has patterned his main characters after a Mosaic model. Does this stylization extend to Luke's portrait of Philip the evangelist? Philip's close connection with Stephen suggests yes. His number two position behind Stephen in the list of seven servants (Acts 6.5) and his appearance as the first fugitive from Jerusalem after Stephen's martyrdom imply that Philip emerges as a kind of successor to Stephen, one who takes up Stephen's mantle, who functions as a 'prophet like Stephen'—and hence, a 'prophet like Moses' as well.[4] Philip, like Stephen and Moses (and, of course, Jesus) is a man of 'wisdom' (6.3, 10; 7.22), a preacher demanding a hearing (ἀκούειν, 8.6; 3.22-23; 6.10-14; 7.54), a worker of 'signs' and mighty deeds (8.6, 13; 6.8; 7.36) and one rejected by Israel (8.1, 4-5; 7.27-28, 35, 39, 54, 57-59).

In some respects, Philip's match with Moses goes beyond Stephen's. For example, Philip's escape to Samaria from hostile Jewish authorities may be linked to Moses' flight to Midian when spurned by fellow-Israelites (Acts 7.24-29). Also, as the angel of the Lord eventually guides Philip to 'a wilderness road' (ἔρημος, 8.26), so 'an angel appeared to him [Moses] in the wilderness (ἔρημος)' (7.30). Finally,

---

1. Moessner, 'Luke 9:1-50', pp. 588-600; cf. R.F. O'Toole, 'Parallels between Jesus and Moses', *BTB* 20 (1990), pp. 22-24.
2. D.P. Moessner, 'Paul and the Pattern of the Prophet like Moses in Acts', in *SBLSP 1983* (ed. K.H. Richards; Chico, CA: Scholars Press, 1983), pp. 203-12; ' "The Christ Must Suffer": New Light on the Jesus–Peter, Stephen, Paul Parallels in Luke–Acts', *NovT* 28 (1986), pp. 220-56.
3. Moessner, '"Christ Must Suffer"', pp. 227-34, 247-48, 255-56.
4. Cf. Minear, *To Heal*, pp. 140-41; L.T. Johnson, *The Literary Function of Possessions in Luke–Acts* (SBLDS, 39; Missoula, MT: Scholars Press), pp. 52-53.

as the one singled out first and foremost among the 'exiles' from hostile Jerusalem, Philip may be loosely regarded as a Moses-like leader spearheading the 'exodus' of God's people from oppressive territory (cf. 7.36).

Generally, then, Philip takes his place in Luke's schema alongside Jesus and other prominent figures as a 'prophet like Moses'. In light of this broad profile, it is reasonable to inquire whether Luke specifically envisaged Moses' competition with Pharaoh's magicians as an analogue to Philip's competition with Simon Magus.

b. *Philip/Simon Magus and Moses/Pharaoh's Magicians*[1]

The Moses-section of Stephen's speech does not specifically mention the contest with Pharaoh's magicians, but the reference to Moses' 'wonders and signs in Egypt' (Acts 7.36) would naturally evoke memories of the classic clash in Pharaoh's court. From the outset of Moses' campaign to free his compatriots, as reported in Exodus, Pharaoh's magicians pit their skills against the Israelite wonder-worker. The Lord predicts that Pharaoh will demand 'a sign or a wonder' (σημεῖον ἢ τέρας, Exod. 7.9 LXX) as proof of Moses' and Aaron's authority, and indeed, at their first meeting Aaron dazzles Pharaoh by transforming his staff into a serpent (7.10). Promptly summoned by the king, the magicians (ἐπαοιδοί) perform the same feat through their 'secret arts' (φαρμαρκείαις), only to find, however, that Aaron's serpent-rod swallows up their own (7.11-12). Still, the competition continues, as the wizards keep pace with the Mosaic acts of polluting the Nile and proliferating frogs (7.22; 8.3 LXX). But the third plague (multiplying gnats) stymies the magicians and forces their confession that a superior power—'the finger of God'—is working through Moses and Aaron (8.14-15 LXX). To add insult to injury, the magicians are personally afflicted by boils (sixth plague) to such an extent that they 'could not stand before Moses' (9.11). Obviously, in the Exodus story, the predominance of Moses (and Aaron) over

---

1. In his commentary on Acts 8.12-13, F.F. Bruce briefly suggests the parallel between Simon and Pharaoh's magicians: 'But Simon Magus himself was influenced by the actions and words of Philip. Like the magicians of Egypt, he recognized that the messenger of the true God had access to a source of power that outstripped his own' (*The Book of the Acts* [NICNT; Grand Rapids: Eerdmans, rev. edn, 1988], p. 167). Bruce, however, does not elaborate on this parallel, and most commentators ignore it altogether.

Egypt's finest sorcerers is a significant factor in vindicating his divine calling and authority.

Surprisingly, then, other parts of the Old Testament which rehearse the Exodus events fail to mention specifically Moses' contest with Pharaoh's magicians. Nevertheless, immediately preceding the announcement of a coming 'prophet like Moses' in Deuteronomy 18 is a stern prohibition against Israel's having anything to do with the magical practices of the Canaanites.

> When you come into the land that the Lord your God is giving you, you must not learn to imitate the abhorrent practices of those nations. No one shall be found among you who. . . practices divination, or is a sooth-sayer or an augur, or a sorcerer (φαρμοκός), or one who casts spells (ἐπαείδων ἐπαοιδήν). . . For whoever does these things is abhorrent to the Lord; it is because of such abhorrent practices that the Lord your God is driving them out before you. . . Although these nations that you are about to dispossess give heed to soothsayers and to diviners, as for you, the Lord your God does not permit you to do so (Deut. 18.9-14).

In effect, the 'prophet like Moses', destined to be God's true spokesman (18.15-19), is directly opposed to the Canaanites' sooth-sayers and diviners,[1] just as Moses rivals Egypt's magicians in the Exodus story.[2] As Moses authenticated his leadership role in the exodus by besting Pharaoh's wizards, so after the conquest his prophetic successor will command greater respect than the local sorcerers. Admittedly, the former incident focuses on Moses' superior miracle-working, whereas the latter accentuates the greater authority of the 'prophet like Moses' to proclaim God's word. But both Exodus and Deuteronomy depict Moses as a prophet mighty in word and deed, such that either dimension virtually presupposes the other (e.g. Exod. 4.1-23; 7.1-7; Deut. 29.1-9; 34.9-12).

Although the Exodus account of Moses' battle with Pharaoh's magicians is not specifically recalled in later strata of the Old Testament, extrabiblical traditions—both Jewish and pagan—surrounding the turn of the eras manifest renewed interest in this clash.

---

1. Although the Canaanites 'give heed' (ἀκούσονται) to wizards, the Lord 'does not permit [Israel] to do so'; rather Israel must 'heed' (ἀκούσεσθε) the 'prophet like Moses' who will be raised up (18.15).

2. There is a linguistic parallel between ἐποίησαν καὶ οἱ ἐπαοιδοὶ τῶν Αἰγυπτίων ταῖς φαρμακείαις αὐτῶν in Exod. 7.11 and φαρμοκός, ἐπαείδων ἐπαοιδήν in Deut. 18.10-11.

For example, as part of its commentary on Exodus 7–12, the *Book of Jubilees* states:

> And Prince Mastema stood up before you and desired to make you fall into the hand of Pharaoh. And he aided the magicians of the Egyptians, and they stood up and acted before you. . . And the Lord smote them with evil wounds and they were unable to stand because we destroyed (their ability) to do any single signs (*Jub.* 48.9-11).[1]

In several places the names of Jannes and/or Jambres (Mambres) came to be associated with the Egyptian magicians, as in the Damascus Document: 'For in ancient times Moses and Aaron arose by the Prince of Lights, and Belial raised Jannes and his brother by his evil device, when Israel was delivered for the first time' (CD 5.17-19).[2] Even the second-century pagan, Numenius, was familiar with the Jannes and Jambres tradition, although he evaluated the two Egyptians more positively than Jewish writers did.

> And next in order came Jannes and Jambres, Egyptian sacred scribes, men judged to have no superiors in the practice of magic, at the time when the Jews were being driven out of Egypt. So then these were the men chosen by the people of Egypt as fit to stand beside Musaeus [Moses], who led forth the Jews, a man who was most powerful in prayer to God; and of the plagues which Musaeus brought upon Egypt, these men showed themselves able to disperse the most violent (*apud* Eusebius, *Praep. Ev.* 9.8).[3]

---

1. Citation is from J.H. Charlesworth (ed.), *The Old Testament Pseudepigrapha* (2 vols.; London: Darton, Longman & Todd, 1983–85), II.

2. Citation is from G. Vermes, *The Dead Sea Scrolls in English* (London: Penguin Books, 3rd edn, 1987). On the Jannes and Jambres tradition, see L.L. Grabbe, 'The Jannes/Jambres Tradition in Targum Pseudo-Jonathan and its Date', *JBL* 98 (1979), pp. 393-401; E. Schürer, *The History of the Jewish People in the Age of Jesus Christ (175 BC–AD 135)*, (3 vols.; rev. and ed. G. Vermes, F. Millar and M. Black; Edinburgh: T. & T. Clark, 1973–87), III.2, pp. 781-83; A. Pietersma and R.T. Lutz, 'Jannes and Jambres', in Charlesworth (ed.), *Old Testament Pseudepigrapha*, II, pp. 427-36.

3. Citation is from Eusebius, *Preparation for the Gospel* (trans. E.H. Gifford; Grand Rapids: Baker, repr. 1981 [1903]). In *Con. Cel.* 4.51 Origen mentions a book by Numenius entitled 'Concerning the Good' in which the pagan author 'quotes the story about Jannes and Jambres'. On Numenius and other pagan writers who refer to Moses' conflict with Jannes and Jambres, see J. Gager, *Moses in Greco-Roman Paganism* (SBLMS, 16; Nashville: Abingdon Press, 1972), pp. 137-40.

According to Josephus's account of the exodus events, the wonder-working Moses was accused by Pharaoh of being an escaped convict now trying to pass himself off 'by juggleries and magic (μαγείαις)' as a divinely-ordained deliverer of Israel (*Ant.* 2.284). To expose Moses' fraud, Pharaoh commissions his magician-priests to emulate Moses' tricks, whereupon they transmute their staves into snake-like objects (2.285). Moses then delivers a forceful defence of his vocation, unparalleled in the canonical story, which accentuates the great gulf between his God-wrought miracles and the base conjuring of Pharaoh's wizards:

> Indeed, O King, I too disdain not the cunning (σοφίας) of the Egyptians, but I assert that the deeds wrought by me so far surpass their magic (μαγείας) and their art as things divine are remote from what is human. And I will show that it is from no witchcraft (γοητείαν) or deception of true judgement, but from God's providence and power (θεοῦ πρόνοιαν καὶ δύναμιν) that my miracles proceed (2.286).

After this, Moses himself (not Aaron acting on his behalf) casts down his rod and orders it to become a serpent; it obeys and proceeds to devour its competitors (2.287).[1]

Strikingly similar language is utilized in Josephus's critique of contemporary Jewish 'sign prophets'[2] or 'popular/action prophets'[3] who spearheaded apocalyptic renewal movements:

> Moreover, impostors (γόητες) and deceivers called upon the mob to follow them into the desert (τὴν ἐρημίαν). For they said that they would show them unmistakeable marvels and signs (τέρατα καὶ σημεῖα) that would be wrought in harmony with God's design (τοῦ θεοῦ πρόνοιαν γινόμενα). Many were, in fact, persuaded and paid the penalty for their folly (*Ant.* 20.167-68; cf. *War* 2.258-60).

Clearly, in Josephus's view, each of these popular leaders purported to

---

1. Cf. G. Delling, 'Josephus und das Wunderbare', *NovT* 2 (1957–58), pp. 297-98; Macrae, 'Miracle in *The Antiquities*', pp. 135-36.

2. So called in P.W. Barnett, 'The Jewish Sign Prophets—AD 40–70: Their Intentions and Origin', *NTS* 27 (1980–81), pp. 679-97.

3. So called in R.A. Horsley and J.S. Hanson, *Bandits, Prophets, and Messiahs: Popular Movements in the Time of Jesus* (New Voices in Biblical Studies; Minneapolis, MN: Winston, 1985), pp. 160-72, 186-87; and R.A. Horsley, '"Like One of the Prophets of Old": Two Types of Popular Prophets at the Time of Jesus', *CBQ* 47 (1985), pp. 435-63. In these studies Horsley contrasts the 'popular/action' prophets with the 'oracular' prophets modelled after the classical biblical tradition.

be the eschatological 'prophet like Moses'. They sought to blaze a new exodus trail 'into the desert' and based their authority, like Moses before them, on 'signs and wonders' allegedly performed in accordance with τοῦ θεοῦ πρόνοιαν.[1] However, Josephus regards them as γόητες (impostors, charlatans) doomed to failure, just like the workers of γοητεία and μαγεία in ancient Egypt who ineffectually aped the miracles of Moses.[2] In short, as P.W. Barnett asserts, 'the Sign Prophets are identified with the Egyptian Court magicians who in the Exodus account of Josephus are contrasted with God's true prophet Moses'.[3]

Two examples which Josephus gives of these false 'prophets like Moses', appraised as mere magicians, are Theudas and an unnamed 'Egyptian'.[4] Theudas was a noted γόης who incited 'the majority of the masses' to pull up stakes and follow him to the Jordan River. He

1. Note also the parallel between 'tokens of deliverance' (σημεῖα ἐλευθερίας) performed by first-century popular prophets (*War* 2.259) and the 'signs' of Moses enacted 'in token of their [the Hebrews'] liberation' (πρὸς τὴν ἐλευθερίαν αὐτοῖς σημείων) from Egyptian bondage (*Ant.* 2.327).

2. According to BAGD, γόης was used in classical literature to denote a 'sorcerer, juggler' and in the New Testament period took on more the connotation of a 'swindler, cheat' (p. 164). In the New Testament itself the term appears only in 2 Tim. 3.13, where the warning is sounded that 'wicked people and impostors (γόητες) will go from bad to worse, deceiving others and being deceived'. Interestingly, a few verses earlier these 'wicked people and impostors' are described as 'people of corrupt mind and counterfeit faith' whose 'folly will become plain to everyone'—just like Jannes and Jambres who opposed Moses (2 Tim. 3.8-9). Cf. Philo, *Spec. Leg.* 1.315.

3. Barnett, 'Jewish Sign Prophets', p. 683; cf. pp. 681-83. Horsley ('"Like One of the Prophets"', p. 455; 'Popular Prophetic Movements at the Time of Jesus: Their Principal Features and Social Origins', *JSNT* 26 [1986], p. 4) flatly rejects Barnett's interpretation, arguing that Josephus's use of Mosaic language to characterize contemporary popular prophets was designed to cast them merely as alleged 'prophets like Moses', not as magicians like those in Pharaoh's service. But Horsley seems to ignore the apparent association of the γόητες-prophets with Egyptian γοητεία and fails to appreciate that as *false and failed* imitators of Moses, the contemporary prophets clearly mirror Pharaoh's court magicians.

4. W. Meeks refers to 'Theudas and the other "magicians" (like Theudas, they doubtless called themselves "prophets") who promised or actively attempted to perform miracles in the wilderness' (*The Prophet-King: Moses Traditions and the Johannine Christology* [NovTSup, 14; Leiden: Brill, 1967], p. 163). Similarly, D.E. Aune speaks of 'demonstrations of magical power' as 'a central feature' of these prophets' activities ('Magic in Early Christianity', *ANRW*, II.23.2, p. 1528).

pronounced himself a prophet capable of dividing the Jordan, thus imagining a new exodus through parted waters with himself in the role of Moses.[1] However, his schemes ultimately fell apart disastrously, making plain the utter 'folly' of his claims (*Ant.* 20.97-98).

The anonymous 'Egyptian' (a possible symbolic designation for a Moses-styled deliverer, reared in Egypt), branded a ψευδοπροφήτης and γόης by Josephus, attracted a large company of Judean peasants and led them on a meandering desert journey to the Mount of Olives. His mission was to conquer Jerusalem after miraculously flattening its walls at his command. While images of Joshua and the conquest spring most readily to mind, the picture of a Moses-led people wandering through the wilderness should also be considered as part of the background to the 'Egyptian's' campaign.[2] Once again, despite his pretensions to be a Moses/Joshua-type leader, the 'Egyptian' was (deservedly in Josephus's thinking) put to flight by Roman armies and his movement crushed (*Ant.* 20.169-70; *War* 2.261-62).[3]

With this widespread currency in Luke's day of retellings and even contemporary applications (in Josephus's case) of the biblical story of Moses' showdown with Pharaoh's magicians, the likelihood is increased that this story forms part of the literary backdrop to the Acts episode of rivalry between Philip and Simon Magus. Such likelihood moves closer to certainty when the Jesus-saying in Lk. 11.20 is taken into account.

> But if it is by the finger of God (δακτύλῳ θεοῦ) that I cast out demons,
> then the kingdom of God has come upon you.

Scholarly debate on this verse has focused typically on whether Luke has retained 'finger of God' from Q or altered the original 'Spirit of God' found in the Mt. 12.28 parallel. The balance of opinion

---

1. In addition to a Moses typology, the pattern of Joshua's parting of the Jordan may also be relevant to Theudas's aspirations, as Josephus conceived them. Cf. Horsley, '"Like One of the Prophets"', pp. 457-58.

2. Cf. Horsley, '"Like One of the Prophets"', pp. 458-59.

3. In addition to the Theudas and 'Egyptian' reports, note the similar account concerning another anonymous γόης:

> Festus also sent a force of cavalry and infantry against the dupes of a certain impostor (γόητος) who had promised them salvation and rest from troubles, if they chose to follow him into the wilderness (τῆς ἐρημίας). The force which Festus dispatched destroyed both the deceiver himself and those who had followed him (*Ant.* 20.188).

still favors the originality of Luke's version, in part because of the unlikelihood that Luke would pass up an opportunity to stress the work of the Spirit.[1] However, on one occasion Luke *omits* a Spirit-reference included in both Mark and Matthew (Mk 12.36; Mt. 22.43; Lk. 20.42),[2] and several times he employs the anthropomorphism 'hand of God/the Lord' (Lk. 1.66; Acts 4.28, 30; 11.21; 13.11), which obviously relates closely to 'finger of God' and appears to be synonymous with 'Spirit of God' in certain Old Testament texts (e.g. Ezek. 3.14; 8.1-3).[3] The 'finger of God' reference, then, even if borrowed rather than created by Luke, fits in well with Lukan interests.[4]

In any event, what is most relevant to the present argument is the consensus view that 'finger of God' in Lk. 11.20 alludes to the recognition by Pharaoh's magicians of the divine authority behind Moses' works: δάκτυλος θεοῦ ἐστὶν τοῦτο (Exod. 8.15 LXX).[5] The link to Exodus becomes especially clear in light of the Lukan setting of Jesus' saying. Jesus is embroiled in debate regarding the source of his exorcising power, with some in the crowd slandering, 'He casts out demons by Beelzebul, the ruler of the demons' (11.15). This is tantamount to a charge that Jesus was functioning as a pagan sorcerer.

---

1. T.W. Manson, *The Teaching of Jesus: Studies of its Form and Content* (Cambridge: Cambridge University Press, 1939), pp. 82-83; Fitzmyer, *Luke*, II, p. 918.

2. Cf. C.S. Rodd, 'Spirit or Finger', *ExpTim* 72 (1960–61), pp. 157-58.

3. Cf. R.G. Hamerton-Kelly, 'A Note on Matthew XII.28 par. Luke XI.20', *NTS* 11 (1964–65), pp. 167-68; G.R. Beasley-Murray, 'Jesus and the Spirit', in *Mélanges bibliques en hommage au R.P. Béda Rigaux* (ed. A. Descamps and A. de Halleux; Gembloux: Duculot, 1970), pp. 469, 474 n. 2. Dunn thinks that the evidence may tilt slightly in favor of the originality of Matthew's 'Spirit' reading but admits that 'the point may be largely academic, since in fact the two concepts ["Spirit" and "finger"] are synonymous' (*Jesus and the Spirit*, pp. 44-46).

4. Cf. A. George, *Etudes sur l'oeuvre de Luc* (Paris: Gabalda, 1978), pp. 127-32.

5. E.g. Fitzmyer, *Luke*, II, p. 922; E.E. Ellis, *The Gospel of Luke* (NCB; London: Nelson, 1966), p. 167; Garrett, *Demise of the Devil*, pp. 44-45; O'Toole, 'Parallels between Jesus and Moses', pp. 23-24. R.W. Wall ('"The Finger of God": Deuteronomy 9.10 and Luke 11.20', *NTS* 33 [1987], pp. 144-50) has recently argued that the primary allusion in Lk. 11.20 is to the 'finger of God' in Deut. 9.10 which wrote the ten commandments. However, the literary setting of Lk. 11.14-23—with its focus on the legitimacy of Jesus' authority to work miracles of deliverance—recalls most directly the controversy between Moses and Pharaoh's magicians (see more below).

Jesus, however, after noting how absurd it would be for Satan to plot his own demise (11.17-19), remonstrates that his exorcisms are in fact genuine demonstrations of the 'finger of God'; that is, they are just like Moses' signs of deliverance in Egypt, wrought by the same divine 'finger' and sharply distinguished from the machinations of Pharaoh's Satan-inspired magicians. Further illustrating his liberation of Satan's captives, Jesus speaks next of plundering the strong man's castle (11.21-22),[1] an image which possibly recalls the despoiling of Pharaoh's household and kingdom during the exodus (Exod. 3.19-22; 11.2-3; 12.35-36).[2]

Beyond Luke 11 there emerges in Acts 4 a similar allusion to the miraculous work of God's 'hand' in emancipating Israel from Egyptian bondage (though not explicitly tied to the discomfiture of Pharaoh's magicians). Under sanction by the local authorities, the Christian community at Jerusalem beseeches the Lord for assistance:

> grant to your servants to speak your word with all boldness, while you stretch out your hand (τὴν χεῖρά [σου] ἐκτείνειν σε) to heal, and signs and wonders (σημεῖα καὶ τέρατα) are performed through the name of your holy servant Jesus' (Acts 4.29-30; cf. Exod. 3.19-20; 7.3-5; 9.3, 15; ἐκτείνας τὴν χεῖρα, 3.20; 7.5; σημεῖα καὶ τέρατα, 7.3).

Given Luke's typological interest in God's mighty finger/hand working through Moses—prompting in particular the correlation of Jesus' victory over Satan with Moses' conquest of Pharaoh's magicians—it appears quite plausible that a similar Exodus connection is implied in Philip's contest with Simon Magus. If so, Philip takes on the role of both a 'prophet like Moses' and a 'prophet like Jesus' who, as a dynamic instrument of the 'finger of God', overwhelms Simon, the 'magus like Pharaoh's magicians'. Interestingly, 'finger of God' (like 'hand of God') is a common scriptural symbol of the 'power of God'.[3] This becomes significant in light of Simon's notoriety as the

---

1. I am following the usual interpretation that the story of the 'strong man' is meant to illustrate Jesus' victory over Satan (cf. Marshall, *Gospel of Luke*, pp. 476-78); contra F.W. Danker (*Jesus and the New Age according to St Luke: A Commentary on St Luke's Gospel* [Philadelphia: Fortress Press, rev. edn, 1988], pp. 233-34) and Wall ('"Finger"', p. 147), who see the story as typifying Satan's threat against Israel.

2. Only Luke depicts the discomfited 'strong man' as an armed warrior guarding his own palace, i.e. a king-like figure, not unlike Pharaoh.

3. Cf. K. Grayston, 'The Significance of the Word *Hand* in the New Testament',

'Great Power of God'. While Simon had given the impression of being divinely empowered, in fact, he—like Pharaoh's wizards—ultimately acknowledges that the Moses-styled prophet—Philip—is a channel of a Higher Power. One might even conceive of Philip as the 'stronger one' who strips Simon the 'strong man' of his authority and frees the Samaritan people long bound under Simon's spell.[1]

Philip's role as a 'prophet like Moses' may also be rooted more specifically in the Deuteronomy 18 tradition demanding that the prophet be heard. For as the Samaritans 'heard' (ἀκούω) and 'listened eagerly to' (προσέχω) Philip's message where formerly they had 'listened eagerly to' (προσέχω) Simon Magus (Acts 8.6, 10-11), so the Israelites were commanded not to 'give heed' (ἀκούω) to the Canaanite sorcerers but rather to 'heed' (ἀκούω) the words of the Mosaic prophet (Deut. 18.14, 15, 18-19).

Having explored the parallel between Philip/Simon Magus and Moses/Pharaoh's magicians in light of various accounts of the Exodus story, we turn finally to consider the potential relevance of Simonian traditions for understanding the 'prophet like Moses' pattern in Acts 8.

c. *Simon Magus and the 'Prophet like Moses'*
While one strand of patristic testimony regards Simon Magus as a Gnostic heretic and thus bears little relation to Acts 8 (see above), another strand, while still embellishing Luke's account, nonetheless builds more directly on the canonical portrait of Simon as a popular Samaritan magician. Upon examining these traditions, we discover possible characterizations of Simon as a self-styled 'prophet like Moses'.

In reporting Celsus's critique of Christianity, Origen cites the objection that 'some thousands will refute Jesus by asserting that the prophecies which were applied to him were spoken of them' (*Con.*

in Descamps and de Halleux (eds.), *Mélanges bibliques*, pp. 479-81. For the equation, finger of God = power of God = Spirit of God, see Dunn, *Jesus and the Spirit*, p. 46; Beasley-Murray, 'Jesus and the Spirit', p. 469. The Psalmist's description of creation as 'the work of your fingers' (Ps. 8.3) establishes a clear symbolic relation between God's 'finger' and his demonstrations of power.

1. Philip's role in Samaria as an exorcist of demons and preacher of the kingdom of God (Acts 8.7, 12) also corresponds with Jesus' statement regarding his own ministry in Lk. 11.20.

Cel. 1.57). Origen scarcely agrees with these numbers, but he does acknowledge some messianic rivals to Jesus: (1) Theudas, 'who said that he was some great one'; (2) Judas of Galilee, who purported to be 'some wise man and an introducer of new doctrines'; (3) Dositheus the Samaritan, who presented himself as 'the Christ prophesied by Moses and. . . appeared to have won over some folk to his teaching'; and (4) Simon 'the Samaritan magician', who endeavored 'to draw away some folk by magic and. . . succeeded in his deception at the time'. However, all of these figures—including Simon—proved to be frauds and failures in Origen's eyes (1.57). Later in the same work Origen again links Simon, 'the so-called Great Power of God', with Dositheus, Theudas and Judas as false claimants to divine authority (6.11).[1]

While it is true that Origen does not spell out precisely that Simon claimed to be the eschatological 'prophet like Moses', the context of Origen's comments suggests such an identity. For Simon is categorized broadly with those who professed to fulfill Old Testament prophecy (e.g. Deut. 18) and linked closely with Dositheus, a fellow Samaritan alleged to be 'the Christ prophesied by Moses'.[2]

A similar, though much more developed, account of Simon's early career emerges in the Pseudo-Clementine literature:

> By nationality he [Simon] is a Samaritan and comes from the village of Gittha, which is six miles distant from the capital. During his stay in Egypt he acquired a large measure of Greek culture and attained to an extensive knowledge of magic and ability in it. He then came forward claiming to be accepted as a mighty power of the very God who has created the world. On occasion he sets himself up for the Messiah and describes himself as the Standing One. He uses this title since he is to

---

1. Cf. also Origen, *Hom. on Luke* 25; *Com. on Matt.*, ser. 33 [on Mt. 24.4ff.], *Com. on John* 13.27 [on Jn 4.25].

2. Note also the report of Eusebius:

> The Samaritans were persuaded that Dositheus, who arose after the times of the savior, was the very prophet whom Moses predicted. Others at the time of the Apostles called Simon the magician the Great Power of God, thinking he was the 'Christ' (*Theophany* 4.35, cited in S.J. Isser, *The Dositheans: A Samaritan Sect in Late Antiquity* [SJLA, 17; Leiden: Brill, 1976], p. 29).

Isser regards Origen's characterization of Dositheus as 'the Christ prophesied by Moses' as 'a Christianized distortion of the eschatological "predicted *prophet*"'— probably the 'prophet like Moses' promised in Deut. 18 (*Dositheans*, pp. 32-33).

exist for ever and his body cannot possibly fall a victim to the germs of corruption (*Hom.* 2.22; cf. *Rec.* 2.7).[1]

The report goes on to place Simon and Dositheus within an elite circle of 30 disciples of John the Baptist and to recount a heated duel between the two Samaritans. The issue at stake was who should rightfully lead the group after John's death as the authorized 'Standing One'. Dositheus initially claimed the position while Simon was away in Egypt studying magic. When Simon returned, he feigned support for Dositheus at first, but eventually plotted to undermine his authority. Matters came to a head when Dositheus, upon discovering his rival's scheme, struck out at Simon with his rod. Amazingly, the rod 'seemed to go through Simon's body as if it were smoke', thus vindicating Simon as the true 'Standing One'. The humiliated Dositheus grudgingly acknowledged Simon's superiority and then died in disgrace a few days later (*Hom.* 2.23-24; cf. *Rec.* 2.8-11).

By making the ability to wield a miraculous staff (like Moses) the critical test of authority, this account implicitly associates the 'Standing One' with the 'prophet like Moses'. In other words, Simon and Dositheus likely claimed both titles or regarded them as alternative expressions of the same identity. This idea may be strengthened by the familiar Old Testament witness that Moses was uniquely called to *stand* in close communion with God (cf. Exod 3.4-6; 33.18-23; Deut. 5.31).[2]

Granting that some early Christian authors viewed Simon and Dositheus as first-century Samaritan magicians pretending to be the end-time 'prophet like Moses', questions arise concerning the historicity of such a conception and the possibility that Luke would have known it. Recent critical analyses of the relevant traditions, notably by S.J. Isser and J.E. Fossum,[3] have indeed tended to regard Simon and

---

1. Citations of Pseudo-Clementine material are from Hennecke and Schneemelcher (eds.), *New Testament Apocrypha*, II.

2. Cf. S.J. Isser, 'Dositheus, Jesus, and a Moses Aretalogy', in *Christianity, Judaism and Other Greco-Roman Cults: Studies for Morton Smith at Sixty. Part 4. Other Greco-Roman Cults* (ed. J. Neusner; SJLA, 12; Leiden: Brill, 1975), pp. 175-77; Fossum, *Name of God*, pp. 117-20.

3. Isser, *Dositheans, passim* (see summary of conclusions, pp. 163-64); Fossum, *Name of God*, pp. 112-29. Cf. also H. Teeple, *The Mosaic Eschatological Prophet* (SBLMS, 10; Philadelphia: SBL, 1957), pp. 64-65; Kippenberg, *Garizim*, pp. 122-36.

Dositheus as historical Samaritan figures around the middle of the first century, known chiefly as wonder-workers who advanced themselves as the expected Mosaic prophet of Deuteronomy 18. While this much appears certain, the precise relationship between the two men remains speculative, not to mention their supposed alliance with John the Baptist.[1]

Supporting and elucidating this plausible connection between the historical Simon/Dositheus and the 'prophet like Moses' are various traditions originating before or within the first century CE.

1. As noted in the previous chapter, a compilation of Deuteronomy citations forms part of the SP expansion to the Exodus Decalogue. Included among these insertions are Deut. 18.18-22—the foundational 'Prophet like Moses' text—and Deut. 5.31, which discloses the Lord's exhortation to Moses, 'But you, *stand here by Me,* and I will tell you the commandments. . . . ' Interestingly, the parallel Qumran cluster of *testimonia* from Exodus 20, Deuteronomy 5 and Deuteronomy 18 (4QTest 175; 4QBibPar 158) does not incorporate Deut. 5.31 in conjunction with the 'prophet like Moses' promises.[2] Thus, the 'prophet like Moses' figure may have been uniquely affiliated in early Samaritan thought with one who *stands*—like Moses—in the presence of God.[3] It would not be surprising, then, to find in first-century Samaria miracle-workers, such as Simon and Dositheus, putting themselves forward as the expected 'prophet like Moses'/'Standing One'.

2. In addition to reporting about various Jewish 'sign prophets', Josephus alludes to an unnamed prophet among the Samaritans, whom Pontius Pilate brutally repressed in 36 CE. This figure had mustered

---

1. The anti-Baptist polemic of the Pseudo-Clementine literature renders suspect the authenticity of associating the Baptist movement with 'heretics' like Simon and Dositheus. Some scholars, however, assume that such a connection is historically valid (e.g. M. Smith, 'The Account of Simon Magus in Acts 8', in *H.A. Wolfson Jubilee Volume* [Jerusalem: American Academy for Jewish Research, 1965], pp. 739-41); cf. the discussion in Fossum, *Name of God*, pp. 115-17.

2. Cf. Isser, *Dositheans*, p. 139; Fossum, *Name of God*, p. 122; R.M. Grant, *Gnosticism and Early Christianity* (New York: Columbia University Press, 1959), pp. 91-92; Kippenberg, *Garizim*, p. 319 n. 72.

3. Later Samaritan traditions represented God himself as the One who 'stands' (lives and reigns) eternally, attended by a 'standing' heavenly court which included angelic intermediaries and, of course, the great prophet Moses. Cf. Kippenberg, *Garizim*, pp. 347-49 n. 136; Isser, *Dositheans*, pp. 138-40; Fossum, *Name of God*, pp. 55-62, 120-24.

his following by claiming to be the restorer of the sacred tabernacle vessels supposedly hidden by Moses on Mt Gerizim (*Ant.* 18.85-89). While the precise nature of his mission remains vague, it appears that he assumed the role of an eschatological Moses *redivivus* or 'prophet like Moses' intent on reinstating true worship on the Samaritans' holy site.[1] Although tapping a somewhat esoteric Mosaic tradition and appearing more as a rabble-rouser than a teacher or miracle-worker, this anonymous leader still witnesses to an early Samaritan interest in Moses-styled prophets which others, like Simon and Dositheus, could have exploited in their own ways.[2]

3. The *Martyrdom of Isaiah*, dating from no later than the first century CE,[3] relates the legend of Isaiah's execution during the reign

1. Cf. M.F. Collins, 'The Hidden Vessels in Samaritan Traditions', *JSJ* 3 (1972), pp. 97-116; note, however, the reservations of B.W. Hall, *Samaritan Religion from John Hyrcanus to Baba Rabba* (Studies in Judaica, 3; Sydney: Mandelbaum Trust, University of Sydney, 1987), p. 295.

2. The eschatological figure most commonly associated with the Samaritans is the *Taheb*, who was expected to usher in the final age of divine favor and judgment. No explicit *Taheb*-references appear prior to the fourth-century *Memar Marqah*. It is noteworthy, however, that the earliest descriptions of the *Taheb* employ Mosaic imagery. For example, the plea in the *Memar Marqah* for the coming of the *Taheb* is matched by a similar prayer for the advent of the great prophet Moses:

> May the Taheb come in peace
> and expose the darkness that has become powerful in the world.
> May the Taheb come in peace
> and destroy the opponents who provoke God (1.9).

> May the great prophet Moses come in peace,
> who revealed truth and abolished falsehood,
> May the great prophet Moses come in peace,
> who glorified righteousness and destroyed the wicked ones (2.8).
> (Citations from Meeks, *Prophet-King*, pp. 248-49).

The most thorough recent examinations of the Samaritan *Taheb*-figure have been conducted by F. Dexinger (see bibliography). Interestingly, Dexinger views the *Taheb*-concept as a direct development of the earlier attested Jewish (including Samaritan) hope in an eschatological 'prophet like Moses', based on Deut. 18.15, 18 ('Der "Prophet wie Moses" in Qumran und bei Samaritanern', in *Mélanges bibliques et orientaux en l'honneur de M. Matthias Delcor* (ed. A. Caquot, S. Légasse and M. Tardieu; AOAT, 215; Neukirchen–Vluyn: Neukirchener Verlag, 1985], pp. 97-111).

3. See the introduction to this work by M.A. Knibb, 'Martyrdom and Ascension of Isaiah', in Charlesworth (ed.), *Old Testament Pseudepigrapha*, II, pp. 143-55. Citations are taken from the translation which follows.

of Manasseh. The evil force behind the throne, according to the tale, was none other than 'the angel of iniquity who rules the world': Beliar (alias Satan, Sammael Malkira, Matanbukus). Beliar had worked through Manasseh to perpetrate throughout Jerusalem 'apostasy' and 'sorcery and magic, augury and divination, fornication and adultery, and the persecution of the righteous' (*Mart. Isa.* 2.4-5). He was aided in his machinations not only by the king, but also by a Samaritan agent named Belkira, a descendant of the false prophet, Chenaanah (2.5, 12). As it turns out, Belkira was responsible for hunting down Isaiah and accusing him (unjustly in the writer's opinion) of false and seditious prophecy (3.1-12; 5.1-16). Among his charges was that Isaiah had blasphemously claimed 'to see more than Moses the prophet' (3.8-9). For his 'crimes' Isaiah was sawed in half, as 'his accuser, Belkira, stood by, and all the false prophets stood by, laughing. . . ' (5.1-3).

Although direct mention of the 'prophet like Moses' is lacking, the collocation of references to 'sorcery and magic', 'false prophets', 'Moses the prophet' and a Samaritan henchman of Beliar suggests some degree of Samaritan notoriety for spawning magic-practicing, Moses-pretending prophets—like Simon and Dositheus.[1]

In the likely event that the related self-conceptions of Simon Magus as the 'prophet like Moses' and 'Standing One' go back in some form to Luke's time, the influence of such ideas on the Acts account of Simon's competition with Philip becomes a real possibility.

Since Philip is cast as a 'prophet like Moses' and his encounter with Simon is modelled after Moses' contest with Pharaoh's magicians, it would follow naturally for Luke to regard Simon as a counterfeit 'prophet like Moses', as did Josephus with respect to Theudas and the 'Egyptian'. And since the μάγος Bar-Jesus is expressly branded a ψευδοπροφήτης in Acts 13.6 (matching the designation of the 'Egyptian' in *War* 2.261), it is reasonable to assume that Luke conceived of Simon Magus in similar terms.[2]

The Samaritan/Simonian concept of the 'Standing One' has seldom been explored in relation to Luke's presentation. But we should not overlook the climactic scene in the Stephen narrative in which the Christian martyr beholds Jesus/Son of Man 'standing at the right hand of God' (Acts 7.55-56). Special attention is drawn to this standing figure by the repetition of ἑστῶτα and the variation from the

---

1. Cf. Garrett, *Demise of the Devil*, pp. 15, 144 n. 32.
2. Garrett, *Demise of the Devil*, p. 68.

customary *seated* position at God's right hand (cf. Lk. 22.69). While numerous opinions have been offered regarding the significance of Stephen's vision,[1] insufficient attention has been paid to possible links between the vision and the preceding speech, particularly between the 'Standing' Christ (vision) and Moses and the Mosaic prophet (speech).

According to Acts 7.33, Moses was appointed to be Israel's deliverer while 'standing' (ἕστηκας) on holy ground in the presence of God. As the speech continues, Moses is further identified as the announcer to the Israelites that 'God will raise up (ἀναστήσει) a prophet. . . as he raised me up' (7.37; Deut. 18.15)—in other words, a 'prophet like Moses' (= Christ, cf. 3.18-22). While this 'raising up' may refer simply to the prophet's appearance in Israel, a more sublime exaltation should not be ruled out. The Stephen discourse ends with a bitter reminder that Israel had always violently rejected its prophets—just as it had recently murdered the 'Righteous One' whom the prophets had anticipated (7.52). And so the promised messiah/Righteous One/'prophet like Moses' meets a shocking and tragic end. But Stephen's ensuing vision of Jesus (alias the 'prophet like Moses') *standing* at God's right hand seems to disclose the prophet's ultimate *raising up* (i.e. resurrection and ascension) to heaven. Moreover, the close alignment of the 'standing' Jesus and the 'glory of God' in this vision (7.55) recalls the unique elements of Luke's transfiguration scene where Jesus—in the company of Moses and in Moses-like fashion—'appeared in glory' while discussing his 'exodus' (Lk. 9.31) and revealed 'his glory' to his disciples and 'the two men who *stood with him* (τοὺς συνεστῶτας αὐτῷ)' (9.32).

In short, the exalted Jesus who appears to Stephen as the 'Standing One' functions in the framework of Luke's larger narrative as the vindicated 'prophet like Moses'.[2]

---

1. See the useful summary of recent explanations in D.L. Bock, *Proclamation from Prophecy and Pattern: Lucan Old Testament Christology* (JSNTSup, 12; Sheffield: JSOT Press, 1987), pp. 222-24; J.D.M. Derrett, 'The Son of Man Standing (Acts 7,55-56)', *Bibbia e Orienta* 30 (1988), pp. 75-77.

2. Isser poses the query—'Could it be that Stephen applied the Standing One tradition. . . to Jesus, whom he saw as the prophet like Moses?' (*Dositheans*, p. 140)—but leaves the matter unelaborated and unresolved; cf. Coggins, 'Samaritans and Acts', pp. 425-26. P. Doble interprets Stephen's vision of the 'Standing' Son of Man as symbolizing the vindication of Christ's authority, but he does not link this idea with the rejected 'prophet like Moses' in Stephen's speech

Is it accidental, then, in the incident which immediately follows Stephen's martyrdom that his associate, Philip—a messenger and emulator of Christ, the true 'Standing One' and 'prophet like Moses'—locks horns in Samaria with Simon Magus who was known (as some sources suggest) for claiming the same titles? Of course, since the only explicit title adopted by Simon in Acts is the 'Great Power', we cannot be certain that Luke had other ideas in mind. But the prospects are enhanced by the likely influence of select Mosaic traditions—including Deuteronomy 18—upon the overall Lukan shape of the Philip–Simon encounter.

Also, R. Pesch has argued that the 'standing' Jesus in Acts 7 plays a critical role in authorizing the impending Samaritan mission. The exalted Christ appears chiefly in Acts to sanction the momentous shift in gospel-proclamation from the Jews in Jerusalem to Gentiles throughout the world. This pattern is particularly evident in the commissioning of Saul (Acts 9.15; 22.21; 26.16-18) and is assumed to underlie Stephen's Christophany as well. In Pesch's view, Jesus/Son of Man stands at Stephen's execution to pronounce judgment against rebellious Israel and to mark a 'salvation-historical turning point': the extension of the gospel beyond Jewish boundaries.[1]

If Pesch is correct, then the 'standing' Christ in Acts 7.55-56 may be regarded (indirectly) as mandating the prophetic mission of Philip the evangelist to Samaria. In such a case, Philip proves worthy of his calling by thoroughly subduing Simon Magus, a usurper of the 'Standing One' and 'prophet like Moses' roles legitimately fulfilled by Christ.

4. *Philip and Simon the 'Apostate'*

The preceding analysis of Philip's juxtaposition with Simon Magus in Acts 8 has uncovered only the highest appraisal of Philip's character and ministry. He appears as both a greater power and greater 'prophet like Moses' than Simon and even converts Simon to Christianity. Simon believes Philip's message, is baptized and follows the evangelist around like a disciple—all typical marks of Christian faith and

('The Son of Man Saying in Stephen's Witnessing: Acts 6.8–8.2', *NTS* 31 [1985], pp. 74-76).
  1. R. Pesch, *Die Vision des Stephanus: Apg 7,55-56 im Rahmen der Apostelgeschichte* (SBS, 12; Stuttgart: Katholisches Bibelwerk, 1966), pp. 38-58.

fellowship in the Christian community.

However, when the following scene in Acts 8.18-24 is considered, an apparent blot on Philip's record emerges. For when the Jerusalem apostles arrive in Samaria, Simon reverts to his old shenanigans and incurs from Peter what amounts to a sentence of excommunication[1]: 'May your silver perish with you. . . . You have no part or share in this [matter], for your heart is not right before God' (8.20-22). Does this 'apostasy'[2] on Simon's part not somehow reflect badly on the caliber of Philip's evangelism? Should not Philip have exercised better judgment, either by refusing to baptize Simon in the first place or by catechizing him more adequately—or at least by personally censuring him instead of leaving the matter to an 'inspector'? Of course, these are all questions arising from a certain ecclesiology which advocates close scrutiny and strict discipline of new converts, and it may be that Luke did not share this perspective.

To discover Luke's understanding of how Simon's 'apostasy' colors Philip's ministry, we must compare this instance with similar cases of 'lapsed' disciples in Luke–Acts connected with the ministries of Jesus and Peter. Also, Luke's Parable of the Sower should prove illuminating, as it delineates different levels of response to the gospel.

1. The Synoptic interpretations of Jesus' Parable of the Sower provide important insights into each evangelist's theology of mission.[3] In Luke's case, the description of the fruitful disciple is particularly revealing: 'But as for that in the good soil, these are the ones who, when they hear the word, hold it fast in an honest and good heart, and

1. Haenchen, *Acts*, p. 305; J.D.M. Derrett, 'Simon Magus (Acts 8.9-24)', *ZNW* 73 (1982), pp. 63-65.

2. S. Brown comments that 'the story of Simon Magus is not strictly an instance of apostasy, since the excommunication formula in v. 20 is not actually carried out' (*Apostasy and Perseverance in the Theology of Luke* [AnBib, 36; Rome: Pontifical Biblical Institute, 1969], p. 110). In view of the prospects for repentance and forgiveness announced in v. 22, it is true that Simon is not expelled once for all from the Christian community. However, Simon still exhibits a marked lapse in his behavior requiring drastic discipline, and it is in this general sense that he may be called an 'apostate'. Moreover, we must appreciate how the story ends: Simon 'resembles a cornered criminal, frightened at the prospects of punishment although not obviously remorseful over his crimes' (Garrett, *Demise of the Devil*, p. 72). In short, Simon remains the villain of the piece.

3. Cf. B. Chilton, *Beginning New Testament Study* (London: SPCK, 1986), pp. 36-39.

bear fruit with patient endurance' (Lk. 8.15). Unique to Luke is the emphasis upon 'holding fast' (κατέχουσιν) to the word and bearing fruit 'in perseverance' (ἐν ὑπομονῇ) from a 'sincere heart' (ἐν καρδίᾳ καλῇ καὶ ἀγαθῇ). The idea of persistent commitment to the word[1] is contrasted with an ephemeral response of joy (χαρά) and faith (πρὸς καιρὸν πιστεύουσιν), capped by a 'falling away' in the hour of testing (8.13).[2] A mature grasp of the word is also opposed to a superficial response susceptible to suffocation by greed and self-indulgence (8.14).

The parallels with Simon's experience in Acts 8 are noteworthy. Simon believes Philip's word (v. 13) and no doubt feels something of Samaria's joy (χαρά, v. 8) over Philip's ministry. As the story unfolds, however, Simon's craving for money and power, stemming from his crooked heart (καρδία, vv. 21, 22), ensnares him. By failing to persevere in faith and obedience, he forfeits his share 'in this word' (ἐν τῷ λόγῳ τούτῳ, 8.21).[3]

2.   The classic apostate in Luke–Acts is, of course, Judas, who through treachery loses his position among the Twelve. The scene in Acts 1.15-26 describing the replacement of Judas displays several points of contact with the Simon story in 8.18-24.[4] Peter announces that, while Judas formerly enjoyed 'a share in this ministry' (τὸν κλῆρον τῆς διακονίας ταύτης, 1.17), his apostolic tenure had been brutally cut short in recent days, fulfilling the judgment of Scripture (1.20). Luke adds parenthetically the financial factor behind Judas's

---

1.   Conzelmann rightly interprets this commitment as primarily ethical, involving obedience and good works, the fruit of a godly character (*Theology*, pp. 103-104, 231-34). S. Brown's ecclesiological conception of perseverance as characterizing those Christians who 'remain [in the church] while others leave' is based heavily on a forced interpretation of ὑπομονή (*Apostasy and Perseverance*, pp. 48-50). See the criticisms of Brown's work in F. Bovon, *Luc le théologien: Vinqt-cinq ans de recherches (1950–1975)* (Neuchâtel: Delachaux & Niestlé, 1978), pp. 407-10.

2.   Cf. S. Brown, *Apostasy and Perseverance*, p. 50.

3.   In light of the multiple references to λόγος in Acts 8.4-25 denoting the gospel word preached to and received by the Samaritans (vv. 4, 14, 25), the same term in v. 21 should no doubt be interpreted along similar lines. Haenchen thinks that 'the λόγος in which Simon is refused a share is Christianity' (*Acts*, p. 305). Stählin proposes that 'this word' refers to a sermon by the apostles which Simon had heard (*Apostelgeschichte*, p. 124).

4.   For the general connection, see Weiser, *Apostelgeschichte*, I, p. 205; S. Brown, *Apostasy and Perseverance*, pp. 82-98.

demise: 'Now this man acquired (ἐκτήσατο) a field with the reward of his wickedness (ἐκ μισθοῦ τῆς ἀδικίας)' (1.18; cf. Lk. 22.3-6). Judas's place is taken by Matthias, chosen by a combined process of prayer (to the Lord who 'knows everyone's *heart'*) and casting lots (ἔδωκαν κλήρους) (1.24-26).

Simon Magus endeavors to purchase (κτάομαι, 8.20) the ability to impart the Spirit, evidently for his own economic profit. As proclaimed by Peter, however, Simon's entanglement in 'the chains of wickedness (ἀδικίας)' (8.23) precludes any partnership (μερὶς οὐδὲ κλῆρος, 8.21) in the apostles' ministry of word and Spirit and merits a penalty of death.[1]

3. According to the opening scene in Acts 5, Ananias and Sapphira, members in (apparently) good standing within the Jerusalem church, sin egregiously against the Holy Spirit by mishandling proceeds from a business transaction (vv. 3, 9). The problem is traced to an evil 'heart' (καρδία) dominated by Satan (vv. 3-4). Peter exposes the offence, and the couple are shockingly struck dead (vv. 5-10).

Again, the correspondence with Simon's impiety is transparent. Although a professing Christian, Simon again becomes Satan's puppet,[2] corrupt in heart and devious in his intent to 'misappropriate' the Spirit. And while he is not smitten on the spot for his perversity, Simon effectively receives a terrifying death sentence which, as far as he knows, has every likelihood of being carried out (8.20-24).[3]

---

1. κλῆρος, κτάομαι and ἀδικία seldom appear in Luke's writing outside of Acts 1.15-26 and 8.18-24. L.T. Johnson especially highlights the parallel between Simon's abortive attempt to buy his way into the apostolic circle and Judas's forfeiture (due to greed) of his share in the apostolic office (*Literary Function of Possessions*, pp. 215-17).

2. Cf. Garrett, *Demise of the Devil*, pp. 65-76.

3. S. Brown contends that Luke distinguishes between Simon and Ananias/Sapphira by denying that the Samaritan magician ever received the Spirit which would have made him a 'full Christian' (*Apostasy and Perseverance*, pp. 111-13). In fact, Luke is vague about whether or not Simon received the Spirit. Still, it could be argued that Simon's preoccupation with imparting the Spirit implies some prior personal experience of the Spirit (why would he seek to transmit what he did not possess?). At any rate, as noted previously, Simon's responses to the gospel in Acts 8.13 are characteristic of 'full Christians'; indeed, they are identical to the other Samaritans who all receive the Spirit through the apostles' hands. Cf. I.H. Marshall, *Kept by the Power of God: A Study of Perseverance and Falling Away* (London: Epworth, 1969), p. 87.

The fundamental point established from these parallels is that Luke did not regard Simon's 'apostasy' as an isolated phenomenon in early Christian history and, consequently, would scarcely have held Philip responsible for its occurrence. If even among Jesus' most intimate disciples one becomes a traitor and among the Spirit-filled Jerusalem congregation headed by Peter two are 'filled with Satan', then nothing derogatory toward Philip necessarily follows his ostensible failure with Simon Magus. It seems inevitable for Luke that the gospel periodically evokes insincere and transitory responses.

Of course, if the end result of a missionary campaign had been *widespread* defection on the part of professing believers, then there would be room for suspecting the missionary's competence. But in the case of Philip's Samaritan mission, Simon stands out among the legion of joyful respondents as the *lone example* of a backslider, even as Judas and Ananias and Sapphira are exceptions among Jesus' disciples and the Jerusalem church. Philip surely should not be blamed for the odd delinquent Samaritan when he has proven successful with the vast majority.

There remains the potential embarrassment for Philip that it is not he but Peter who disciplines the reprobate Simon. But the same situation applies to Jesus' treatment of Judas. The betrayed Master actually rebukes his followers for retaliating against Judas and his arrest party (Lk. 22.47-53), leaving Peter to assess Judas's true condition in Acts 1. It may in fact be a Lukan *Tendenz* to stress Peter's role as the staunch opponent of pretenders to the faith. This pattern is suggested by the unique saying of the Lukan Jesus when predicting Peter's denial: 'Simon, Simon, listen! Satan demanded to sift all of you like wheat, but I have prayed for you that your own faith may not fail; and you, when once you have turned back, strengthen your brothers' (Lk. 22.31). The book of Acts demonstrates that Jesus' prayer was answered, as a renewed Simon Peter, now strong and bold, exposes others whom Satan has claimed and whose faith has failed. When it comes, then, to censuring Simon Magus, Luke's assignment of the task to Peter seems more designed to reinforce a particular portrayal of Peter than to denigrate Philip in any way.

5. *Conclusion*

The principal features of Philip's portrait in Acts discernible from his encounter with Simon Magus include an emphasis on his greatness and on his continuity with the 'prophet like Moses' and other key figures in Luke–Acts.

1. That Luke esteems Philip the evangelist as one of the truly great figures in early Christianity is evident in the presentation of Philip's superiority, both in terms of power and motivation, over the likes of Simon Magus, the self-acclaimed and self-absorbed 'Great Power'. Philip's notable achievement culminates in Simon's rapt response to his mighty works and submission to his ministry of proclamation and baptism. Although later in the story Simon fails to measure up to Christian standards, this should not be taken as disparaging Philip's reputation, any more than Judas's 'apostasy' tarnishes Jesus' ministry or the hypocrisy of Ananias and Sapphira casts suspicion on the whole Jerusalem church. Admittedly, however, there persists the thorny problem of why Philip does not impart the Spirit to his Samaritan converts, which will be discussed thoroughly in Chapter 5.

2. Luke buttresses Philip's greatness by patterning his exploits after those of a 'prophet like Moses'. In particular, Philip's subduing of the Samaritan magician appears analogous to Moses' victory over Pharaoh's magicians in the well-known Exodus story. Also, Luke may have subtly counterpointed Philip's vocation as a true 'prophet like Moses' and servant of Jesus Christ—the pre-eminent 'prophet like Moses'—and Simon's insidious masquerade as the expected Mosaic prophet and 'Standing One'.

3. Philip's triumphant contest with Simon Magus closely associates his work with the ministries of both Jesus and Paul in Luke–Acts. Like Jesus, Philip stands out as a Moses-styled instrument of the 'finger of God' (cf. Lk. 11.20), wielding his authority against a formidable evil 'Power'. Like Paul, Philip successfully eliminates the impediment of magic-oriented religion to the worldwide advance of the gospel.

Chapter 4

PHILIP AND THE ETHIOPIAN EUNUCH

1. *Introduction*

By virtue of his pioneering outreach to the Samaritans, Philip the evangelist takes his place within Luke's narrative as one of the leading trailblazers of the universal Christian mission. He yields the spotlight temporarily to the Jerusalem apostles (Acts 8.14-25) but subsequently re-emerges as the missionary protagonist in the conversion story surrounding the Ethiopian eunuch (8.25-40). The present chapter focuses on this second Philip episode, with an eye to determining its significance within Luke's unfolding drama of the global extension of the gospel. Particular attention will be given to correlating Philip's evangelization of the Ethiopian eunuch with his prior Samaritan mission and with subsequent missionary milestones in Acts 9–11 associated with Peter, Paul and the community at Antioch.

Both Philip incidents in Acts 8 highlight his ministry of gospel-proclamation (εὐαγγελίζομαι, vv. 4, 12, 35, 40) and baptism (vv. 12-13, 36-39) beyond the borders of Jerusalem (Samaria/road to Gaza). But despite this correspondence, the two episodes are far from identical. In the first place, while the Samaritan account is a brief, generalized summary of events exclusively in the third person, the eunuch story is much more detailed and centers around an extended dialogue between Philip and his inquirer. Secondly, there are differences in the setting and scope of Philip's respective missions. On the one hand, Philip journeys to 'the city of Samaria' and ministers to 'the crowds' (8.4-8); on the other hand, he goes down to 'a wilderness road' to witness solely to an isolated traveller (8.26-29). Thirdly, different impulses trigger Philip's actions. He is driven to Samaria on account of domestic hostilities (8.1, 3-5), whereas he is directed to the Ethiopian eunuch by divine mandate (8.26, 29). Finally, and most significantly, Philip's converts vary in terms of their ethno-religious status. We have already noted the ambiguous position of the Samaritans vis-à-vis Jews and Gentiles. In the case of the Ethiopian eunuch, his African heritage tips off his indisputable Gentile identity. To be sure, he appears as a Gentile interested in Jewish worship and Scripture, but one of the specific expressions of this attraction to Judaism—his pilgrimage to Jerusalem (8.27)—again distinguishes him from the Gerizim-honoring Samaritans.

Because of these noteworthy differences between Philip's two missions, they should not simply be lumped together as parts of a single, transitional step beyond Jewish boundaries. It is thus an important aim of this chapter to clarify what Luke regards as Philip's distinctive and innovative achievement in evangelizing the Ethiopian eunuch.

In relating the Philip–eunuch encounter to the following events in Acts 9–11, the critical issue concerns the opening of the church's doors to the Gentiles. In ch. 9 Paul is dramatically converted and commissioned to be the Lord's 'instrument. . . to bring my name before Gentiles' (v. 15), thus setting the stage for his monumental mission across the Mediterranean world in the latter half of Acts. In 10.1–11.18 Peter's witness to the Roman centurion, Cornelius, receives extended treatment. This event is normally interpreted as officially inaugurating the Gentile mission, and in any case, it has a poignant impact upon the church's developing mission policy (11.1-18; cf. 15.7-9). In 11.19-21 missionaries—including 'men of Cyprus and Cyrene'—establish a vibrant Christian community at Antioch comprised of Greek as well as Jewish members.

How then does Philip's outreach to the Ethiopian eunuch fit in with these beginning incidents of the Gentile mission?[1] Some scholars essentially deny any connection, since they regard the eunuch as a full proselyte to Judaism.[2] Others, however, see him as more marginally attached to Judaism and mark his conversion as a 'stepping-stone'

1. Among those who appreciate this link between the eunuch incident and the mission stories in Acts 9–11, see Stählin, *Apostelgeschichte*, p. 116; R.F. O'Toole, 'Philip and the Ethiopian Eunuch (Acts VIII 25-40)', *JSNT* 17 (1983), pp. 29-31; B. Gaventa, *From Darkness to Light: Aspects of Conversion in the New Testament* (OBT, 20; Philadelphia: Fortress Press, 1985), pp. 123-25.

2. E.g. S.G. Wilson, *The Gentiles and the Gentile Mission in Luke–Acts* (SNTSMS, 23; Cambridge: Cambridge University Press, 1973), pp. 171-72; Sanders, *Jews*, pp. 151-53. J. Dupont (*The Salvation of the Gentiles: Studies in the Acts of the Apostles* [New York: Paulist Press, 1979], pp. 11-33) curiously leaves the eunuch narrative out of his discussion altogether.

between the Samaritan and Gentile missions, a move beyond the 'semi-Jewish' Samaritans but still shy of reaching full-fledged Gentiles.[1] Yet another approach positions the eunuch closer to the edge of the Jewish–Gentile divide, viewing Philip's mission as a *Vorspiel*,[2] *Präludium*,[3] or *Auftakt*[4] (German synonyms roughly equivalent to 'prelude') to the fuller work of Peter and Paul among the Gentiles.

The difficulty with these 'stepping-stone' and 'prelude' perspectives lies in both cases with their imprecision and, consequently, the questions they leave unanswered. For example, if evangelizing the eunuch slots somewhere between the Samaritan and Gentile missions, to which is it closer? Is it more a tentative inching beyond Samaritan boundaries, a bold new advance just this side of a Gentile breakthrough, or something in between? Likewise, if Philip's witness to the eunuch harbingers the flowering of the Gentile mission, does this make Philip the originator of a new missionary program which Peter, Paul and certain preachers in Antioch simply carry on and complete? Or should Philip's contribution be judged more modestly as a chance encounter with an isolated foreigner before the serious seeking after Gentiles commences in Acts 9–11?

In short, we must clarify precisely how Philip's mission to the Ethiopian eunuch functions as a narrative bridge from the Samaritan mission in the first half of Acts 8 to the early stages of the Gentile mission in Acts 9–11. To this end, it will be useful to analyze the eunuch incident from a variety of angles, starting with a literary investigation of the story's structure, style and parallels with other accounts (Old Testament and Lukan) and then proceeding to explore several key issues—including matters pertaining to geography, divine intervention, the eunuch's status and Philip's ministry of proclamation and baptism—all of which have a bearing on defining Philip's strategic role in advancing the gospel around the world.

---

1. E.g. Haenchen, *Acts*, p. 314; Roloff, *Apostelgeschichte*, p. 139; W. Schmithals, *Die Apostelgeschichte des Lukas* (Zürich: Theologischer Verlag, 1982), p. 86; M. Dömer, *Das Heil Gottes: Studien zur Theologie des lukanischen Doppelwerkes* (BBB, 51; Bonn: Hanstein, 1978), p. 167.

2. Bauernfeind, *Kommentar*, p. 123; G. Schneider, *Apostelgeschichte*, I, p. 498.

3. Conzelmann, *Apostelgeschichte*, p. 63.

4. E. Plümacher regards the eunuch's conversion as at least 'eine Auftakt', if not the 'eigentliche Heidenbekehrung im lukanischen Sinn' (*Lukas als hellenistischer Schriftsteller: Studien zur Apostelgeschichte* [Göttingen: Vandenhoeck & Ruprecht, 1972], p. 90).

2. *Structure and Style of Acts 8.25-40*

A word of explanation must first be offered for opening the story at v. 25. μὲν οὖν characteristically signals the start of a new section in Acts (cf. above on 8.4), and the circumstances of v. 25 dovetail nicely with v. 26 to introduce the following narrative.[1] The two verses chart the courses of the missionary protagonists upon leaving Samaria. The first relates Peter and John's movement back to Jerusalem, while the second, by way of contrast ('*But* [δέ] an angel of the Lord said to Philip. . . '), announces Philip's separate journey toward the coastal plain where the next scene will occur. To be more precise, v. 25 functions as a transitional 'hinge', aptly wrapping up the Samaritan episode (as noted above) and pointing ahead to a new story. This dual purpose is suggested by its marking as a self-contained paragraph in most modern texts and translations.

A helpful approach to structuring Acts 8.25-40 maps out an intricate chiastic pattern. The detection of chiasm, including its use in the eunuch story, is nothing new in Lukan scholarship.[2] Drawing in particular on the work of D. Mínguez and R. O'Toole, the following schema may be sketched.[3]

1. Cf. W.C. van Unnik, 'Der Befehl an Philippus', in *Sparsa Collecta*, I, pp. 332-34.

2. Cf. C.H. Talbert, *Literary Patterns: Theological Themes and the Genre of Luke–Acts* (SBLMS, 20; Missoula, MT: Scholars Press, 1974), pp. 51-58; K.E. Bailey, *Poet and Peasant: A Literary Cultural Approach to the Parables in Luke* (Grand Rapids: Eerdmans, 1976), pp. 79-85; C.L. Blomberg, 'Midrash, Chiasmus, and the Outline of Luke's Central Section', in *Gospel Perspectives. III. Studies in Midrash and Historiography* (ed. R.T. France and D. Wenham; Sheffield: JSOT Press, 1983), pp. 233-48.

3. D. Mínguez, 'Hechos 8,25-40: Análisis estructural del relato', *Bib* 57 (1976), pp. 168-91; O'Toole, 'Philip', pp. 25-29. The two analyses are not identical, and O'Toole's is the more helpful (it is actually a refinement of Mínguez's). See also P. de Meester, ' "Philippe et l'eunuque éthiopien" ou "Le baptême d'un pèlerin de Nubie"?', *NRT* 103 (1981), pp. 366-67, whose chiastic schema is simpler and focuses more on thematic rather than linguistic connections.

v. 25　　Α ὑπέστρεφον εἰς Ἱεροσόλυμα
　　　　　Β πολλάς τε κώμας τῶν Σαμαριτῶν
　　　　　C εὐηγγελίζοντο
v. 26　　D ἐλάλησεν πρὸς Φίλιππον
　　　　　Ε πορεύου... ἐπὶ τὴν ὁδὸν
v. 27　　F καὶ ἰδοὺ ... εὐνοῦχος
v. 29　　G εἶπεν δὲ τὸ πνεῦμα τῷ Φιλίππῳ
v. 31　　Η ἀναβάντα καθίσαι σὺν αὐτῷ
v. 32　　I ἡ δὲ περιοχὴ τῆς γραφῆς
vv. 32-35　　J Isa. 53.7-8: citation and discussion
v. 35　　Ι´ ἀπὸ τῆς γραφῆς ταύτης
v. 39　　Η´ ἀνέβησαν ἐκ τοῦ ὕδατος
　　　　　G´ πνεῦμα κυρίου ἥρπασεν τὸν Φίλιππον
　　　　　F´ καὶ οὐκ εἶδεν αὐτὸν οὐκέτι ὁ εὐνοῦχος
　　　　　Ε´ ἐπορεύετο γὰρ τὴν ὁδὸν αὐτοῦ
v. 40　　D´ Φίλιππος δὲ εὑρέθη εἰς Ἄζωτον
　　　　　C´ εὐηγγελίζετο
　　　　　Β´ τὰς πόλεις πάσας
　　　　　Α´ τοῦ ἐλθεῖν αὐτὸν εἰς Καισάρειαν

Arranging a text chiastically reveals both its central focus—at the pivot-point—as well as important subsidiary ideas flagged through repetition on either side. The hub of the eunuch narrative may thus be located at Acts 8.32-35, dealing with the citation and discussion of Isa. 53.7-8 (J).[1] This emphasis on the Isaiah text is reinforced by the closely linked repetition of γραφή (I/I´). Such a direct appeal to Scripture, especially prophetic passages, represents a favorite Lukan tendency at large, but interestingly, in Acts 8–11 this tendency surfaces again only in Peter's instruction to Cornelius, and even then only in a general fashion ('All the prophets testify about him', 10.43). Certainly, grasping the significance of the Isaiah reference is critical to interpreting the eunuch episode.

Auxiliary concerns reflected in the chiastic structure of Acts 8.25-40, along with their echoes in the surrounding scenes in chs. 8–11, may be enumerated as follows.

1.　Luke characteristically focuses on principal cities within a region as bases of missionary operation (e.g. Jerusalem, Antioch,

---

1.　In addition to O'Toole and Mínguez, on the story's center see G. Schneider, *Apostelgeschichte*, I, p. 498; C.H. Lindijer, 'Two Creative Encounters in the Work of Luke: Luke xxiv 13-15 and Acts viii 26-40', in *Miscellanea Neotestamentica* (ed. T. Baarda, A.F.J. Klijn and W.C. van Unnik; NovTSup, 48; Leiden: Brill, 1987), pp. 80-81.

Ephesus).[1] In the eunuch incident, while the main action takes place on 'a wilderness road', the movement of the narrative as a whole is from one great urban center to another: Jerusalem to Caesarea (A/A'; cf. Jerusalem in vv. 26-27). The Jerusalem connection appears in all the stories of Acts 8–11, but the additional association with Caesarea emerges only in the Cornelius episode.

2. The stress on εὐαγγελίζομαι is evident not only at the beginning and end (C/C'), but also very near the heart of the eunuch story (v. 35). The term also characterizes the previous Philip incident (8.4, 12) and recurs in Peter's sermon to Cornelius (in connection with God's announcement of peace through Christ, 10.36) and in the reported witness of the first missionaries to Antioch (11.20).

3. Repeated references to Philip and the eunuch (D/D'; F/F') are scarcely surprising. The particular use of εὐνοῦχος, however, as the dominant appellation for the latter figure (overshadowing ἀνὴρ Αἰθίοψ and δυνάστης, v. 27) is quite striking and potentially significant. The one-to-one evangelistic encounter is typical of Acts 8–11, as seen in the interactions between Philip/Peter and Simon Magus, Ananias and Saul, and Peter and Cornelius.

4. The recurrence of πορεύομαι (E/E'; cf, vv. 27, 36) and ὁδός (E/E'; cf. v. 36; ὁδηγέω, v. 31) is redolent of the familiar journey motif throughout Luke–Acts.[2] In the immediate context of Acts 8–11, the two terms cluster again in the account of Saul's conversion and commission (9.3, 11, 15, 17, 21). With respect to the eunuch narrative, Bauernfeind has made the interesting suggestion that πορεύεσθαι ἐπι τὴν ὁδόν signals the movement of the gospel on the way to the Gentiles, thus contravening the mission imperatives of Mt. 10.5-6.[3]

5. The focus on the Spirit as the agent of divine guidance (G/G') undergirds the emphasis on providential direction which permeates

---

1. Cf. Conzelmann, *Apostelgeschichte*, p. 61.

2. Cf. F.V. Filson, 'The Journey Motif in Luke–Acts', in *Apostolic History and the Gospel: Essays in Honor of F.F. Bruce* (ed. W. Gasque and R.P. Martin; Grand Rapids: Eerdmans, 1970), pp. 68-77; Moessner, *Lord of the Banquet*, pp. 26-33, 289-325; O'Toole, 'Philip', pp. 30-31.

3. εἰς ὁδὸν ἐθνῶν μὴ ἀπέλθητε. . . πορεύεσθε δὲ μᾶλλον πρὸς τὰ πρόβατα τὰ ἀπολωλότα οἴκου Ἰσραήλ (Mt. 10.5-6). Bauernfeind's view is tied in with the observation (noted previously) that the Matthean text also prohibits preaching to the Samaritans, unlike the Philip narrative which promotes such a mission (*Kommentar*, p. 122; cf. Hengel, *Between Jesus and Paul*, pp. 111-12).

this Philip story and also the following Peter and Paul stories in Acts 9–11.

6. ἀναβαίνω denotes action linking together Philip and the eunuch (H/H'). Philip 'comes up' to sit with the eunuch in his chariot, enabling the pair to discuss the Isaiah passage (v. 31). Later, just before Philip is snatched from the scene, he and the eunuch 'come up' out of the water together, picturing their common faith and baptism. Elsewhere in Acts 8–11, ἀναβαίνω occurs only in the Cornelius incident (10.4, 9; 11.2), but with no apparent significance.

Apart from those terms which strictly conform to a chiastic pattern in Acts 8.25-40, there are other repeated words reflecting key ideas.

1. The multiple use of both προφήτης (vv. 28, 30, 34) and ἀναγινώσκω (vv. 28, 30, 32) in reference to the Isaiah reading confirms the pivotal place which it holds within the narrative.

2. The recurrence of ὕδωρ (vv. 36 [twice], 38, 39) and βαπτίζω (vv. 36, 38) directly following Philip's proclamation accentuates the act of baptism as a requisite response to the gospel. Baptism likewise demonstrates the faith of Saul and Cornelius' household in Acts 9–10.

3. The double-mention of ἰδού (vv. 27, 36) highlights the occurrence of unexpected phenomena in the eunuch story (the presence of a traveller and water in the desert) which serves to reinforce the major theme of supernatural guidance. The term surfaces frequently in the surrounding stories, especially calling attention to the unusual events prompting Peter's visit to Cornelius (10.17, 19, 21, 30; 11.11; cf. 7.56; 9.10-11).

To complete this linguistic analysis of Acts 8.25-40, two additional features should be noted.

1. *Word-plays.* Cleverly the author describes the traveller on the road from Jerusalem to Γάζαν (v. 26) as an official in charge of all the queen's γάζης (v. 27); later, Philip's terse question to this man evinces a similar literary flair: ἆρά γε γινώσκεις ἃ ἀναγινώσκεις; (v. 30).[1]

2. *Optative + ἄν.* The eunuch responds to Philip's query using a construction alien to *koine* Greek and found nowhere else in

---

1. Cf. Stählin, *Apostelgeschichte*, pp. 127-28.

the New Testament outside of Luke's writings: πῶς γὰρ ἂν δυναίμην... (v. 31a).[1]

No great significance should be read into these characteristics, but they both represent samples of literary sophistication, suggesting a particular slant toward an educated audience.

In conclusion, this investigation of the internal structure and style of the eunuch narrative has pointed consistently to its highly artistic design. This is not to deny the use of source material, but, as so often in Luke's work, it makes the task of distinguishing between tradition and redaction exceedingly difficult. Also emerging in this study has been an indication of the story's leading ideas, meriting further examination below, and a preliminary demonstration of continuity among the various mission episodes in Acts 8–11.

3. *Literary Analogues to Acts 8.25-40*

In addition to (and ultimately informing) the connection between Acts 8.25-40 and the companion mission accounts in chs. 8–11 are possible parallels between the eunuch incident and selected stories from both the Old Testament and Luke's Gospel. Of particular significance to understanding Luke's perspective on Philip's mission are the comparisons with the Elijah/Elisha material in Kings and the Emmaus narrative in Luke 24.

a. *The Elijah/Elisha Narratives*
The dynamic prophets, Elijah and Elisha, and the lively incidents surrounding them in 1 Kings 17–2 Kings 9 clearly captured the attention of Luke, who utilized this material both explicitly (Lk. 1.17; 4.25-27; 9.8, 19, 30-33) and in more allusive fashion.[2] Both Philip narratives in Acts 8 show signs of this influence, but it is the eunuch story which most extensively associates the Christian evangelist with the two venerable Israelite prophets.

E. Trocmé has noted a number of striking affinities between the eunuch incident and the Elijah episode in 1 Kings 18: (1) events set in

---

1. Cf. Haenchen, *Acts*, p. 311; J.H. Moulton, *A Grammar of New Testament Greek*. I. *Prolegomena* (Edinburgh: T. & T. Clark, 3rd edn, 1908), pp. 197-99.

2. See generally R.E. Brown, 'Jesus and Elijah', pp. 90-93; J.-D. Dubois, 'La Figure d'Elie dans la perspective lucanienne', *RHPR* 53 (1973), pp. 155-76; Evans, 'Luke's Use of the Elijah/Elisha Narratives'.

motion by divine command (1 Kgs 18.1; Acts 8.26); (2) desert setting
(1 Kgs 18.2, 5; Acts 8.26); (3) prophet encounters pious, royal official
(Obadiah, 1 Kgs 18.3-4, 7; Ethiopian eunuch, Acts 8.27-28); (4)
prophet outruns chariot (1 Kgs 18.46; Acts 8.30); (5) prophet engages
official in conversation (1 Kgs 18.7-15; Acts 8.30-35); (6) sacrificial
act forms core of the narrative (1 Kgs 18.20-40; Acts 8.32-35); (7)
provision of necessary water (1 Kgs 18.41-45; Acts 8.36); (8) exit of
prophet through divine intervention (1 Kgs 18.46, 12; Acts 8.39).[1]
   This list may be supplemented by the following items:

9. The mysterious movements of Elijah are attributed to the
    vehicle of the 'Spirit of the Lord' (1 Kgs 18.12), just as in
    Philip's case (Acts 8.39). A similar reference emerges in 2 Kgs
    2.16, accounting for Elijah's whereabouts after his heavenly
    assumption.[2]

10. The royal official, Obadiah, encountered by Elijah, demon-
    strates his piety by attending to the Lord's prophets (1 Kgs
    18.4, 13), a devotion which is mirrored in the eunuch's interest
    in the prophet Isaiah.

11. Both Elijah's ordeal on Mt Carmel and Philip's adventure in
    the desert take place at noon-time (μεσημβρία), which proves
    to be an hour of divine testing (1 Kgs 18.26-29; Acts 8.26).

Admittedly these parallels are not equally compelling, but together
they are sufficient to confirm some coloring of Philip's ministry to the
eunuch with Elijah-like characteristics. As Trocmé contends, this
depiction of Philip as an Elijah-styled prophet should probably be
linked both to his role in the Samaritan mission, marked by miracle-
working and outdoing the 'false prophet' Simon, and to his association
with a circle of prophets (including his own daughters) in Acts
21.8-11.[3]
   T.L. Brodie has recently drawn attention to the correspondence
between the eunuch incident and the story of Elisha's dealings with
Naaman in 2 Kings 5. Brodie in fact understands the Naaman narrative as a major source underlying the whole of the Philip cycle in Acts

   1. Trocmé, *'Livre des Actes'*, p. 180.
   2. Noting the parallel between this Elijah reference and Philip's experience are
Pesch (*Apostelgeschichte*, I, p. 294), G. Krodel (*Acts* [Augsburg Commentary on
the NT; Minneapolis, MN: Augsburg, 1986], p. 171) and many other commentators.
   3. Trocmé, *'Livre des Actes'*, p. 180.

8.9-40, though the bulk of the influence concentrates in the final episode.[1] Moreover, this analysis is part of a much larger agenda in which Brodie has sought to demonstrate the widespread effects of the Elijah/Elisha narratives upon a number of Lukan stories.[2] In light of the extent and innovation of his work, a brief assessment of Brodie's methods and conclusions seems appropriate.[3] Brodie starts from the double premise that Luke was a Greco-Roman author employing rhetorical conventions popular in his day and that he was also a Christian theologian seeking to interpret the Jewish Scriptures for his post-resurrection community. Along the first line, Brodie concludes that Luke was particularly indebted to the ancient literary practice of *imitatio*. Integral to this method was the technique of 'internalization', which involved 'taking an existing text, especially a text that was old, and reworking it in a way which emphasized values that were internal' (in other words, inward, spiritual values).[4] Additional processes of adaptation included 'abbreviation, elaboration, division. . . fusing of diverse characters' and 'modernization'.[5] One ancient text from which Luke frequently 'has distilled the essence. . . and has used that essence as a basic component, a skeletal framework, around which he has grafted other material'[6] is the block of Elijah/Elisha narratives in the LXX.

As Brodie himself admits, his approach needs some refinement in

---

1. T.L. Brodie, 'Towards Unraveling the Rhetorical Imitation of Sources in Acts: 2 Kgs 5 as One Component of Acts 8,9-40', *Bib* 67 (1986), pp. 41-67.

2. Brodie's work stems from his 1981 dissertation from the Pontifical University of St Thomas Aquinas ('Luke the Literary Interpreter: Luke–Acts as a Systematic Rewriting and Updating of the Elijah–Elisha Narrative') and has been published in a series of articles from 1983–89 (see bibliography).

3. Cf. the basically positive appraisal in Evans, 'Luke's Use of the Elijah/Elisha Narratives', pp. 75-83.

4. Brodie, '2 Kgs 5', p. 44. In an article on Lk. 7.36-50, Brodie suggests that Luke has taken 'external' elements pertaining to 'financial debt' and 'physical life' from 1 Kgs 17.17-24 and 'internalized' them to correspond to matters related to 'moral debt' and 'spiritual life' ('Luke 7,36-50 as an Internalization of 2 Kings 4,1-37: A Study of Luke's Rhetorical Imitation', *NTS* 32 [1986], p. 457). On the use of this rhetorical technique in ancient literature, see T.L. Brodie, 'Greco-Roman Imitation of Texts as a Partial Guide to Luke's Use of Sources', in Talbert (ed.), *Luke–Acts: New Perspectives*, pp. 17-32.

5. '2 Kgs 5', pp. 44, 53.

6. '2 Kgs 5', p. 41.

terms of unravelling the precise operations which Luke has performed on his Old Testament model. Also, he occasionally succumbs to the trap of 'parallelomania', drawing excessively tenuous and far-fetched links between incidents in the LXX and Luke–Acts (see p. 139 n. 2). Nevertheless, on the whole, Brodie's working hypothesis is an illuminating one based on sound principles and careful examination. He has correctly recognized the Greco-Roman and Jewish literary backgrounds which, as most scholars agree, inform Luke's writing, but he advances the discussion by positing a satisfying integration, functional in a broad sample of cases, which few have attempted, much less achieved.

Regarding the example of Acts 8.25-40, three principal themes (to be examined more fully in due course) appear to be influenced by the material in 2 Kings 5.

1. The status and condition of the inquirers in the two stories are demonstrably parallel. Naaman and the Ethiopian eunuch are both prominent, chariot-riding foreigners employed as royal officials. True, Naaman is a military officer and the eunuch a treasurer, but Naaman also superintends large amounts of his monarch's money (2 Kgs 5.5)—a function more vital to the story than his service in the army (2 Kgs 5.15-27). The conditions of the two men are not identical, but neither are they dissimilar. Both need cleansing—one outwardly, the other internally—which is effected through immersion in water (καὶ κατέβη. . . καὶ ἐβαπτίσατο [2 Kgs 5.14]/καὶ κατέβησαν. . . ἐβάπτισεν αὐτόν [Acts 8.38]).[1] Also, assuming one interpretation of εὐνοῦχος, we may add to Brodie's observations that both Naaman and the Ethiopian suffer from physical afflictions (leprosy/castration) which legally exclude them from Israel's assembly (Lev. 13–14/Deut. 23.1).

2. A similar emphasis on providential guidance emerges in both narratives. At just the point when Naaman appears thwarted in his quest for healing, two directional instructions come from Elisha, the 'man of God', setting the leprous official on the road to recovery (2 Kgs 5.8-10). The first beckons Naaman to come to Elisha's house, 'that he may learn that there is a prophet in Israel'; the second comes via a messenger (ἄγγελος) of Elisha, enjoining Naaman to wash in the Jordan seven times. This prophetic message is not readily appreciated

---

1. Brodie, '2 Kgs 5', pp. 51-54. On the connection between baptism and cleansing in Luke's understanding, see Acts 22.16; cf. 2.38.

by Naaman, but after discussion with his servants (2 Kgs 5.11-13) he proceeds to the river to perform the required ritual and is cured—'according to the word of the man of God' (v. 14). Likewise, the Ethiopian eunuch's need for salvation is miraculously answered by a double-command (angel [ἄγγελος] of the Lord [Acts 8.26]/Spirit of the Lord [8.29]) which brings Philip to provide the necessary counsel. The discussion turns on the significance of the prophetic word, in this case the message of Isaiah 53; it, like Elisha's prescription to Naaman, is not immediately understood, but eventually the eunuch is enlightened by Philip's explanation and responds by submitting himself to baptism (8.30-38).[1]

3. An additional point of contact (in terms of both comparison and contrast) between the Naaman and eunuch incidents—which Brodie fails to recognize—relates to a pattern of resisting or obstructing God's purpose. As is well-known, Naaman at first indignantly refuses to go and wash in the Jordan; he must finally be persuaded (2 Kgs 5.11-13). At this point Naaman appears as quite the opposite, indeed an antitype, of the Ethiopian eunuch. The latter figure is positively eager to be baptized, even taking the initiative with Philip the evangelist: 'Look here is water! What is to prevent me from being baptized?' (Acts 8.36). Implied in this query, however, is the notion that something may still be obstructing (preventing) the eunuch's baptism—if not his own obedience (as in Naaman's case), then something else (such as restrictive Jewish legislation). In any event, certain barriers hindering washing/baptism must be broken down for both Naaman and the eunuch.

Whether or not we accept Brodie's view that Acts 8.25-40 (along with 8.9-24) represents a conscious, extensive and sophisticated rewriting of 2 Kings 5,[2] the evidence at least indicates that Luke took some notice of Elisha's dealings with Naaman as suitably analogous to

---

1. Brodie, '2 Kgs 5', pp. 54-58.

2. One point where Brodie may be pressing his case too far relates to Luke's alleged adaptation of βιβλίον from the Kings story. To court the favor of the king of Israel, Naaman brings money and a βιβλίον, a letter of recommendation from the king of Syria (2 Kgs 5.6-7). In Brodie's opinion, the reading of this letter 'has been fused [by Luke] to become the single complex idea of reading (a *biblion*) of the prophet Isaiah' in the eunuch episode ('2 Kgs 5', p. 54). However, the connection between a royal letter and a book of prophetic Scripture seems tenuous at best and is all the more difficult to accept in view of the complete absence of βιβλίον-terminology in the eunuch story.

Philip's encounter with the Ethiopian eunuch. That Luke had reflected on the contemporary relevance of the Naaman episode is certified by Lk. 4.27 and suggested by the probable correspondence to the cleansing of the Samaritan leper in Luke 17 (see Chapter 2 above).

Curiously, in their focus on the influence of either an Elijah or Elisha story on the eunuch incident, neither Trocmé nor Brodie seriously entertains the possibility that Luke had in view both prophetic traditions. However, since the materials surrounding the two prophets are so closely related in Kings and since Luke evinces a tendency to juxtapose allusions to both figures (Lk. 4.25-27; 9.51-57), it is quite reasonable that a similar juxtaposition underlies the eunuch story. At certain points, items from each half of the Elijah/Elisha cycle even appear to coalesce in their parallels to the Acts account. For example, both Elijah and Elisha function as literary models for the Lukan Philip, as do Obadiah and Naaman for the Ethiopian eunuch, and there are additional common elements such as the prophetic word, divine guidance and the significance of water.

Given this shaping of the account of Philip's mission to the Ethiopian eunuch, a significant link may be made to Luke's earlier adumbration of the Gentile mission. As noted previously, Jesus' appeal to Elijah and Elisha in Lk. 4.25-27 serves to foreshadow (and legitimate) the church's eventual turn toward the Gentiles. As a counter-response to rejection by his own people, Jesus recalls that during rebellious days in Israel's history two of her most revered prophets had bypassed their compatriots to minister instead to selected Gentiles: a Sidonian widow and the Syrian officer, Naaman. At this stage Jesus himself does not actively turn to the Gentiles, but the implication is clear: Jewish repudiation of his mission will in time precipitate a move to the more receptive Gentiles. Within the Lukan schema this move is normally judged to have begun officially with Peter's witness to Cornelius,[1] but if the Elijah/Elisha paradigm from Lk. 4.25-27 is taken seriously, then Philip's evangelization of the eunuch also appears to mark an important breakthrough to the Gentiles. For Philip functions as both an Elijah- and Elisha-styled prophet, in the latter case exhibiting a direct connection to the Naaman incident cited in Lk. 4.27. While Philip's association with Elijah seems generally unrelated to the particular story mentioned in Lk. 4.25-26 (miraculous feeding

1. Cf. Crockett, 'Luke 4.25-27', pp. 177-83.

of the widow at Zarephath), it is noteworthy that both the LXX story of the widow's provision and the Acts account of the eunuch's conversion commence with identical mandates to the Lord's messengers—ἀνάστηθι καὶ πορεύου—followed by prompt obedience—'he rose and went' (3 Kgdms 17.8-10; Acts 8.26-27).[1] Remembering also that the outcome of Jesus' pronouncements in Nazareth—his violent expulsion from the city (Lk. 4.28-30)—is matched by Philip's forced flight from Jerusalem which sparks his evangelistic ministry (Acts 8.4-40), the conclusion presents itself that Luke likely regarded Philip as one of the fulfilling agents of Jesus' projected mission to the Gentiles.

b. *The Emmaus Narrative (Luke 24.13-35)*
Further evincing the narrative unity of Luke–Acts is the striking parallelism between Philip's encounter with the Ethiopian eunuch in Acts 8 and Jesus' interaction with the Emmaus disciples in Luke 24.[2] A variety of common linguistic features tie the stories together,[3] but the most impressive linking factor pertains to a shared sequence of similar events.

1. Two disciples on the way from Jerusalem to Emmaus are joined by Jesus (Lk. 24.13-16; ὁδός, v. 32); the eunuch travelling from Jerusalem to his homeland is joined by Philip (Acts 8.29-30; ὁδός, vv. 26, 36).
2. Jesus and Philip both engage their fellow-wayfarers in conversation with a probing question (Lk. 24.17; Acts 8.30).

---

1. Cf. van Unnik, 'Befehl an Philippus', pp. 335-36. It is also interesting that earlier in Acts Philip functions as a supplier of food to needy widows (though not through miraculous means) (6.1-7).

2. See J. Dupont, 'Les pèlerins d'Emmaüs (Luc, xxiv, 13-35)', in *Miscellanea Biblica B. Ubach* (Scripta et Documenta, 1; Montisserrati, 1953), pp. 361-64, 370-73; *idem*, 'The Meal at Emmaus', in *The Eucharist in the New Testament: A Symposium* (ed. J. Delorme *et al.*; London: Geoffrey Chapman, 1964), pp. 116-21; J. Grassi, 'Emmaus Revisited (Luke 24,13-35 and Acts 8,26-40)', *CBQ* 26 (1964), pp. 463-67; Lindijer, 'Two Creative Encounters'; J. Kremer, *Die Osterevangelien: Geschichten um Geschichte* (Stuttgart: Katholisches Bibelwerk, 1977), pp. 129-30; X. Léon-Dufour, *Resurrection and the Message of Easter* (New York: Holt, Rinehart & Winston, 1975), pp. 160-63; J. Wanke, '"... wie sie ihn beim Brotbrechen erkannten": Zur Auslegung der Emmauserzählung Lk 24,13-35', *BZ* 18 (1974), p. 102; R.J. Dillon, *From Eye-witnesses to Ministers of the Word: Tradition and Composition in Luke 24* (AnBib, 82; Rome: Biblical Institute, 1978), pp. 111-12.

3. See Lindijer, 'Two Creative Encounters', pp. 77-79.

3. Discussion ensues in the Emmaus story over the significance of
    Jesus' recent death and alleged resurrection, which Jesus him-
    self illuminates through scriptural—especially prophetic—
    exposition (Lk. 24.18-27). Similarly, Philip proclaims Jesus to
    the eunuch, starting[1] from the Isaianic reference to the suffer-
    ing and exaltation of the Lord's Servant (Acts 8.32-35).
4. Both encounters culminate in 'Sacred Acts'[2] signifying the
    traveller's new-found fellowship with Jesus. In the Gospel
    story, Cleopas and his companion break bread with Jesus
    (24.28-30); in Acts the eunuch submits to Christian baptism
    (8.36-39).
5. Jesus suddenly vanishes from the scene (Lk. 24.31) and then
    re-appears in another place and resumes his revelatory min-
    istry (24.36-43); likewise, Philip abruptly disappears from the
    eunuch's sight and rematerializes in another location where he
    continues to proclaim the gospel (Acts 8.39-40).
6. The travellers are deeply affected emotionally by their
    'recognitions' of Jesus.[3] The Emmaus disciples recall their
    'hearts burning within' them (Lk. 24.32), and the eunuch pro-
    ceeds on his way 'rejoicing' (Acts 8.39).

By so modelling the Emmaus and eunuch narratives after a common
pattern, Luke no doubt betrays his customary concern to demonstrate
continuity between the experiences of Jesus and the early church. But
which experiences are particularly in view? J. Grassi fixes on the
provision of hospitality to travelling missionaries: as the Emmaus
disciples hosted Jesus, so Christian communities should receive itinerant evangelists, like Philip, as they would receive Christ himself.[4]
However, while hospitality is an important Lukan theme and contributes to the portrayal of Philip in Acts 21.8-9 (see Chapter 6
below), it simply is not a factor in the eunuch episode (Philip does not
linger long enough to require lodging!).

---

1. Cf. ἀρξάμενος ἀπὸ Μωϋσέως καὶ ἀπὸ πάντων τῶν προφητῶν (Luke
24.27) and ἀρξάμενος ἀπὸ τῆς γραφῆς ταύτης. . . (Acts 8.35).
2. Lindijer, 'Two Creative Encounters', p. 79.
3. On the 'recognition' motif in the Emmaus and eunuch incidents, see
B.P. Robinson, 'The Place of the Emmaus Story in Luke–Acts', *NTS* 30 (1984),
p. 483-85.
4. Grassi, 'Emmaus Revisited', pp. 465-67.

J. Dupont stresses the corresponding ministries of word and sacrament carried out by Jesus and the church, giving clear priority, however, to the sacramental element.

> The story of the Ethiopian eunuch is the story of his baptism; the whole story leads to the baptism. . . Great prominence is given to the explanation of the Scriptures. . . but these explanations, important as they are, are only a preparation for the baptism, the conclusion and climax of the passage.
>
> In the story of disciples on the way to Emmaus the explanation of the Scriptures plays a similar role, to which Luke attaches great importance. . . But the explanation of the Scriptures is only a preparation. . . there is still need of the sacrament of breaking of bread. Apart from the salvation which is taught on the basis of scriptural evidence, there is the salvation which acts and operates in the sacraments.[1]

Apart from doubts concerning the eucharistic interpretation of 'breaking bread' in Luke 24 (or anywhere else in Luke–Acts), not to mention the assumption that Luke envisaged a distinctively sacramental link between breaking bread and baptism,[2] Dupont's position may be challenged at the point of subordinating scriptural proclamation to sacramental practice in the Emmaus and eunuch incidents. 'Opening the Scriptures' is more than just preparation for the eunuch's baptism; it is the *centerpiece* of the story, as Luke's chiastic arrangement makes clear. And in the Emmaus narrative, despite the undeniable emphasis on recognizing Jesus 'in the breaking of the bread' (Lk. 24.35; cf. vv. 30-31), the wider context of Luke 24 fortifies the 'fulfillment of prophecy' motif more than the idea of table fellowship (vv. 6-8; 44-47).[3]

Indeed, a major clue to Luke's purpose in linking the Emmaus and eunuch incidents may lie in this emphasis on scriptural fulfillment *as it relates to the Gentile mission*. The Emmaus story is very closely tied to the following scene in Luke's narrative (Lk. 24.33-49). Among the

---

1. Dupont, 'Meal at Emmaus', p. 120.

2. For a critique of eucharistic interpretations of Lk. 24 and other Lukan texts dealing with bread and feeding, see B.P. Robinson, 'Place of the Emmaus Story', pp. 487-94; C.K. Barrett, *Church, Ministry and Sacraments in the New Testament* (Didsbury Lectures, 1983; Exeter: Paternoster Press, 1985), pp. 60-63.

3. Cf. P. Schubert, 'Structure and Significance of Luke 24', in *Neutestamentliche Studien für Rudolf Bultmann* (ed. W. Eltester; Berlin: Töpelmann, 1957), pp. 173-77; Parsons, *Departure*, pp. 83-91; B.P. Robinson, 'Place of the Emmaus Story', pp. 482-83.

most obvious parallels between the two episodes is Jesus' appeal to the Scriptures as predicting his passion and resurrection.

> Then he said to them, 'Oh, how foolish you are, and how slow of heart to believe all that the prophets have declared! Was it not necessary that the Messiah should suffer these things and then enter into his glory?' Then beginning with Moses and all the prophets, he interpreted to them the things about himself in all the scriptures (24.25-27).

> Then he said to them, 'These are my words that I spoke to you while I was still with you—that everything written about me in the law of Moses, the prophets, and the psalms must be fulfilled'. Then he opened their minds to understand the scriptures, and he said to them, 'Thus it is written, that the Messiah is to suffer and to rise from the dead on the third day . . . ' (24.44-46).

Jesus has more to say, however, in this latter (climactic) passage. He also brings into the orbit of biblical prophecy the impending mission to the Gentiles:

> 'Thus *it is written*. . . that repentance and forgiveness of sins is to be proclaimed in his name *to all nations*, beginning from Jerusalem. You are witnesses of these things. And see, I am sending upon you what my Father promised; so stay here in the city until you have been clothed with power from on high' (24.46-49).

Thus, Scripture—christologically interpreted—legitimates the Gentile mission.[1]

Within Luke's narrative, these words at the end of the Gospel apply primarily to the eleven apostles. They receive almost identical instruction in Acts 1.4-8, and Peter in particular alludes to Christ's commission and preaches 'forgiveness of sins' to the Gentile Cornelius (Acts 10.41-43). And certainly Paul is not far from view as the Christ-appointed 'light for the Gentiles' in Acts, in accordance with Isaiah's prophecy (Acts 13.47; Isa. 49.6).

But what about Philip the evangelist who, utilizing the testimony of Isaiah, proclaims Christ's suffering and exaltation to the Ethiopian eunuch and, more clearly than any other Lukan character, emulates Christ's role in the Emmaus story? Does he not also fulfill Christ's scriptural mandate in Luke 24 by witnessing to a Gentile official? Part of the conclusion to J. Wanke's study of the Emmaus story supports this hypothesis:

---

1. Cf. Tyson, 'Gentile Mission and Scripture'.

Was in der Äthiopiergeschichte exemplarisch als missionarisches Bemühen der Kirche herausgestellt wird, hat nach Auskunft des Evangelisten seine Grundlegung im Tun (Lk. 24,25ff) und Auftrag (Lk. 24,44ff) des Auferstandenen.[1]

Philip, then, effectively takes his place alongside Peter and Paul in Luke's mission history as one authorized by the resurrected Christ to evangelize the Gentile nations. Moreover, as Jesus legitimated Philip's Samaritan mission by his teaching and example in Luke 9–17, so he legitimates Philip's witness to the Ethiopian eunuch in Luke 24.

c. *Conclusion*

The literary models which Luke employs in shaping Acts 8.25-40 help to clarify Philip's role in relation to both Jesus' earthly ministry and the developing mission of the early church. On the one hand, the parallels between the eunuch story and the Elijah/Elisha cycle associate Philip's mission with the *beginning* of Jesus' public ministry in Nazareth. By appealing to Elijah and Elisha as precedents (Lk. 4.25-27), Jesus forecasts a turn to the Gentiles which Philip apparently fulfills. On the other hand, the correspondence between the eunuch and Emmaus narratives links Philip's work to the *climax* of Jesus' earthly activity. Once again Jesus utilizes Scripture to predict (and prescribe) the commencement of the Gentile mission (Lk. 24.44-47), and once again Philip's witness to the eunuch seems to realize (at least in part) this goal.

Although final and more precise conclusions regarding Philip's contribution to the Gentile mission in Luke–Acts must await a thorough assessment of the eunuch's social status, this preliminary literary investigation intimates a more significant, pioneering role than is often assumed.

4. *Geographical Elements in Acts 8.25-40*

Several items of geographical interest emerge in Acts 8.25-40. The brief travel notes, κατὰ μεσημβρίαν and αὕτη ἐστὶν ἔρημος (8.26) will be examined in a later section, but for now I will explore three larger matters: (1) the reference to Jerusalem; (2) the eunuch's Ethiopian homeland; and (3) the setting of the Philip–eunuch encounter along Israel's coastal plain.

---

1. Wanke, '" . . . wie sie ihn beim Brotbrechen erkannten"', p. 192.

a. *Jerusalem*

The importance of Jerusalem (and the temple) in Luke–Acts as the geographical center of salvation history and starting point of the church's mission is well known;[1] thus, any references to the Holy City in the Philip narratives should not be passed over lightly. The connection between Jerusalem and Philip's first mission has been acknowledged above (Philip ventures to Samaria after fleeing Jerusalem [Acts 8.1, 4-5], and two Jerusalem apostles complement Philip's work [8.14-17]). In the second Philip story, the Jerusalem link continues. The opening three verses each mention the city in relation to the movements of different characters: (1) Peter and John return to Jerusalem after preaching in Samaritan villages (8.25); (2) Philip is directed to the road which runs *from* Jerusalem to Gaza (8.26); and (3) the Ethiopian eunuch journeys home after worshipping *in* Jerusalem (8.27).

Interestingly, these references to Jerusalem appear in two distinct lexical forms: Ἱεροσόλυμα (8.25) and Ἰερουσαλήμ (8.26, 27). This variation occurs throughout Luke–Acts and has given rise to no end of ingenious explanations. Older literary studies supposed that different sources accounted for the variant terms, but such an approach has commanded little support in recent years as scholars have devoted more attention to Luke as redactor and composer. For example, J.K. Elliott contends that Luke consciously utilizes the more Hebraic form—Ἰερουσαλήμ—in obviously Jewish contexts, specifically, when a Jewish audience is being addressed by a Jewish speaker or when a story takes place in Jewish territory. In Elliott's opinion, 'the church is still on Jewish soil' in Acts 7.8–9.31—hence the preponderant use of Ἰερουσαλήμ in this section.[2] Alternatively, I. de la Potterie distinguishes between the more 'religious' or 'sacred' Ἰερουσαλήμ and the more 'profane', Hellenized term, Ἱεροσόλυμα. Accordingly, the former name appears in settings which memorialize Jerusalem as the Holy City of Israel where Jesus accomplished his

---

1. Cf. M. Bachmann, *Jerusalem und der Tempel: Die geographisch-theologischen Elemente in der lukanischen Sicht des jüdischen Kultzentrums* (BWANT, 109; Stuttgart: Kohlhammer, 1980); J.B. Chance, *Jerusalem, the Temple, and the New Age in Luke–Acts* (Macon, GA: Mercer University Press, 1988); Brawley, *Luke–Acts*, pp. 118-32.

2. J.K. Elliott, 'Jerusalem in Acts and the Gospels', *NTS* 23 (1976–77), pp. 462-65.

salvific work and the apostles based their ministry. When the church's mission extends beyond Jerusalem into the Diaspora, any continued reference to Jerusalem is in the 'profane' form. Thus, the argument goes, only Ἱεροσόλυμα appears in Acts 8.1-25—where the focus falls on the church's dispersion from the Holy City—while the 'religious' Ἱερουσαλήμ re-emerges as the dominant name in 8.26-11.26—where mission concerns have subsided and Jerusalem stands out again as the sacred center of Israel.[1]

Despite the attempt to be comprehensive, it is doubtful whether either of these schemes adequately accounts for all the evidence, especially Acts 8. In response to Elliott, we must certainly question whether the Samaritan mission, much less Philip's witness to the eunuch, should be situated *wholly* within a Jewish environment. And his case is further undermined by having to accept as original the poorly attested reading of Ἱερουσαλήμ in both 8.14 and 8.25.[2] De la Potterie likewise seems weak in his handling of Acts 8. His notion that Ἱεροσόλυμα appears when apostolic activity moves beyond Jerusalem scarcely fits the report in 8.25 of Peter and John's *return to* Ἱεροσόλυμα, and in the Ἱερουσαλήμ section in 8.26–11.26 an interest in mission matters outside Jerusalem certainly does not diminish and, if anything, intensifies. The Ethiopian official may travel to Ἱερουσαλήμ to worship (8.27), but the key events of this man's story—his discussion with Philip and subsequent baptism—take place on the return trip—*away from* the Holy City.

The string of 11 consecutive occurrences in Acts 1–6 of the more Semitic, 'biblical' Ἱερουσαλήμ[3] may well relate to Luke's emphasis in these chapters on the church's early continuity with Judaism.[4] However, as the church breaks out of its Jewish shell in Acts 8ff., the more random use of two names for Jerusalem seems to follow no prescribed pattern. As Cadbury states, 'probably the two forms owe their

---

1. I. de la Potterie, 'Les deux noms de Jérusalem dans les Actes des Apôtres', *Bib* 63 (1982), pp. 153-65.

2. Neither the Nestlé–Aland nor United Bible Societies text even cites Ἱερουσαλήμ as a variant in these cases.

3. This is the only form for 'Jerusalem' found in the LXX.

4. Acts 1.8, 12 (twice), 19; 2.5, 14; 4.5, 16; 5.16, 28; 6.7. (The first reference to 'Jerusalem' in Acts [1.4], however, utilizes the more 'Hellenized' form, Ἱεροσόλυμα.) Cf. Schneider, *Apostelgeschichte*, I, pp. 199-200; Jeremias, 'ΙΕΡΟΥΣΑΛΗΜ/ΙΕΡΟΣΟΛΥΜΑ', *ZNW* 65 (1974), pp. 273-76.

adoption to the changing fancy of the writer in each several instance'.[1]

In the case of Acts 8.25-27, the important distinction among the three Jerusalem references has to do not so much with terminology as with the orientation of key personnel in relation to the Holy City. As noted above, Peter and John head back to Jerusalem after their brief preaching stint in Samaria (v. 25), whereas Philip and the eunuch meet while travelling away from Jerusalem toward the Mediterranean coast (vv. 25-30). It may be thought that Philip's order to follow the Jerusalem–Gaza road implies that he must first go back to Jerusalem from Samaria (a puzzling itinerary in light of his recent expulsion from Jerusalem) and then proceed from there toward Gaza.[2] In fact, however, the angel simply directs Philip to 'go. . . to the road' (πορεύου. . . ἐπὶ τὴν ὁδόν) which runs from Jerusalem to Gaza. This can easily be taken to mean that Philip should proceed directly from Samaria to some point of intersection along the Jerusalem–Gaza road, thereby bypassing Jerusalem altogether.[3] Be that as it may, Philip's final destination places him once more beyond the perimeters of Jerusalem, while the apostles remain stationed inside the city, as in 8.1. Philip is thus positioned again at the forefront of the church's centrifugal mission beyond Jerusalem.

In Acts 9–11 other Christian missionaries follow Philip's lead in venturing outside Jerusalem. Saul, newly converted and commissioned, proclaims Christ to Jews in Damascus; Peter ministers in Lydda and Joppa and eventually evangelizes Cornelius's household in Caesarea; and some anonymous missionaries find a welcome reception in Antioch. But for both Paul and Peter, there is still a strong counterpull back to Jerusalem at this stage of the narrative (9.26-29; 11.2). Only Philip and the missionaries to Antioch—both fugitives from

---

1. Cadbury, 'Four Features of Lucan Style', p. 91. Cf. E. Lohse, 'Σιών, κτλ.', *TDNT*, VII, pp. 327-28; Harnack, *Acts*, p. 81. For other views and discussion of the problem of Jerusalem-terminology in Luke–Acts, see Bachmann, *Jerusalem*, pp. 13-66; D.D. Sylva, 'Ierousalēm and Hierosoluma in Luke–Acts', *ZNW* 74 (1983), pp. 207-21.

2. Cf. Schmithals, *Apostelgeschichte*, p. 84.

3. Although Luke charts no specific course for Philip, one might imagine a journey from Samaria which ran southwest to Antipatris and then due south through Lydda and along the edge of the Shephelah to Eluetheropolis (Betogabris), which marked an intersection with the Jerusalem–Gaza road at approximately its mid-point.

Jerusalem—seem permanently assigned to mission fields outside the Holy City.

b. *Ethiopia*

In the ancient world 'Ethiopia' designated the land of Nubia (Old Testament Cush) located due south of Egypt between the first and sixth cataracts of the Nile. Its principal cities were Napata and Meroe. The Ethiopian kingdom was typically ruled in the New Testament era by queens assuming the dynastic title of Candace, such as the figure mentioned in Acts 8.27.[1] Luke's story contains the only references to Αἰθίοψ in the New Testament, but this region and its inhabitants were featured more frequently in both the Old Testament and Greco-Roman literature.[2]

The biblical tradition portrays Ethiopia as a remote and distant land (Ezek. 29.10; Esth. 1.1; 8.9; cf. Jdt. 1.10) renowned for its wealth (Job 28.19; Isa. 45.14), military prowess (2 Kgs 19.9; 2 Chron. 14.9-13; Isa. 37.9; Jer. 46.9) and dark-complexioned people (Jer. 13.23). The prophets repeatedly class Ethiopia with other wicked nations of the world, such as Egypt and Sheba, who have opposed God's people and merited his judgment (Isa. 20.3-5; 43.3; Ezek. 30.1-9; Nah. 3.9; Zeph. 2.11-12). However, a more positive note is also sounded, in that Ethiopians are reckoned among those foreign peoples destined to be converted and acknowledge the true God of Israel.

> Let bronze be brought from Egypt;
>> let Ethiopia hasten to stretch out its hands to God.
> Sing to God, O kingdoms of the earth;
>> sing praises to the Lord (Psa. 68 [67].31-32).

---

1. Strabo, *Geog.* 17.2.1-3; Pliny, *Nat. Hist.* 6.35; Dio Cassius, *Hist.* 54.5. Cf. E. Dinkler, 'Philippus und der ΑΝΗΡ ΑΙΘΙΟΨ (Apg 8,26-40): Historische und geographische Bemerkungen zum Missionsablauf nach Lukas', in *Jesus und Paulus*, pp. 89-94; P.T. Crocker, 'The City of Meroe', *BurH* 22 (1986), pp. 53-66; S. Lösch, 'Der Kämmerer der Königin Kandake (Apg. 8,27)', *TQ* 111 (1930), pp. 477-519; F.F. Bruce, 'Philip and the Ethiopian', *JSS* 34 (1989), pp. 380-81.

2. Cf. various studies by F.M. Snowden, Jr: *Blacks in Antiquity: Ethiopians in the Greco-Roman Experience* (Cambridge, MA: Harvard University Press, 1970), pp. 169-95; *Before Color Prejudice: The Ancient View of Blacks* (Cambridge, MA: Harvard University Press, 1983), pp. 46-59; 'Ethiopians and the Graeco-Roman World', in *The African Diaspora* (ed. M.L. Kilson and R.I. Rotberg; Cambridge, MA: Harvard University Press, 1976), pp. 11-36.

> Thus says the Lord:
>> The wealth of Egypt and the merchandise of Ethiopia,
>> and the Sabeans [from Sheba], tall of stature,
>> shall come over to you and be yours,
>> they shall follow you;
>> they shall come over in chains and bow down to you.
> They will make supplication to you, saying,
>> 'God is with you alone, and there is no other;
>> there is no god besides him' (Isa. 45.14).

> At that time I will change the
>> speech of the people to a pure speech,
> that all of them may call on the name of Lord
>> and serve him with one accord.
> From beyond the rivers of Ethiopia
>> my suppliants, my scattered ones,
>> shall bring my offering (Zeph. 3.9-10).

In classical writings, the Ethiopians were idealized as people of great piety and beauty. Homer spoke of 'blameless Ethiopians' (*Iliad* 1.423-24); Herodotus extolled the 'burnt-skinned' Ethiopians as the tallest and most handsome of all human beings (3.20); and Diodorus Siculus commented that 'it is generally held that the sacrifices practiced among the Ethiopians are those which are most pleasing to heaven' (3.3.1).[1] Adding to their mystique in Greco-Roman society was the common perception that the Ethiopians lived 'at the end of the habitable earth',[2] on the very edge of civilization. Homer, for example, regarded the Ethiopians as 'the furthermost of men (ἔσχατοι ἀνδρῶν)' (*Odyssey* 1.22-24), and the geographer Strabo placed Ethiopia at the 'extreme limits' of the Roman Empire (τὰ ἄκρα τῆς οἰκουμένης, *Geog.* 17.2.1).[3] Further arousing the curiosity of the educated classes in exotic Ethiopia were reports of two Roman expeditions into the region, one military (under Gaius Petronius, 23 BCE) and the other scientific (to discover the source of the Nile, 62 CE).[4]

---

1. Citation is from Diodorus of Sicily (ed. and trans. C.H. Oldfather *et al.*; LCL; Cambridge, MA: Harvard University Press; London: Heinemann, 1933–67).

2. Hengel, *Between Jesus and Paul*, p. 111.

3. See also Herodotus 3.114; Strabo, *Geog.* 17.1.13; Philostratus, *Apol.* 6.1; cf. Hengel, *Between Jesus and Paul*, p. 200 n. 85; T.C.G. Thornton, 'To the End of the Earth: Acts 1.8', *ExpTim* 89 (1977–78), pp. 374-75; Snowden, 'Ethiopians', p. 22.

4. Dio Cassius, *Hist.* 54.5; Pliny, *Nat. Hist.* 6.35; Seneca, *Nat. Quest.* 6.8.3;

As an educated and sophisticated author in his own right, Luke no doubt exploited this interest in Ethiopia in various ways.

1. Assuming that part of Luke's overall purpose was to press the claims of Christianity before a cultured Hellenistic audience (represented by Theophilus, Lk. 1.3; Acts 1.1), he needed to present not only a convincing and accurate narrative (Lk. 1.1-4), but also a compelling and interesting one which would capture the imagination. Certainly one reason for relating the conversion story of a leading official from mysterious Ethiopia was precisely because of its guaranteed dramatic appeal.[1]

2. As noted previously, Acts 1.8 plots the trajectory of the church's mission in Acts from Jerusalem and Judea to Samaria and ultimately out 'to the ends of the earth' (ἕως ἐσχάτου τῆς γῆς), to the farthest reaches of the Gentile nations.[2] Since Luke reports the Ethiopian's conversion immediately after the mission to Samaria, it is reasonable to assume that he has in view Ethiopia's fame as a distant borderland and thus regards the second Philip incident as an initial outreaching step 'to the ends of the earth'.[3]

Strabo, *Geog.* 17.1.54. Cf. Dinkler, 'Philippus', pp. 91-92; Plümacher, *Lukas*, pp. 12-13.

1. Dinkler, 'Philippus', pp. 90-94; Plümacher, *Lukas*, pp. 12-13; Cadbury, *Book of Acts*, pp. 15-18; R.I. Pervo, *Profit with Delight: The Literary Genre of the Acts of the Apostles* (Philadelphia: Fortress Press, 1987), pp. 70-71.

2. D.R. Schwartz has advanced the view that Acts 1.8 presents as the goal of apostolic witness 'the end of the land', that is, the land of *Israel* ('The End of the ΓΗ [Acts 1.8]: Beginning or End of the Christian Vision?', *JBL* 105 [1986], pp. 669-76). However, among other things, this thesis founders on Luke's own commentary on Acts 1.8 in 13.47, where the gospel's extension to the ends of the earth is unmistakeably linked to the church's light-bearing mission to the *Gentiles*. Cf. Davies, *Gospel and Land*, pp. 279-80; Dupont, *Salvation*, pp. 18-19.

3. Thornton, 'To the End of the Earth', pp. 374-75; Tannehill, *Narrative Unity*, II, pp. 108-12, 134-35; C.J. Martin, 'A Chamberlain's Journey and the Challenge of Interpretation for Liberation', *Semeia* 47 (1989), pp. 110-20.

A link to Luke's Gospel may also be envisaged. As 'the queen of the South [= Sheba] . . . came from *the ends of the earth* (ἐκ τῶν περάτων τῆς γῆς) to listen to the wisdom of Solomon' (Lk. 11.31), so a confidant of the queen of Ethiopia (a region proximate to Sheba) comes from the world's farthest reaches to hear Philip's proclamation concerning one 'greater than Solomon'. In early Abyssinian Christianity there was in fact a tendency to fuse the figures of Candace and the queen of Sheba (cf. E. Ullendorff, 'Candace [Acts VIII.27] and the Queen of Sheba', *NTS* 2 [1955–56], pp. 53-56).

On this reading of Acts, Philip appears as a trailblazer for both the Samaritan and Gentile missions. However, the extent of this latter breakthrough should not be overestimated. For in spite of the understandable deduction of patristic writers that the eunuch went on to bear witness to Christ in his native land,[1] Luke does not say this and in fact restricts the scope of Philip's mission to a single Ethiopian on Palestinian soil. Philip certainly propels the gospel on its way toward the earth's outer limits, but he can hardly be credited with bringing the church's global mission to full flower. This only comes in the second half of Acts with the efforts of Paul, fulfilling his commission 'to be a light for the Gentiles' and herald of salvation 'to the ends of the earth' (ἕως ἐσχάτου τῆς γῆς, 13.47; cf. Isa. 49.6).

3. Given Luke's tendency to interpret the missions of Jesus and the early church as fulfilling Old Testament prophecy, it is conceivable that he views the eunuch's conversion as a first-fruit of the forecasted harvest of the Ethiopian nation.[2] Significantly, however, Luke adjusts the biblical scenario by associating the Ethiopian's evangelization not so much with his pilgrimage to Jerusalem, but with his encounter with Philip while returning home from Jerusalem. Further insight into Luke's understanding of this event in relation to Old Testament expectation will follow the discussion below of the Ethiopian's identity as a eunuch.

c. *The Coastal Plain*

After baptizing the eunuch at a spot near the Jerusalem–Gaza highway, Philip is carried away by the Spirit to Azotus (Acts 8.39-40). First-century Azotus was located due west of Jerusalem and north of Gaza on the Mediterranean coast. Thus, Philip remains in the general vicinity of where he ministered to the eunuch. A final note discloses that from Azotus Philip moved north along the coastal plain to Caesarea, 'proclaim[ing] the good news to all the towns' *en route* (8.40). Apparently, then, Luke has summarized an extended missionary campaign of Philip's along the coast and chosen to focus on the

---

1. Irenaeus, *Adv. Haer.* 3.12.8; 4.23.2; Eusebius, *Eccl. Hist.* 2.1.13.
2. On the linguistic links between Acts 8.26-40 and Zeph. 2–3, see W.K.L. Clarke, 'The Use of the Septuagint in Acts', in Foakes Jackson and Lake (eds.), *Beginnings of Christianity.* II. *Prolegomena 2. Criticism*, p. 102. On the eunuch incident as the fulfillment of Ps. 68(67).31-32, see Eusebius, *Eccl. Hist.* 2.1.13; Dinkler, 'Philippus', p. 85; Martin, 'Chamberlain's Journey', p. 109.

eunuch encounter as a representative incident.

The particular coastal cities mentioned in conjunction with Philip's ministry—Gaza and Azotus (both former Philistine strongholds) and Caesarea (the provincial Roman capital)—were all Hellenistic centers with substantial *Gentile* populations in the first century.[1] That Luke would have known these demographic facts is likely, since he generally demonstrates a first-hand acquaintance with the coastal region.[2] Accordingly, it is also likely that Luke regarded Philip's outreach to the eunuch as part of a wider mission in Gentile territory.

Another important feature of Philip's coastal mission is its parallel to Peter's itinerary in Acts 9.32–10.48. Peter leaves Jerusalem and proceeds to Lydda (9.32-35), Joppa (9.36–10.23) and Caesarea (10.24-48). The first two stops are at the most prominent *Jewish* centers along the coastal plain,[3] located between Gaza and Azotus to the south and Caesarea to the north. While Luke reports that many are converted as a result of Peter's ministry in these places (9.35, 42), it is noteworthy that in each case Peter works initially within a community of believers which has already been established (9.32, 36, 38, 41). Indeed, the impression is given that Peter is making an 'inspection' tour of local churches outside Jerusalem.[4] Who founded these communities then? Luke does not explicitly tell us, but the earlier announcement of Philip's proclamation to 'all the towns' between Azotus and Caesarea (8.40) certainly implies that, in addition to working in the Hellenistic centers of the coastal plain, Philip also contributed to the growth of the Jewish-Christian communities at Lydda and Joppa prior to Peter's arrival. Therefore, a similar situation to that in Samaria presents itself where Philip establishes a beachhead for the gospel, and Peter comes along later to nurture and expand the young congregations.[5]

---

1. On these ancient cities, see Hengel, *Between Jesus and Paul*, pp. 110-16; Schürer, *History*, II, pp. 98-103, 108-109, 115-18.

2. See the detailed study by Hengel, *Between Jesus and Paul*, pp. 111-28.

3. Hengel, *Between Jesus and Paul*, pp. 116-17.

4. Peter's visits to Lydda and Joppa are representative of a much larger mission to established churches outside of Jerusalem. Acts 9.31 summarizes the growth and stability of 'the church throughout Judea, Galilee and Samaria'. The very next verse, before introducing Peter's work at Lydda, first discloses that 'Peter went here and there *among all the believers*'—that is, presumably, among all those suggested in 9.31.

5. Cf. Dietrich, *Petrusbild*, p. 258.

Likewise, Peter comes to Caesarea only after Philip has been stationed there (8.40; cf. 21.8). In this place, however, Peter does not minister to an established local church; rather he witnesses solely to the Gentile inquirer, Cornelius, and his family. Thus, Peter now functions not as a pastor complementing Philip's former work in Samaritan or Jewish areas, but as an evangelist matching Philip's previous activity in Hellenistic coastal centers. More specifically, Peter's witness to Cornelius, a foreign official with Jewish sympathies, may be compared to Philip's mission to the Ethiopian eunuch. The significance of this comparison will be explored more fully below.

5. The Theme of Supernatural Guidance in Acts 8.25-40

Although Philip performs no miracles for the eunuch as he did for the Samaritans (healings and exorcisms), the element of the supernatural is by no means absent from the eunuch incident. It simply takes a different form, that of supernatural guidance.[1] From start to finish the events in the eunuch story unfold according to a divinely ordered agenda. Philip's mission is set in motion by a peculiar angelic directive. The heavenly messenger instructs Philip to head toward the Jerusalem–Gaza road without giving any details concerning what he should expect along the way (Acts 8.26). Philip simply obeys without hesitation, and 'behold' (ἰδού) he comes upon a traveller who just happens to be reading the Bible (8.27-28). Another divine mandate, this time from the Spirit, leads Philip to confront the traveller (8.29-30). What then follows is a beautifully orchestrated exchange of questions and answers centering around Isa. 53.7-8—which happens to be the particular text being read at precisely the moment when Philip arrives—thus affording Philip a golden opportunity to proclaim the good news of Jesus (8.30-35). Upon hearing the message, the eunuch promptly desires baptism, and 'behold' (ἰδού) there is water (8.36). No sooner is the baptism administered than the Spirit miraculously posts Philip to another station (8.39-40).

This marked emphasis on the Spirit's guidance once again links Philip's work to that of the foremost characters in Luke–Acts: Jesus, Peter and Paul. Just before Jesus' public ministry commences in Galilee, he is 'led by the Spirit in the wilderness' for a season of

---

1.   See Haenchen, *Acts*, pp. 314-15; Stählin, *Apostelgeschichte*, pp. 127-28; Plümacher, *Lukas*, pp. 90-91; O'Toole, 'Philip', pp. 29-30.

testing (Lk. 4.1-2). After passing the test, Jesus returns to Galilee 'filled with the power of the Spirit' and begins to teach in the synagogues (4.14-15). At Nazareth he announces his personal fulfillment of Isa. 61.1-2 and, in so doing, places his entire mission under the banner of the Spirit's authority: 'The Spirit of the Lord is upon me, because he has anointed me to bring good news. . . ' (4.18). Likewise, at a critical juncture in Peter's career culminating in his witness to the Gentile, Cornelius, it is the Spirit who provides the decisive impulse (Acts 10.19-20; 11.12). The pattern continues with Paul's mission. The Spirit's sovereign will is the determining factor in his venture into Asia Minor, his trek further west into Greece and his final journey to Jerusalem (13.2, 4; 16.6-10; 19.21; 20.22-23).

While it is customary in Luke–Acts for the Spirit to authorize new advances in mission, the 'transportational' dimension of the Spirit's work is more distinctive to Philip's coastal campaign. As suggested above, a parallel is provided in the mysterious movements of the resurrected Jesus (Lk. 24.31, 36-37; though not explicitly related to the Spirit), but no comparable phenomenon appears in conjunction with the travels of Peter or Paul or any other missionary in Acts. Apart from the connection to Jesus, Philip's relocation by the Spirit recalls most readily the experiences of biblical prophets, such as Elijah (1 Kgs 18.12; 2 Kgs 2.16; cf. above), Ezekiel (Ezek. 3.12, 14; 8.3; 11.1, 24) and Habakkuk (Bel 36–39).[1]

As for the significance of Philip's 'uplifting' experience, it certainly illustrates his spontaneity and availability as an instrument of the Spirit. R. Pesch takes the matter further, however, and again relates the Spirit's activity to legitimation of mission. He regards the snatching away of Philip immediately after the eunuch's baptism as a vindicating sign of Philip's bold outreach to a Gentile formerly 'hindered' from the way of salvation (cf. Acts 8.36).[2] In an act of approval—not

---

1. G. Friedrich thinks that Philip is 'caught up' (ἁρπάζω) in an ecstatic vision, like the experience of the one 'caught up (ἁρπάζω) to the third heaven' according to 2 Cor. 12.2 ('Die Gegner des Paulus im 2. Korintherbrief', in *Abraham unser Vater: Juden und Christen im Gespräch über die Bibel* [ed. O. Betz, M. Hengel and P. Schmidt; AGJU, 5; Leiden: Brill, 1963], pp. 200-201). However, the two situations are quite different. Philip is physically moved by the Spirit from one earthly place to another; there is no mention of 'seeing' or 'hearing' special phenomena. The heavenly traveller, on the other hand, is transported to Paradise—'whether in the body or out of the body'—and exposed to unutterable revelations.

2. Pesch, *Apostelgeschichte*, I, p. 294.

dismissal—following a job well done, Philip is reassigned to continue his evangelistic work elsewhere.

In addition to being led by the Spirit, Philip is also guided by the angel of the Lord. Although outlining no detailed itinerary, the angel does tell Philip to 'get up and go' (ἀνάστηθι καὶ πορεύου) to the Jerusalem–Gaza road κατὰ μεσημβρίαν, to an area described as ἔρημος (Acts 8.26).[1] The meaning of both of these travel notes is disputed, but W.C. van Unnik has supplied a satisfying interpretation which coordinates well with the theme of supernatural guidance.[2]

On purely lexical and grammatical grounds κατὰ μεσημβρίαν can either denote 'toward the south' or 'about noon'.[3] Either reading makes sense in the present context, but the case for the temporal meaning appears stronger. In its only other New Testament usage— also in Acts (22.6)—μεσημβρία clearly refers to 'midday', again in the context of travel. Likewise, most of the' LXX instances suggest 'noon-time'.[4] Still, it is most unusual for Philip's journey to be deliberately scheduled at this hour—the least comfortable time to travel and thus the least favorable time to encounter anyone else.[5] Why should an evangelist be out and about when there is likely to be no one around to evangelize? As strange as it seems, however, the description of the Jerusalem–Gaza road as ἔρημος confirms the picture of loneliness. ἔρημος, taken as a noun, represents a desert or wilderness region. But since the route in question did not really traverse such terrain, it seems best to take the term as an adjective meaning 'deserted, abandoned, vacated' (*menschenleer*): that is, *without people*.[6]

---

1. The ἔρημος-reference can either be included in the angel's command or treated as a parenthetical elaboration of that command by the narrator. The former option is supported by van Unnik ('Befehl', p. 332) and Haenchen (*Acts*, p. 309), the latter by the NRSV.

2. Van Unnik, 'Befehl', pp. 328-39; cf. Gaventa, *From Darkness to Light*, pp. 101-103.

3. BAGD, p. 506.

4. E.g. Gen. 18.1; 43.16, 25; Deut. 28.29; 2 Kgdms 4.5; 3 Kgdms 18.26, 27; Ps. 36(37).6; Amos 8.9; Isa. 18.4; 58.10; Jer. 15.8; Sir. 43.4.

5. Objectors to the 'noon-time' rendering of μεσημβρία in Acts 8.26 often cite this fact (e.g. Bauernfeind, *Kommentar*, p. 128).

6. Van Unnik, 'Befehl', pp. 328-34. I am assuming with van Unnik and most recent commentators that αὕτη in 8.26 refers back to ὁδόν and not to Γάζαν (see e.g. Pesch, *Apostelgeschichte*, I, p. 290; Schneider, *Apostelgeschichte*, I, p. 501; Stählin, *Apostelgeschichte*, p. 127; contra Lake and Cadbury [eds.], *Beginnings of*

Why then would the angel issue this 'absurd command' (*widersinnige Befehl*) directing Philip to an isolated spot? This peculiarity is best explained as a dramatic means of enhancing the supernatural dimension of Philip's encounter with the eunuch. In a setting most unsuited to finding any human ear for the gospel, Philip in fact meets a receptive Ethiopian. That Luke wants his readers to register this element of surprise is signalled in the ἰδού exclamation of the eunuch's sudden appearance on the scene (Acts 8.27; cf. v. 36).[1]

A similar focus on shocking heavenly orders may be discerned in the accounts of Saul's conversion/call and Peter's witness to Cornelius in Acts 9–11.[2] Saul, on his way to Damascus to arrest Christians, suddenly finds himself arrested by a heavenly vision and commanded by the very Jesus he opposes to 'get up and enter (ἀνάστηθι καὶ εἴσελθε) the city' where he would receive further instructions (9.3-6). Subsequently, one of the Damascene disciples, Ananias, is also confronted by the exalted Jesus and given perplexing orders. He is to 'get up and go' (ἀναστὰς πορεύθητι) to Judas's home to find the villainous Saul, who now, lo and 'behold' (ἰδού), is praying and expecting Ananias to restore his sight (9.11-12). Moreover, following Ananias's protests, the Lord repeats the command to 'go' (πορεύου) and reveals the astonishing new destiny mapped out for Saul as missionary to the Gentiles and martyr for Christ's name (9.15-16).

While praying on a housetop in Joppa 'about noon' (Acts 10.9), Peter receives a bewildering vision of unclean animals accompanied by the unthinkable mandate to 'get up. . . kill and eat' (10.10-13). As he ponders the meaning of this experience, the Spirit intervenes and informs Peter that—'behold' (ἰδού, 10.19; cf. v. 17)—even now at his doorstep are three men with whom he is to 'get up. . . and go' (ἀναστὰς. . . καὶ πορεύου σὺν αὐτοῖς) without delay (10.20). He learns that these men's master, a 'God-fearing' Gentile named Cornelius, had himself been directed by 'a holy angel' to seek out Peter's counsel (10.22; cf. vv. 3-8).

Christianity, IV, p. 95). The story explicitly states later that Philip encounters the eunuch 'along the road' (κάτα τὴν ὁδόν, 8.36); no further mention is made of Gaza.

1. Cf. Tannehill, *Narrative Unity*, II, pp. 248-49.
2. Cf. O'Toole, 'Philip', pp. 29-30; Plümacher, *Lukas*, pp. 90-91; K. Haacker, 'Dibelius und Kornelius: Ein Beispiel formgeschichtlicher Überlieferungskritik', *BZ* 24 (1980), pp. 246-47.

Clearly, the theme of supernatural guidance binds together the conversions of the Ethiopian eunuch, Saul and Cornelius as divinely engineered events critical to the development of the Gentile mission. However, while such unity marks the ministries of Philip, Paul and Peter in Acts 8–11, Philip still stands apart from both Peter and Paul in an important respect. Simply put, Philip promptly obeys the puzzling angelic orders without a fuss. Note the repetition of verbs in 8.26-27a: he who was instructed to 'get up and go' (ἀνάστηθι καὶ πορεύου) in fact 'got up and went' (ἀναστὰς ἐπορεύθη), pure and simple.[1] In a similar vein, when directed by the Spirit to intercept the eunuch's chariot, Philip *runs* to fulfill his appointed task (8.30). What a contrast this eager reaction poses to the initial hostility of Saul toward Christianity and the impulsive indignation of Peter at the thought of mingling with 'unclean' Gentiles (note also the contrast to Ananias's misgivings over ministering to Saul). These resistant attitudes must be overcome before the Gentile mission can move forward. Philip, on the other hand, enthusiastically preaches Christ to a stranger (foreigner). To draw on prophetic models, Peter and Paul appear as Jonah-type figures requiring considerable heavenly persuasion before heeding the Lord's missionary call;[2] Philip, however, acts more like Isaiah in his willing compliance with the Lord's purpose ('Here am I! Send me').

6. *The Social Status of the Ethiopian Eunuch*

The significance of Philip's evangelization of the Ethiopian eunuch is naturally tied closely to the convert's social status, as portrayed by Luke. His ethnic status as an Ethiopian has already been considered. It is now necessary to examine briefly his economic and occupational position and, more fully, his religious status vis-à-vis Judaism. The critical factor in this analysis concerns the socioreligious import of the dominant label: εὐνοῦχος.

---

1. Van Unnik, 'Befehl', pp. 335-37.

2. R.W. Wall in fact argues for a strong typological connection in Luke's mind between the Jonah story and Peter's outreach to Cornelius ('Peter, "Son" of Jonah: The Conversion of Cornelius in the Context of Canon', *JSNT* 29 [1987], pp. 79-90); cf. C.S.C. Williams, *A Commentary on the Acts of the Apostles* (BNTC; London: A. & C. Black, 1957), pp. 152-53; M.D. Goulder, *Type and History in Acts* (London: A. & C. Black, 1964), pp. 176-77.

a. *Finance Minister*

In Acts 8.27 the Ethiopian eunuch is described as δυνάστης Κανδάκης βασιλίσσης Αἰθιόπων, ὃς ἦν ἐπὶ πάσης τῆς γάζης αὐτῆς: a leading official in Candace's court, specifically, the head of the treasury. Consequently, he appears as a man of high social standing and great wealth. Other details in the story confirm this appraisal. The Ethiopian dignitary obviously has the means to travel in style ('seated in his chariot') a long distance and to obtain an expensive Greek scroll of Isaiah for personal study.[1] Moreover, the fact that in transit he leisurely reads and converses with Philip implies the aid of attending servants (8.28-31).

The reported conversion of such a figure coincides with Luke's general interest in the attraction of foreign officials and other prominent citizens to Christianity.[2] Jesus and Peter both reach out to Roman centurions who demonstrate exemplary faith and humility (Lk. 7.1-10; Acts 10–11; cf. Lk. 23.47). Jesus receives support from the wife of Herod's steward (Lk. 8.3), and a member of Herod's court stands out as one of the leaders in the church at Antioch (Acts 13.1). Paul preaches at Cyprus to the inquiring proconsul, Sergius Paulus (13.7), and at Berea to 'not a few Greek women and men of high standing' (17.12; cf. 17.4). He also numbers among his friends some Asiarchs in Ephesus (19.31) and is graciously entertained by 'the leading man of the island' of Malta, named Publius (28.7).

As is well known, however, Luke also takes pains to demonstrate the great reversal of social patterns—the humbling of the powerful and exalting of the downtrodden—touched off by Christ's advent. Indeed, the only other occurrence of δυνάστης in Luke–Acts outside the eunuch story surfaces in Mary's classic pronouncement, 'he has brought down the powerful (δυνάστας) from their thrones, and lifted up the lowly (ταπεινούς)' (Lk. 1.52). The stage is thus set for repeated warnings to the rich concerning their precarious position in God's kingdom and assurances to the poor of their acceptance (Lk. 4.18-19; 6.20; 7.22; 12.13-34; 14.7-24; 16.19-31; 18.18-30).

In light of this perspective, it is important to realize with respect to the Ethiopian minister that, although he ranks high on the social ladder and superintends a considerable fortune, he does not depend

---

1. Cf. K. Bornhäuser, *Studien zur Apostelgeschichte* (Gütersloh: Bertelsmann, 1934), p. 96.
2. Cf. Esler, *Community and Gospel*, pp. 183-85.

upon these for his salvation. He trusts in the Lord's humiliated (ταπείνωσις) and exalted servant (Acts 8.33) and makes no attempt to curry divine favor with the queen's money. Implicitly, then, a striking contrast emerges with the manipulative Simon Magus.[1]

b. *The Proselyte/'God-fearer' Question*
Determining the socioreligious status of the Ethiopian eunuch inevitably entails a discussion of two categories of Gentiles sympathetic to Judaism: proselytes and 'God-fearers'. While προσήλυτος consistently refers in the LXX to the 'resident alien' in Israel, it soon acquires a more technical sense of a Gentile convert to Judaism.[2] Philo, for example, speaks of '"proselytes", or newly-joined (προσηλύτους ἀπὸ τοῦ προσεληλυθέναι καινῇ)' members of 'the new and godly commonwealth' who merit great respect for abandoning 'their country, their kinsfolk and their friends for the sake of virtue and religion' (*Spec. Leg.* 1.51-52).[3] In another place Philo adds that these 'incomers' have forsaken 'the ancestral customs in which they were bred' and 'have crossed over to piety in whole-hearted love of simplicity and truth' and worshipped the one true God (*Spec. Leg.* 1.308-309). No doubt for Philo this 'cross-over' to the Jewish community involved circumcision and allegiance to the Torah (cf. *Migr. Abr.* 89-94).[4] In rabbinic tradition, proselytes were also required to undergo a purificatory baptism (cf. *m. Pes.* 8.8; *m. Ed.* 5.2).[5] While,

---

1. Note R.B. Rackham's comment: 'There is a contrast between Simon Magus and the Ethiopian treasurer which recalls the contrast between Gehazi and the stranger Naaman who was baptized in the Jordan' (*The Acts of the Apostles* [London: Methuen, 1901], p. 120).
2. See K.G. Kuhn, 'προσήλυτος', *TDNT*, VI, pp. 730-42; Jeremias, *Jerusalem*, pp. 320-34.
3. Texts and translations of Philo in this chapter are from Philo, *Works* (10 vols.; ed. and trans. F.H. Colson and G.H. Whitaker; LCL; Cambridge, MA: Harvard University Press; London: Heinemann, 1929–43).
4. See P. Borgen, *Paul Preaches Circumcision and Pleases Men and Other Essays on Christian Origins* (Trondheim: TAPIR, 1983), pp. 16-18; T.M. Finn, 'The God-fearers Reconsidered', *CBQ* 47 (1985), pp. 82-83; J.L. Nolland, 'Uncircumcised Proselytes?', *JSJ* 12 (1981), pp. 173-79. (All discuss the difficult text related to Philo's view of circumcision in *Quaest. Exod.* 2.2 [on Exod. 22.21 LXX].)
5. Jeremias, *Jerusalem*, pp. 320-21. On the necessity of circumcision for proselytes, see J.J. Collins, 'A Symbol of Otherness: Circumcision and Salvation in the First Century', in *'To See Ourselves as Others See Us': Christians, Jews, 'Others'*

generally speaking, these converts were accepted as partners in the Jewish community and no longer classed as Gentiles, continuing debates over their precise status suggest that they remained marked off in some respects from native Jews (cf. *Mek. Mishpat.* 18; *m. Qidd.* 4.1; *m. Nid.* 7.3). Jeremias classifies proselytes with various Israelites set apart by 'a slight blemish'.[1]

'God-fearers' (φοβούμενοι/σεβόμενοι τὸν θεόν), by contrast, typically designate those Gentiles more marginally attached to Judaism, who supported the local synagogue and complied with certain Jewish beliefs (e.g. monotheism) and customs (e.g. Sabbath observance, food laws), but for one reason or another stopped short of total conversion. Legally they remained Gentiles in the eyes of Jewish society; to call them 'half'- or 'semi-proselytes' is a misnomer.[2] While the paucity of archaeological evidence has prompted some recent doubts about the existence of 'God-fearers' as a distinct group in first-century Judaism, ancient literary testimony as well as certain inscriptional data still adequately support the consensus position.[3]

---

in Late Antiquity (ed. J. Neusner and E.S. Frerichs; Chico, CA: Scholars Press, 1985), pp. 170-71; Nolland, 'Uncircumcised Proselytes?'. On the requirement of proselyte baptism, see Epictetus, *Diss.* 2.9.20 and comment on this text in M. Stern, *Greek and Latin Authors on Jews and Judaism* (3 vols.; Jerusalem: Israel Academy of Science and Humanities, 1976–84), I, pp. 543-44.

1. Jeremias remarks that the rabbinic consideration of a converted Gentile 'in all things as an Israelite' (*b. Yeb.* 47b) does not imply a parity of status between proselyte and native-born Jew, but merely underscores the proselyte's duty to keep the whole law (*Jerusalem*, p. 323).

2. Cf. F. Siegert, 'Gottesfürchtige und Sympathisanten', *JSJ* 4 (1973), p. 163; K. Lake, 'Proselytes and God-Fearers', in Lake and Cadbury (eds.), *Beginnings of Christianity*, V, p. 76.

3. See Juvenal, *Sat.* 14.96-106; Josephus, *Ant.* 3.127; 14.110; *Apion* 2.282; and the important inscription from the synagogue at Aphrodisias discussed at length in J.M. Reynolds and R. Tannenbaum, *Jews and God-Fearers at Aphrodisias: Greek Inscriptions with Commentary* (Cambridge Philological Society Sup., 12; Cambridge: Cambridge Philological Society, 1987) (see the useful summary in P.R. Trebilco, 'Studies on Jewish Communities in Asia Minor' [unpublished PhD thesis, University of Durham, 1987], pp. 161-64).

The major objector to the traditional perspective on 'God-fearers' has been A.T. Kraabel (see 'The Disappearance of the "God-fearers"', *Numen* 28 [1981], pp. 113-26; 'Greeks, Jews, and Lutherans in the Middle Half of Acts', *HTR* 79 [1986], pp. 147-57). His challenge has been successfully countered, however, by

Josephus's story of the interplay between Izates and certain Jewish missionaries provides a detailed illustration of the proselyte/'God-fearer' options available to Gentiles interested in Judaism.[1] As a Jewish sympathizer and foreigner of high rank (the king of Adiabene), Izates represents a useful test case for comparison with the Ethiopian eunuch. His mother and wives had been instructed by a Jewish merchant named Ananias 'to worship God (τὸν θεὸν σέβειν) after the manner of the Jewish tradition'. Then Izates himself became attracted to Judaism and desired circumcision, 'since he considered he would not be genuinely a Jew unless he was circumcised'. Fearing, however, that such a decision might not be appreciated by Izates' subjects, Ananias advised the king against becoming a proselyte, assuring him that he could 'worship God even without being circumcised (καὶ χωρὶς τῆς περιτομῆς τὸ θεῖον σέβειν) if indeed he had fully decided to be a devoted adherent to Judaism, for it was this that counted more than circumcision'. At this stage Izates appears to be a 'God-fearing' Gentile still on the periphery of Jewish society.

Subsequently, however, a Pharisaic teacher from Galilee, named Eleazar, passed through Adiabene. Upon encountering Izates reading the law of Moses, Eleazar exhorted the king to fulfill the Torah's requirements, particularly that of circumcision. Setting aside any former misgivings, Izates now submitted to circumcision and, in so doing, accepted the badge of the Jewish covenant and became a bona fide proselyte (*Ant.* 20.34-48).

Josephus sheds further light on the eunuch's situation in his report of certain Gentiles who made pilgrimages to Jerusalem.[2] He specifically mentions a group of foreigners who made the arduous journey to the temple only to find themselves barred from full participation in the cultic ceremonies:

Finn ('God-fearers'), J. Gager ('Jews, Gentiles, and Synagogues in the Book of Acts', *HTR* 79 [1986], pp. 91-99) and Trebilco ('Studies on Jewish Communities', pp. 154-77), among others.

1. See the brief but helpful discussion of this story in J.J. Collins, *Between Athens and Jerusalem: Jewish Identity in the Hellenistic Diaspora* (New York: Crossroad, 1983), p. 164.

2. See S. Safrai, *Die Wallfahrt im Zeitalter des Zweiten Tempels* (Forschungen zum jüdisch-christlichen Dialog, 3; Neukirchen–Vluyn: Neukirchener Verlag, 1981), pp. 108-109; 'Relations between the Diaspora and the Land of Israel', in *The Jewish People in the First Century* (ed. S. Safrai and M. Stern; Assen: Van Gorcum, 1974), I, pp. 199-200.

certain persons from beyond the Euphrates, after a journey of four months, undertaken from veneration of our temple and involving great perils and expense, having offered sacrifices, could not partake of the victims, because Moses had forbidden this to any of those not governed by our laws nor affiliated by the customs of their fathers to ourselves (*Ant.* 3.318-19).

Similar alienation is described in *The Jewish War*. Among the pilgrims at Passover season, as recorded in a public census during Nero's reign, was a large contingent of 'foreigners (ἀλλόφυλοι) present for worship', who alongside lepers and other defiled persons 'were not permitted to partake of this sacrifice' (*War* 6.426-27).[1]

Given this background, what can be said about the status of the Ethiopian eunuch? Was he, in Luke's eyes, a proselyte or 'God-fearer'? A major problem clouding this issue is the usage of προσήλυτος or φοβούμενος/σεβόμενος τὸν θεόν terminology elsewhere in Luke's writing—but *not* in Acts 8. This has prompted Haenchen and others to conclude that Luke has purposefully blurred the socioreligious status of the eunuch.[2] According to this view, the tradition of Philip's evangelization of the eunuch marked the first conversion of a Gentile (i.e. 'God-fearer') in Hellenist–Christian circles. Luke, however, regarded Peter's convert, Cornelius, as the first Gentile believer and so was compelled to reformulate the eunuch incident in such a way as to leave the eunuch's status ambiguous. By avoiding 'God-fearer' language in Acts 8 which he used in 10.2, 22 (cf. v. 35), Luke effectively distanced Philip's convert from Cornelius and other Gentile Christians.

The lack of customary labels to identify the Ethiopian eunuch may well be grounds for concluding that Luke did not regard him as a proselyte. Gentile converts to Judaism are consistently designated as προσήλυτοι in Acts (2.10; 6.5; 13.43),[3] and there is no obvious case

---

1. On temple restrictions against 'God-fearers', see Esler, *Community and Gospel*, pp. 145-67.

2. Haenchen, *Acts*, p. 314; Schneider, *Apostelgeschichte*, I, pp. 498-500; Weiser, *Apostelgeschichte*, I, pp. 208-209; J.-W. Taeger, *Der Mensch und sein Heil: Studien zum Bild des Menschen und zur Sicht der Bekehrung bei Lukas* (SNT, 14; Gütersloh: Gutersloher/Gerd Mohn, 1983), pp. 208-10.

3. Cf. M. Wilcox, 'The "God-Fearers" in Acts—A Reconsideration', *JSNT* 13 (1981), p. 108; Kuhn, 'προσήλυτος', pp. 742-43. J.A. Overman contends that, because Luke distinguishes προσήλυτος from Ἰουδαῖος in Acts 2.10 and 13.43, he never employs προσήλυτος in the technical sense of a Gentile convert to

where Luke envisages a proselyte without using the appropriate term. Moreover, proselytes, like Nicolaus of Antioch, were already part of the Christian community before Acts 8 (6.5; cf. 2.10, 41), thus making it difficult to account for Luke's failure to classify the eunuch as a proselyte if such was his conception of the man.

Concerning the 'God-fearer' question, however, the linguistic argument from silence is not so convincing. Luke identifies Cornelius as a φοβούμενος τὸν θεόν (Acts 10.2, 22) and as a devout (εὐσεβής, 10.2, 7), upright (δίκαιος, 10.22), Jewish-sympathizing—but still *uncircumcised* (10.45; 11.3) Gentile: in other words, a 'God-fearer', according to the description given above. Generally speaking, however, Luke does not employ φοβούμενος/σεβόμενος τὸν θεόν as a clear-cut *terminus technicus* for a class of Gentiles marginally devoted to Judaism.[1] Lydia and Titius Justus are both characterized as σεβόμενοι τὸν θεόν (16.14; 18.7) and may fit the conventional 'God-fearer' category, but in fact too little is known about them (had Justus been circumcised?) to ascertain their precise relationship to Judaism. Elsewhere in Luke–Acts φοβέομαι and σέβομαι are applied broadly to 'anyone' who reveres God (Acts 10.35; 18.13; Lk. 1.50)[2] as well as to the native Jew (Jesus, Lk. 23.40) and proselytes (τῶν σεβομένων προσηλύτων, 13.43).[3]

Moreover, Luke does not always apply the 'God-fearer' tag when referring to Gentiles attracted—but not converted—to Judaism. In other words, one does not have to be called a 'God-fearer' in Luke–Acts to be a 'God-fearer', as defined by modern scholarship. On two occasions Gentile worshippers at Diaspora synagogues are simply

Judaism ('The God-Fearers: Some Neglected Factors', *JSNT* 32 [1988], p. 20). However, Overman fails to appreciate the social status of proselytes discussed above: while they were fully accepted into the Jewish community, at the same time they continued to be classed in a distinct, slightly inferior, category from native-born Jews.

1. See Wilcox, ' "God-Fearers" ', pp. 102-22; Lake, 'Proselytes and God-fearers', pp. 85-88.

2. Note even the context of pagan worship in Acts 19.27: 'the great goddess Artemis. . . she will be deprived of her majesty that brought all Asia and the world to worship (σέβεται) her'.

3. Realizing the generalized, non-technical meaning of σέβομαι in Luke–Acts, there is no need to follow scholars such as Kuhn ('προσήλυτος', p. 743) who regard προσήλυτος in 13.43 as an inaccurate Lukan slip or later textual gloss. Cf. Wilcox, ' "God-Fearers" ', pp. 108-109.

identified as 'Greeks' ("Ελληνες, Acts 14.1; 18.4). The centurion in Luke 7 is not labelled a 'God-fearer', but as an honored lover of the Jewish nation and patron of the Capernaum synagogue (7.5), he closely parallels Cornelius, the 'God-fearing' centurion in Acts.[1] Finally, P.F. Esler suggests that Naaman represents a prototypical 'God-fearer' in Luke's eyes—although no such terminology emerges in Lk. 4.27—since the underlying Kings story recounts the Syrian general's acknowledgment of Israel's God (5.15) and yet gives no hint of circumcision or incorporation into the Israelite community.[2] This example is particularly instructive in view of the correspondence between Naaman and the Ethiopian eunuch sketched above.

This fluidity in terminology cautions against hinging one's judgment concerning the eunuch's social status on the presence or absence of φοβούμενος/σεβόμενος τὸν θεόν in Acts 8. If such language had been employed, he could not automatically be classified as a 'God-fearer' in the technical sense; by the same token, the lack of 'God-fearer' language does not preclude from Luke's perspective a fundamental link in status between the eunuch and Cornelius. Other criteria than word choice must come into play.

The eunuch's pilgrimage to worship at Jerusalem demonstrates in principle that he 'feared' God (although προσκυνέω is used instead of φοβέομαι/σέβομαι) and corresponds to the practice of other 'God-fearers' outlined above (cf. *Ant.* 3.318-19; *War* 6.426-27; Jn 12.20). Also, his high rank as a court official and serious interest in the Jewish Scriptures both recall the example of the 'God-fearer' Izates—before he was circumcised. Thus, the possibility that Luke regarded the eunuch as a 'God-fearing' Gentile—on a par with Cornelius—should not be dismissed. On the other hand, at this stage in the discussion neither can the possibility of the eunuch's proselyte status be ruled out completely (although it seems unlikely). A conclusive decision must await a careful examination of the key term in Acts 8 designating Philip's convert: εὐνοῦχος.

---

1. As the Jewish elders report to Jesus that the Capernaum centurion 'loves our people (τὸ ἔθνος)' (Lk. 7.4-5), so members of Cornelius's household inform Peter that their master 'is well spoken of by the whole Jewish nation (τοῦ ἔθνους)' (Acts 10.22). For an extended treatment of the links between the two centurion incidents, see G. Muhlack, *Die Parallelen von Lukas-Evangelium und Apostelgeschichte* (Theologie und Wirklichkeit, 8; Frankfurt: Lang, 1979), pp. 39-71.

2. Esler, *Community and Gospel*, p. 35.

c. *The Meaning and Social Significance of* Εὐνοῦχος

The term εὐνοῦχος can refer to a castrated man, a public official or both, since court attendants in antiquity were often eunuchs in the physical sense.[1] In the LXX εὐνοῦχος uniformly renders the Hebrew *saris*, whose meaning is also variable. Applied to the married Potiphar (Gen. 39.1) εὐνοῦχος patently denotes only a military officer; other references are plainly limited to *castrati* (Isa. 56.3-4; Sir. 30.20). Most instances, however, refer broadly to military and political officials, especially those serving as palace courtiers; in these contexts, both physical and vocational notions could easily apply.[2]

Since in Acts 8 the Ethiopian εὐνοῦχος is also characterized as a queen's δυνάστης, some have thought that the εὐνοῦχος designation merely reinforces the chamberlain's official status and does not suggest any physical handicap.[3] On one occasion the LXX renders *saris* with δυνάστης (Jer. 41[34].19), instead of the more customary εὐνοῦχος, so it is possible that Luke understood the two Greek terms as interchangeable. Nevertheless, a stronger case can be made supporting Luke's emphasis on the physical connotation of εὐνοῦχος. First, Luke periodically features public figures as beset by some bodily 'defect'. Naaman, the Syrian general afflicted with leprosy, is the most obvious example (Lk. 4.27), but not to be ignored are the cases of the Capernaum centurion; the synagogue ruler, Jairus; and Publius, the 'chief man' of Malta—all of whom, though not personally debilitated, are deeply distressed over the infirmities of a close friend or relative which they appear helpless to remedy (Lk. 7.2-3; 8.41-42; Acts 28.7-8). Secondly, the deployment of εὐνοῦχος and δυνάστης Κανδάκης in immediate succession in Acts 8.27 most naturally communicates two discrete characteristics; otherwise, if the designations were

---

1. Especially in oriental societies (e.g. Persia). On εὐνοῦχος in the ancient world, see J. Schneider, 'εὐνοῦχος, εὐνουχίζω', *TDNT*, II, pp. 765-68; G. Petzke, 'εὐνοῦχος', *EWNT*, II, pp. 202-204; 'Eunuchen', in A.F. Pauly, G. Wissowa *et al.* (eds.), *Real-Encyclopädie der klassischen Altertumswissenschaft*, Sup. vol. III, cols. 449-55; L.H. Gray, 'Eunuch', *Encyclopedia of Religion and Ethics*, V, pp. 579-84.

2. See numerous references in the book of Esther (1.1, 10, 12, 15, 21; 2.3, 14, 15, 21, 23; 4.4, 5; 6.2, 14; 7.9); 4 Kgdms 8.6; 9.32; 20.18; 2 Chron. 18.8; Jer. 36 (29).2.

3. Wilson, *Gentiles*, p. 171; Hahn, *Mission*, p. 62 n. 2; R.N. Longenecker, 'The Acts of the Apostles', in *The Expositor's Bible Commentary*, IX, p. 363; de Meester, '"Philippe"', p. 363.

identical, one would seem to be semantically superfluous.[1] Thirdly, if Luke desired only to stress the Ethiopian's courtly position and not to raise the question of his sexual identity as well, it is difficult to see why he repeatedly utilized the ambiguous εὐνοῦχος and allowed it to stand alone in four out of five occurrences without any clarifying term like δυνάστης. Finally, the Ethiopian's role as servant of an oriental queen also intimates his status as a physically-impaired eunuch. For obvious reasons, the male attendants to a female royal figure were often castrated.[2]

In view of this apparent characterization of the Ethiopian as a castrated man, we are pressed to explore the place of such a figure within ancient society. In brief, as G. Petzke states, eunuchs in antiquity typically 'gehörten. . . zu den am meisten verachteten und verspotteten Menschengruppen'.[3] Often they were slaves who had been brutalized by other men as a form of punishment or subjugation.[4] Even those eunuchs who were fortunate enough to rise to positions of power and responsibility could not wholly escape the stigma associated with their

1. Cf. Petzke, 'εὐνοῦχος', p. 204; Dinkler, 'Philippus', p. 92.

2. As in the book of Esther. Among those supporting the status of the Ethiopian official as a eunuch in the physical sense, see (in addition to the sources in the previous note) Bornhäuser, *Studien zur Apostelgeschichte*, pp. 95-99; K. Löning, 'Der Stephanuskreis und seine Mission', in *Die Anfänge des Christentums: Alte Welt und neue Hoffnung* (ed. J. Becker *et al.*; Stuttgart: Kohlhammer, 1987), p. 88; Bachmann, *Jerusalem*, pp. 290-91; Taeger, *Mensch*, p. 209 n. 867; Krodel, *Acts*, p. 168.

3. Petzke, 'εὐνοῦχος', p. 202; cf. Gray: 'The social status of the eunuch has always been of the lowest' ('Eunuch', p. 582).

4. Cf. Petzke, 'εὐνοῦχος', p. 202; 'Eunuchen', in Pauly, Wissowa *et al.* (eds.), *Real-Encyclopädie*, col. 449. It should also be mentioned that certain men voluntarily submitted to castration (including self-castration in some cases) for religious reasons, such as priests in Asiatic fertility cults (e.g. Cybele) and some distinguished early Christian bishops (e.g. Melito, Origen; cf. Eusebius, *Eccl. Hist.* 5.24.5; 6.8.2-3). However, despite some tendency to spiritualize castration, the attitude toward eunuchs in the ancient world remained basically negative. As P. Brown states after discussing Origen's case:

> The eunuch was notorious (and repulsive to many) because he had dared to shift the massive boundary between the sexes. He had opted out of being male. By losing the sexual 'heat' that was held to cause his facial hair to grow, the eunuch was no longer recognizable as a man. He was a human being 'exiled from either gender' (*The Body and Society: Men, Women and Sexual Renunciation in Early Christianity* [New York: Columbia University Press, 1988], p. 169; cf. pp. 9-11, 17-19, 66-69, 168-69).

peculiar condition.[1] Herodotus tells of a eunuch in Xerxes' court, named Hermotimus, who enjoyed the special favor of the king. However, when opportunity presented itself, Hermotimus exacted vicious revenge on the man who was responsible for his castration and enslavement, for making him 'to be no man. . . a thing of nought'. Exercising his acquired authority, Hermotimus eventually sought out this practitioner of 'the wickedest trade on earth' and forced him to castrate his own sons and they in turn their father (8.104-106). Closer to the New Testament period, the satirist Lucian narrates a tale of a (supposed) eunuch who was in the running for one of the chairs of philosophy at Athens. Despite his intellectual qualifications for the post, the eunuch's physical condition proved to be a serious liability. Witness the scornful remarks of his chief competitor in Lucian's story: '. . . such people [eunuchs] ought to be excluded. . . not simply from all that [philosophy] but even from temples and holy-water bowls and all the places of public assembly' (*The Eunuch* 6).[2]

Eunuchs fared no better, if not worse, in ancient *Jewish* society. The stark Mosaic mandate in Deut. 23.1 (23.2 LXX) was fundamental: 'No one whose testicles are crushed or whose penis is cut off shall be admitted to the assembly of the Lord'. The rationale for this exclusionary policy presumably had to do with a eunuch's incapacity for procreation and (in the case of dismemberment) circumcision, both of which were regarded as sacred acts vital to the identity of every Jewish male.[3] B. Malina (following Jeremias) classifies eunuchs within first-century Judaism alongside bastards, orphans and foundlings as unfortunates who

> had a grave genealogical impediment about them: they were simply not whole and complete. They could not properly trace their ancestry, might derive from highly disreputable ancestors, and in the case of the eunuch, could no longer transmit covenant status.[4]

1. On the role of eunuchs in the Roman court, see J.P.V.D. Balsdon, *Romans and Aliens* (Chapel Hill: University of North Carolina, 1979), pp. 227-30. Following Titus's reputation for favoring eunuchs, Domitian officially prohibited castration throughout the empire. Hadrian later bolstered this edict with the death penalty for violators.

2. Citations are from Herodotus (ed. and trans. A.D. Godley; LCL; Cambridge, MA: Harvard University Press; London: Heinemann, 1920–26); and Lucian (ed. and trans. Harmon, Kilburn and MacLeod; LCL).

3. Schneider, 'εὐνοῦχος', p. 766.

4. B. Malina, *The New Testament World: Insights from Cultural Anthropology*

Also, an emasculated man was certainly judged to be physically blemished or deformed and thus in a permanent state of ritual impurity (cf. Lev. 21.20; 22.24).[1]

That this ban on eunuchs within the Jewish community was current during the New Testament era is plainly manifest in comments from Josephus and Philo.[2] The former writer vigorously enjoined total separation from eunuchs, principally because of their perceived opposition to the created order.

> Shun eunuchs and flee all dealings with those who have deprived themselves of their virility and of those fruits of generation, which God has given to men for the increase of our race; expel them even as infanticides who withal have destroyed the means of procreation. For plainly it is by reason of the effeminacy of their soul that they changed the sex of their body also. And so with all that would be deemed a monstrosity by the beholders. Ye shall castrate neither man nor beast (*Ant.* 4.290-91).

Similarly, in the category of 'all the unworthy' barred from entering the sacred congregation, Philo placed

> the men who belie their sex and are affected with effemination, who debase the currency of nature and violate it by assuming the passions and the outward form of licentious women. For it [the law] expels those whose generative organs are fractured or mutilated (*Spec. Leg.* 1.324-25).

In marked contrast, however, to this Torah-based exclusion of eunuchs, advocated by most Jewish authorities, at least two voices registered a counter-opinion supporting a legitimate place for devout eunuchs within the covenant community. In the first, the postexilic 'Isaiah' announced to 'God-fearing' eunuchs—alongside foreigners—

(Atlanta: John Knox, 1981), p. 133; cf. Jeremias, *Jerusalem*, pp. 337-44.

1. Cf. G. Stählin ('ἀποκόπτω', *TDNT*, III, p. 854), who also points out the probable association in Jewish law between emasculation and other forbidden 'cutting' operations characteristic of pagan practice (cf. Lev. 19.28; Deut. 14.1).

2. The Mishnah also enforces the Deuteronomic ban against eunuchs (*m. Yeb.* 8.1-2), although there was some tendency to distinguish between the status of those who were eunuchs 'by nature' (i.e. from birth) and those who had been mutilated by men (*m. Yeb.* 8.4-6; cf. Mt. 19.12, no Lukan parallel). Cf. Jeremias, *Jerusalem*, pp. 343-44.

the blessed prospects of 'spiritual fruitfulness'[1] and incorporation into
God's household:

> Do not let the *foreigner* joined to the Lord say,
> 'The Lord will surely separate me from his people';
> and do not let the *eunuch* say,
> 'I am just a dry tree'.
> For thus says the Lord:
> To the *eunuchs* who keep my sabbaths,
> who choose the things that please me
> and hold fast my covenant,
> I will give, in my house and within my walls,
> a monument and a name better than sons and daughters;
> I will give them an everlasting name
> that shall not be cut off.
> And the *foreigners* who join themselves to the Lord,
> to minister to him, to love the name of the Lord, and to be his servants,
> all who keep the sabbath,
> and do not profane it,
> and hold fast my covenant—
> these I will bring to my holy mountain,
> and make them joyful in my house of prayer;
> their burnt offerings and their sacrifices
> will be accepted on my altar;
> *for my house shall be called a house of prayer*
> *for all peoples* (Isa. 56.3-8).

Similar hopes were held out for eunuchs (alongside barren women) in
a Hellenistic–Jewish piece from the first century BCE:

> Blessed also is the eunuch whose hands have done no lawless deed,
> and who has not devised wicked things against the Lord;
> for special favor will be shown him for his faithfulness, and a
> place of great delight in the temple of the Lord.
> For the fruit of good labors is renowned, and the root of
> understanding does not fail (Wis. 3.14-15; cf. vv. 13-19).

Considering these divergent views on the socioreligious status of
eunuchs within ancient Judaism, Luke's treatment of the Ethiopian
eunuch clearly reflects a closer leaning to the more 'liberal' stance of
Trito-Isaiah and the Wisdom writer. Indeed, as many have supposed,
it is likely that Luke was directly influenced by the material in Isaiah

---

1. Cf. M. Callaway, *Sing, O Barren One: A Study in Comparative Midrash*
(SBLDS, 91; Atlanta: Scholars Press, 1986), pp. 91-94.

56, given its proximity to the cited passage from Isaiah 53[1] and obvious relevance to the God-worshipping foreigner–eunuch–pilgrim featured in Acts 8.[2] Thus, it appears that Luke conceived of Philip's evangelization of the Ethiopian eunuch as the realization (at least in part) of the expected opening of God's household to 'all peoples' (πᾶσιν τοῖς ἔθνεσιν, Isa. 56.7).

Still, it is important to appreciate that, despite the similarities between Luke and Isaiah, Luke goes significantly further in endorsing open access for eunuchs into the covenant community. As H. Kee notes, while Isaiah 56 opens the covenant door to the same outcast groups (foreigners/eunuchs) welcomed by Luke, the requirements for entry remain restrictively tied to the Jewish cult; these obligations 'include observing the Sabbath, bringing the proper sacrifices to the temple, and offering prayer and worship in the holy mountain'.[3] By contrast, Luke imposes no such duties on would-be converts.

In the case of the Ethiopian eunuch, his trek to Jerusalem—for all its show of genuine piety—does not make him a part of God's covenant people. In Luke's eyes, this covenant status is conferred through receiving the Christian gospel and baptism along a 'deserted' path outside Holy City limits. The Judaism known to Luke still 'prevented' (κωλύω, Acts 8.36) the full acceptance of eunuchs, even devout ones. The Jerusalem temple never fulfills its destiny of becoming a 'house of prayer for all peoples', irrespective of sexual (eunuchs) and racial (foreigners) identity (cf. Lk. 19.46; Mk 11.17; Isa. 56.7).[4] The Jews

---

1. Luke, of course, would not have been greatly bothered by our modern distinctions between 'Second' and 'Third' Isaiah.

2. Cf. Esler, *Community and Gospel*, pp. 160-62; Sanders, *Jews*, p. 152; Bornhäuser, *Studien zur Apostelgeschichte*, pp. 96-97; Martin, 'Chamberlain's Journey', pp. 108-109. In a brief article, R.J. Porter suggests that, in addition to Isa. 54.4-8, the Isaianic background to the eunuch story includes 54.9-10 and 55.1— passages supposedly applicable to Christian baptism ('What Did Philip Say to the Eunuch?', *ExpTim* 100 [1988–89], pp. 54-55). However, the baptismal connection is tenuous at best: the 'waters of Noah' seem far removed from the eunuch episode. If another text relevant to the eunuch's situation is sought in Isa. 53–56, a better choice would be 54.1-3, proclaiming the marvelous fecundity of the formerly 'barren one'.

3. Kee, *Knowing the Truth*, p. 94.

4. In the Lukan account of the temple-cleansing, Jesus appeals to Isa. 56.7 ('My house shall be a house of prayer', Lk. 19.46) *without* the final phrase—'for all the nations'—included in the Markan parallel (11.17). In Marshall's opinion (*Gospel of*

in Luke–Acts—especially the Pharisees—are greatly concerned with maintaining standards of cultic purity and thus may be assumed to uphold the segregating stipulations of Deut. 23.1. They would no more sanction covenant partnership with defiled and disfigured eunuchs than with lepers, cripples, harlots, tax collectors and other such 'sinners' (cf. Lk. 7.36-50; 14.1-24; 15.1-32; 17.11-19; 18.9-14; 19.1-10).[1] The impossibility of circumcision for many eunuchs would particularly (and permanently) certify their outsider status (cf. Acts 15.1, 5). And since such a separatist stance would be taken against Jewish eunuchs, how much more against a Gentile eunuch like the Ethiopian!

Consequently, in relation to the Judaism familiar to Luke, the foreign official encountered by Philip could not have become a proselyte even if he wanted to. He must have remained a 'God-fearer', barred from access to the inner courts of the temple and the inner circles of Jewish society.[2] Only in the newly constituted messianic community established through Jesus Christ (whom Philip proclaims) does the Ethiopian eunuch at last find a home among the people of God.

d. *Conclusion*

This extended investigation into the social status of the Ethiopian eunuch has uncovered a multi-dimensional character eminently suited

---

Luke, p. 721), this omission has to do with Luke's awareness that the Jerusalem temple never became a gathering center of worship for all peoples. This accords with the view that Luke especially sees Isaiah's hope of 'multi-national' restoration realized in the Ethiopian eunuch's acceptance of the Christian gospel—apart from the temple!

1. J.A. Ziesler has correctly demonstrated that Luke's portrait of the Pharisees is by no means a wholly negative one. Particularly in Acts certain Pharisees (e.g. Gamaliel) appear on the side of the Christian movement (5.33-39; 23.6-10) ('Luke and the Pharisees', *NTS* 25 [1978–79], pp. 146-57). However, alongside this more positive presentation, one must not overlook Luke's recurrent and poignant critique of certain Pharisees and scribes for their self-righteous and exclusivist demeanor in relation to impure 'sinners' (cf. J.T. Sanders, *Jews*, pp. 84-131; Saldarini, *Pharisees*, pp. 174-87; Moxnes, *Economy*, pp. 10-21).

2. Cf. Esler, *Community and Gospel*, pp. 154-63; Bachmann, *Jerusalem*, pp. 291-97; contra Cadbury: 'Whether in point of fact a eunuch could have become a proselyte or been admitted to the service of the Temple is a query which probably did not interest Luke' ('The Hellenists', in Lake and Cadbury [eds.], *Beginnings of Christianity*, V, p. 66).

to Luke's presentation of the early church's expanding mission. He is, as B. Gaventa puts it, a 'symbolic convert'—symbolic of the inclusive and barrier-breaking thrust of the Christian gospel.[1] He appears as a well-to-do public official of some prominence, and yet at the same time, he bears as a castrated man a certain ignominy reserved only for the lowest classes in the ancient world. What is more, he is a foreigner—a Gentile—who, whatever his devotion to the God of Israel, is doomed as a eunuch to remain forever on the margins of Jewish society. No attempt is made to blur or play down this outsider status. The Ethiopian eunuch fits the same basic category of 'God-fearer' (the absence of the term notwithstanding) as the Roman centurion, Cornelius. If anything, the Ethiopian is more alienated from Judaism than Cornelius, because Cornelius could presumably become a proselyte if he so desired, whereas this option is closed to the eunuch.

In sketching this social profile of the Ethiopian eunuch, we gain further valuable insight into the significance of Philip's evangelistic ministry. By reaching out in proclamation and baptism to such a distinctive individual, Philip stands out once again in Luke's narrative as a pioneering minister of the gospel to 'all flesh'. We must especially underscore Philip's achievement in converting a Gentile ('God-fearer') to Christianity. Accordingly, Philip must be allowed his fair share of the credit, normally reserved exclusively for Peter, for inaugurating the early church's Gentile mission in Acts.

7. *Philip's Ministry to the Ethiopian Eunuch*

After examining a variety of literary, theological, geographical and social elements related to Acts 8.25-40, we must finally focus directly on the heart of the story in 8.30-38. In particular, I will examine the nature and significance of the two main components of Philip's evangelistic ministry: proclamation and baptism.

a. *Proclamation*
As in the report of Philip's Samaritan mission, so in the present

---

1. Gaventa, *From Darkness to Light*, p. 106; contra W.H. Willimon, who classifies the Ethiopian official only as 'a well-placed and significant person' and plays down any notions of the figure as 'despised or deprived' (*Acts* [Interpretation; Atlanta: John Knox, 1988], p. 72).

narrative, no speech is placed in the evangelist's mouth disclosing the content of his preaching. A general description, however, is provided, once again identifying Philip's message as 'the good news about Jesus' (Acts 8.35; cf. 8.5, 12). More specifically, this proclamation is linked to a foundational prophetic text: Isa. 53.7-8a (Acts 8.30-35).

As sketched above, the citation and discussion of Isa. 53.7-8a marks the structural pivot of the entire eunuch story. The exchange between Philip and the eunuch revolves around the proper interpretation of the Isaiah text, especially pertaining to the identity of the afflicted 'servant'.[1] When Philip first meets him, the eunuch is riding in a chariot and reading from Isaiah. This situation prompts Philip's first words, a query as to whether the eunuch comprehends what he is reading; the reply comes back: 'How can I, unless someone guides me?' Philip then climbs aboard at the eunuch's behest, clearly assuming the role of the required interpreter (Acts 8.30-31). Directly, Philip's specific interpretive assignment is revealed. It concerns a selected Isaianic text and a pointed question regarding its referent: 'About whom. . . does the prophet say this, about himself or about someone else?' Philip responds by proclaiming Jesus—'starting with this Scripture' (8.34-35). Although the substance of Philip's preaching is not recounted in detail, we are left with little doubt that Jesus is identified as a 'suffering servant' whose recent experiences parallel those of the mysterious figure in Isaiah 53.[2] In short, Jesus is the answer to the eunuch's exegetical question and, as it turns out, to his spiritual quest as well.

A thorough delving into the significance of the Acts citation of Isa. 53.7-8a demands careful consideration of the function of this text within the wider literary context of Luke–Acts and the immediate social context of evangelizing a Jewish-sympathizing foreigner and eunuch. These matters have rarely been given sufficient attention in scholarly discussion. Investigations into the New Testament's use of Isaiah 53 have tended to serve predominantly historical and dogmatic interests, such as whether Jesus himself and/or the earliest Jewish-

---

1. The terminology of 'servant' or 'suffering servant', while not a part of the Acts citation from Isa. 53 (cf. C.K. Barrett, 'Luke/Acts', in *It is Written: Scripture Citing Scripture: Essays in Honour of Barnabas Lindars, SSF* [ed. D.A. Carson and H.G.M. Williamson; Cambridge: Cambridge University Press, 1988], p. 239), may still be used as a convenient shorthand for the featured figure.

2. Cf. Bock, *Proclamation*, pp. 229-30.

Christian communities conceived of Jesus as the promised servant–messiah whose vicarious death effectively atoned for sin.[1] Increasingly, however, doubts have been raised concerning the primitive origins of a servant Christology,[2] and evidence has been marshalled supporting a striking *Lukan* interest in Isaianic prophecy in general and servant Christology in particular beyond that of merely preserving early traditions.[3] Even so, little has been done to demonstrate how the particular text (not the full-blown servant image) quoted from Isaiah 53 coordinates with salient Lukan themes and the eunuch's peculiar social identity.[4]

The Acts citation of Isaiah 53 reproduces the LXX text virtually verbatim,[5] commencing just after the reference to the servant's sin-bearing in v. 6 (καὶ κύριος παρέδωκεν αὐτὸν ταῖς ἁμαρτίαις ἡμῶν, 'and the Lord laid on him the iniquity of us all') and cutting off just before a similar reference in v. 8b (ἀπὸ τῶν ἀνομιῶν τοῦ λαοῦ μου ἤχθη εἰς θάνατον, 'because of the iniquities of my people he was led to death'). Thus, with respect to the servant's death, Luke seems studiously to avoid any hint to atoning efficacy, highlighting instead the element of ταπείνωσις (vv. 7-8a).[6] R. Leivestad has

1. E.g. Cullmann, *Christology*, pp. 51-82; Jeremias, 'παῖς θεοῦ', *TDNT*, V, pp. 700-17; Longenecker, *The Christology of Early Jewish Christianity* (Grand Rapids: Baker, repr. 1981 [1970]), pp. 104-109.

2. Cf. Cadbury, 'Titles of Jesus', pp. 364-70; M.D. Hooker, *Jesus and the Servant: The Influence of the Servant Concept of Deutero-Isaiah in the New Testament* (London: SPCK, 1959); O'Neill, *Theology*, pp. 133-39; D. Juel, *Messianic Exegesis: Christological Interpretation of the Old Testament in Early Christianity* (Philadelphia: Fortress Press, 1988), pp. 119-33.

3. On Luke's interest in Isaiah, see Dupont, *Salvation*, pp. 141-46; J.A. Sanders, 'Isaiah in Luke', *Int* 36 (1982), pp. 144-55; D. Seccombe, 'Luke and Isaiah', *NTS* 27 (1980–81), pp. 252-59. On Luke's servant Christology, see E. Franklin, *Christ the Lord: A Study in the Purpose and Theology of Luke–Acts* (London: SPCK, 1975), pp. 60-64; D.L. Jones, 'The Title "Servant"', in Talbert (ed.), *Luke–Acts: New Perspectives*, pp. 148-65; Tiede, *Prophecy and History*, pp. 43-46; Fitzmyer, *Luke*, I, pp. 211-13.

4. P.B. Decock does carefully examine the citation's overarching Lukan context, but he fails to analyze adequately the function of the quotation in its immediate setting of the eunuch story ('The Understanding of Isaiah 53:7-8 in Acts 8:32-35', *Neot* 14 [1981], pp. 111-33).

5. Luke makes only two minor changes in the LXX: adds αὐτοῦ and alters κείροντος to κείραντος.

6. Cf. Hooker, *Jesus and the Servant*, pp. 113-14; Cadbury, *Making of Luke–*

argued that in biblical usage ταπείνωσις (and cognates ταπεινόω and ταπεινός) consistently retains its negative, 'secular' connotation of 'humiliation' or 'debasement' (*Niedrigkeit*) and has not become colored by the more noble, 'theological' shades of 'humility' or 'meekness' (*Demut*), as in the case of ταπεινόφρων/ταπεινοφροσύνη.[1] Like a helpless sheep led to the slaughter, the Isaianic servant experiences unmitigated oppression and degradation (Acts 8.32-33a).

But such is not the whole story. The servant's humiliation, while not leading directly to the expiation of sin, apparently does give way to something positive: the servant's personal exaltation. This reversal of the servant's bad fortune may be envisaged already in the phrase—ἡ κρίσις αὐτοῦ ἤρθη—from the opening line of Acts 8.33, which can be rendered, 'his judgment/condemnation was taken away'.[2] However, κρίσις can also connote the idea of 'justice' (cf. Lk. 11.42), in which case the phrase in question simply reinforces the servant's debasement (NRSV: 'In his humiliation justice was denied him'; cf. REB, JB, NIV). In any case, whatever the interpretation of 8.33a, the final statement in v. 33 seems to strike a hopeful note regarding the servant's ultimate destiny: ὅτι αἴρεται ἀπὸ τῆς γῆς ἡ ζωὴ αὐτοῦ (8.33c). Here, too, an element of ambiguity must be acknowledged. The verb αἴρω used both in 8.33(a) and (c) can signify either 'take away' (remove, deprive) or 'take up' (lift, raise), While the former meaning alone fits the context of the first line in 8.33, either meaning could logically govern the last line. Still, within Luke's overall presentation, the notion of 'lifting up' the servant's life in exaltation is the more convincing option, as it calls to mind the peculiarly Lukan account of Jesus' ascension into heaven (Lk. 24.51; Acts 1.2, 9-11)[3] and the

---

Acts, pp. 280-81 n. 2; M. Rese, *Alttestamentlich Motive in der Christologie des Lukas* (SNT, 1; Gütersloh: Gerd Mohn, 1969), pp. 98-100; E. Kränkl, *Jesus der Knecht Gottes: Die heilsgeschichtliche Stellung Jesu in den Reden der Apostelgeschichte* (Biblische Untersuchungen, 8; Regensburg: Pustet, 1972), p. 115; R.J. Dillon, 'Acts of the Apostles', in *The New Jerome Biblical Commentary* (ed. R.E. Brown, J.A. Fitzmyer and R.E. Murphy; Englewood Cliffs, NJ: Prentice–Hall, 1990), p. 743.

1. R. Leivestad, 'Ταπεινός-ταπεινόφρων', *NovT* (1966), pp. 36-47. On humility/humiliation in the biblical world, see K. Wengst, *Humility: Solidarity of the Humiliated* (Philadelphia: Fortress Press, 1988).

2. So Haenchen, *Acts*, p. 312; G. Schneider, *Apostelgeschichte*, I, pp. 504-505; Roloff, *Apostelgeschichte*, p. 141.

3. Juel, *Messianic Exegesis*, p. 128.

emphasis on 'raising up' (glorifying) God's prophet/servant in the Petrine speeches in Acts (2.22-24, 31-36; 3.13-15, 22-26). By concluding his citation of Isa. 53.8 with an upward focus, Luke accentuates the crowning transformation of the servant-Jesus' humiliation into exaltation. A similar emphasis emerges in the Emmaus narrative, where the Lukan Jesus expounds the prophetic Scriptures to demonstrate how necessary it was 'that the messiah should suffer. . . and then enter into his glory' (Lk. 24.25-27).

The humiliation–exaltation pattern is featured repeatedly in Luke's writing.[1] In the Magnificat Mary exults over the Lord's thoughtful consideration of her 'lowliness' (ταπείνωσις), evidenced in his extraordinary blessing destined to be remembered by all future generations (Lk. 1.48). Moreover, Mary regards her experience as typical of the Lord's dealings with humankind: 'he has brought down the powerful (δυνάστας) from their thrones, and lifted up the lowly (ταπείνωσις)' (1.52). This inversion of traditional societal positions is also a key part of Jesus' agenda in Luke's Gospel, as disclosed in John the Baptist's poetic prediction of the effects of Jesus' work (drawn from Isaiah and cited only by Luke): 'Every valley shall be filled, and every mountain and hill shall be made low (ταπεινωθήσεται). . . and all flesh shall see the salvation of God' (Lk. 3.5-6; Isa. 40.4-5). This pattern of ministry is fulfilled in both Jesus' action and teaching. He restores the ill to health (e.g. Lk. 5.12-26), accords love and dignity to notorious 'sinners' (e.g. 7.36-50) and enables hopeless outcasts to re-enter the mainstream of society (e.g. 8.26-39). And especially in parables addressed to Pharisees, Jesus drives home the thrust of his social program: 'For all who exalt themselves will be humbled (ταπεινωθήσεται) and those who humble themselves (ὁ ταπεινῶν) will be exalted' (14.11; 18.14). That is, those in the lowest places at the wedding banquet will be promoted (14.6-10), and those alienated from worship in the temple will be accepted (18.9-14).[2]

---

1. See Decock, 'Understanding of Isaiah 53:7-8', pp. 115-22.

2. Another way of approaching the humiliation–exaltation motif is through the honor–shame code characteristic of first-century Mediterranean culture. On the general importance of these 'pivotal values' in antiquity, see Malina, *New Testament World*, pp. 25-50. Applied more specifically to Luke (e.g. the 'Pharisee' parables in Lk. 14.7-24 and 18.9-14), see D. Daube, 'Shame Culture in Luke', in *Paul and Paulinism: Essays in Honour of C.K. Barrett* (ed. M.D. Hooker and S.G. Wilson; London: SPCK, 1982), pp. 355-72; Moxnes, *Economy*, pp. 134-38; Gowler,

Not only, however, does Jesus act and speak on behalf of the oppressed in order to elevate their social status; he also personally identifies with their plight in a dramatic way. 'He [is] counted among the lawless' in his death (Lk. 22.37; Isa. 53.12),[1] literally crucified between two convicted criminals (23.32). Yet he rises again to new life (24.1-53) and paves the way to 'paradise' not only for himself, but also for one of the felons who died with him (23.43).[2] A bridge is thus built from Luke's Gospel to the portrait of Jesus in Acts 8. Jesus himself underwent ταπείνωσις in death, yet ultimately was 'taken up' (αἴρεται) in renewed life to an exalted state.

Another important line cited from Isaiah 53 in the eunuch narrative, whose meaning must be ascertained in relation to the literary context of Luke–Acts, is the enigmatic query in Acts 8.33b: τὴν γενεὰν αὐτοῦ τίς διηγήσεται; the interpretive crux is the sense of γενεά in this setting. The term can be a temporal one, denoting an 'age' or 'era'—past, present or future—roughly equivalent to a life-span, or it can refer to the existing population within any given generation, frequently in a pejorative sense ('You faithless and perverse generation', Lk. 9.41; cf. 11.29-32).[3] Neither of these options, however, seems to fit the case in Acts 8. Here, as most commentators and modern versions agree, γενεά takes on more of a strictly *genea*-logical meaning, such as 'descendants' (NIV, JB) or 'posterity' (REB). But the question is then raised once again of whether a negative or positive connotation is in view. Should we read, 'Who will describe his descendants?' as a *lamentation*, bemoaning the fact that because of the servant's untimely death he will leave behind no progeny? Or should we think in diametrically opposite terms of an *exultation*, marvelling at the 'indescribable' (incalculable) number and scope of 'spiritual

'Characterization in Luke', pp. 57-62.

1. Note that this other Lukan reference to Isa. 53 also stresses the ignominy Jesus suffered in death and has nothing directly to do with the notion of atonement.

2. Fitzmyer notes that Luke essentially equates being 'in paradise' with other pictures of Christ's exaltation, such as 'exalted at God's right hand', 'taken up', 'entering into his glory' and 'ascending' ('"Today you Shall Be with me in Paradise" (Luke 23:43)', in *Luke the Theologian: Aspects of his Teaching* [New York: Paulist Press, 1989], pp. 218-22).

3. BAGD, pp. 153-54; F. Büchsel, 'γενεά, γενεαλογία, γενεαλογέω, κτλ.', *TDNT*, I, pp. 662-63; R. Morgenthaler and C. Brown, 'Generation', *NIDNTT*, II, pp. 35-39.

offspring' to be generated as a result of the servant's humiliation and ultimate vindication?

The latter interpretation seems more aligned with Lukan interests.[1] The opening chapter of the Gospel emphasizes the remarkable generative power of God in the most problematic situations. Elizabeth is barren, and both she and her husband, Zechariah, are too advanced in years to expect children through natural means. But, nonetheless, a divine messenger appears and promises Zechariah a son. The old man is completely taken back by this announcement and even struck dumb for his incredulity. Still, John the Baptist is miraculously born on schedule, at which time both the stigma of Elizabeth's barrenness is removed,[2] and Zechariah's muteness gives way to exclamations of praise for God's merciful intervention (Lk. 1.5-25, 57-80). As amazing as this birth is, however, it sets the stage for an even more wondrous event: the nativity of Jesus, the Son of God, to the virgin Mary. In short, Luke's infancy narrative underscores the theological point made by Gabriel: 'For nothing will be impossible with God' (1.37).

In the rest of Luke's narrative, the phenomenon of miraculous generation shifts from the physical to the spiritual realm. Luke is scarcely preoccupied with Jesus' earthly ties or physical family. Jesus, of course, never marries or establishes a permanent home of his own (cf. Lk. 9.57-62). When it comes to family matters, he attends strictly to the business of his heavenly Father, ignoring his earthly parents, if necessary (2.41-52), and embracing as his true relatives 'those who hear the word of God and do it' (8.21). It is the 'household of God' with which Jesus is concerned and to which he consistently adds new members, including the impoverished and infirm from the 'highways and hedges' of society (14.20-23). Even in his death, where one might expect the tragic end of his influence upon humanity, spiritual ties are established with unlikely parties. The convict hanging adjacent to Jesus

---

1. Commentators favoring this interpretation include Roloff (*Apostelgeschichte*, p. 141) and Schneider (*Apostelgeschichte*, I, p. 505). Haenchen (*Acts*, p. 312) and Kränkl (*Jesus der Knecht*, p. 115) admit to its plausibility.

2. Luke identifies the shame of Elizabeth's barrenness as ὄνειδος (1.25) instead of ταπείνωσις; however, the two terms are closely related in meaning, and ταπείνωσις is used in the LXX in connection with Elizabeth's counterpart, Hannah (1 Kgdms 1.11), whose story surely influenced Luke's infancy narratives (cf. R.E. Brown, *The Birth of the Messiah* [London: Geoffrey Chapman, 1977], pp. 268-69, 281, 288-89, 335-36, 357-63; Callaway, *Sing, O Barren One*, pp. 100-107).

is guaranteed fellowship with him in paradise (23.43), and the centurion standing below is inspired to praise God and proclaim Jesus' innocence (23.47).

All of this, however, is only a prelude to the story in Acts of the great accession of Christ's dedicated followers or 'spiritual descendants' touched off by his death, resurrection and ascension (cf. Acts 2.41, 47; 4.4). Indeed, in Luke's estimation, the Christ who had suffered and become 'the first to rise from the dead' was himself still actively at work in reaching out and gathering his 'family'. He was, to be more specific, 'proclaim[ing] light both to our people and to the Gentiles', thus fulfilling a missionary role originally assigned to the Lord's servant in Deutero-Isaiah (Acts 26.23; Isa. 49.6).

Against this backdrop of Luke's wider perspective on the generative work of God, the meaning of γενεά in Acts 8.33b as Christ's 'spiritual offspring' seems confirmed. Outside of Luke's work in the New Testament, the idea is not far in import from the Pauline conception of the resurrected Christ as the 'first-fruits' or 'firstborn within a large family' (cf. Rom. 8.29; 1 Cor. 15.20, 23; Col. 1.15, 18).

The use of Isaianic ideas to characterize the developing Christian mission, particularly as it aggressively reaches out to 'all people'— including the disabled, the disadvantaged and the foreigner—is central to Luke's presentation.[1] In other words, the brief citation in the eunuch story is symptomatic of a much wider missionary agenda in Luke–Acts based on Isaiah. Simeon's first oracle, for example, comprises a pastiche of Isaianic allusions, identifying the newborn Jesus as the long-awaited agent of God's salvation, 'prepared in the presence of all peoples [Isa. 40.5 LXX; 52.9-10], a light for revelation to the Gentiles [Isa. 42.6; 49.6 LXX], and for glory to your people Israel [Isa. 46.13]' (Lk. 2.30-32).[2] Another reference to Isa. 40.5 (LXX), spoken this time by John, again anticipates the impending redemption of 'all flesh' (Lk. 3.6). In the pivotal Nazareth pericope, the essence of Jesus' ministry is disclosed in Isaianic language, emphasizing the

---

1. Cf. D.P. Moessner, 'Ironic Fulfillment of Israel's Glory', in *Luke–Acts and the Jewish People: Eight Critical Perspectives* (ed. J.B. Tyson; Minneapolis, MN: Augsburg, 1988), pp. 46-50, 140.

2. Tiede suggests that this Isaiah-laden oracle 'might well be regarded as a thematic statement of Luke's entire narrative: the call of the servant (*pais*) to restore the diaspora of Israel and to be a light to the Gentiles to the end of the earth' (*Prophecy and History*, p. 31). Cf. R.E. Brown, *Birth*, pp. 458-60.

liberation of the poor, the enslaved, the blind and the oppressed (Lk. 4.17-19; Isa. 61.1-2 LXX; 58.6). Jesus claims not only to fulfill Isaiah's prophecy (4.21); he also 'exegetes' this material, by appealing to other scriptural traditions (from Kings), in a way which poignantly associates the beneficiaries of liberation with needy persons existing outside the social and geographical boundaries of Israel (i.e. Gentiles, 4.25-27).[1]

Toward the end of the Stephen speech in Acts 7, an Isaiah passage supports the emphasis on God's universal presence, unrestricted to any one people or locale (Acts 7.49-50; Isa. 66.1-2), and sets the stage for Stephen's stinging castigation of those Jews who rejected Jesus (7.51-53) as well as Philip's mission beyond Jewish borders in ch. 8. Not surprisingly, Luke also characterizes the Gentile mission of Paul as realizing Isaianic hopes. Ultimately spurned by a vocal Jewish contingent in Pisidian Antioch, the Lukan Paul announces his decision to 'turn to the Gentiles' (13.46), citing Isa. 49.6 as his divine warrant: 'I have set you to be a light for the Gentiles, so that you may bring salvation to the ends of the earth' (13.47). Similarly, before Agrippa, Paul portrays his work in Isaianic terms as a light- and sight-giving mission among the nations, authorized by Jesus himself (26.16-18; cf. Isa. 42.6-7, 16). Finally, Paul appeals to Isa. 6.9-10 at the end of Acts to legitimate once more the Gentile thrust of his mission (28.25-28).

In relating the Acts citation of Isa. 53.7-8a to leading ideas and patterns characterizing Luke's work as a whole, we must not lose sight of the immediate context of Philip's encounter with the Ethiopian eunuch. Why is the eunuch preoccupied with precisely this passage from Isaiah 53, and why does the correspondence between Jesus and Isaiah's 'suffering servant' precipitate the decision to be baptized? Although Luke is not explicit at this point, surely the centrality of the Isaiah citation to the overall incident (see chiasm above) suggests that this text is especially relevant to the eunuch's particular situation. Recalling the foregoing discussion, such relevance is not hard to find.

As one well-acquainted with humiliation and ostracism from the covenant community on account of his irremediable deformity, the eunuch no doubt reads the account of the servant's ταπείνωσις with intense interest and sympathy. As Philip interprets the prophetic text,

---

1. See J.A. Sanders, 'From Isaiah 61 to Luke 4', in *Christianity, Judaism and Other Greco-Roman Cults: Studies for Morton Smith at Sixty*. Part I. *New Testament* (ed. J. Neusner; SJLA, 12; Leiden: Brill, 1975), pp. 92-104.

the eunuch learns that this mysterious figure, of whom Isaiah speaks, was recently revealed in the person of Jesus. As predicted, this one had suffered the kind of humiliation to which the eunuch could easily relate, but more than that, he subsequently experienced a glorious exaltation of which the eunuch could only dream. No wonder, then, that in this servant-Jesus the eunuch finds the basis for hope and acceptance, 'good news' indeed.

Furthermore, as one impotent and therefore 'barren', the Ethiopian eunuch is no doubt also intrigued by the prospects of the servant's indescribable γενεά. The dumbness of the lamb before its shearer ('cutter') could perhaps symbolize the silent shame of childlessness, the stigma—well-known to the eunuch—of having one's name 'cut off', as well as the disbelief, like Zechariah's, that such a condition could effectively be reversed. But in contrast to this speechless despair, Philip 'opens his mouth'[1] and proclaims the good news of the humiliated servant's remarkable generative ability. The eunuch is thus enlightened concerning the access into God's household graciously provided by the servant-Christ and also encouraged by the potential renewal of his own generative capacity. In effect, with nothing now 'hindering' his progress (κωλύω, Acts 8.36), he becomes through faith and baptism one of the numerous 'spiritual descendants' of Christ featured in Acts, and with his new-found joy (8.39) he becomes a potential witness to Christ in his native land, one who might bear, so to speak, his own children in the faith.

The way to acceptance and fruitfulness, formerly denied to the foreigner/eunuch within a restrictive community, is at last opened wide through the salvific work of the humiliated–exalted servant, Jesus Christ.

The role of Philip the evangelist in this episode may be viewed as that of a 'midwife', facilitating the eunuch's incorporation into the family of Christ's descendants. In more traditional terms, Philip functions as the messenger of the servant-Christ, announcing to the eunuch the good news of God's universal salvation effected through Christ's

---

1. Note the play on words: Philip 'opens his mouth' (ἀνοίξας δὲ ὁ Φίλιππος τὸ στόμα αὐτοῦ) to proclaim the good news of the servant-Jesus who had shut his mouth in humiliation, like the lamb facing slaughter (οὐκ ἀνοίγει τὸ στόμα αὐτοῦ, Acts 8.32, 35). In this connection Luke may be stressing Philip's function as Jesus' mouthpiece: one who speaks *for* Jesus as well as *about* him (cf. Pesch, *Apostelgeschichte*, I, p. 292).

humiliation and exaltation. Therefore, like Paul, Philip may be regarded as a missionary-servant in his own right, a 'light for the Gentiles [the eunuch]' who 'brings salvation to the ends of the earth [Ethiopia]' (cf. Acts 13.47).

b. *Baptism*
As with Philip's Samaritan mission, so with his outreach to the Ethiopian eunuch, baptism is administered as a sign of both receiving the gospel message and entering the Christian community. Luke does not refer explicitly to the eunuch's faith (except according to later 'Western' readings, Acts 8.37), but it is surely presupposed in the forthright initiation of his own baptism (8.36, 38a).

The significance of Philip's baptism of the eunuch may be profitably explored in relation to the eunuch's critical query: 'What is to prevent (κωλύει) me from being baptized?' (Acts 8.36). Posing the request for baptism in these terms implies a persisting element of doubt in some minds regarding the eunuch's qualifications for community membership. Indeed, as suggested above, the implicit background to this scene seems to be the denial of proselyte status (achieved through baptism?) to the eunuch on account of his irreparable physical blemish. However, when Philip arrives and announces the good news of God's salvation proffered in Jesus Christ, all impediments to the eunuch's baptism are removed. The requisite water is amazingly ready-to-hand at the opportune moment (ἰδοὺ ὕδωρ); Philip performs the ritual act; and the eunuch proceeds on his way rejoicing (8.36-39).

Related occurrences of κωλύω[1] in Luke–Acts confirm and illuminate further the boundary-breaking nature of the eunuch's baptism. The term appears twice on the lips of Jesus as a mandate to his disciples not to exclude (μὴ κωλύετε) certain parties seeking to associate with him. In the first instance, Jesus decries the attempt to prohibit an outsider from exorcising demons in his name (Lk. 9.49-50). In the second example, he chides his followers for hindering the approach of little children who serve as models for all who would enter the kingdom of God (18.15-17). On yet another occasion, the Lukan Jesus

---

1. κωλύω is a favorite term in Luke–Acts, appearing 12 times (about half of all New Testament occurrences) in a variety of contexts, e.g., forbidding taxes (Lk. 23.2), preventing assistance (Acts 24.23) and thwarting an intent to kill (Acts 27.43). Our concern, of course, is with those instances which closely parallel the situation reflected in the eunuch story.

denounces a company of hypocritical lawyers who, despite their pretensions to wisdom, remain ignorant of God's ways and impede those seeking entrance into the covenant community (τοὺς εἰσερχομένους ἐκωλύσατε, Lk. 11.52; cf. Mt. 23.13). Thus, Jesus sets the example—followed by Philip in dealing with the eunuch—of clearing the path into the household of God for those whose access had been blocked in some way by insiders' prejudice.

This pattern is also reflected in Peter's involvement with Cornelius in Acts 10–11. In this case, of course, while Peter ultimately endorses the unhindered acceptance of uncircumcised Gentiles, his own reservations must be overcome first. It is only when the Spirit spontaneously falls on Cornelius and family that Peter is driven to ask whether anyone can legitimately 'withhold (δύναται κωλῦσαι) the water for baptizing these people' (10.47). When Peter is later questioned by the 'circumcision party' in Jerusalem, he rehearses the miraculous events in Cornelius's home and frankly confesses, 'who was I that I could hinder (δυνατὸς κωλῦσαι) God?' (11.17). To persist in preventing uncircumcised Gentiles from entering God's household is now tantamount in Peter's mind to hindering the realization of God's sovereign purpose.

This common emphasis on removing traditional barriers to baptism once more closely connects the missions of Philip to the Ethiopian and Peter to Cornelius in Luke's narrative.[1] Such a parallel supports the conclusion reached above that both cases have to do with evangelizing 'God-fearing' foreigners apart from the customary requirements of Jewish law, especially circumcision.

Finally, the import of the very last word in Acts—an adverbial

---

1. O. Cullmann has theorized that the use of κωλύω in the eunuch and Cornelius stories reflects the language of a primitive baptismal liturgy designed to test the fitness of candidates seeking church membership (*Baptism in the New Testament* [SBT; London: SCM Press, 1950], pp. 71-80). A.W. Argyle ('O. Cullmann's Theory Concerning κωλύειν', *ExpTim* 67 [1955–56], p. 17) has properly challenged this view, however, pointing to the usage of κωλύω in Luke–Acts and other ancient Greek literature in a wide range of contexts having nothing to do with baptism. He thinks that the LXX likely influenced Luke's treatment of κωλύω more than Christian liturgical tradition. Without elaboration, Argyle notes a suggestive parallel between the κωλύω-reference in the eunuch story and Isa. 43.6: 'I will say to the north, "Give them up", and to the south, "Do not withhold (μὴ κώλυε); bring my sons from far away and my daughters from the end of the earth"' (cf. references to 'pass[ing] through the waters' and 'Ethiopia' in Isa. 43.2-3).

form of κωλύω (ἀκωλύτως, 'unhinderedly', 28.31)—should not be missed. While some regard Luke's ending as strangely abrupt and awkward, F. Stagg perceives that ἀκωλύτως aptly concludes Paul's boundary-breaking mission to the Gentiles (cf. 28.23-31) and indeed 'epitomizes' the prominent Lukan accent on extending the gospel to all peoples:

> Throughout his two volumes, Luke never lost sight of his purpose, and he planned well the conclusion to it all, achieving the final effort by the last stroke of the pen. 'Unhinderedly', Luke wrote, describing the hard-won liberty of the gospel. This liberty came only after many barriers had been crossed, and it was won because its first home was in the mind and intention of Jesus himself.[1]

By reaching out 'unhinderedly' to the marginalized Ethiopian eunuch,[2] Philip the evangelist once more emerges in Luke's presentation as a notable proponent of the liberating Christian gospel and a worthy partner with Paul in advancing the early church's universal mission.

8. *Conclusion*

Having examined Philip's outreach to the Ethiopian eunuch from a variety of angles, we may finally attempt to assess its overall significance within Luke's mission history. The balance of evidence suggests that Luke presents this episode as a pioneering missionary breakthrough to the Gentiles. Literarily, it seems to fulfill Jesus' expectations in Lk. 4.25-27 and 24.47 of a developing Gentile mission; geographically, the gospel reaches an exotic representative of 'the ends of the earth'; thematically, the elements of supernatural guidance and humiliation/exaltation correlate elsewhere in Luke–Acts with an emphasis on extending God's salvation to 'all flesh'; and socially, the Ethiopian eunuch may be classed as a 'God-fearing' foreigner who at last finds acceptance among God's people through Jesus Christ—an acceptance formerly denied him under traditional Jewish law on account of his incorrigible 'defect'.

As for the connection between the Philip story involving the eunuch and the other mission stories in Acts 8–11, time and again we have

---

1. F. Stagg, *Book of Acts: The Early Struggle for an Unhindered Gospel* (Nashville: Broadman, 1955), p. 1; cf. pp. 1-4, 263-66.
2. Stagg, *Book of Acts*, pp. 106-109.

discovered a forward link with the narratives in chs. 9–11 dealing with the origins of the Gentile mission. The tie to the prior Philip story in Acts 8, involving the Samaritans, is in fact more tenuous. By evangelizing the Ethiopian eunuch, Philip takes a 'leap to the extreme'[1] beyond his own Samaritan mission in advancing the gospel to all humankind. From a people (Samaritans) stationed socially within a vague, marginal realm between Jews and Gentiles, the Christian mission now extends to an individual who, despite his attraction to Judaism, is no Jew at all but rather a full-fledged Gentile from a far-flung land.

The parallels drawn between Philip's mission to an Ethiopian treasurer and Peter's outreach to a Roman centurion (Acts 10–11) are especially striking. For example, both incidents are part of larger missionary tours along Israel's coastal plain; both are marked by the Spirit's guidance; both involve the conversion and baptism of uncircumcised, Jewish-sympathizing foreign officials; and both dismantle traditional socioreligious barriers preventing (κωλύω) full incorporation of 'God-fearing' Gentiles into the fellowship of God's household. I have contended that such links between the eunuch and Cornelius narratives are notably transparent—not blurred or downplayed. Accordingly, the conclusion presents itself that Luke has deliberately set up a dramatic correspondence between the missionary achievements of Philip and Peter. The glory is not all Peter's in inaugurating the early church's Gentile mission. Philip the evangelist must also be given his due.

Indeed, because Philip's story is recounted first, it might be thought that primary credit for the Gentile breakthrough should go to him, not Peter. However, such an arrangement is too simplistic. Although the common perception that Luke gives Peter *exclusive* credit for bringing the gospel to the Gentiles must be challenged, we cannot deny that Peter's witness to Cornelius marks a watershed event in Luke's narrative. The entire episode (Acts 10.1–11.18) is four times as long as the Philip/eunuch story, and its impact is much greater. Philip certainly evangelizes the first Gentile in Acts, but this is an isolated case, mentioned no more after ch. 8. It is Peter who spearheads the first Gentile baptism which attracts others' attention and eventually sparks the landmark decision of the Jerusalem church

---

1. Tannehill, *Narrative Unity*, II, p. 107.

endorsing the wider Gentile mission of Paul and Barnabas (15.7-11). Philip's pioneering step to the Gentiles should not be overlooked or minimized, but it must be kept in perspective. Philip blazes a trail, so to speak into Gentile territory which Peter then follows and expands. In other words, Philip functions as Peter's forerunner (see also the Samaria incident in 8.4-25). His outreach to the Ethiopian eunuch sets the stage for (or serves as a 'prelude' to) Peter's climactic mission to the Gentiles, represented by Cornelius and family. This forerunner role for Philip in relation to Peter will be further explored and clarified in the next chapter.

Chapter 5

PHILIP AND PETER

1. *Introduction*

My investigation thus far has revealed a number of contact points between the Lukan portraits of Philip and Peter. They both proclaim the gospel of Jesus Christ and perform similar miracles; they both feature prominently among the first wave of missionaries outside the boundaries of Jerusalem-based Judaism, first to the Samaritans and then to 'God-fearing' Gentiles; they are both 'men of Spirit', supernaturally guided and empowered to execute their ministries; and true to their prophetic vocations, they both encounter persecution from hostile opponents.

While a certain parity is thus established between Philip and Peter in Acts, the dominant role of Peter in chs. 1–12 can scarcely be overlooked, and a case can even be made that, whatever the resemblances between the two characters, Luke still purposefully subordinates Philip to Peter and (in certain respects) plays down the significance of Philip's ministry. In the Simon Magus case, where Peter 'disciplines' one of Philip's apparent converts, I have already demonstrated that no necessary aspersions are cast on the integrity or importance of Philip's work. I have also argued that, in Luke's eyes, Peter's witness to Cornelius more accurately complements rather than eclipses Philip's mission to the Ethiopian eunuch. But two additional elements remain within the portraits of Philip and Peter in Acts which might suggest at first glance an undervaluing, if not degrading, of Philip's ministry compared to Peter's.

First, Philip initially appears in Acts as one of the seven table-servants appointed to assist the twelve apostles—led by Peter—in the pastoral care of the Jerusalem community. Does the 'ordination' of the Seven (6.6) to a menial task, thus freeing the apostles to devote themselves to the vital ministries of proclamation and prayer (6.2-4), not imply a clear-cut 'subordination' of the Seven to the Twelve? And are Philip's subsequent achievements as an evangelist (ch. 8) not deliberately toned down by first associating him with his 'lesser' vocation of caterer?

Secondly, while Philip proclaims the gospel, works wonders and baptizes with water, his prowess as a missionary apparently fails to match Peter's at the crucial point of imparting the Spirit to his converts. This pattern is especially evident in Samaria, where Peter (along with John) discovers that the believers baptized by Philip have not yet received the Spirit and, consequently, supplies what is lacking through prayer and the laying on of hands (Acts 8.14-17). Similarly, with respect to the Gentiles, Peter is present when the Spirit falls on Cornelius and his household, whereas according to the best text no mention is made of the Spirit's outpouring upon the Ethiopian eunuch. Is it not an odd feature of the Acts narrative that a charismatic missionary like Philip, so evidently imbued with the Spirit (6.3; 8.29, 30), does not himself administer the Spirit to those he evangelizes? Is Philip's competence perhaps brought into question and his dependence upon Peter accentuated?

While it may appear that Luke purposefully subordinates Philip to Peter and even stigmatizes the former's work, a closer analysis of the relevant materials reveals a different perspective. This chapter aims to clarify Philip's role both as Peter's 'diaconal' assistant and as precursor to Peter's Spirit-imparting mission, demonstrating in the process that Philip remains an exemplary Lukan character and functions more as Peter's co-laborer than his underling.

2. *Philip, Peter and the Jerusalem Community (Acts 6.1-7)*

In the list of seven servants chosen to assist the twelve apostles, Philip is placed second, immediately after Stephen. Since extended narratives pertaining to Stephen and Philip directly follow, the snippet in Acts 6.1-7 serves to introduce these characters into Luke's story.[1] Their initial table-waiting role is thus juxtaposed with their subsequent identities as martyr and missionary. Luke confirms this link with respect to Philip in a terse description later in Acts: 'Philip the evangelist, who was one of the seven' (21.8). There is also the connection

---

1. Cf. J.T. Lienhard, 'Acts 6.1-6: A Redactional View', *CBQ* 37 (1975), pp. 228-30; Wilson, *Gentiles*, p. 130.

with Peter and the other apostles. Philip first helps the Twelve in the pastoral care of the Jerusalem community, and then Peter and John help Philip in evangelizing the Samaritans.

Investigations of Acts 6.1-7 have typically aimed at reconstructing historical conditions within the primitive Jerusalem church. Accordingly, the text has been viewed as a window into this situation, made visible by drawing back the curtains of Lukan redaction. Commonly perceived as underlying tradition is the report of two competing factions within the developing Jerusalem community, one led by Peter and his eleven fellow-apostles and the other headed by a seven-member body, including Stephen and Philip (6.1, 5). Redactional material may be detected principally in 6.2-4, 6-7, where Luke, true to his idealistic and 'catholic' tendencies, restores harmony to the church by reducing the seven to mere table-waiters under the apostles' authority.[1]

In the present section I will test this common perception of Luke's agenda in Acts 6.1-7, utilizing a variety of analytical methods. Rarely in discussions of this passage—preoccupied as they are with quests for historical data—is sufficient attention paid to literary concerns related to (1) the function of the text within Luke's narrative and (2) the influence of Old Testament models on its composition.[2] By attending to these matters, we may hope to gain a clearer view of the Lukan picture of community relations in Jerusalem.

a. *The Twelve and the Seven*
Does Acts 6.1-7 in fact betray a received tradition pitting the seven leaders of the 'Hellenist' wing of the Jerusalem church against the twelve governors of the 'Hebrew' wing? And, if so, was Luke's concern to reconcile these two groups within a hierarchical structure,

---

1. See, e.g., Lienhard, 'Acts 6.1-6', pp. 228-36; Weiser, *Apostelgeschichte*, I, pp. 162-69; M. Simon, *St Stephen and the Hellenists in the Primitive Church* (Haskell Lectures, Oberlin College, 1952; London: Longmans, Green, 1958), pp. 4-9; E.S. Fiorenza, *In Memory of Her: A Feminist Theological Reconstruction of Christian Origins* (London: SCM Press, 1983), pp. 162-66.

2. Notable exceptions include J.B. Tyson, 'Acts 6.1-7 and Dietary Regulations in Early Christianity', *PerRelSt* 10 (1983), pp. 145-61 (literary analysis); and D. Daube, 'A Reform in Acts and its Models', in *Jews, Greeks and Christians: Religious Cultures in Late Antiquity: Essays in Honor of William David Davies* (ed. R. Hamerton-Kelly and R. Scroggs; Leiden: Brill, 1976), pp. 151-63 (use of Old Testament models).

casting the Seven as submissive servants under the Twelve's jurisdiction?

While Luke transparently refers to an altercation between 'Hellenist' and 'Hebrew' factions (Acts 6.1), he nowhere identifies the leaders of these parties nor does he make plain that such leaders directly promoted the present crisis. Thus, it must be admitted that interpretations which link the Seven and the murmuring 'Hellenists' and drive a wedge between the Seven and the twelve 'Hebrews' are based at best on inferences from Luke's account, not explicit statements.

1. The fact that Stephen, Philip and all the others listed in Acts 6.5 have Greek names may point, as many have supposed, to the homogeneous, 'Hellenist' character of the seven-member committee. But this evidence is not conclusive. Two members of the Twelve—Andrew and Philip (Lk. 6.14; Acts 1.13)—also bear Greek appellations, and the wide currency of the Greek language throughout the ancient world made Greek names commonplace, even among the Jews.[1]

2. Describing the Stephen–Philip group as 'seven men of good standing, full of the Spirit and of wisdom' (Acts 6.3) may suggest a recognition on Luke's part that this company already constituted an acknowledged leadership body distinct from, though not necessarily in competition with, the Twelve. Town councils comprising seven men were common administrative entities in first-century Israel,[2] and the particular qualities characterizing the Seven are appropriate not only to table-service, but also to the exercise of more extensive charismatic authority within the congregation.[3] Moreover, it is assumed that such

---

1. J. Munck calls attention to inscriptional evidence from ancient Jewish tombs in Jerusalem indicating the widespread use of both Greek and Semitic names within individual Jewish families (*Acts*, p. 57).

2. Cf. Josephus, *Ant.* 4.214, 287; *War* 2.569-71; G. Alon, *The Jews in Their Land in the Talmudic Age (70–640 C.E.)* (trans. and ed. G. Levi; Jerusalem: Magnes, 1980), I, pp. 176-79. For rabbinic references to the 'Seven of a City', see H.L. Strack and P. Billerbeck, *Kommentar zum Neuen Testament aus Talmud und Midrasch* (Munich: Beck, 1924), II, p. 641.

3. Cf. Dunn, *Jesus and the Spirit*, p. 181. The 'wisdom' of the Seven should not be reduced to 'worldly prudence' (so Haenchen, *Acts*, p. 262), suitable only to practical duties such as table-service. As seen especially with Stephen, σοφία is also a dynamic quality inspiring persuasive proclamation (Acts 6.10; cf. Lk. 21.15; O. Glombitza, 'Zur Charakterisierung des Stephanus in Act 6 und 7', *ZNW* 53 [1962], pp. 238-44).

qualities had been manifest long enough to gain community respect.

3. It is often surmised that Luke's report of the persecution which breaks out against the Jerusalem church implies an underlying rift between the Seven and the Twelve.[1] It all begins with the stoning of Stephen, the leading representative of the Seven. This tragic event then precipitates a general attack on the wider Christian community, prompting the dispersion of 'all (πάντες) except the apostles (πλὴν τῶν ἀποστόλων)' (Acts 8.1). While at this point the story clearly distinguishes the Twelve from the *entire* scattered community (not strictly from the Seven or the 'Hellenists'), it is important to note that succeeding chapters do not present the Twelve as the last remnant of a ravaged church. Assisted by a body of elders and such notable ministers as James, Barnabas and Agabus (9.26-30; 11.27-30; 15.2-29), they still preside over a company of disciples, such as the prayer group based in Mary's home (12.12-17). Moreover, the only fugitives from Jerusalem following Stephen's death featured specifically in Acts are Philip, Stephen's partner (8.4-5), and the founders of the church at Antioch, among whom number Greek-speaking ('Hellenist'?) Cypriots and Cyrenians (11.19-20). Taken together, these data may indeed point to a polarization between the Twelve and their followers (the 'Hebrews'?), on the one hand, who withstand or avoid the fiercest wave of persecution in Jerusalem, and the Seven and their affiliates (the 'Hellenists'?), on the other hand, who are forced to flee.

J.D.G. Dunn also perceives a trace of this community division in the note that 'devout men (εὐλαβεῖς) buried Stephen, and made loud lamentation over him' (Acts 8.2). εὐλαβής is not a distinctively Christian term in Luke–Acts (cf. Lk. 2.25; Acts 2.5) and could refer in this instance to pious Jews (not Jewish Christians) committed to upholding Mosaic burial laws. Why is there no mention of disciples or apostles lending a helping hand or of the church bemoaning Stephen's death? 'Is Luke perhaps trying to cloak the fact that the Hebrew Christians had virtually *abandoned* Stephen?'[2] This is a provocative idea, but of course care must be taken not to build too much on presumed silences in the text.

---

1. See the discussion in Wilson, *Gentiles*, pp. 142-53; Hengel, *Between Jesus and Paul*, p. 13; J.D.G. Dunn, *Unity and Diversity in the New Testament: An Inquiry into the Character of Earliest Christianity* (London: SCM Press, 1977), pp. 273-75.

2. Dunn, *Unity and Diversity*, p. 273.

4. Understanding Luke's conception of the 'Hebrews' and 'Hellenists' may provide additional clues linking the two groups to the Twelve and the Seven respectively. As is well known, determining the meaning of Ἐβραῖος and Ἑλληνιστής is a long-standing and complex problem in *Actaforschung*.[1] In recent years, however, a certain view, typically associated with M. Hengel, has emerged as the dominant, if not consensus, interpretation.[2] The 'Hebrews' in Acts 6.1 are taken to be native Aramaic-speaking Jewish Christians[3] of Judean and Galilean origin whose worship remained centered in the Jerusalem temple, while their 'Hellenist' counterparts are identified as Greek-speaking[4] Jewish Christians from the Diaspora who migrated to

---

1. See surveys of the debate in H.-W. Neudorfer, *Der Stephanuskreis in der Forschungsgeschichte seit F.C. Baur* (Giessen: Brunner, 1983), pp. 329ff.; Grässer, 'Acta-Forschung', pp. 17-25; E. Ferguson, 'The Hellenists in the Book of Acts', *ResQ* 12 (1969), pp. 159-80.

2. Hengel, *Between Jesus and Paul*, pp. 1-29. Regarding the widespread acceptance of Hengel's argument, E. Larsson wittily remarks: 'Es sieht aus, als ob sich die Forscher-Kollegen in einer ähnlichen Situation befanden wie die Gegner des Stephanus in Jerusalem: Sie können der Weisheit und dem Geist, der heraus spricht, nicht widerstehen' ('Die Hellenisten und die Urgemeinde', *NTS* 33 [1987], p. 207). Among those who either anticipated Hengel's conclusions or have since built upon them, see C.F.D. Moule, 'Once More, Who Were the Hellenists?', *ExpTim* 70 (1958–59), pp. 100-102; J.N. Sevenster, *Do You Know Greek? How Much Greek Could the First Jewish Christians Have Known?* (NovTSup, 19; Leiden: Brill, 1968), pp. 28-38; I.H. Marshall, 'Palestinian and Hellenistic Christianity: Some Critical Comments', *NTS* 19 (1972–73), pp. 277-79; R. Pesch, E. Gerhardt and F. Schilling, ' "Hellenisten" und "Hebräer": Zu Apg 9,29 und 6,1', *BZ* 23 (1979), pp. 87-92.

3. N. Walter has recently argued that the 'Hebrew'–'Hellenist' controversy should be viewed not as an inner-Christian conflict but as a problem within the wider Jewish community ('Apostelgeschichte 6.1 und die Anfänge der Urgemeinde in Jerusalem', *NTS* 29 [1983], pp. 370-93). However, from Luke's point of view at least, the situation appears restricted to the context of a growing company of 'disciples' (= Christian believers, 6.1a; cf. 6.2a: 'the whole community of the disciples'). For a critique of Walter's thesis and the related stance of N. Hyldahl, see Larsson, 'Hellenisten', pp. 208-11.

4. The term Ἑλληνιστής does not occur in extant Greek literature of antiquity prior to Acts. It appears, however, to be coined from ἑλληνίζω, whose primary meaning was 'to speak Greek' (hence the rendering of Ἑλληνιστής as a [Jewish] Greek-speaker). Cf. BAGD, p. 252; Sevenster, *Do You Know Greek?*, pp. 28-29; W. Jaeger, *Early Christianity and Greek Paideia* (Cambridge, MA: Belknap, 1961), pp. 107-109.

Jerusalem (before becoming Christians) and naturally became attached to local Greek-speaking synagogues. The social differences, therefore, between the two groups are judged to be principally linguistic and liturgical, although many would feel that matters of distinctive culture and theology also entered the picture.[1] Given this profile, the twelve 'men of Galilee' (1.11; cf. 2.7) whose Jerusalem ministry is based in the temple (2.46; 3.1-11; 5.12-16, 42) appear to be aligned with the 'Hebrews' in Luke's presentation. The Seven are more difficult to categorize, but Stephen's interaction with members of the Diaspora synagogue in Acts 6.9-10, although ending in disaster, implies a certain sociocultural common ground for debate between him and these 'Hellenist' Jews (cf. 9.29).[2] Another representative of the Seven, Nicolaus, is designated 'a proselyte of Antioch' (6.5), suggesting that he too was a Greek-speaking Jew (albeit a convert) with roots outside the land of Israel.[3]

1. That is, some regard the 'Hellenists' as more open to practicing Greek customs and more critical of venerated Jewish institutions, such as Torah and Temple. See, e.g., E.E. Ellis, *Prophecy and Hermeneutic in Early Christianity: New Testament Essays* (WUNT, 18; Tübingen: Mohr [Paul Siebeck], 1978), pp. 118-23; W. Schmithals, *Paul and James* (SBT, 46; London: SCM Press, 1965), pp. 16-37; Wilson, *Gentiles*, pp. 138-52; C.S. Mann, ' "Hellenists" and "Hebrews" in Acts VI 1', in Munck, *Acts*, pp. 301-304. It should be noted, however, that some Diaspora Jews who had settled in Jerusalem are portrayed in Acts as tenaciously loyal to the temple and the laws of Moses (cf. Acts 6.8-15; 21.27-29).

2. Cf. the appraisal of M. Simon:

> the term Hellenists, as used by Luke, includes all Greek-speaking Jews, whether already converted, as in the case of the Seven, or still opposing the Christian message. It must be conceded that to the author of Acts, the word apparently has no other meaning (*St Stephen*, p. 15).

Cadbury ('Hellenists', pp. 70-74) and more recently Tyson ('Acts 6.1-7', pp. 155-61) have concentrated on the reference to Ἑλληνιστής in Acts 11.20— where the term seems to denote 'Greeks' (i.e. Gentiles) in opposition to 'Jews' (Ἰουδαῖοι) in 11.19—and argued that the same meaning applies to the 'Hellenists' in 6.1 and 9.29. However, there is reasonable doubt concerning the authenticity of the Ἑλληνιστάς-reading in 11.20 (the variant is Ἕλληνας), and Luke has provided no other transparent clues to the presence of Gentiles within either the earliest church or synagogue(s) in Jerusalem. For an alternative social-historical analysis of the 'Hellenists' in 6.1 which supports Hengel's basic position but goes further to posit a contingent of 'God-fearers' within the group alongside Greek-speaking Jews, see Esler, *Community and Gospel*, pp. 136-39, 154-63.

3. E.C. Blackman ('The Hellenists of Acts vi.1', *ExpTim* 48 [1936–37],

On the whole then, the evidence—though more allusive and sketchy than scholars tend to concede—does point to Luke's apparent consciousness of a historic division between the Twelve and the Seven in the primitive Jerusalem church, connected in some way with the reported tension between the 'Hebrews' and 'Hellenists'. But ultimately Luke has sought to play down this division by depicting a scene of harmony between the two groups and their leaders. This leads us to explore the question of exactly how Luke brings the Seven and Twelve together in Acts 6.1-7. N. Walter speaks for many scholars when he propounds in one place, 'it is generally recognized that Luke endeavors not only to relate (*zuordnen*) but also to subordinate (*unterzuordnen*) the Seven to the twelve apostles, in that he allows them to be appointed by the apostles. . . '[1] And in another place: 'everything in 6.1-7 which amounts, so to speak, to an "official" subordination (*"dienstliche" Unterordnung*) of the Seven under the Twelve and which seems to force down (*herabdrücken*) the function of the Seven to that of social-helpers, springs from the efforts of Luke. . . '[2] Walter also admits, however, that in the ensuing material in chs. 6–8 Luke virtually subverts his own plan in 6.1-7 by allowing Stephen and Philip to function more like dynamic ministers of the word, like the twelve apostles, than menial table-servants.[3]

Does Luke in fact construct a hierarchical unity between the Twelve and Seven in Acts 6.1-7 which then disintegrates in the more developed stories of Stephen and Philip which follow? It is true that the Twelve take charge and play a leading role in healing the breach between 'Hellenists' and 'Hebrews' in the Jerusalem community. They initiate reconciliation by proposing to the congregation that they—the Twelve—appoint (καταστήσομεν) a committee of seven to oversee the care of widows (6.2-3). Elsewhere in Luke–Acts καθίστημι occasionally denotes a ruler's assignment of duty to one of his subjects—for example, a householder's charging his steward to

---

pp. 524-25) and B. Reicke (*Glaube und Leben der Urgemeinde: Bemerkungen zu Apg. 1–7* [ATANT, 32; Zürich: Zwingli, 1957], pp. 115-17) suggest that all of the Seven and their fellow-'Hellenists' should be regarded as proselytes. However, Nicolaus's proselyte status appears to be singled out as an exception among the Seven, rather than the rule.

1. Walter, 'Apostelgeschichte 6.1', p. 370.
2. Walter, 'Apostelgeschichte 6.1', pp. 372-73.
3. Walter, 'Apostelgeschichte 6.1', p. 370.

manage the estate (Lk. 12.42, 44) or a king's installing a governor to administrate the realm (Acts 7.10). Such notions of a formal chain of command may possibly inform the Twelve's appointment of seven servants to pastoral duty.

However, we must not slight the important contribution which the larger assembly also makes to the proceedings in Acts 6. The account is framed in vv. 1 and 7 by a similar focus on the burgeoning company of disciples comprising the Jerusalem congregation (πληθυνόν-των τῶν μαθητῶν; ἐπληθύνετο ὁ ἀριθμὸς τῶν μαθητῶν). These disciples represent more than mere 'extras' on the scene; they are very much involved in solving the crisis which threatens their fellowship. The 'whole community' of believers, 'Hellenists' and 'Hebrews' together,[1] ratify the apostles' recommendation (καὶ ἤρεσεν ὁ λόγος ἐνώπιον παντὸς τοῦ πλήθους, 6.5)[2] and then carry it out. The community selects (ἐξελέξαντο) the seven candidates of its choice, sets them (ἔστησαν) before the apostles, and finally: προσευξάμενοι ἐπέθηκαν αὐτοῖς τὰς χεῖρας (6.6). It is often assumed that these consecratory acts of prayer and the laying on of hands should be understood as ecclesiastical rites performed by the apostles. But the grammar of the sentence by no means requires this interpretation. Indeed the most natural reading of Acts 6.6 would take the subjects of ἔστησαν, προσευξάμενοι and ἐπέθηκαν to be the same, namely, the congregation.[3] Accordingly, the same assembly which brings forward the seven nominees also prays collectively for God's blessing upon them; likewise, the imposition of hands betokens the congregation's solidarity with and support of its chosen representatives.[4] The apostles

---

1. Contra P. Gaechter, who argues unconvincingly that only the 'Hellenists' are assembled by the apostles and take part in selecting the Seven (*Petrus und seine Zeit: Neutestamentliche Studien* [Innsbruck: Tyrolia, 1958], pp. 128-30).

2. What 'pleases' (ἀρεστόν, Acts 6.2) the apostles must also 'please' (ἀρέσκω, 6.5) the congregation.

3. Cf. Dunn, *Jesus and the Spirit*, p. 181; D. Daube, *The New Testament and Rabbinic Judaism* (Jordan Lectures, 1952; London: Athlone, 1956), pp. 237-39; Barrett, *Church*, p. 50. The 'Western' text makes it clear that only the apostles laid hands upon the Seven, but this seems to reflect a later tendency toward a more rigid institutionalization of church authority.

4. Daube understands the congregation's laying on of hands in terms of the Jewish *samakh*, which symbolized identification and representation (*New Testament and Rabbinic Judaism*, pp. 236-39). The people '"leaned their hands on them", thus making them into their representatives. . . The distribution of charity was now

still approve and oversee the church's action, but not in a domineering way. As it turns out, their appointment of the Seven appears to be more of a collaborative venture with the congregation than an expression of independent authority.

Given this cooperation between apostles and assembly in commissioning the Seven, the resulting relationship between the Twelve and Seven appears to be more fraternally based than officially structured.[1] That is, Luke depicts the two groups of ministers as colleagues, fellow-laborers united in serving the entire congregation. The Twelve certainly command special respect by virtue of their unique witness to the earthly ministry and resurrection of Jesus (cf. Acts 1.21-23), but this does not entitle them to absolute control over church business nor accord them superior ecclesiastical ranking over other ministers, such as the Seven. A brief look at three other incidents in Acts dealing with decision-making in the church will further confirm the point.

1. The appointment of a successor for Judas occurs not behind closed apostolic doors but 'among the believers' numbering about 120 (Acts 1.15). Peter, to be sure, takes the lead and stipulates the qualifications for enrollment in the Twelve, but ultimately 'they propose' (ἔστησαν)[2] two candidates (1.23; cf. 6.6), 'they pray' (προσευξάμενοι) for divine guidance (1.24), and 'they cast (ἔδωκαν) lots' to determine the choice (1.26). 'They' in each case seems to refer to the entire congregation which participates in selecting Matthias, thus matching the community in ch. 6 which chooses and sets apart the Seven.[3] As to who has supreme authority in ch. 1 to appointment Judas's replacement, the spotlight falls on *the Lord himself* (σὺ κύριε. . . ἀνάδειξον ὃν ἐξελέξω, 1.24) rather than on a particular cadre of ecclesiastical officials, apostolic or otherwise.[4]

2. Barnabas and Saul are commissioned for missionary service at

in the hands of the community—the community living in its deputies' (p. 237).

1. Cf. K. Giles, 'Is Luke an Exponent of "Early Protestantism"? Church Order in the Lukan Writings', part 2: *EvQ* 55 (1983), pp. 16-17.

2. The 'Western' variant, ἔστησεν, focuses on Peter's leading role in the proceedings. Once again the 'Western' reading reflects later ecclesiastical practice, in this case the tendency to exalt Peter as the chief monarchical bishop. Cf. Metzger, *Textual Commentary*, p. 288.

3. Cf. Pesch, *Apostelgeschichte*, I, p. 90.

4. On the parallel between the appointment of Matthias in Acts 1 and the Seven in Acts 6, see B. Domagalski, 'Waren die "Sieben" (Apg 6,1-7) Diakone?', *BZ* 26 (1982), pp. 26-29.

Antioch without any contribution from the Twelve (Acts 13.1-3). As
the Antioch community, led by recognized prophets and teachers,
gathers for worship,[1] the Holy Spirit instructs the assembly to 'set
apart *for me* Barnabas and Saul for the work to which *I have called
them*' (13.2). Once again the emphasis falls on the Lord's sovereignty
to appoint his ministers. The church, however, must still play its part
in carrying out the divine plan, and it seems to be the entire worshipping body which takes the appropriate action: 'after fasting and praying *they* laid their hands on them and sent them off' (13.3).[2] Such a
procedure (praying/laying on of hands) obviously echoes the
Jerusalem community's dealings with the Seven in Acts 6.

3. The so-called 'Apostolic Council' in Acts 15 is in fact not exclusively an apostolic affair. Coming to Jerusalem, Paul and Barnabas
report their missionary experiences to 'the church and the apostles and
the elders' (15.4) As debate ensues, Peter and James emerge as the
principal spokesmen for the Jerusalem church, but 'the whole assembly' (πᾶν τὸ πλῆθος) remains attentively on the scene (15.12). When
a verdict is finally reached, it represents the collective will of 'the
apostles and the elders, with the... whole church (σὺν ὅλῃ τῇ
ἐκκλησίᾳ)' (15.22). This entire company chooses (ἐκλεξαμένους)
two representatives and dispatches them with a letter to the Pauline
communities in Syria and Cilicia (15.22-23).

In short, throughout the book of Acts a non-hierarchical, democratic process characterizes church government in general and the
appointment of ministers in particular. Peter and the apostles play a
leading role but do not lord their authority over fellow-believers in
Jerusalem or elsewhere. Persons chosen and commissioned to specific
tasks—such as Philip and the other table-servants—are not so much

---

1. There is some ambiguity regarding the subject of λειτουργούντων in 13.2. Is
it the entire 'church at Antioch' (13.1) or strictly the five prophets and teachers
gathered in closed session? Marshall's judgment on the matter seems best:

> Since the list of names in verse 1 is primarily meant to show who was available for
> missionary service, and since changes of subject are not uncommon in Greek, it is
> preferable to assume that Luke is thinking of an activity involving the members of the
> church generally (*Acts*, p. 215).

2. The same group which worships and fasts in 13.2—namely, the congregation
together with its leaders—appears to be the same body who fasts and prays in 13.3
and by the laying on of hands commissions Barnabas and Saul for missionary
service.

placed under the Twelve as alongside them *and* the larger community of disciples, all of whom work together as partners in the service of the church's sovereign Lord.

Having concluded that Luke does not 'officially' assign a subordinate *status* to the Seven with respect to the Twelve, we must still address the practical issue of whether or not dividing the labor in Acts 6 between proclaiming the word and waiting on tables implies a subordinate *function* for the Seven.

b. *Proclaiming the Word*[1] *and Waiting on Tables*

The value which Luke places on the work assigned to the Seven may be ascertained by isolating particular dimensions of their prescribed *diakonia* and interpreting them in the context of Luke's overall perspective on Christian service. First, we must appreciate that the ministry of the Seven is directed especially to neglected widows in the community (6.1). No New Testament writer demonstrates a greater concern for the plight of widows than Luke. Outside the material in Lk. 20.45–21.4, shared with Mark, the several passages in Luke–Acts focusing on widows are unique. Anna, an elderly widow and prophet, appears as a model of devotion and key witness to the redemptive vocation of the Christ-child (Lk. 2.36-38). In the critical Nazareth scene where Jesus begins and defines the character of his public ministry, he invokes the precedent of Elijah's mission to a destitute, famine-stricken widow (4.25-27). Later, Jesus encounters a bereaved widow at the funeral of her only son and, in Elijah-like fashion, he resuscitates the child and reunites the family (7.11-17).[2] In his teaching, Jesus links spirituality and justice towards widows. He emphasizes importunate prayer and vindicating the oppressed in the parable of the mistreated widow and callous judge (18.1-8), and he exposes the pretentious praying of the scribes known for their deplorable habit of 'devour[ing] widows' houses' (20.47). Finally, as in Mark, the Lukan Jesus commends a poor widow for her remarkable generosity (21.1-4).

---

1. In Acts 6.4 the Twelve's commitment to proclamation is connected with their devotion to *prayer*. However, in 6.2 the contrast is between the ministry of the word (only) and table-service, and it is this fundamental distinction which will occupy our attention in this section.

2. Cf. T.L. Brodie, 'Towards Unraveling Luke's Use of the Old Testament: Luke 7.11-17 as an *Imitatio* of 1 Kings 17.17-24', *NTS* 32 (1986), pp. 247-67.

The Jesus portrayed by Luke obviously manifests a deep sensitivity to the vulnerable position of widows in ancient society.[1] It is especially relevant to our present interests that this concern for widows is part and parcel of Jesus' overall outreach to the disadvantaged which itself is integrally connected to his proclamation of the gospel. The Jesus who restores the widow's son to life is the same Jesus who restores lepers and other outcasts and brings good news to the poor (Lk. 7.21-22; cf. 4.18-19).[2] Without a doubt, authentic gospel ministry for Luke is more than uttering a message; it includes acting in mercy towards helpless widows and others in need.

If Luke makes no essential value distinction between Jesus' proclamation of the word and his support of widows, then surely no such distinction should be read into the situation in Acts 6.[3] Although for pragmatic reasons (such as community growth) the Twelve and Seven divide the labor between them, there is no notion that the Seven are saddled with lowly, onerous duty (watching over widows) while the Twelve get on with the really important work (preaching and teaching). As for relating the ministerial assignments in Acts 6 and subsequent chapters, the tension is not as great as often assumed. Philip's prophetic ministry of word and deed to the marginalized Samaritans and eunuch is entirely of a piece with his care of needy widows. And in Acts 9.32-43 Peter appears less as a proclaimer of the word than as a pastoral servant to suffering disciples, *including bereft widows* (v. 39-41).[4] The point is this: in the course of Acts both Philip and Peter, following Jesus' lead, participate in the vital and intertwined tasks of preaching the word and ministering to widows.

Additional features of the Seven's work are disclosed in two διακονία-phrases: ἡ διακονία ἡ καθημερινή (Acts 6.1) and

---

1. On the plight of widows in the ancient world, see G. Stählin, 'Das Bild der Witwe: Ein Beitrag zur Bildersprache der Bibel und zum Phänomen der Personifikation in der Antike', *JAC* 17 (1974), pp. 5-20.

2. Note also the Nazareth pericope where Jesus implicitly relates Elijah's ministry to the widow (with which he identifies, Lk. 4.25-26) to his vocation of proclaiming good news to the poor and liberating the oppressed (4.18).

3. Cf. the discussion in Tyson, 'Acts 6.1-7', pp. 158-59.

4. Although Peter does not directly assist widows, he does so in an indirect way by raising up Dorcas, who herself had been 'devoted to good works and acts of charity' toward needy widows (9.36, 39-41). As Haenchen puts it, 'for them [widows] the restoration to life of their benefactress is especially important' (*Acts*, p. 340).

διακονεῖν τραπέζαις (6.2). Significantly, the ministry of the Twelve is also designated as ἡ διακονία τοῦ λόγου (6.4). In a sense, then, whatever may distinguish the two callings, they are both perceived as 'diaconal' in Luke's view. Formal ecclesiastical notions of the Seven as holding the office of deacon under the episcopacy of the Twelve appear anachronistic to Acts.[1]

Specifically regarding the table-service of the Seven, a τράπεζα can refer to a bank (Lk. 19.23) or money-changer's table (Mk 11.15; Mt. 21.12; Jn 2.15), but more commonly in Luke–Acts it denotes a dinner table (Lk. 16.21; 22.21, 30) or, by extension, the meal placed on the table (Acts 16.34). Since διακονία and διακονέω also frequently occur in Luke's narrative in the context of meal-service and hospitality (Lk. 4.39; 8.3; 10.40; 12.37; 17.8; 22.26, 27),[2] it seems most likely that διακονεῖν τραπέζαις identifies the Seven's duty as that of distributing food to the needy. As a 'daily' (καθημερινή) chore, this ministry may be linked to the 'day by day' (καθ' ἡμέραν) fellowship meals in the Jerusalem church (Acts 2.46). Perhaps the Seven are to make sure that widows and other poor members of the community are invited to these home gatherings and receive their fair share.[3] The rabbinic system of Jewish poor-relief, whereby indigent vagrants were supplied with a daily ration of food, may also provide relevant background to the 'daily distribution' in Acts 6.1.[4]

According to conventional social standards, ancient and modern, the

1. Cf. Larsson: 'Die alte Frage, ob Apg 6 die Gründung des Diakonats schildert, sollte heute nicht mehr aktuell sein' ('Hellenisten', p. 211); Barrett, *Church*, pp. 49-51.

2. H. Beyer ('διακονέω, διακονία, διάκονος', *TDNT*, II, pp. 81-93) has demonstrated that throughout the range of Greek literature, including Luke–Acts, the διακονέω word-group is associated primarily with food-service or table-waiting.

3. Fiorenza (*In Memory of Her*, pp. 165-66) thinks that the problem in Acts 6 concerned a specifically eucharistic meal in which 'Hellenist' widows were either not properly served themselves or excluded from participating in serving others. However, as noted above, it is questionable whether formal eucharistic connotations lie behind references to 'breaking of bread' or meal-time observances in Luke–Acts (cf. Barrett, *Church*, pp. 60-63; Robinson, 'Place of the Emmaus Story', pp. 487-94).

4. There was also a weekly distribution in which the local poor received requisite food and clothing. See the discussion in Jeremias, *Jerusalem*, pp. 130-32; A. Strobel, 'Armenpfleger "um des Friedens willen" (Zum Verständnis von Act 6.1-7)', *ZNW* 63 (1972), pp. 271-76.

task of doling out food or waiting on tables is a lowly one, scarcely comparable in value to acts of public-speaking and policy-making performed by community leaders. Even in the church the influential ministry of the word—largely the province of ordained officials—has tended to be prized above the admittedly necessary but menial work of Christian charity carried out by laypeople, including women. But Luke must be allowed his own perspective on the matter.

On the basis of three accounts in Luke's Gospel, two of which are unique, it might well be construed that he regards table-service as suitable 'women's work', inferior to the preaching and healing exploits of Jesus and his male disciples. In reporting the cure of Simon's mother-in-law, Luke follows Synoptic tradition in indicating that, once her fever miraculously broke, the woman immediately 'got up and began to serve (διηκόνει)' her guests (Lk. 4.39; Mk 1.31; Mt. 8.15). A special summary statement of Jesus' activities discloses that he was preaching the gospel throughout Galilee, accompanied by the Twelve and a group of women (Lk. 8.1-3).[1] Finally, in an incident which E.S. Fiorenza explicitly compares to Acts 6, Jesus chides Martha for being 'distracted with much serving (πολλὴν διακονίαν)' at the same time he commends Mary for attending to the 'good portion' of Jesus' word (10.38-42).[2]

On closer examination, however, these examples do not necessarily subordinate women's table-service to the preaching ministry of Jesus and the apostles. In the cases of Simon's mother-in-law and the women in Luke 8, their διακονία stands not so much in contrast to Jesus' ministry as complementary to it. Through table-service, these women show their gratitude for Jesus' help and commitment to support his mission. Moreover, B. Witherington has argued convincingly that in Luke's eyes Mary Magdalene, Joanna, and company represent 'more than just a hospitality or catering service for the men and Jesus'.[3]

---

1. M. Hengel ('Maria Magdalena und die Frauen als Zeugen', in Betz, Hengel and Schmidt [eds.], *Abraham unser Vater*, pp. 247-48) suggests that this account parallels the report in Acts 6.1-7 as 'eine paradigmatische Vorstufe des späteren Diakonenamtes'. As the diaconal ministry of the Seven in Acts 6 is designed to free the Twelve to pursue their ministry of the word without encumbrance, so the service of the women in Luke 8 enables Jesus and the apostles to carry out their task of proclaiming the kingdom of God.

2. Fiorenza, *In Memory of Her*, p. 165; cf. Schneider, *Apostelgeschichte*, I, p. 426 n. 48.

3. B. Witherington, 'On the Road with Mary Magdalene, Joanna, Susanna, and

Introduced as members of Jesus' band of disciples in Lk. 8.1-3, these women typify the fruitful receptors of the word in Jesus' ensuing parable (8.4-15) and prepare for the critical role of certain women— including Mary Magdalene and Joanna—later in the narrative as the first *witnesses* (= ministers of the word) to Jesus' resurrection (24.8-11).[1]

The snippet set in Mary and Martha's home does contrast the latter's absorption in table-service and the former's devotion to Jesus' word. But the distinction is not between two ministries—table-service and proclaiming the word (= Acts 6)—but rather between two expressions of love for Jesus—serving him dinner or listening to his word. Jesus does not fault the work of table-service *per se*; he simply rebukes Martha for becoming so preoccupied with this work that she slights the cardinal duty of all disciples: to attend to Jesus' instruction. By commending Mary's choice, Jesus does not reject Martha but rather invites her to join her sister in the fellowship of Jesus' word. In no way does the Lukan Jesus relegate women to catering duties or block them from sharing in his word.[2]

There are four other passages in Luke's Gospel dealing with table-service or food-provision[3] which must be considered, especially as they relate to the ministry of the twelve apostles.

1.   Luke's version of the feeding of the five thousand focuses more

Other Disciples—Luke 8.1-3', *ZNW* 70 (1979), p. 244 n. 6.

1.   Witherington, 'On the Road', pp. 243-48. Note that in Lk. 24.8-11 the women are portrayed as witnesses of Jesus' resurrection to the eleven apostles, who initially respond to this testimony with incredulity.

2.   Cf. Fitzmyer: 'Luke in this scene does not hesitate to depict a woman as a disciple sitting at Jesus' feet. . . the episode is scarcely introduced to instruct women about the proper entertainment of traveling preachers. Jesus rather encourages a woman to learn from him' (*Luke*, II, p. 893).

3.   The themes of food and table-fellowship are pervasive in Luke's Gospel and relate to a wide range of issues. As R. Karris remarks, 'The extent. . . of Luke's use of the theme of food is appreciated only when the reader realizes that the aroma of food issues from each and every chapter' (*Luke: Artist and Theologian: Luke's Passion Account as Literature* [New York: Paulist Press, 1985], p. 47; cf. pp. 47-78 for an extended treatment of the motif). D.E. Smith ('Table Fellowship as a Literary Motif in the Gospel of Luke', *JBL* 106 [1987], pp. 613-38) divides his analysis of table-fellowship into five distinct categories. Our discussion is limited to only one of these areas—'Table Service as a Symbol for Community Service' (pp. 629-33)— which is most directly relevant to the situation in Acts 6.

emphatically on the Twelve than the other Gospels. Only Luke explicitly designates the apostles as οἱ δώδεκα (9.12) and further features the number as the very last word in the account (κλασμάτων κόφινοι δώδεκα: the twelve apostles take up the twelve leftover baskets [9.17]). Multiple emphatic pronouns with reference to the Twelve (ὑμεῖς, ἡμῖν, ἡμεῖς, 9.13) also highlight their role in the narrative.[1] What this role amounts to is that of resisting Jesus' intention to feed the crowd at the end of a full day of preaching and healing (9.11-13). The Twelve, who themselves have just returned from a preaching and healing campaign (9.1-6, 10),[2] balk at Jesus' plan because of what they perceive to be a grave shortage of resources. As is well known, they fail to reckon with the breadth of Jesus' power and depth of his compassion for the hungry throng (9.14-17). One lesson which clearly emerges from this miracle story is Jesus' determined blending of gospel-proclamation and food-provision in his ministry. The two tasks stand side by side as important components of his mission of mercy. The Twelve's slowness to appreciate this dual aspect of service provides an interesting prelude to their activity in Acts 6.

2. In the parable of the watchful servants, Jesus tells of an estate owner who will 'sit down to eat. . . and serve (διακονήσει)' his servants if he finds them alert to their business (Lk. 12.37). Peter then asks the Lord if this parable is 'for us [= the disciples, including the Twelve] or for everyone [= the crowd]' (12.41),[3] whereupon Jesus clarifies the duty of faithful stewards, with obvious application to the leaders of his people.[4] They must superintend the members of his household, 'to give them *their allowance of food* at the proper time' (12.42). Obviously, Jesus again pinpoints table-service/food-provision as honorable and necessary employment for himself and his ministers.[5]

---

1. Cf. Tannehill, *Narrative Unity*, I, pp. 216-17.

2. The opening statement in Lk. 9.10a—'On their return the apostles told Jesus all they had done'—clearly links the feeding story back to the report of the Twelve's preaching mission in 9.1-6. And Luke's connection between these preaching and feeding episodes is much closer than Mark's because of the greatly abbreviated intervening account of Herod's troubles with John the Baptist (Lk. 9.7-9; cf. Mk 6.14-29).

3. Cf. Fitzmyer, *Luke*, II, p. 989.

4. Cf. Tannehill, *Narrative Unity*, I, p. 217.

5. The picture of table-service in the parable no doubt has a figurative application

3. In a short parable unique to Luke, Jesus tells of a slave who returns to his master's home after working in the field. The master, Jesus suggests, will hardly invite his hired hand to dine with him but rather will insist, 'Prepare supper for me... and serve (διακόνει) me, while I eat and drink'. Such is the required duty of 'worthless slaves' (Lk. 17.7-10). The story seems to be addressed especially to Jesus' apostles (cf. 17.5, 7), exhorting them to fulfill their servant-vocation, which includes waiting on tables. More specifically, P.S. Minear thinks that Jesus aims to check the apostles' tendency to under-value domestic and 'diaconal' work in relation to their prized calling of proclaiming the gospel on the 'mission field':

> The parable distinguishes the duties in the field from those in the house. This distinction agrees with the line drawn between the duties of traveling evangelists (cultivating the field, searching for lost sheep, inviting people to the banquet table, 14.21-23) and the duties of the more sedentary deacons. The parable presupposes that the apostolic evangelists have a penchant for claiming that their work is finished when they come from the field into the house; they also have a tendency to assign priority and supe-riority to their 'field work'. The parable counters this tendency with the insistence that the same servants must fulfill both extramural and intramu-ral duties to the lord.[1]

4. In Luke, unlike the other Synoptics, the apostles' dispute over greatness takes place around the table at the Last Supper (Lk. 22.14-23), and in response Jesus holds up a table-servant (rather than a martyr-servant as in Mark and Matthew) as the model of true great-ness (22.25-27). Indeed, Jesus himself provides the supreme example of ὁ διακονῶν (22.27) by his recent service of bread and wine to his authority-minded apostles (22.17-20).[2]

These selected materials are sufficient to demonstrate Luke's appreciation of waiting on tables as a significant part of Jesus' mission

---

to all forms of ministry within the community, but this does not preclude an application to literal table-service as well. Cf. D.E. Smith: 'The text surely correlates with the reference in Acts 6.1-6 to actual table service in the early church. In addition, however, it can be interpreted as a symbol of servanthood as a whole' ('Table-Fellowship', p. 630).

1. P.S. Minear, 'A Note on Luke 17.7-10', *JBL* 93 (1974), p. 85; cf. p. 86, where an explicit connection is made between this text and Acts 6.1-6.

2. On the connection between the Last Supper scene and Jesus' statement in Lk. 22.27, see D.J. Lull, 'The Servant-Benefactor as a Model of Greatness (Luke 22.24-30)', *NovT* 28 (1986), pp. 297-99.

alongside proclaiming the word. Moreover, we have noted Jesus' repeated attempts to correct the apostles' proclivity to elevate kerygmatic ministry over domestic service. As the narrative of Acts unfolds, we begin to glimpse that in some respects the apostles have learned their lesson. While taking the lead in proclaiming the Christian message, they also attend to the material welfare of the fledgling Jerusalem church, supplying funds to anyone in need (χρεία) (4.34-35; cf. 2.43-45). In Acts 6, the Twelve affirm the priority of preaching, but still, to their credit, they continue to aid the poor by initiating the appointment of the Seven to superintend the 'need' (χρεία, 6.3) of food-provision. This division of labor perhaps betrays the apostles' abiding reluctance to participate personally in table-service, but at least they now recognize the importance of such ministry and take action to insure its efficient performance.

Certainly from Luke's perspective, revealed in the portraits of the (always) reliable Jesus and (sometimes) fallible apostles, the proclaiming and catering 'services' (διακονία) of the Twelve and Seven respectively are esteemed as complementary facets of holistic community care. More particularly, the fact that Philip waits on tables while Peter preaches the word does not subordinate the former to the latter, and the fact that Philip later launches a successful preaching mission is not at all incompatible with his earlier vocation. In short, Philip 'the evangelist who was one of the Seven' emerges in Luke's narrative as a prime model of the dutiful servant in Jesus' parable who both sows the word in the field and waits on tables in the house.[1]

c. *Pentateuchal Parallels*

Having illumined Acts 6.1-7 by exploring its wider Lukan setting, I will now attempt to interpret the passage in relation to its larger canonical framework. In particular, certain Pentateuchal accounts featuring Moses seem to have influenced the composition of Acts 6.1-7. Once again, then, I will investigate the possible Mosaic background to Luke's portrait of Philip.

A number of scholars note the apparent link between the installment of the Seven and the appointment of Joshua as Moses' successor in

---

1. Note also that after his presentation in Acts 8 as a dynamic evangelist, Philip returns in 21.8 to a domestic role as provider of hospitality (see the full discussion of this role in Chapter 6).

Num. 27.15-23.[1] The verb ἐπισκέπτομαι appears in both accounts (Acts 6.3; Num. 27.16); the Seven and Joshua are similarly portrayed as anointed by the Spirit (Acts 6.3; Num. 27.18); and they are formally set before (ἵστημι, Acts 6.6; Num. 27.22) a congregation and commissioned through the laying on of hands (Acts 6.6; Num. 27.23). While such parallels are indeed striking, they must not blind us to important differences between the two cases, especially pertaining to the roles of the assembly and its leaders.

In the Numbers incident, Moses consults directly with the Lord and assumes total control of the situation. He asks the Lord to appoint a successor, and the Lord promptly singles out Joshua and outlines the ordination process (27.15-21). The assembly is gathered but plays a strictly passive role. Moses is the one who takes Joshua, sets him before the congregation (and Eleazar the priest) and lays hands upon him (27.22-23). In so doing, Moses invests Joshua with his personal, God-given authority (cf. 27.20). By marked contrast, the congregation in Acts 6 participates much more actively. As we have seen, the entire Christian community selects the Seven, presents them before the Twelve and lays hands upon them. The Twelve play their part, but in this case they should not be facilely identified with Moses as exclusive agents of God's authority. The Seven are not cast as official successors to the Twelve, but rather as representatives of the larger assembly. If Luke did compose Acts 6.1-7 with an eye to Num. 27.15-23 (which seems likely), he clearly adapted his biblical model to feature a more egalitarian, cooperative relationship between God's people and their leaders.

In a fresh analysis of Acts 6.1-7, D. Daube examines the literary links with three Mosaic episodes dealing with the appointment of administrative assistants.[2] In Exodus 18 Moses' father-in-law, Jethro, observes a typical workday for Israel's leader. Jethro concludes that

---

1. E.g. Haenchen, *Acts*, p. 262; Marshall, *Acts*, pp. 126-27; Daube, *New Testament and Rabbinic Judaism*, pp. 238-39; Roloff, *Apostelgeschichte*, p. 119.

2. Daube, 'Reform'. This article (published in 1976) updates and expands the author's earlier discussion of Acts 6.1-7 in *New Testament and Rabbinic Judaism* (1956), pp. 237-39. Daube's insights have been incorporated into two recent German commentaries: Schneider, *Apostelgeschichte*, I, pp. 422-30; and Pesch, *Apostelgeschichte*, I, pp. 225-26. (These two works also discuss Pharaoh's appointment of Joseph to oversee the distribution of grain in Gen. 41.29-43 as a possible literary background to Acts 6.1-7.)

Moses' frenetic schedule of settling disputes from dawn to dusk 'is not good', since it will eventually sap his strength (18.14-18). Jethro then devises a plan to ease Moses' burden involving the selection (σκέπτομαι) of 'able men' to be placed over (καθίστημι) segments of the population to judge their petty conflicts. Only critical cases must be brought to Moses (18.19-23). Such a proposal pleases Moses, and he proceeds to choose his own helpers (18.24-27).

In a related but not identical passage from Deuteronomy 1, Moses rehearses the process of appointing managerial aides. Here Jethro is not mentioned. Moses simply refers to his growing awareness that he needed assistance in governing the Israelite horde (πλῆθος) whom God had steadily multiplied (πληθύνω) (1.10). So, according to this review, he instructed the people to choose for themselves 'wise (σοφία), discerning and reputable' judges (1.13). They endorsed the plan (1.14), and Moses installed (καθίστημι) the judges to settle disputes of 'the small and the great alike', except for difficult cases which Moses would still decide (1.15-17).

It is clear that a number of linguistic and thematic elements link these two Pentateuchal incidents and Acts 6.1-7. But once again there are important distinctions. Daube recognizes the greater involvement of the congregation in Acts 6 but fails to appreciate a further difference in the assignments of duty. He sees a close parallel between Moses' delegation of lesser matters to his assistants so he could attend to weightier decisions and the Twelve's relinquishment of 'the smaller, controversial business' of table-service to the Seven[1] in order to devote themselves to the vital tasks of preaching and prayer.[2] In fact, although Moses' helpers and the Seven are both appointed to solve administrative crises within expanding communities, their specific duties are quite different. Israel's judges oversaw small units

---

1. Daube thinks that Acts 6.3 should be taken to mean that the apostles had been trying to manage the table ministry themselves: 'it is no good that, having abandoned preaching, we are engaged in the distribution of supplies' ('Reform', p. 155). But the majority of scholars would follow Haenchen's interpretation:

> These words do not mean that the Apostles gave up this service because they were overworked; καταλείψαντας does not express past action: the Apostles are not reproaching themselves with having taken over the serving of tables (with unhappy results, at that) and therefore neglected their preaching. Luke is rather explaining to the reader why the Apostles did not themselves assume this responsibility (*Acts*, p. 262).

2. Daube, 'Reform', pp. 154-55.

of people within an elaborate corporate structure topped by Moses, the chief executive, legislator and judge. Stephen, Philip and company, however, constitute a service organization—not a judicial body—for the entire congregation—not merely a sub-group. Moreover, the 'business' of table-service appears to be transferred wholly and exclusively to the Seven; no stipulation is introduced suggesting that the Seven bring difficult matters to the Twelve for final adjudication. As argued above, the Seven are cast more as the apostles' partners than their employees in the work of community care. Once again we must conclude that, if Luke did depend on Mosaic models from Exodus and Deuteronomy, he freely adjusted the hierarchical community structure which they assume.

The third Old Testament incident which Daube discusses as a model for Acts 6.1-7 again comes from Numbers. The parallel here is especially noteworthy in that both episodes are sparked by grumbling (γογγύζω, Num. 11.1; γογγυσμός, Acts 6.1) over food supply. In Numbers the Israelites plead for meat to supplement the manna they had already received (11.1-9). Such murmuring prompts Moses to protest his heavy burden of leading the nation, whereupon the Lord instructs him to share the load with seventy elders (11.16-17). When Moses assembles these elders, the Lord 'comes down' and imparts to them a portion of the Spirit possessed by Moses, causing them to *prophesy* (11.24-25). Interestingly, nothing is said about the Seventy's assistance in the immediate dietary crisis. This the Lord handles himself with a mighty gust of wind which brings a flock of quail into the camp (11.31-32; cf. 11.18-23).

Yet again the evidence suggests a broad correspondence but not a perfect match between the Pentateuchal narrative and Acts 6.1-7. A notable difference (which Daube does not point out) pertains to the ultimate outcomes of the two incidents. In Numbers the complainers are struck down by the Lord 'while the meat [is] still between their teeth' (11.33-34), whereas in Acts the widows' grumbling is treated sympathetically, and the final result of satisfying their need is community growth (6.7). An essentially tragic Old Testament story finds a positive counterpart in Acts.

Even with these divergent endings, the two accounts remain closely tied in their portraits of the Seventy (Numbers) and Seven (Acts). Apart from the obvious numerical connection, the two groups function in similar ways. The Seventy, chosen to aid Moses during a crisis over food supply and cast ultimately as Spirit-anointed prophets, provide an interesting biblical precedent for Stephen and Philip among the Seven, who likewise emerge as Spirit-empowered prophets after their appointment as table-servants.[1]

The special case of the two prophesying elders, Eldad and Medad, defended by Moses against Joshua in Numbers 11, may intimate a further link to Stephen and Philip.

> And Joshua son of Nun, the assistant of Moses, one of his chosen men, said, 'My lord Moses, stop them (κώλυσον αὐτούς)!' But Moses said to him, 'Are you jealous for my sake? Would that all the Lord's people were prophets, that the Lord would put his spirit upon them!' (11.28-29).

There is some evidence of early Christian interest in Eldad and Medad (Modad), even to the point of circulating a book (no longer extant) allegedly detailing their prophecies (cf. Hermas, *Vis.* 2.3.4).[2] In Luke's case, the Eldad/Medad story seems to inform the brief report of Jesus' rebuke of John (one of his 'chosen' apostles, Lk. 6.13-14) for forbidding (κωλύω) an outsider to minister in Jesus' name (9.49-50).[3] Is it possible, then, that Eldad and Medad also underlie the Acts narratives of Stephen and Philip—two men outside the circle of the Twelve who function, however, not only as table-servants but also— just like the Twelve—as Spirit-inspired prophets? Daube specifically compares Joshua's resistance to Eldad and Medad *for Moses' sake* with the attack on Stephen for uttering 'blasphemous words against *Moses* and God' (Acts 6.11).[4] In any event, it is quite certain that Luke does not regard the prophetic activities of Stephen and Philip as in any sense improper or inconsistent with their former catering duties or

---

1. For a discussion of Luke's typological method which correlates the seventy elders (seventy-two with Eldad and Medad?) in Num. 11 with the seventy(-two) messengers in Lk. 10 and the seven servants in Acts 6, see A.M. Farrer, 'The Ministry in the New Testament', in *The Apostolic Ministry: Essays on the History and the Doctrine of the Episcopacy* (ed. K.E. Kirk; London: Hodder & Stoughton, new edn, 1957 [1946]), pp. 133-50.

2. See E.G. Martin, 'Eldad and Modad', in Charlesworth (ed.), *Old Testament Pseudepigrapha*, II, pp. 463-65.

3. Cf. Marshall: 'The background of the story lies. . . in the appointment of the Twelve to mission, and their incredulity that one who had not been authorised in the same way should be doing the same work. It is thus a NT parallel to the situation in Nu. 11.24-30' (*Gospel of Luke*, p. 398).

4. Daube, 'Reform', pp. 158-59.

lack of apostolic status. Speaking through the voice of the apostle Peter—the leader of the Twelve—as well as the prophet Joel, Luke announces in the Pentecost sermon the fulfillment of Moses' wish cited above: 'that all the Lord's people were prophets, that the Lord would put his spirit upon them!'

> In the last days it will be, God declares, that I will pour out my Spirit upon all flesh, and your sons and your daughters shall prophesy. . . even upon my slaves, both men and women, in those days I will pour out my Spirit; and they shall prophesy (Acts 2.17-18).

d. *Conclusion*

The foregoing analysis of Acts 6.1-7 has confirmed the consensus view that Luke has broadly shaped his portrait of the Jerusalem community to camouflage the conflict and highlight the harmony between the Twelve and the Seven. However, I have interpreted the precise dimensions of this portrait in a distinctive way. Luke does not erect a rigid hierarchical structure with the Twelve at the summit, fulfilling top priority assignments, and the Seven underneath them, tending to more menial matters. Rather, he takes a more egalitarian line affirming the executive authority of the entire Christian assembly (supported but not dominated by its leaders) and the comparability of proclaiming the word and waiting on tables as valued expressions of Christian (= Christ-like) service ($\delta \iota \alpha \kappa o \nu \iota \alpha$).[1]

Accordingly, as key representatives of the Seven and Twelve, Philip and Peter appear in Acts 6 as partners in ministry, cooperative and complementary servants of Christ and his church. This relationship must be kept in mind when evaluating the overlapping missions of the same two figures in chs. 8–11. Here, however, an important new factor complicates the situation: the respective functions of Philip and Peter as channels of the Spirit. It is to this issue that I now turn.

3. *Philip, Peter and the Spirit (Acts 8–11)*

a. *Statement of the Problem*

Earlier I adumbrated the apparent incongruity of Philip's lack of involvement in conferring the Spirit upon his converts compared with

---

1. Cf. J. Koenig, *New Testament Hospitality: Partnership with Strangers as Promise and Mission* (OBT, 17; Philadelphia: Fortress Press, 1985), pp. 107-10, 122 n. 36.

his otherwise dynamic evangelistic efforts. I must now expose the problem in more detail. The case of the Samaritan mission poses a particularly perplexing 'riddle'.[1] It appears anomalous within the New Testament in its temporal dissociation of Spirit-reception from the moment of conversion-initiation (typically linked closely to water-baptism). Paul and John certainly think that the true believer automatically possesses the Spirit (e.g. Gal. 3.2, 5; Rom. 8.9; Jn 3.5-8; 7.38-39), but evidently so does Luke, according to the key statement in Acts 2.38: 'Repent, and be baptized every one of you in the name of Jesus Christ so that your sins may be forgiven you; and you will receive the gift of the Holy Spirit'. How then do we explain the lapse of time (of unspecified duration) between the Samaritans' faith and baptism in 8.12-13 and their reception of the Spirit in 8.14-17?

Various attempts to diminish the problem have focused on some kind of two-stage schema of the Spirit's manifestation. In other words, the Spirit is perceived as coming in some measure upon the Samaritans when they believe and are baptized, only to be poured out later in some degree of greater fullness. Particular theological constructions undergirding this perspective include: (1) the classical Pentecostal understanding of Spirit-baptism (usually accompanied by speaking in tongues) as a 'second blessing' experienced only by select believers, marking a higher level of spirituality than that attained at conversion;[2] (2) the classical Catholic position regarding confirmation, whereby the separate rite of the laying on of hands 'completes' the believer's relationship to the Spirit begun in baptism;[3] and (3) the view that Acts 8.14-17 merely recounts the added experience of external phenomena (not the Spirit itself) to authenticate the Spirit's presence within the Samaritan disciples and legitimate a new

---

1. Cf. ch. 5, 'The Riddle of Samaria', in Dunn, *Baptism in the Holy Spirit*, pp. 55-68.

2. E.g. H.D. Hunter, *Spirit-Baptism: A Pentecostal Alternative* (Lanham, MD: University Press of America, 1983), pp. 83-84; H.M. Ervin, *Conversion-Initiation and the Baptism in the Holy Spirit* (Peabody, MA: Hendrickson, 1985), pp. 25-40.

3. E.g. N. Adler, *Taufe und Handauflegung: Eine exegetisch-theologische Untersuchung von Apg. 8,14-17* (NTAbh, 19/3; Münster: Aschendorff, 1951), pp. 109-17; J. Coppens, 'L'imposition des mains dans les Actes des Apôtres', in Kremer (ed.), *Les Actes des Apôtres*, pp. 423-32; L. Dewar, *The Holy Spirit and Modern Thought* (New York: Harper, 1959), pp. 51-57; cf. discussion in Bovon, *Luc le théologien*, pp. 244-52.

missionary advance beyond Jerusalem.[1]

However distinct from one another these theories may be and whatever their individual difficulties, an insuperable problem plaguing them all is the plain reading of Luke's text. One simply cannot get around the stark statement in Acts 8.16 concerning the Spirit:

οὐδέπω γὰρ ἦν ἐπ᾽ οὐδενὶ αὐτῶν ἐπιπεπτωκός, μόνον δὲ βεβαπτισμένοι ὑπῆρχον εἰς τὸ ὄνομα τοῦ κυρίου Ἰησοῦ.

The words οὐδέπω, οὐδενί and μόνον all drive home the absoluteness of the Spirit's *absence* among the believing and baptized Samaritans. The first term, very rare in the New Testament, is also combined with οὐδείς in a version of Lk. 23.53 to describe the tomb of Jesus 'where no one had ever been laid'[2] (cf. Jn 19.41). Clearly Acts 8.16 communicates in exclusive terms that *no one* converted in Philip's Samaritan mission *had ever* received the gift of the Spirit. It is likely that what Simon sees in 8.18 are the outward signs of the Spirit's presence,[3] but as with similar scenes in Acts (2.1-4; 10.44-48; 19.1-7), the visible signs are manifested precisely at the time of the Spirit's coming.

A more feasible attempt to explain the oddity of the so-called 'Samaritan Pentecost' questions whether chronological concerns matter that much in Luke's accounts of the Spirit's operations. We need only compare the Samaritans' situation with that of Cornelius and family in Acts 10, which displays the Spirit's spontaneous effusion *before* baptism, to detect a certain flexibility in scheduling the Spirit's activities in relation to new believers. The important thing for Luke seems to be the *total experience* of respondents to the gospel, including such typical components as repentance, faith, water-baptism and forgiveness of sins, along with possession of the Spirit—but not

1. E.g. G.R. Beasley-Murray, *Baptism in the New Testament* (Exeter: Paternoster Press, 1972), pp. 119-20; J.E.L. Oulton, 'Holy Spirit, Baptism and Laying on of Hands in Acts', *ExpTim* 66 (1954–55), pp. 236-40; and more recently Gourges:

> The Samaritans had only received individually the gift of the 'quiet Spirit' linked with baptism. The laying on of hands performed by Peter and Paul [*sic*] coincides with a 'Pentecost' or manifestation of the 'shattering Spirit' which indicates that the time has come to move into the second stage of mission ('Esprit des commencements', p. 376).

2. οὗ οὐκ ἦν οὐδεὶς οὐδέπω κείμενος (attested in Sinaiticus and incorporated into the Westcott–Hort text).

3. Oulton, 'Holy Spirit', p. 238.

ordered according to any rigidly determined pattern. Accordingly, the fact that the Samaritans *eventually* receive the promised gift of the Spirit may be viewed as adequate fulfillment of Acts 2.38.[1]

Whatever the merits of such an approach to handling certain soteriological (*ordo salutis*) questions surrounding the time lag between the Samaritans' conversion-initiation and reception of the Spirit, there remains a critical ministerial problem regarding the role of human agents as channels of the Spirit. Here is where doubts may arise as to Philip's competence as a missionary. For Luke outlines a series of events in which the Samaritans receive the Spirit not only at a different time than their baptism, but also at the hands of different ministers—Peter and John—than the one who baptized them—Philip. Indeed, it could easily be inferred that the Samaritans must wait for the Spirit precisely because they must wait for the arrival of authorized ministers—distinct from Philip!—to impart the Spirit to them. Philip's lack of participation in bestowing the Spirit becomes even more puzzling in comparison with his otherwise charismatic role in Acts 8 as wonder-worker and beneficiary of the Spirit's guidance (8.6-7, 13, 29, 39),[2] and with the portrait of Ananias, a devoted but scarcely dynamic disciple,[3] in ch. 9 as the instrument through which no less a one than Saul receives the Spirit in abundance (9.17). Why does Philip the mighty evangelist fail where a lesser light like Ananias succeeds? Are we pressed at last to agree with Käsemann that Luke has 'stigmatized' Philip's ministry as 'defective'?[4]

Whatever his shortcoming with the Samaritans, Philip's reputation as a channel of the Spirit might be vindicated in his encounter with the Ethiopian eunuch. First, some have argued for the priority of the longer 'Western' reading in Acts 8.39, which depicts the Spirit not as snatching Philip away but rather as *falling upon the eunuch* immediately after his baptism (an angel then relocates Philip). Nevertheless,

---

1. Cf. S. New, 'The Name, Baptism, and the Laying on of Hands', in Lake and Cadbury (eds.), *Beginnings of Christianity*, V, pp. 136-37.

2. Cf. Schmithals: 'das Manko der Samaritaner unbegreiflich bleibt, da ja Philippus "voll von Geist". . . wirkt und tauft' (*Apostelgeschichte*, p. 81).

3. Acts presents Ananias as 'a disciple' (9.10) and 'a devout man according to the law and well spoken of by all the Jews' (22.12)—but nowhere is he portrayed as being Spirit-empowered or performing miraculous deeds.

4. E. Käsemann, *Essays on New Testament Themes* (Philadelphia: Fortress Press, repr. 1982 [1964]), p. 146.

most commentators and all modern texts and translations opt in favor of the shorter standard text. Its external attestation is considerably stronger, and it stakes a better claim to being the *lectio difficilior*. It is hard to imagine why any scribe would uniquely characterize the Spirit as a transporter of missionaries[1] or arbitrarily omit an explicit reference to the Spirit's outpouring in Acts.[2]

The text-critical issue aside, some interpreters take the concluding note that the eunuch 'went on his way rejoicing' as evidence that he had indeed received the Spirit.[3] Certainly in Luke's understanding joy flows as a natural result of possessing the Spirit (cf. Acts 13.52), but in fact rejoicing is no automatic guarantee of the Spirit's presence. We have only to recall the previous Philip narrative in which the Samaritans experience 'great joy' (8.8) over the gospel and yet still at this point do not possess the Spirit (8.16). The eunuch seems to be in a similar state when he and Philip part company.

Although we learn nothing, as with the Samaritans, of the Ethiopian treasurer's subsequent reception of the Spirit, we do read soon of the Spirit's descent upon that other foreign official, Cornelius. But, of course, in this case the 'minister-in-charge' is the apostle Peter. Philip the evangelist, although situated in the city of Caesarea (Acts 8.40; cf. 21.8), plays no role at all in the Cornelius affair. As with the Samaritans, so with the Gentiles Philip paves the way through his work of gospel-preaching and water-baptism but then gives way to Peter's climactic ministry of imparting the Spirit. Despite the interpretation of Acts 6.1-7 offered above, must we now conclude from Acts 8–11 that in the final analysis Luke has subordinated Philip to Peter? In any event, we must attempt to account for Philip's peculiar

---

1. The 'rapture' idea associated with ἁρπάζω does appear in 2 Cor. 12.2, 4, 1 Thess. 4.17 and Rev. 12.5—but not in conjunction with the Spirit or missionary travel. Cf. Coppens, 'L'imposition des mains', p. 411.

2. Lake and Cadbury (*Beginnings of Christianity*, V, p. 98) suggest that the 'Western' reading is the more difficult since it clashes with Acts 8.14-17. It does conflict with the Samaritan story by associating Philip with the Spirit's coming, but 8.14-17 and the 'Western' text of 8.39 agree that the Spirit is poured out upon believers, whereas the shorter text of 8.39 diverges from 8.14-17 in that the Spirit, as far as we are told, does not come at all—immediately or later—upon the eunuch.

3. Marshall, *Acts*, pp. 165-66; Bruce, *Book of Acts*, p. 178; G.W.H. Lampe, *The Seal of the Spirit: A Study in the Doctrine of Baptism and Confirmation in the New Testament and the Fathers* (London: SPCK, 2nd edn, 1967), pp. 65-67; Beasley-Murray, *Baptism*, pp. 118-19.

dissociation from Peter in the matter of transmitting the Spirit to Samaritan and Gentile converts.

A typical approach to this conundrum focuses on Philip's status as an independent, itinerant evangelist in comparison with Peter's role as the established Jerusalem apostle. I now turn to evaluate this approach and to set the stage for proposing a more distinctive solution to the problem in the following section.

b. *Philip the Independent Evangelist and Peter the Jerusalem Apostle*
Käsemann's opinion that Luke has purposefully downgraded Philip's evangelistic achievements springs from a particular understanding of Lukan ecclesiology. According to this view, Luke conceives of the church as the *Una sancta catholica* built on the foundation of the twelve apostles and rigidly exclusive of all divergent ideologies, such as Gnosticism. More specifically, Luke makes his point by magnifying the apostles' centralized, Jerusalem-based authority over the expanding church, including their unique prerogative to impart the Spirit to new believers. Thus, 'freelance' missionaries like Philip and Apollos (Acts 18.24-28), who strike out on their own with alarming success, are deliberately diminished and brought under the ecclesiastical umbrella by making their converts wait to receive the Spirit through official channels (the Twelve/Paul).[1] In a similar vein, Haenchen contends that Luke's account of the Spirit's outpouring in Acts 8.14-17 is designed to emphasize that 'the mission to the Samaritans was not completed by any subordinate outsider [= Philip], but was carried out in due form by the legal heads of the Church [= the Twelve]'.[2]

The connection between Philip and Apollos is noteworthy and merits further attention below, but the portrait of the apostles as Spirit-dispensing executives who sanction the work of maverick missionaries and safeguard the unity of the church simply does not match the full presentation in Acts. Lowly Ananias, for example, heals and confers the Spirit on Saul in Acts 9.17 without any apostolic aid. Barnabas, an emissary of the Jerusalem church (though not one of the Twelve), instructs and encourages the young Antiochene Christians

---

1. Käsemann, *Essays*, pp. 90, 136-48; cf. *idem*, *New Testament Questions of Today* (Philadelphia: Fortress Press, repr. 1979 [1969]), pp. 236-43.

2. Haenchen, *Acts*, p. 306; cf. also Conzelmann, *Apostelgeschichte*, pp. 61-62; Koch, 'Geistbesitz', pp. 69-82; Weiser, *Apostelgeschichte*, I, pp. 200, 203.

but does not transmit the Spirit to them (11.22-25).[1] The Spirit's presence in Antioch is simply assumed in 13.2 without any formal account of its descent. Repeated references to the Spirit as God's 'gift' (δωρεά/δίδωμι: Acts 2.38; 8.20; 10.45; 11.17; 15.8; cf. Lk. 11.13) suggest that bestowing the Spirit is ultimately not a human prerogative at all, apostolic or otherwise. This point is forcefully driven home in the larger Samaritan episode. Simon Magus desires the authority to confer the Spirit and is willing to pay for it. He is sternly rebuffed, however, since anything to do with the Spirit as δωρεὰ τοῦ θεοῦ (8.20) is by definition not for sale, not disposable by human means.[2] Only God can bestow the Spirit; thus, any attempt to manipulate the Spirit for personal ends represents a perverse usurpation of divine privilege (8.21-24).

Even the Lord's apostles must recognize the sovereignty of God in matters concerning the Spirit. Hence their primary response to a need for the Spirit is *prayer* (Acts 8.15),[3] beseeching God for what he alone can give. The Spirit is 'given' (δίδωμι, 8.18) and 'received' (λαμβάνω, 8.15, 17, 19), not strictly administered and obtained. It is perceived as 'falling' (ἐπιπίπτω, 8.16) from heaven rather than being brought down. With all of these emphases on the Spirit's freedom within the Samaritan incident and throughout Acts (cf. 21.4; 10.44-47; 11.15-17), it is most difficult to sustain an 'early Catholic' interpretation of the Spirit's management by apostolic officials.[4]

---

1. Cf. Dunn, *Baptism*, pp. 58-59; Beasley-Murray, *Baptism*, pp. 114-15; H. von Baer, *Der Heilige Geist in den Lukasschriften* (BWANT, 39; Stuttgart: Kohlhammer, 1926), pp. 172-73; M. Quesnel, *Baptisés dans l'Esprit: Baptême et Esprit Saint dans les Actes des Apôtres* (LD, 120; Paris: Cerf, 1985), pp. 60-61.

2. Cf. Barrett, 'Light on the Holy Spirit', pp. 292-95; Dietrich, *Petrusbild*, pp. 253-56.

3. 'The two. . . *prayed* for them that [so that, ὅπως] they might receive the Holy Spirit' (Acts 8.15). The laying on of hands follows immediately as an accompanying activity, but it appears to be less directly connected to the actual transmission of the Spirit: 'then Peter and John laid their hands on them, and (καί) they received the Holy Spirit' (8.17). Of course, Simon Magus interprets the Spirit as coming through the laying on of hands. But this may be viewed as part of his skewed perspective on the whole event.

On the connection between prayer and the activity of the Spirit in Luke–Acts see Lk. 11.13; Acts 1.14 and 2.1-4; 4.31; 13.1-3; and S. Smalley, 'Spirit, Kingdom and Prayer in Luke–Acts', *NovT* 15 (1973), pp. 59-71.

4. Cf. Barrett, 'Light on the Holy Spirit', pp. 292-95; *idem*, *Church*, pp. 58-59,

W. Dietrich realizes that on the whole Luke does not restrict the Spirit's transmission to the apostles, but he does argue that underlying Acts 8.14-17 was an early Jerusalem tradition which did credit the apostles with exclusive authority to impart the Spirit.[1] As for Philip's role in the Samaritan mission, Dietrich suggests that it betrays a 'limitation of competence' (*Kompetenzbegrenzung*) compared with the 'competence' of the Jerusalem apostles to confer the Spirit, but he also claims that Philip's ministry is thereby 'in no way discredited'.[2] Apparently, Dietrich means that just because Philip and Peter perform different tasks is no reason to assume that one task is necessarily more important than the other.[3]

As for the hypothesis that Acts 8.14-17 stems from a primitive source which singled out the apostles as authorized agents of the Spirit, the problem of anachronism rears its head. Solid evidence for rigid institutionalization of ministry only surfaces toward the end of the first century and into the second. Certainly the undisputed letters of Paul bear witness to a rather fluid church structure marked by charismatic instead of institutional authority.[4] The Spirit is sovereignly bestowed by the Lord himself, not funnelled through any hierarchy (cf. Gal. 3.5; Rom. 8.14-17; 12.3-8; 1 Cor. 2.10-14; 12.1-31). Another difficulty with Dietrich's analysis is the opinion that Luke has incorporated without alteration an early tradition regarding the Spirit which stands in contrast to his overall presentation. My earlier analysis of Acts 8.4-25 demonstrated that, whatever the sources at his disposal, Luke has thoroughly shaped the material into a unified story with numerous links to the rest of his narrative. In 8.14-17 elements such as the word of God, prayer, baptism in Jesus' name and the

78-80; Dunn, *Unity and Diversity*, pp. 356-58.

1. Dietrich, *Petrusbild*, pp. 248-51. He notes in particular the divergence of the supposed traditional remnant in Acts 8.14-17 from Luke's own view in 9.17, for example, which allows for someone who was not an apostle (Ananias) to transmit the Spirit (p. 251 n. 160). Cf. Lake, 'The Holy Spirit', in Lake and Cadbury (eds.), *Beginnings of Christianity*, V, pp. 108-10.

2. Dietrich, *Petrusbild*, pp. 249-51.

3. Dietrich speaks of the 'Ausbleiben jeglicher abträglichen Bewertung oder positiven Beurteilung' in the portrait of Philip's ministry in Acts 8. Moreover, 'hat Philippus das Vorrecht der Apostel respektiert und seine Tätigkeit auf Verkündigung und Taufe beschränkt, ohne dass diese Kompetenzbegrenzung für ihn zu einem offenen oder latenten Problem geworden wäre' (*Petrusbild*, pp. 249-50).

4. Cf. Dunn, *Unity and Diversity*, pp. 106-14.

laying on of hands, not to mention the outpouring of the Spirit, are echoed repeatedly throughout Acts. On a matter of such seminal importance to Luke as the coming of the Spirit, we would expect more coherence of presentation than Dietrich seems to allow.[1] With these criticisms aside, Dietrich makes a useful observation in noting that the distinctive roles assigned to Philip and Peter in Samaria need not be differentiated in importance. I made a similar point above in relation to the division of labor in Jerusalem between Philip's table-service and Peter's ministry of the word.

While Acts 8.14-17 does not appear to portray Peter and John as sacramental officials monopolizing the administration of the Spirit, it may reflect a Lukan interest in the apostolic pair as representatives of the resident 'Hebrew' faction of the Jerusalem church. Thus, the Samaritan incident would illustrate the unity which remained between this group and the scattered 'Hellenists', represented by Philip, after Stephen's death.[2] The acts of praying and laying on of hands performed by the visiting apostles in 8.15, 17 may once again be viewed as gestures of solidarity (cf. 6.6) as well as catalysts of the Spirit's outpouring. The two representatives of the Twelve proffer the hand of fellowship both to the outcast Samaritans[3] and (implicitly) to Philip, the architect of the Samaritan mission who himself had been recently estranged from Jerusalem. Notions of Philip's subordination to Peter and John need not enter the picture. The apostles may simply be acknowledging the evangelist as a partner in mission.

The acceptance of Philip's Samaritan enterprise by leaders of the Jerusalem church may also demonstrate Luke's 'salvation-historical' interest in establishing the continuity of every new phase of the Christian mission with the earthly ministry of Jesus—which culminated in Jerusalem—and with the first community of Jesus' disciples—localized in Jerusalem.[4] To be sure, Jerusalem does not function in

---

1. Cf. Oulton, 'Holy Spirit', p. 236; Beasley-Murray, *Baptism*, pp. 104-12.

2. Cf. Stählin, *Apostelgeschichte*, pp. 122-24; Barrett, 'Light on the Holy Spirit', pp. 281-82.

3. For the emphasis on fellowship in this encounter, see Lampe, *Seal*, pp. 69-72; F.F. Bruce, 'The Holy Spirit in the Acts of the Apostles', *Int* 27 (1973), p. 174.

4. See E. Schweizer, 'πνεῦμα, πνευματικός', *TDNT*, VI, pp. 411-13; Löning, 'Lukas—Theologe', pp. 205-10, 228; S. Brown, '"Water-Baptism" and "Spirit-Baptism" in Luke–Acts', *ATR* 59 (1977), p. 149; W. Wilkens, 'Wassertaufe und Geistempfang bei Lukas', *TZ* 23 (1967), pp. 26-27.

Acts like some kind of grand ecclesiastical see ruling over all Christendom. For instance, the give-and-take negotiations between Jerusalem leaders and Paul over the Gentile mission in chs. 15 and 21 chart a relationship of mutual respect and cooperation. It likewise follows, as already suggested, that the Jerusalem apostles do not function in Acts as episcopal officers for the whole church, roaming about the empire imposing their will.[1] They simply represent the interests of Jewish Christians based in Jerusalem, and then not exclusively. Ambassadors from Jerusalem also include ministers outside the Twelve, such as Barnabas, Agabus, Judas and Silas, all dispatched to Antioch (11.22, 28; 15.27, 32). So Luke still allows for a measure of independence and diversity within early Christianity. But for all this, we must not minimize Luke's overriding emphasis that a cooperative tie is never broken between the various mission congregations (and their leaders) and the mother church (and her leaders) in Jerusalem.

Granting that the Samaritan episode in Acts 8 displays a mutual rather than hierarchical relationship between Philip and Peter and a continuity between Philip's mission and the center of 'salvation history' in Jerusalem, the question still remains: why the focus on the Samaritans' reception of the Spirit? An apostolic visit to Samaria exhibiting friendly relations with Philip and integrating his mission into God's redemptive plan could have easily been recounted without bringing in the controversial matter of the Samaritans' lack of the Spirit. For example, bridges are built between Jerusalem and Paul without making Paul dependent on the Twelve for supplying the Spirit. Paul himself receives the Spirit at the hands of a Damascene disciple unconnected to Jerusalem and later conveys the Spirit to a group of Ephesian believers without any outside intervention. What then is the significance of forging the bond between Philip and Peter around the issue of Spirit-transmission? A special literary pattern in Luke–Acts may provide some helpful clues.

c. *Philip the Forerunner and Peter the Culminator*
In the preceding chapter I broadly characterized Philip in Acts 8–11 as Peter's forerunner in Samaria and the coastal plain. In the present chapter, I will probe more fully a particular aspect of this Philip–

---

1. Cf. Dunn, *Baptism*, p. 59; S.G. Wilson: 'Luke himself has left hints which show that Jerusalem did not enjoy such a ubiquitous role as overseer of all missionary development as his overall scheme implies' (*Gentiles*, p. 240).

Peter relationship in Acts 8–11: Philip's initial mission of preaching and baptizing (with water) followed by Peter's climactic work of imparting the Spirit to Samaritan and Gentile converts. When we combine these elements, an interesting relational pattern emerges:

Philip	=	the *forerunner* who proclaims the gospel and baptizes with water
Peter	=	the *culminator* who comes after and 'baptizes' with the Spirit

R. Tannehill detects a similar, though not identical, 'initiator–verifier' pattern.[1] While such terminology (especially 'verifier') may conjure up hierarchical images of official, apostolic authorization or inquisitorial inspection, this is not Tannehill's intention. He very much affirms an abiding, 'cooperative' relationship between Philip and the Jerusalem apostles:

> through the arrival of Peter and John, and through their important action on behalf of the Samaritans, the mission becomes a cooperative undertaking. Philip is the initiator, but Peter and John also make an important contribution. Philip's mission does not become an independent operation, for the apostles quickly establish contact and help the Samaritans to share in the Holy Spirit. The result is a cooperative mission in which an established church affirms and contributes to the establishment of new churches.[2]

In my opinion, the model of 'forerunner–culminator' more clearly reveals the cooperative dimension of the interplay between Philip and Peter and is less open to misinterpretation. More than that, it readily recalls a potentially illuminating Lukan parallel which Tannehill neglects to discuss: the relationship between John the Baptist and Jesus.

In Luke 3 John comes on the scene 'proclaiming a baptism of repentance' and 'prepar[ing] the way of the Lord', as Isaiah had predicted (3.3-4). More specifically, John prepares the way for Jesus the messiah and delineates his relationship to this coming one in the well-known formula: 'I baptize you with water; but one who is more powerful than I is coming. . . He will baptize you with the Holy Spirit and fire' (3.16). All of the Gospel writers in some fashion set forth John's role as Jesus' forerunner, typified in the distinction between John's water-baptism and Jesus' Spirit-baptism (Mt. 3.3, 11; Mk 1.2-4,

---

1. Tannehill, *Narrative Unity*, II, pp. 102-12.
2. Tannehill, *Narrative Unity*, II, p. 104.

7-8; Jn 1.6-8, 15, 23, 26-34). But Luke makes much more of this relational pattern than the other evangelists, especially when we consider the material in his second volume.

Just before his ascension to heaven, the risen Jesus instructs his apostles to tarry in Jerusalem and 'wait there for the promise of the Father' which he had previously announced (Acts 1.4; cf. Lk. 24.49). Jesus then identifies this anticipated blessing as the Holy Spirit and separates its provision from the ministry of John in terms clearly echoing John's own earlier prediction: 'for John baptized with water, but you will be baptized with the Holy Spirit not many days from now' (Acts 1.5; cf. Lk. 3.16). Once again the antithesis presented here is strictly between one who baptizes with water and one who baptizes with the Spirit.[1] No variation is suggested as yet between two types of water-baptism (one 'of repentance' and the other 'in the name of Jesus').

As the Acts narrative unfolds, the Pentecost event marks the initial fulfillment of Jesus' announcement of the Spirit's coming. The apostles had formerly encountered the baptizing mission of John (Acts 1.21-22) but had not yet been baptized with the Spirit. Assembling together on the day of Pentecost, they now receive—through Jesus—the promised Holy Spirit (2.33; cf. 1.4-5). Later, Peter recalls this 'beginning' of his experience of the Spirit and its connection to 'the word of the Lord' concerning Spirit-baptism as distinct from John's water-baptism (11.15-16). Significantly, the particular context for these reflections is Peter's report to the Jerusalem church about his recent mission to Caesarea, in which he compares his own Pentecostal experience to the Spirit's surprising descent upon the Gentile Cornelius before water-baptism even came up for discussion:

> And as I began to speak, the Holy Spirit fell on them [Cornelius and his household] just as it had upon us at the beginning. And I remembered the word of the Lord, how he had said, 'John baptized with water, but you will be baptized with the Holy Spirit' (11.15-16; cf. 10.44-48).

Another reference to John's baptism surfaces earlier in the Cornelius story as part of Peter's message about Jesus (10.37). Similarly, on two occasions later in Acts, Paul reiterates the preparatory vocation of John in relation to Jesus (13.24-25; 19.4), and in the latter instance he

---

1. The precise identity of the baptizer with the Spirit remains unclear in Acts 1.5, but 2.32-33 clearly attributes this work to the risen and exalted Christ.

proceeds to impart the Spirit to a group of Ephesian disciples who had received John's baptism but knew nothing of the Spirit's presence in their lives (19.1-7).

Given this evidence that Acts continues to feature John the Baptist as Jesus' forerunner and specifically recalls the contrast between John's water-baptism and Jesus' Spirit-baptism at three principal stages of early Christian mission—Jerusalem, Caesarea and Ephesus—it seems plausible that a similar 'Baptist-factor' also underlies the episode at Samaria, where Philip baptizes in water and prepares the way for Peter's transmission of the Spirit.[1] Consequently, a vital clue to uncovering Luke's assessment of Philip (the forerunner) in relation to Peter (the culminator) may be found in closely comparing the portrait of John in relation to Jesus. In particular, we must investigate (1) the infancy narratives in Luke 1–2, (2) the description of John's ministry in Luke 3, culminating in Jesus' baptism, and (3) additional isolated texts in Luke 7 and 16.

1. Only Luke gives special consideration to relating the narratives of John and Jesus. The result is a parallel characterization of the two infants.[2] Both experience miraculous births (1.57-66; 2.1-20) heralded by angels (1.5-25; 1.26-55); both are circumcised (1.59-63; 2.21), and both inspire prophetic oracles regarding their appointed service of the Lord (1.67-80; 2.25-35). Like Jesus, John is destined for greatness (μέγας, 1.15, 32) and is filled with the Spirit from birth (1.15, 35). Finally, their nativities are both occasions for jubilant rejoicing (1.14, 58; 2.10-14).

But within this comparative framework, a pattern of distinction also emerges.[3] Both children are great, but one is greater; both have their

---

1. S. Brown (' "Water-Baptism" and "Spirit-Baptism" ') and Wilkens ('Wasser-taufe und Geistempfang') both discuss Luke's distinction between water-baptism and Spirit-baptism and its foundational link with the portraits of John the Baptist and Jesus. They also acknowledge the basic fit of the Samaritan episode within this pattern, but they fail to explore the possible connection between the vocations of Philip and John the Baptist.

2. See R. Laurentin, *Structure et théologie de Luc I–II* (EBib; Paris: Gabalda, 1957), pp. 36-42; R.E. Brown, *Birth*, pp. 246-53; A. George, 'Parallele entre Jean-Baptiste et Jésus', in Descamps and de Halleux (eds.), *Mélanges bibliques*, pp. 147-71.

3. See P. Benoit, 'L'enfance de Jean-Baptiste selon Luc 1', *NTS* 3 (1956–57), pp. 191-93; Dömer, *Heil Gottes*, pp. 18-25; H.H. Oliver, 'The Lucan Birth Stories and the Purpose of Luke–Acts', *NTS* 10 (1963–64), pp. 215-26; W.B. Tatum, 'The

roles to play in God's work of salvation, but only Jesus is called 'a Savior, who is the messiah, the Lord' (2.11). John is born to a barren woman advanced in years (1.17); Jesus, however, is born of a virgin (1.26-38). Friends and neighbors rejoice over John's birth (1.58); the whole host of heaven exults over Jesus' advent (2.13-14). John is appointed as prophet of the Most High to prepare the way for the Lord (1.76; cf. 1.17); Jesus is the very Son of the Most High (1.32, 34), the Lord himself (1.43; 2.11). And most critically for our interests, John is imbued with the Spirit from birth (1.15) and will conduct his mission 'in the spirit and power of Elijah' (1.17); but Jesus is conceived by the Spirit, supernaturally brought into being by 'the power of the Most High' (1.35).

How should we evaluate this parallel-yet-distinct portrayal of John and Jesus? Some scholars have posited a 'Baptist' source behind the Lukan birth stories stemming from circles devoted to John as master, if not messiah. Accordingly, Luke's redaction of this material to accentuate the pre-eminence of Jesus the Christ-child supposedly represents a polemical offsetting of rival Baptist claims.[1] Apart from the difficulties, however, of detecting the existence, much less the messianic beliefs, of Baptist sects before the second century,[2] the narrative in Luke 1–2 simply does not convey a polemical tone. As we have seen, although cast as Jesus' forerunner, John is highly esteemed as a great and dynamic prophet in his own right. In addition, there is little in the presentation of John's nativity which cannot be accounted for by scriptural models of miraculous births and Baptist traditions from Mark and Q.[3]

Epoch of Israel: Luke I–II and the Theological Plan of Luke–Acts', *NTS* 13 (1966–67), pp. 184-95.

1. Cf. E. Bammel, 'The Baptist in Early Christian Tradition', *NTS* 18 (1971–72), pp. 105-109; and the survey of research in Oliver, 'Lucan Birth Stories', pp. 205-15.

2. Solid evidence for the existence of Baptist sects claiming John as the messiah first emerges in the Pseudo-Clementine and Mandean literature. On Baptist movements in ancient history, see generally J. Thomas, *Le mouvement baptiste en Palestine et Syrie (150 AV. J.-C.–300 AD. J.-C.)* (Gembloux: Duculot, 1935); C.H. Kraeling, *John the Baptist* (New York: Charles Scribner's Sons, 1951), pp. 158-87; C.H.H. Scobie, *John the Baptist* (London: SCM Press, 1964), pp. 187-202.

3. Cf. R.E. Brown, *Birth*, pp. 245-50; W. Wink, *John the Baptist in the Gospel Tradition* (SNTSMS, 7; Cambridge: Cambridge University Press, 1968), pp. 58-72.

H. Conzelmann recognizes that Luke's opening chapters manifest a 'typological correspondence' or 'analogy' between John and Jesus, but he also thinks that this material stands in 'direct contradiction' to the balance of Luke–Acts, in which John and Jesus are sharply segregated from one another as representatives of distinct epochs of salvation history (John = period of Israel; Jesus = 'the Middle of Time').[1] H.H. Oliver and W.B. Tatum have both challenged Conzelmann's disjunction of Luke 1–2 from the rest of Luke–Acts, while at the same time affirming his basic salvation-historical schema. These scholars interpret the infancy stories as reinforcing John's separation from the messianic kingdom inaugurated by Jesus. Oliver speaks of 'a conscious suppression of the relationship between Jesus and John' on Luke's part which 'had *already been well established* in the birth stories' (his emphasis).[2] For example, by describing John as the '*prophet* of the Most High' (versus Jesus, the '*Son* of the Most High', 1.32) who 'will go before the Lord to prepare his ways' (1.76), Luke is thought to be 'establish[ing] the subordinate and preliminary role of John to that of Jesus and the Middle of Time'.[3] Tatum, focusing chiefly on the Spirit-motif, likewise perceives 'the subordination of John to Jesus' in Luke 1–2 and contends that any correspondence between the two figures is 'superficial'.[4]

Obviously, Oliver and Tatum have highlighted the distinctions between John and Jesus in Luke's birth narrative at the expense of the parallels. But in so doing they have failed to appreciate the fine balance of Luke's literary artistry. The comparisons between John and Jesus as great, Spirit-endowed servants of God are plainly presented in Luke's narrative and should not be dismissed or diminished. Moreover, the equally evident distinctions between John and Jesus are hardly of such a black-and-white variety as to drive a thick wedge between the two figures; rather, they mark differences in *degree of greatness*. As noted above, Jesus outshines John in Luke 1–2 at a number of points, but these are always points at which John is exalted in his own right. To repeat but one example, Jesus may rank higher by virtue of his conception by the Holy Spirit (1.35), but John certainly runs a close second with his fullness of the Spirit from his

---

1. Conzelmann, *Theology*, pp. 24, 172.
2. Oliver, 'Lucan Birth Stories', p. 217.
3. Oliver, 'Lucan Birth Stories', p. 217; cf. overall discussion, pp. 216-26.
4. Tatum, 'Epoch of Israel', p. 189; cf. overall discussion, pp. 184-95.

mother's womb (1.15). The two pre-natal experiences are more alike than dissimilar in designating both John and Jesus as special instruments of the Spirit.[1] Thus, it seems best to set the nativities of John and Jesus not so much within a system of opposition and distinction as within a framework of 'climactic parallelism',[2] in which one figure (Jesus) surpasses the other (John) in various respects, even as both largely mirror one another and share in a noble, common enterprise.

P.S. Minear takes a similar stance, arguing for both the coherence of Luke 1–2 with the rest of Luke–Acts (against Conzelmann) and the comparability of John and Jesus within the birth narratives (against Oliver and Tatum):

> Although the prologue [Luke 1–2] preserves a distinction between the tasks of the two figures, at no point does it make an invidious or apologetic effort to downgrade or to deny the eschatological significance of John . . . The work of both men is seen as essential to the fulfillment of the promise, as ground for the joy of redemption. Both are included within the same consolation of Israel. In fact, the mood, resonance, and thrust of the birth narratives are such as to discourage the neat assignment of John and Jesus to separate epochs.[3]

---

1. Tatum goes too far when he concludes that 'the role played by the Spirit here in relation to Jesus [Lk. 1.35] is to be *sharply distinguished* [emphasis added] from the role it plays in relation to John [in Lk. 1.15]' ('Epoch of Israel', p. 187). More specifically, he sets up an unnecessary dichotomy between the Spirit of prophecy, which engulfs John in his mother's womb, and the Spirit as divine creative power, operative in Jesus' conception. Passages like Lk. 4.14-19, Acts 1.8, 2.17 and 4.31, taken together, demonstrate the close link between the Spirit of prophecy and power in Luke's presentation.

2. On the technique of 'climactic parallelism', in Luke–Acts, see Tannehill, *Narrative Unity*, I, p. 216; H. Flender, *St Luke: Theologian of Redemptive History* (London: SCM Press, 1967), pp. 20-27. However, when assessing the 'climactic parallelism' structuring the portraits of John and Jesus in Lk. 1–2, Flender exaggerates the distinctive dimension: 'Obviously, Luke is very interested in showing that the Baptist stands shoulder to shoulder with Jesus, but at the same time they are poles apart' (p. 22). In my view, the transparent 'shoulder to shoulder' comparison of John and Jesus at a number of points precludes a gaping polarization between the two figures. Distinction—yes; polarization—no.

3. P.S. Minear, 'Luke's Use of the Birth Stories', in Keck and Martyn (eds.), *Studies in Luke–Acts*, pp. 122-23; cf. overall discussion (pp. 118-30) and Minear's more recent comment: 'Certainly Luke did not encourage his readers to promote Jesus by demoting John. To him the association of the two prophets did not demean either' (*To Heal*, p. 97). Cf. also Wink, *John the Baptist*, p. 71.

2. The distinction between John's water-baptism and Jesus' Spirit-baptism in Lk. 3.16 must be carefully considered within its literary setting of 3.1-22, where John's public ministry is most fully detailed, culminating in the baptism of Jesus. Initially, Luke sets John's work in a broader context than the other Gospel writers. The political situation throughout the land of Israel is sketched (3.1-2), and John's baptismal activity, launched by divine directive in the wilderness (ἔρημος, 3.2b; cf. 3.4b), is described as an itinerant mission throughout '*all* (πᾶσαν) the region around the Jordan' (3.3a). Again, through the extended quotation from Isaiah 40 (unique to Luke), the effects of John's preparatory ministry are depicted in the widest possible terms: '*Every* (πᾶσα) valley shall be filled, and *every* (πᾶν) mountain and hill shall be made low. . . and *all* (πᾶσα) flesh shall see the salvation of God' (3.4-6). This universal impact of John's ministry is characteristic of Luke–Acts (cf. πᾶς: Lk. 3.15, 16a; 7.29; 20.6; Acts 13.24)[1] and warns us against defining the scope of John's vocation too narrowly.

John's ascetic garb and diet receive no mention in Luke (cf. Mt. 3.4; Mk 1.6), as the narrative moves directly to focus on John's proclamation of repentance. As in Matthew, Luke generally presents John's message as stressing the importance of righteous conduct over ethnic heritage, implying that repentant Gentiles as well as Jews will be included among God's covenant people ('God is able from these stones to raise up children to Abraham', 3.8; cf. 3.7-9). Only Luke, however, spells out some of John's more specific exhortations to the crowds at large and to designated groups. Sharing food and clothing with the needy befits true repentance for everyone, and tax collectors and soldiers are especially reminded to be just in their financial dealings with others (3.10-14).

As for John's ensuing pronouncements about Jesus, including the prediction of his Spirit-baptizing ministry, several characteristic elements may be enumerated in comparison with Matthew and Mark.

a. Only Luke stages John's evaluation of Jesus against a background of pervasive speculation concerning his own messiahship (3.15).[2] Thus, as in the infancy narratives, no attempt is made to conceal John's attractiveness even while distinguishing him from the Stronger One who is to come.

---

1. Cf. Dömer, *Heil Gottes*, p. 31.
2. At this point Luke is closer to the Fourth Gospel (cf. Jn 1.19-28).

228   The Portrait of Philip in Acts

b. In John's self-reference to his baptizing mission, Luke places ὕδατι in a more prominent syntactical position than Matthew or Mark (ἐγὼ μὲν ὕδατι βαπτίζω ὑμᾶς, 3.16; cf. βαπτίζω ἐν ὕδατι, Mt. 3.11; ἐβάπτισα ὑμᾶς ὕδατι, Mk 1.8);[1] thereby, Luke possibly accentuates the distinction between the *watery* substance of John's baptism and the *Spirit* element in which Jesus will baptize.

c. Luke's omission of ὀπίσω μου in 3.16 (cf. Mt. 3.11; Mk 1.7) may reflect an attempt to play down Jesus' role as John's disciple, if ὀπίσω is taken in the sense of 'following after'.[2] But if a more temporal distinction is in view, positioning Jesus *later than* (after) the forerunning John, then little importance should be attached to the omission. For even without ὀπίσω, Luke clearly presents Jesus' public mission as coming after John's preparatory mission (cf. Lk. 3.18-23; Acts 13.25 [μετ' ἐμέ]; 19.4 [μετ' αὐτὸν]).

d. Luke follows Mark in declaring John's unworthiness to *untie* (λύω) the Coming One's sandals. However, by omitting Mark's κύψας (1.7), Luke softens an undue emphasis on John's subordination to Jesus.

e. Luke follows Q in announcing that Jesus will baptize with the Holy Spirit *and with fire* (3.16). The latter element may symbolize the judgmental character of the Stronger One's ministry, as elaborated in 3.17: 'the chaff he will burn with unquenchable fire'.[3] Thus, important continuity is maintained between the vocations of Jesus and John (cf. 3.9: 'every tree therefore that does not bear good fruit is cut down and thrown into the

---

1. Cf. H. Schürmann, *Das Lukasevangelium: Kommentar zu Kap. 1.1–9.50* (HTKNT, 3/1; Freiburg: Herder, 1969), pp. 172, 186.

2. Cf. W. Grundmann, *Das Evangelium nach Lukas* (THKNT, 3; Berlin: Evangelische, 1971), p. 105; and Marshall: 'the phrase ὀπίσω μου is omitted, possibly as conveying a sense of inferiority' (*Gospel of Luke*, p. 146).

3. Cf. Scobie, *John the Baptist*, pp. 67-73; Schürmann, *Lukasevangelium*, pp. 174-75. This judgmental dimension of the predicted Spirit-and-fire baptism does not preclude an accompanying salvific (purifying/refining) dimension as well (note the manifestation of Spirit and 'fire' in the Pentecost scene [Acts 2.1-4, 17-21]). Cf. J.D.G. Dunn, 'Spirit-and-Fire Baptism', *NovT* 14 (1972), pp. 85-92 (though the discussion focuses chiefly on what the 'historical' John might have meant by his baptismal announcement).

fire') amid the discontinuity over the matter of the Spirit's bestowal.

f. Only Luke, after reporting John's appraisal of Jesus, appends a summary statement of John's preaching: 'So, with many other exhortations, he proclaimed the good news (εὐηγγελίζετο) to the people' (3.18). There is no warrant for bracketing off this use of εὐηγγελίζετο as unique within Luke–Acts, denoting the activity of preaching—but not its content.[1] As we have seen, throughout Luke's writings εὐαγγελίζομαι is virtually a technical term for proclaiming the gospel of Christ and the kingdom of God. Thus, as W. Wink states, 'by deliberately applying the word to John's preaching Luke makes him the first preacher of the Gospel, the prototype of the Christian evangelist'.[2]

In conclusion, Lk. 3.15-18 unmistakeably presents Jesus as 'more powerful' than his forerunner, John, principally in his Spirit-baptizing vocation in contrast to John's water-baptizing mission. But within this relational structure Luke still seems to resist a tendency to denigrate John or to segregate him altogether from Jesus' evangelical mission. In short, John and Jesus remain cooperative partners in ministry.

The report of Jesus' baptism and anointing with the Spirit in Lk. 3.21-22 further clarifies the relationship between John and Jesus. It is most striking here that Jesus' own baptism and attendant reception of the Spirit are set apart from John's influence to a degree unparalleled in the other Gospels. The Baptist has already completed his preaching mission (3.18) and been imprisoned by Herod (3.19-20).[3] Jesus' baptism is then described in very impersonal and imprecise terms: 'Now when all the people were baptized, and when Jesus had also been baptized. . . ' (3.21). No mention is made of the Jordan setting or the activity of John. The outpouring of the Spirit occurs *after* Jesus is *baptized* (βαπτισθέντος, aorist participle) and *while* he is *praying* (προσευχομένου, present participle),[4] with no reference to human assistants. In a sense, Jesus precipitates—through prayer—his own

---

1. So Conzelmann, *Theology*, pp. 23 n. 1, 221.

2. Wink, *John the Baptist*, p. 53; cf. Talbert, *Reading Luke*, pp. 27-30.

3. Matthew and Mark treat the imprisonment (and eventual beheading) of John the Baptist much more extensively than Luke and at a much later point in their narratives (Mt. 14.3-12; Mk 6.17-29).

4. Cf. Marshall, *Gospel of Luke*, p. 152; Wilkens, 'Wassertaufe', p. 29.

baptism with the Spirit as a distinct experience from his baptism with water. As a result, John's forecast of Jesus' Spirit-baptizing work receives its initial fulfillment, and Jesus' personal experience provides something of a model for the early Christians' baptism with the Spirit in Acts.[1]

3. Although Lk. 3.21-22 climaxes in a scene which stresses the gulf between John's baptizing with water and Jesus' baptizing with the Spirit, it should still not be concluded that Luke is downgrading John or confining him to a bygone age of Israelite prophecy. While John's task as the messiah's forerunner is essentially completed, Luke does not hesitate later to disclose Jesus' continuing high esteem for the Baptist: 'What then did you go out to see? A prophet? Yes, I tell you, and more than a prophet... I tell you, among those born of women no one is greater than John' (7.26, 28a). The next statement—'yet the least in the kingdom of God is greater than he' (7.28b)—despite appearances, is not meant to nullify the previous comments or to diminish John's role in the kingdom. Promoting the status of the 'least' echoes Jesus' familiar perspective in Luke that the kingdom of God is an inclusive community open as much to social and religious outcasts as to more established groups. Witness, for example, Jesus' incorporation of despised tax collectors into the fellowship of God's kingdom (Lk. 5.27-32; 19.1-10). Far from setting Jesus apart from John, this acceptance of tax collectors as well as 'all the people' represents a significant extension of John's ministry: 'And all the people who heard this [i.e. Jesus' appraisal of John in 7.24-28], *including the tax collectors*, acknowledged the justice of God, *because they had been baptized with John's baptism*' (7.29).[2]

Another reference to John appears in Lk. 16.16, a verse made famous as the linchpin of Conzelmann's epochal structure of Luke–Acts, dividing the age of John and Israel from that of Jesus and the kingdom of God.[3] Linguistically, however, the meaning of the verse is

---

1. On Luke's understanding of Jesus' reception of the Spirit at the Jordan as a 'Spirit-baptism' paradigmatic of the early Christians' experience at Pentecost, see Dunn, *Baptism*, pp. 23-54. For an alternative view, see M.M.B. Turner, 'Jesus and the Spirit in Lucan Perspective', *TynBul* 32 (1981), pp. 10, 28-29, 40, who stresses more the uniqueness of the Lukan Jesus' anointing with the Spirit.

2. Further continuity between John and Jesus is suggested in Lk. 11.1 regarding the practice of prayer.

3. Conzelmann, *Theology*, pp. 21-27, 112, 160-62.

far from clear and may even be taken to support the very opposite of what Conzelmann contends:

> The law and the prophets were in effect until John came [μέχρι Ἰωάννου: up to but *not* including John?]; since then [ἀπὸ τότε: from John onwards?] the good news of the kingdom of God is proclaimed. . .

In any event, Minear's cutting criticism of Conzelmann's use of Lk. 16.16 must be borne in mind: 'It must be said that rarely has a scholar placed so much weight on so dubious an interpretation of so difficult a logion'.[1]

Having sketched the main contours of the forerunner–culminator relationship between John and Jesus in Luke's Gospel, we may now determine the extent to which this relationship both mirrors and illuminates the Philip–Peter connection in Acts.

The principal factor correlating the two pairs of ministers remains the basic distinction between the forerunner who baptizes with water (John/Philip) and the culminator who confers the Spirit (Jesus/Peter). More specifically, we may compare the circumstances surrounding the Spirit's outpouring upon Jesus and the Samaritans: just as Jesus receives the Spirit while he is praying at a point in time after his baptism with water and after John's exit from the scene (Lk. 3.18-22), so the Samaritans receive the Spirit in answer to Peter's praying on an occasion following their baptism with water by Philip, who then plays no further part in the proceedings (Acts 8.14-17). In addition, several other elements linking the missions of John and Philip may be observed.

1. John and Philip both conduct itinerant preaching and baptizing missions throughout the land of Israel, including specifically desert/deserted areas; in fact, Philip is the only missionary in Acts reported to have worked in such a spot (ἔρημος, Lk. 3.2, 4; Acts 8.26).

2. In reaching out to the Samaritans and Ethiopian treasurer, Philip matches John's ministry to religious outcasts within Judaism, such as tax collectors, and endorses John's implicit critique of Jewish nationalism (Lk. 3.7-14; 7.29; Acts 8.4-40).

3. John and Philip are both noted for 'proclaiming good news'

---

1. Minear, 'Luke's Use of the Birth Stories', p. 122; cf. Marshall, *Gospel of Luke*, pp. 628-29; Wink, *John the Baptist*, pp. 51-57.

(εὐαγγελίζομαι, Lk. 3.18; Acts 8.4, 12, 35, 40).

4. Both John and Philip are characterized as 'filled with the Spirit' (Lk. 1.15; Acts 6.3; 8.29, 39), even though they are not direct channels of the Spirit's bestowal on others.

5. John's distinction as 'great' (μέγας in God's sight, Lk. 1.15; cf. 7.28) and 'powerful' (δύναμις like Elijah, Lk. 1.17) is matched by Philip's dynamic overwhelming of Simon, the so-called 'Great Power of God' (ἡ δύναμις τοῦ θεοῦ ἡ καλουμένη μεγάλη, Acts 8.10).[1]

In short, if John the Baptist functions as a 'prototype of the Christian evangelist' for anyone in Luke–Acts, it would appear to be Philip the 'baptist' evangelist to the Samaritans and Ethiopian eunuch. As John paves the way for the Spirit-baptizing Jesus through his ministry of proclamation and water-baptism, so Philip similarly prepares for Peter's Spirit-imparting mission to the Samaritans and Gentiles. And just as the forerunner–culminator arrangement between John and Jesus is not designed to slight John's achievements or down-grade his status within God's kingdom, so a similar arrangement between Philip and Peter should not be viewed as stigmatizing Philip's competence or minimizing the importance of his pioneering mission work. To be sure, Peter (like Jesus) plays the larger and more drama-tic 'culminator' role, including his unique involvement in channelling the Spirit to new believers. But Philip's lesser 'forerunner' role (like John the Baptist's) is by no means a negligible one; neither does it nullify the numerous parallels (proclaiming Christ, working miracles, supernatural guidance, etc.) which tie the ministries of Philip and Peter together. As with John and Jesus in Luke 1–2, Philip and Peter in Acts 8–11 may be viewed as knit together in a pattern of 'climactic parallelism', a pattern which admits a certain distinction in importance ('climactic') between two figures, but not at the expense of their basic unity and comparability ('parallelism'). Indeed, the overriding picture of relations between the forerunner Philip and the culminator Peter remains one of partnership and cooperation, rather than polarity and competition.

This proposal that Luke has utilized a 'forerunner–culminator' model, in conjunction with a literary pattern of 'climactic paral-

---

1. Recall also the portrait of Philip as an Elijah-styled prophet (Chapter 4 section 3a above).

lelism', to display the correlation between both John/Jesus and Philip/Peter would doubtless be strengthened and clarified if another similar case could be uncovered. As it happens, a promising analogue does appear in Acts 18.19–19.7 involving Apollos and Paul and the familiar motifs of Johannine baptism and the outpouring of the Spirit. Upon arriving in Ephesus, Paul proceeds first (as usual) to the synagogue to debate with the Jews. However, despite the invitation that he remain longer, Paul leaves the synagogue and the city after only a brief stay. He promises to return 'if God wills' and leaves behind his trusted colleagues, Priscilla and Aquila (Acts 18.19-23). He eventually does return, of course, and conducts a long and fruitful mission in the Asian capital (19.1-40; cf. 20.17-38). After his short initial visit, however, no conversions are reported, and no Christian community appears to be established.

Apollos comes to Ephesus after Paul's departure (18.24). On a historical level, considerable debate has surrounded the question of whether Apollos was simply a Jew or a Jewish Christian at this time.[1] However one settles this issue, there is little doubt regarding Luke's perception of Apollos's status. Although his rhetorical skill and biblical expertise may be claimed by any devout Jew, Apollos's knowledge of the 'Way of the Lord' (τὴν ὁδὸν τοῦ κυρίου),[2] his fervency in the Spirit (ζέων τῷ πνεύματι, cf. Rom. 12.11) and his accurate teaching of 'the things concerning Jesus' (ἐδίδασκεν ἀκριβῶς τὰ περὶ τοῦ Ἰησοῦ) (18.25) could only characterize a bona fide Christian missionary. The last item echoes especially the closing description of Paul's ministry in Acts (διδάσκων τὰ περὶ τοῦ κυρίου Ἰησοῦ Χριστοῦ, 28.31).[3]

---

1. Schweizer ('Die Bekehrung des Apollos, Apg 18,24-26', in *Beiträge zur Theologie des Neuen Testaments: Neutestamentliche Aufsätze [1955–70]* [Zürich: Zwingli, 1970], pp. 75-79) emphasizes the introduction of Apollos as a 'Jew' and attempts to demonstrate how ζέων τῷ πνεύματι and ἡ ὁδὸς τοῦ κυρίου (Acts 18.25) could have originally been interpreted in a strictly Jewish sense. However, most other commentators accept Apollos's 'Christian' status from the start; see, e.g., C.K. Barrett, 'Apollos and the Twelve Disciples of Ephesus', in Weinrich (ed.), *New Testament Age*, I, pp. 29-39; Dunn, *Baptism*, pp. 88-89; H. Preisker, 'Apollos und die Johannesjünger in Act 18.24–19.6', *ZNW* 30 (1931), pp. 301-304.

2. 'The Way' for Luke is something of a technical term designating the Christian movement; cf. Acts 9.2; 19.9, 23; 22.4; 24.14, 22.

3. Note also the common element of 'boldness' in the proclamation of Apollos

As a Jewish-Christian evangelist, Apollos proclaims his message in the local synagogue (18.26), just as Paul had previously done. Although again no specific conversions are reported, it is clear from the mention of 'brothers'[1] in 18.27 that a Christian community has sprung to life in Ephesus. Since these new believers encourage Apollos and recommend his service to others (18.27), they obviously think highly of him; and some, we might plausibly deduce, even owe their Christian faith to Apollos's witness. In any case, Acts 18.24-28 presents a generally favorable picture of Apollos as a foundational missionary in the Ephesian church.

Still, we cannot ignore three items in Luke's report which seem to suggest certain deficiencies in Apollos and his work:

1. 'He knew only the baptism of John' (18.25c).
2. He requires a 'more accurate' explanation of the way of God by Aquila and Priscilla (18.26).
3. He takes a letter of recommendation to Corinth (18.27; cf. 19.1).

Working in reverse order through this list, the letter of recommendation (unique in Acts), while revealing the support of the Ephesian community, may also suggest a degree of skepticism about how the Corinthians would receive Apollos. However, we soon learn that Apollos proves to be a glowing success in Corinth (18.27-28), and the use of an introductory letter may simply reflect traditional policy regarding the reception of itinerant missionaries (cf. 2 Cor. 3.1-3). It is more difficult to account for Apollos's being instructed 'more accurately' (ἀκριβέστερον, 18.26) by Aquila and Priscilla when he already teaches 'accurately' (ἀκριβῶς, 18.25) about Jesus. How can information be 'more accurate' than 'accurate'? Luke seems to be treading on delicate ground here, not wanting to impugn Apollos's grasp of the Christian gospel but still desiring to supplement his understanding with insights from Paul's colleagues. Finally, the note that Apollos 'knew *only* (μόνον) the baptism of John' certainly defines the limits of Apollos's religious background, but without necessarily implying any judgment about it. Most likely, the point is that Apollos both experienced the rite of John's baptism and 'knew'

(18.26) and Paul (28.31); cf. Barrett, 'Apollos', p. 30.
    1. Cf. Cadbury, 'Names for Christians and Christianity in Acts', in Lake and Cadbury (eds.), *Beginnings of Christianity*, V, pp. 378-79.

(understood, ἐπιστάμενος) the baptismal message which John proclaimed.[1] An important link is thus established between the ministries of John and Apollos which may further clarify the role of Apollos in the Ephesian story.[2]

As John prepared 'the way of the Lord' (Lk. 3.4), acting as forerunner for the culminating mission of Jesus, so Apollos, instructed in 'the way of the Lord', breaks ground for the gospel at Ephesus which Paul will cultivate and bring to full harvest. And as John and Jesus are both extolled by Luke in similar ways, but with Jesus manifesting the greater glory, so Apollos is commended for his proclamation ('accurate') while also being cast as dependent upon Pauline representatives for deeper ('more accurate') insight. The operation of the Spirit, so critical to the distinction between John and Jesus, also affects the characterization of Apollos and Paul. Like John, Apollos himself is imbued with the Spirit (Acts 18.25), but no mention is made of his conveying the Spirit to others in Ephesus. This ministry is reserved for Paul when he returns to Ephesus after Apollos has departed for Corinth (19.1-7). Scholars disagree over the precise connection between the Apollos story and the following incident involving Paul and the Ephesian disciples, with some going so far to discount any substantial tie other than geographical.[3] But the presence of two important elements—the baptism of John and the activity of the Spirit—in both episodes suggests some closer linkage beyond the shared Ephesian locale.[4]

Upon returning to Ephesus, Paul initially encounters τινας μαθητάς, no doubt referring (according to typical Lukan usage) to specifically Christian disciples.[5] Just a few lines earlier the narrator identified the μαθηταί in Achaia as 'those who through grace had become believers' (τοῖς πεπιστευκόσιν διὰ τῆς χάριτος, 18.27). So, too, the Ephesian 'disciples' are addressed by Paul as 'believers'

---

1. On baptism as the object of John's preaching as well as practice, see Lk. 3.3; Acts 10.37; 13.24.
2. For a similar recognition of the John/Apollos parallel, see Pereira, *Ephesus*, pp. 61-65.
3. E.g. Beasley-Murray, *Baptism*, pp. 108-11; Roloff, *Apostelgeschichte*, p. 181.
4. Cf. Barrett, 'Apollos', pp. 36-37; M. Wolter, 'Apollos und die ephesinischen Johannesjünger (Act 18.24–19.7)', *ZNW* 78 (1987), pp. 61-62.
5. Cf. Cadbury, 'Names', pp. 375-78.

(πιστεύσαντες, 19.2).[1] But no sooner has their Christian identity been suggested than these Ephesians prove themselves to be peculiar disciples indeed. They respond to Paul's query with the astonishing admission that they had never heard of the Holy Spirit (19.2). The sense of this declaration is commonly interpreted as ignorance not of the Spirit's existence but of the Spirit's special outpouring in the last days.[2] In any case, it is clear that these disciples had not yet personally received the Spirit. Upon learning of this deficiency, Paul immediately inquires about the Ephesians' baptism and uncovers its link to John (19.3).

Why this concern with baptism? In the present context, it must have something to do with the Ephesians' lack of the Spirit, most logically relating to the established Lukan viewpoint that John's baptism with water, whatever else it accomplished, did not lead to the Spirit's outpouring. Responding further to the Spirit-less Ephesians, Paul spells out for them the significance of John's baptism: 'John baptized with the baptism of repentance, telling the people to believe in the one who was to come after him, that is, in Jesus' (Acts 19.4). This stress on repentance and faith in Jesus should probably not be understood as a disclosure of new information to the Ephesians, which they then embrace. The only reported reaction to Paul's message is re-baptism in Jesus' name, with no mention of repenting or believing (indeed, Paul assumes that they had already believed in 19.2). Still, there were limits to John's ministry. As the 'prototype Christian evangelist', John had truly called the people to testify to their repentance and faith in Jesus through the rite of baptism in water; but this baptism, significant though it was, did not transmit the Spirit. Hence the Ephesian disciples must now be baptized by Paul in the name of the One (Jesus) who alone baptizes with the Spirit (19.5-6).

How does Apollos fit into this scenario? Although we are never told

---

1. Dunn suggests that 'Luke's description of the twelve as τινες μαθηταί . . . probably implies that the twelve did *not* belong to "the disciples" in Ephesus. . . ' (*Baptism*, p. 84). However, in this context the use of τινες (even without the definite article) most naturally means that Paul simply met 'some'—that is, not all, only a portion, a particular group of—members within the larger Ephesian community. Most commentators on Acts 19.1-7 support the reading of 'disciples' as true believers.

2. Cf. the clarification of the 'Western' reviser: 'We have not even heard whether people are receiving [λαμβάνουσίν τινες] the Holy Spirit'.

explicitly who evangelized the Ephesian disciples, Apollos appears to be the prime candidate. He represents the principal witness to Jesus in Ephesus up to this point,[1] and his background includes a direct link to John's baptismal mission. Apollos himself possesses the Spirit without any (recorded) supplemental baptism in the name of Jesus and in this respect occupies a similar position to John as a specially anointed prophet of God. But also like John, Apollos cannot participate in conveying the Spirit to others. He can effectively bring his hearers to believe in Jesus as the Christ, but when it comes to imparting the Spirit, he can only pave the way for the climactic minister of Christ, in this case, Paul. Thus, the 'forerunner–culminator' pattern which structures relations between John and Jesus in Luke's narrative also appears to couple Apollos and Paul.

Such a conclusion generally supports Käsemann's opinion that the ministries of Apollos and Paul are purposefully intertwined in Acts 18–19 to promote Luke's well-known interest in Christian unity. The two ministers are effectively brought together as co-laborers within the developing Ephesian community. But we need not endorse Käsemann's additional viewpoint that Luke has established a hierarchical unity by placing the maverick Apollos (as well as 'heretical' Baptist sects) under the aegis of Paul's apostolic authority.[2] If Luke had really purposed to bring Apollos under Paul's ecclesiastical wing, it is strange that he would cast a couple of Paul's associates, rather than Paul himself, in the role of Apollos's instructors.[3] Moreover, Apollos is still allowed independent movement ('when *he wished* to cross over to Achaia', 18.27a) and heads to Corinth, where he in fact supplements Paul's earlier ministry (Apollos 'greatly helped' the disciples, 18.27b). A more mutual and cooperative bond than Käsemann allows seems to characterize relations between Apollos and Paul. As we have seen, the two celebrated ministers appear as fellow, Spirit-inspired preachers of 'the things concerning Jesus' and partners in the work of evangelizing Ephesian Jews within the synagogue,

---

1. Paul had only been in Ephesus for a brief visit at this stage, and the only recorded ministry of Aquila and Priscilla was directed to Apollos himself. Certainly neither Paul nor his companions would have converted the twelve disciples and left them in the state in which Paul later finds them.
2. Käsemann, *Essays*, pp. 136-48.
3. Cf. Barrett, 'Apollos', pp. 38-39; Schweizer, 'Bekehrung', p. 75.

although admittedly Paul's vocation as a channel of the Spirit is more climactic.

In a more recent study M. Wolter likewise underplays the egalitarian dimensions of Luke's portrayal of Apollos and Paul. While Wolter does not wholly accept Käsemann's sweeping 'early Catholic' interpretation, he still contends that the principal redactional concern in Acts 18.24–19.7 is 'die paulinische Dominanz über Apollos zum Ausdruck zu bringen'.[1] In particular, Wolter thinks that Luke has in mind the historical situation behind 1 Corinthians 1–4, in which an Apollos faction had troubled the Corinthian church by touting themselves as inspired pneumatics while denying this status to Paul. Luke, in Wolter's estimation, aimed to turn the tables on this situation by subtly devaluing Apollos's pneumatic abilities and by depicting Paul as the exclusive administrator of the Spirit.[2]

However, apart from the difficulties in unravelling the history of the Corinthian church from Paul's letters and in determining Luke's knowledge of that history, it is hard to see how an account which so clearly extols Apollos's virtues can at the same time serve (even tacitly) a polemical, anti-Apollos intention. It is true that Paul surpasses Apollos as a conduit of the Spirit, but not in a way which effaces Apollos's own personal gifts and his missionary achievements in Ephesus and Corinth.[3] If Luke was aware of past tensions between rival Corinthian parties associated with Apollos and Paul, then his attitude would appear to be more in line with Paul's own expressed democratic stance in 1 Corinthians 3 than with Wolter's hierarchical reading.

> What then is Apollos? What is Paul? Servants through whom you believed, as the Lord assigned to each. I planted, Apollos watered [or in the case of the Ephesus incident in Acts, the roles would be reversed: Apollos planted, Paul watered], but God gave the growth. So neither the one who plants nor the one who waters is anything, but only God who gives the growth. The one who plants and the one who waters *have a common purpose*, and each will receive wages according to the labor of each. For we are God's servants, *working together* (1 Cor. 3.5-9).

Since the characterization of Apollos and Paul in Acts 18–19

---

1. Wolter, 'Apollos', p. 68; cf. pp. 67-71.
2. Wolter, 'Apollos', pp. 72-73.
3. Cf. Tannehill: 'Apollos is not a problem but an asset' (*Narrative Unity*, II, p. 232).

corresponds with that of John the 'forerunner' and Jesus the 'culminator' in Luke's Gospel, we would expect a similar connection to the portrayal of Philip and Peter. To be sure, there are some obvious differences between Philip and Apollos, notably that Philip receives no supplemental instruction and is not said to have personally experienced John's baptism. But such distinctions should not obscure the several parallels which emerge between the two missionaries and the Samaritan and Ephesian 'Pentecosts'.

1. Philip and Apollos both possess the Spirit and impress their audiences with dynamic preaching about Jesus.
2. Philip and Apollos both function as Baptist-styled forerunners who mirror their missionary successors in many respects even as they prepare the way to be surpassed by them ('climactic parallelism').
3. Their Samaritan and Ephesian converts must both wait beyond the experience of water-baptism to receive the Spirit at the hands of other ministers (Peter and Paul).
4. The incompleteness of Apollos's Johannine baptism and the Samaritans' baptism by Philip is suggested in both cases by the use of μόνον (Acts 8.16; 18.25).[1]
5. For both the Samaritans and Ephesians, the imposition of hands accompanies the Spirit's outpouring.[2]

The fact that the Ephesian disciples lack the Spirit after the *baptism of John* and the Samaritans find themselves in the same condition after *baptism in the name of Jesus* does not substantially weaken the tie between the two situations. In general, Acts expounds no necessary causal connection between water-baptism *in any form* and Spirit-reception, although it assumes that all Spirit-filled believers have submitted or will submit to baptism at some time (2.38).[3] The Cornelius incident most clearly reveals the freedom of the Spirit's work apart from water-baptism, be it John's baptism which Peter explicitly distinguishes from Spirit-baptism (11.16) or baptism in

---

1. Cf. Käsemann, *Essays*, pp. 144-45.
2. The only other occurrence in Acts where the imposition of hands accompanies the reception of the Spirit emerges in the case of Saul (Acts 9.17).
3. Cf. Schweizer, 'πνεῦμα', pp. 414-15, and the fuller discussions in S. Brown, ' "Water-Baptism" and "Spirit-Baptism" ', and Wilkens, 'Wassertaufe und Geistempfang'.

Jesus' name which follows the Spirit's spontaneous effusion (10.47-48). The Ephesian episode comes close to linking the Spirit's coming directly to baptism in the name of Jesus (19.5-6), but, as discussed above, the main thrust of Paul's instruction here has to do with affirming the 'Christian' focus of John's baptismal mission as well as its limited potential to confer the Spirit. Although the Ephesians proceed to be (re-)baptized in Jesus' name, they are not actually commanded to do so by Paul, and their subsequent reception of the Spirit is associated more immediately with the laying on of Paul's hands than with the act of (re-)baptism. Moreover, the intent of the Ephesian story in 19.1-7 can hardly be to promote baptism in Jesus' name as either an indispensable requirement or automatic guarantee of Spirit-possession when the preceding story presents Apollos as a dynamic instrument of the Spirit who 'knew only the baptism of John'.

Therefore, whatever may distinguish them on other grounds, there appears to be little difference in Luke's view between the baptism of John and baptism in the name of Jesus in terms of their direct connection to the outpouring of the Spirit. Both are important acts of water-baptism representing outward testimonies of repentance and faith in Jesus, which, however, do not instantaneously or mechanically effect the Spirit's coming. With this outlook on the limits of water-baptism in Luke–Acts, there is no real disparity between the basic structures of the Samaritan and Ephesian missions conducted by Philip/Peter and Apollos/Paul.

d. *Conclusion*

The presentation of Philip's ministry as one of proclaiming the gospel and baptizing with water—but not conferring the Spirit upon new converts—need not betray a Lukan tendency to smear Philip's reputation as an evangelist or to cast Philip in a starkly subordinate role to the superior, Spirit-imparting missionary, Peter. Conceiving of the Spirit in no uncertain terms as a gift of God freely poured out upon all believers ('all flesh'), Luke has little interest in establishing an ecclesiastical caste system in which any group or individual—apostolic or otherwise—appears to monopolize the Spirit's activity. Philip, as surely as Peter, is a man filled with and empowered by the Spirit in Acts. His lack of participation in channelling the Spirit to new believers does not reflect a deficiency or abnormality in his mission;

rather, it fits into a literary schema within Luke's narrative which depicts an overarching compatibility and continuity between pairs of prominent ministers.

The primary model integrates the missions of John the Baptist and Jesus. The two characters share much in common as notably great and Spirit-endowed prophets in the kingdom of God. But they also fulfill distinctive roles in relation to each other. John functions as the *forerunner* who baptizes in water, preparing the way for Jesus the *culminator* who will baptize with the Spirit. Such a distinction, however, while pointing to Jesus' supremacy, does not minimize John's own eminence in Luke's eyes nor impair the essential bond which holds John and Jesus together. Indeed, it may be viewed as supporting this bond by showing how the two ministers complement one another within a cooperative enterprise of ushering in God's kingdom.

In a similar fashion, Philip functions as a Baptist-styled forerunner to Peter's Spirit-imparting mission in Acts 8–11 (as does Apollos in relation to Paul in Acts 18–19) and thereby displays another facet of his mutual rather than subordinate relationship to the Jerusalem apostle. As Philip's local ministry of table-service was presented as a worthy vocation complementing Peter's ministry of the word, so on the mission field in Samaria and the coastal plain, Philip's trail-blazing work of proclamation and baptism marks an important missionary achievement both individually and cooperatively in relation to Peter's culminating work of Spirit-transmission. In short, Philip plants and Peter waters, but ultimately God gives the increase—even in the matter of the Spirit's outpouring. Philip and Peter remain co-laborers, fellow-workers in God's field.

EXCURSUS: *THE LETTER OF PETER TO PHILIP*

The Letter of Peter to Philip designates a Christian-Gnostic tractate originally written in Greek in the late second or early third century CE. It was eventually translated into Coptic and incorporated into Codex VIII of the Nag Hammadi library.[1] Although *The Letter of Peter to Philip* post-dates Luke's writings by a century or so, its focus on the figures of Peter and Philip and inclusion of several other items reminiscent of the canonical Acts make it an interesting text with which to compare and contrast Luke's depiction of Philip–Peter relations.

---

1.   Cf. M.W. Meyer and F. Wisse, 'The Letter of Peter to Philip (VIII,2)', in *The Nag Hammadi Library in English* (ed. J.M. Robinson; San Francisco: Harper & Row, 3rd edn, 1988), p. 433.

The tractate opens with the superscription: 'The Letter of Peter Which He Sent to Philip'.[1] What immediately ensues is a standard epistolary greeting from (pseudo-) author (Peter) to (pseudo-)recipient (Philip) and a cordial plea on Peter's part that Philip 'our beloved brother and fellow apostle' rejoin the apostolic assembly which he had recently shunned.

> Now I [Peter] want you [Philip] to know, our brother [that] we received orders from our Lord and the Savior of the whole world that [we] should come [together] to give instruction and preach in the salvation which was promised us by our Lord Jesus Christ. But as for you, you were separate from us, and you did not desire us to come together and to know how we should organize ourselves in order that we might tell the good news. Therefore, would it be agreeable to you, our brother, to come according to the orders of our God Jesus? (132.16–133.8).

At this juncture, the epistolary form is abandoned in favor of a third-person narrative which runs to the end of the document. Philip is described as receiving and reading the correspondence and duly responding to Peter's wishes of reunion. We then learn that Peter convenes Philip and the other apostles on the Mount of Olives to await Christ's instructions (132.9–133.9). From this point on, Peter clearly dominates the apostolic group as its chief spokesman and leader. After the opening two paragraphs, neither Philip nor any apostle other than Peter is singled out or mentioned by name again.

As the apostles gather in prayer on the Mount of Olives, the risen Christ appears and speaks to them. The apostles respond by asking a series of questions related to typically Gnostic concerns, such as 'the deficiency of the aeons and their pleroma' and 'why do the powers fight against us?' (134.19–135.2). One by one 'our illuminator, Jesus' addresses the apostles' queries, following the basic form of a standard Gnostic 'dialogue' (135.3–138.3).[2]

When the discussion concludes, Christ is 'taken up to heaven', and the apostles return to Jerusalem. Along the way they confer with one another concerning the revelation they had just received, focusing in particular on the suffering of Christ and the prospects for their own persecution as his disciples. Once again, an illuminating 'voice' breaks in to instruct the confused apostles (138.4–139.4).

With great joy the apostles arrive in Jerusalem. They proceed to the temple where they offer 'instruction in salvation in the name of [the] Lord Jesus Christ' and administer healing to a multitude of people (139.4-9). Then Peter, 'filled with a holy spirit', addresses his fellow disciples, proclaiming the crucified and risen 'Lord Jesus, the Son of the immeasurable glory of the Father. . . the author of our life'

---

1. All citations from *The Letter of Peter to Philip* are taken from the translation by F. Wisse, in Robinson (ed.), *Nag Hammadi Library*, pp. 434-37. For other modern translations, see M.W. Meyer, *Letter of Peter to Philip: Text, Translation, and Commentary* (SBLDS, 53; Chico, CA: Scholars Press, 1981), pp. 17-33; J.E. Ménard, *La Lettre de Pierre à Philippe: Texte établi et présente* (Bibliothèque Copte de Nag Hammadi; section 'Textes' 1; Quebec: Laval University, 1977), pp. 10-29; H.-G. Bethge, 'Die Sogennante "Brief des Petrus an Philippus"', *TLZ* 103 (1978), pp. 166-68.

2. Cf. Meyer, *Letter of Peter to Philip*, p. 92.

and petitioning Christ 'to give us a spirit of understanding in order that we also may perform wonders' (139.9–140.7). As a result, all the apostles are 'filled with a holy spirit' and empowered to work miraculous healings and preach the message of Jesus (140.7-13).

At the close of the narrative, Jesus appears yet again to his apostles, giving them a special blessing of peace and assuring them of his abiding presence. The apostles then scatter 'to preach. . . by a power of Jesus, in peace' (140.15-27).

Several elements within *The Letter of Peter to Philip* manifest an obvious resemblance to certain features of the narrative in Luke 24 and the first half of Acts, for example: (1) the discussion concerning Jesus' death on the Emmaus road, (2) the disciples' joyous return to Jerusalem, (3) Peter's Spirit-filled leadership and Pentecost sermon, (4) the apostles' Spirit-empowered ministry in the temple (including miraculous healings) and (5) the apostles' commission to preach the gospel. These affinities have prompted the consensus view that the author of *The Letter of Peter to Philip* was directly dependent upon segments of Luke–Acts or at least closely related early Christian traditions.[1] Of particular interest to us is the apparent connection between the Peter and Philip referred to in the Gnostic tractate and the same two characters featured in Acts 8. To be sure, the former Philip is designated an apostle (unlike Philip 'the evangelist' in Acts), but this may simply reflect a developing tendency in early Christianity to blur the historical distinction between Philip the apostle and evangelist (cf. Eusebius, *Eccl. Hist.* 3.31, 39; Clement, *Strom.* 3.6).[2]

If *The Letter of Peter to Philip* did draw upon the Acts accounts of Peter and Philip the evangelist, then it also adapted these accounts to suit its own purposes. M.W. Meyer contends that by accentuating Philip's initial separation from Peter and the apostolic circle *The Letter of Peter to Philip* 'indicates more clearly than Luke the independence of Philip and his mission', although it ultimately follows Luke's 'early catholic' agenda by bringing Philip back into the apostolic fold under Peter's supreme authority.[3] My view, however, expounded above is that, while Luke does emphasize the unity and complementarity of Peter's and Philip's ministries, he has no desire in the process to denigrate or cover up Philip's independent mission. Moreover, we must appreciate that *The Letter of Peter to Philip* only acknowledges

---

1. See the discussion in G.P. Luttikhuizen, 'The Letter of Peter to Philip and the New Testament', in *Nag Hammadi and Gnosis: Papers Read at the First International Congress of Coptology* (ed. R.McL. Wilson; NHS, 14; Leiden: Brill, 1978), pp. 96-102; K. Koschorke, 'Eine gnostische Pfingstpredigt: Zur Auseinandersetzung zwischen gnostischem und kirchlichem Christentum am Beispiel der "Epistula Petri ad Philippum" (NHC VIII,2)', *ZTK* 74 (1977), pp. 325-32; T.V. Smith, *Petrine Controversies in Early Christianity: Attitudes towards Peter in Christian Writings of the First Two Centuries* (WUNT, 15; Tübingen: Mohr [Paul Siebeck], 1985), pp. 122-26; Meyer, *Letter of Peter to Philip*, pp. 94-98. *The Letter of Peter to Philip* also shows signs of adapting other New Testament materials besides Luke–Acts, such as the Johannine prologue.

2. For a summary of references to the two Philips in early Christian literature, see P.W. Schmiedel, 'Philip, the Apostle, and Philip, the Evangelist', *Encyclopaedia Biblica*, III, cols. 3697-3701; F. Bovon, 'Les Actes de Philippe', *ANRW* II.25.6, pp. 4456-60; H.H. Platz, 'Philip', *IDB*, III, pp. 784-85.

3. Meyer, *Letter of Peter to Philip*, pp. 95-97.

Philip's dissociation from the apostles in order to criticize it (as a violation of 'the orders of our God Jesus') and correct it (by reuniting Philip with the apostles and subordinating him to Peter). If anything, by not referring to Philip again after his return to the apostolic company, *The Letter of Peter to Philip* effectively effaces Philip's independent status to a degree unparalleled in Luke–Acts.

In addition, T.V. Smith correctly perceives that the apostle Peter emerges in the Gnostic 'letter' as a figure of much greater authority than we find in Acts, especially in relation to the Spirit. Unlike its source in Acts 2, *The Letter of Peter to Philip* portrays Peter as being filled with the Spirit, delivering his Pentecost-type sermon and praying for his fellow apostles before they are similarly endowed with the Spirit's power. Accordingly, the author would no doubt have regarded Peter's Spirit-imparting mission to the Samaritans as a further example of the apostles'—in this case Philip's—dependence upon Peter's superior ability and subordination to Peter's pre-eminent authority.[1]

The Letter of Peter to Philip is first and foremost a Petrine document designed to promote Peter's primacy in the early church.[2] As such it has moved far beyond its more egalitarian Lukan *Vorlage*. The opening scenes, where Philip is featured as joyfully returning to Peter and the other apostles, may as Ménard suggests, intimate an attempted 'rapprochement' between contemporary Petrine and Philippine circles,[3] but scarcely in a way which accords comparable, much less equal, status to the party devoted to Philip.

---

1. Smith, *Petrine Controversies*, pp. 124-25; cf. Koschorke, 'Gnostische Pfingstpredigt', p. 328.

2. Other ancient Petrine or pseudo-Petrine documents would include 1–2 Peter, *Apocalypse of Peter*, *The Acts of Peter and the Twelve Apostles* and *Epistula Petri* (at the beginning of the Pseudo-Clementine literature).

3. Ménard, *Lettre de Pierre à Philippe*, p. 7.

Chapter 6

PHILIP AND PAUL

1. *Introduction*

A large measure of Philip's significance in Acts derives not only from his relationship with Peter, but also from his association with Paul, the chief missionary to the Gentiles. We have already noted certain parallels between the missions of Philip and Paul, such as their common efforts of proclamation and miracle-working and similar confrontations with misguided magicians. We now turn to consider a brief scene in Acts 21.8-9 in which Philip and Paul are brought into direct contact with one another.

This report of Paul's sojourn at Philip's home in Caesarea has excited little scholarly discussion. For the most part it is treated as an incidental segment of an extended travelogue charting Paul's journey from Greece to Jerusalem (Acts 20.4–21.16).[1] But the presentation of Philip's hospitality toward Paul merits closer attention as the final image of Philip which Acts impresses upon its readers. It may, of course, be objected that this image has little connection with the much earlier and fuller characterization of Philip in ch. 8. In fact, however, a number of literary features link the Philip scenes in chs. 8 and 21.

1. The designation of Philip as εὐαγγελιστής in Acts 21.8 recalls his 'evangelistic' exploits in ch. 8 (ἐκ τῶν ἑπτά likewise recalls Philip's role in 6.5).

2. Philip's residence at Caesarea in Acts 21 matches the last-mentioned site of his preaching ministry (8.40).

3. A similar proximity to Jerusalem characterizes the earlier and later Philip narratives in Acts. In the first instance, Philip's

1. The most immediate context is the travel report of stations from Miletus to Jerusalem in 21.1-16; cf. the title for this section in Lüdemann's commentary: 'Reise von Milet nach Jerusalem' (*Frühe Christentum*, p. 238).

mission to Samaria marks the church's *first* step beyond Jerusalem. Ties with Jerusalem are still maintained, however, through the follow-up work of Peter and John in Philip's territory (8.4-25). Philip's later ministry of hospitality in Caesarea represents the last stage before the action in Acts moves back to Jerusalem for the final time;[1] and here in Philip's home the outreach of the Jerusalem church is felt once again, this time through the prophet Agabus (21.8-16).

4.	The intersection of the careers of Philip and Paul in Acts 21 also has an interesting counterpart earlier in the first half of the book. The large Philip cycle in 8.4-40 is framed most immediately by references to Paul's former campaign of violence against the early church (8.1-3; 9.1-2). Although Philip does not encounter Paul directly in ch. 8, his entire evangelistic ministry in Samaria and along the coastal plain may be viewed as falling under the threat of Paul's persecution.[2]

Despite these literary ties between the earlier and later portraits of Philip in Acts, it may still be argued that the reference in 21.8 is more reflective of Luke's source or personal reminiscence than his redactional artistry. Such a conclusion is related in part to the 'we' section in which this reference appears.

In Acts 20.5 the first-person plural pronoun re-emerges in the narrative after its last occurrence in 16.17. The 'we'-group now

1. The expanded 'Western' version of Acts 21.16-17 discloses that in fact Mnason's home was the final resting-place for Paul's travel party *before* entering Jerusalem: 'And these [the Caesarean disciples] brought us to those with whom we were to lodge; and when we arrived at a certain village, we stayed with Mnason of Cyprus, an early disciple. And when we had departed thence we came to Jerusalem' (cf. Metzger, *Textual Commentary*, p. 483). Roloff (*Apostelgeschichte*, pp. 313-14) thinks that this reading presents the correct itinerary. I am following, however, the view of Lake and Cadbury that 'a linguistically more natural exegesis would place Mnason's house in Jerusalem' (*Beginnings of Christianity*, IV, p. 270). The mention in 21.17 of the travellers' arrival in Jerusalem and warm welcome by 'the brothers' most logically does not begin a new section in a new setting but rather describes what happened when the Pauline party reached Mnason's dwelling (cf. 21.15-16). The shift in setting does not occur until 21.18, where on 'the next day' Paul and company visit James and the elders of the Jerusalem church (cf. discussion in Stählin, *Apostelgeschichte*, pp. 275-76).

2. On the link between Paul and Philip in conjunction with Stephen's death, see Brawley, *Luke–Acts*, p. 44; Richard, *Acts 6.1–8.4*, p. 312.

designates a Pauline travel party moving east from Macedonia (20.6). This 'we' style continues to be used through 20.15, after which comes the Miletus episode recounted in the third person (20.16-38). The 'we' report then resumes in 21.1-18. Because of the rather lengthy hiatus marked by the Miletus incident, some scholars envisage two discrete 'we' sections in Acts 20–21.[1] But a better case can be made for a single continuous 'we' narrative.[2] According to 20.15 the 'we'-party came with Paul to Miletus, and 21.1 reports that 'we. . . parted from them [i.e. the Ephesian elders assembled at Miletus] and set sail'. Obviously, then, Paul's companions ('we') remained with him throughout his reunion with the Ephesian elders. The fact that they recede into the background for a while, so that the focus may be placed on Paul and his contacts, is not untypical of the 'we' passages in Acts.[3]

The placement of Acts 21.8-9 within the extended 'we' section running from 20.5–21.18 raises a number of literary and historical questions regarding this closing Philip scene. Does the use of 'we' reveal the author's historical participation in the events being reported?[4] Does it betray an underlying source, say a travel diary kept by one of Paul's companions (not the author of Acts)? Or is the employment of 'we' merely a narrative device, designed to give the impression (illusion) of eyewitness testimony,[5] to conform to a

---

1. Acts 20.5-15 and 21.1-18. These together with 16.10-17 and 27.1–28.16 comprise the 'we' passages in Acts. Cf. V.K. Robbins, 'By Land and by Sea: The We-Passages and Ancient Sea Voyages', in Talbert (ed.), *Perspectives on Luke–Acts*, p. 216; Lüdemann, *Paul: Apostle to the Gentiles: Studies in Chronology* (London: SCM Press, 1984), pp. 25-26; E. Plümacher, 'Wirklichkeitserfahrung und Geschichtsschreibung bei Lukas: Erwägungen zu den Wir-Stücken der Apostelgeschichte', *ZNW* 68 (1977), p. 2.

2. Cf. H.J. Cadbury, ' "We" and "I" Passages in Luke–Acts', *NTS* 3 (1956–57), p. 130 n. 1.

3. This happens also at Troas on the present journey (20.9-12); cf. 27.9-12, 21-26, 30-36; 28.3-6.

4. See general discussion of the 'we'-problem in Dupont, *Sources of Acts*, pp. 75-165; D.E. Aune, *The New Testament in its Literary Environment* (LEC, 8; Philadelphia: Westminster Press, 1987), pp. 122-24; R. Jewett, *A Chronology of Paul's Life* (Philadelphia: Fortress Press, 1979), pp. 13-17; Schneider, *Apostelgeschichte*, I, pp. 89-95.

5. Haenchen, *Acts*, p. 85.

recognized 'sea-voyage genre'[1] or to present the author as an experienced traveller (seaman) and therefore a reliable historian?[2]

Luke's sporadic deployment of 'we' argues in favor of his membership in the 'we'-group or his takeover of an eyewitness source.[3] All purely redactional theories founder on having to explain why Luke did not utilize the 'we' device more often, particularly if its purpose was as important as authenticating his entire work. The suggestion that 'we' is specifically limited to accounts of sea voyages ignores the absence of such language during the sailing segments of Paul's first missionary journey (Acts 13.4, 13; 14.26) and the dominant focus of the first 'we' passage on movements *within* the city of Philippi (16.12-17). Also problematic is the nature of the Hellenistic parallels which supposedly point to 'we' as a purely stylistic ploy. Ancient reports of sea voyages may often have been told in dramatic, first-person style, but this hardly establishes *ipso facto* that the author was not personally on board during the voyage; indeed, readers would have probably assumed just the opposite.[4]

While granting that the 'we' sections in Acts likely derive from eyewitness testimony, we must also appreciate the notable coherence of this material with the larger Lukan narrative.[5] In the case of Acts 20.5–21.18, we discover not only typical Lukan vocabulary but also prominent Lukan themes (such as Spirit-inspired guidance, 20.22-23; 21.4, 11-14)[6] as well as an overarching structure patterned after the

1. Robbins, 'By Land and by Sea', pp. 215-42.
2. Plümacher, 'Wirklichkeitserfahrung', pp. 16-22.
3. Cf. Jewett, *Chronology*, p. 13.
4. See the useful critique of Robbins's theory in C.K. Barrett, 'Paul Shipwrecked', in *Scripture: Meaning and Method: Essays Presented to Anthony Tyrrell Hanson for his Seventieth Birthday* (ed. B.P. Thompson; Hull: Hull University Press, 1987), pp. 51-64; cf. Marshall, *Acts*, pp. 38-39; and W.S. Kurz:

> All literary critics whose treatment of the Acts 'We' passages I have discovered interpret them as a claim of the implied author's presence in those Acts events. Whether or not this claim is verified historically for the real author as distinct from the implied author, literary criticism clearly establishes the fact that the implied author is making such a claim and not automatically using a sea voyage convention forced on him by his environment ('Narrative Approaches to Luke–Acts', *Bib* 68 [1987], p. 210).

5. See the extensive linguistic investigation in A. Harnack, *Luke the Physician: The Author of the Third Gospel and the Acts of the Apostles* (CTL, 20; London: Williams & Norgate; New York: Putnam's Sons, 1911), pp. 26-120.
6. Evidence of literary design in the report of Paul's final journey to Jerusalem

story of Jesus in Luke's Gospel (cf. Paul's 'passion' with that of Jesus).[1] Luke does not merely chronicle Paul's final journey to Jerusalem, but shapes it to fit his entire two-volume work. The 'we' narrative is clearly *his* narrative; likewise, the 'we' references are *his* references.

In all probability, therefore, the 'we' sections of Acts represent reflective recollections of Luke's own experiences of missionary travel with Paul. They are eyewitness testimonies, reported not in wooden, journalistic fashion, but rather adapted creatively to coordinate with Luke's overall literary and theological interests. As for the episode in Acts 21.8, it is reasonable to number Luke among the 'we' who 'came to Caesarea and. . . went into the house of Philip the evangelist'. Thus, we may assume with Harnack and others that Luke met Philip personally, visited with him for several days (21.10a) and obtained valuable information about Philip's missionary activity (and possibly other material pertaining to the 'Hellenists').[2] However, the mention of Philip in Acts 21 should not be regarded merely as Luke's identification of an informant. As part of a 'we' passage, the closing Philip scene is also part of a carefully designed narrative in which the hospitable evangelist appears not simply as a historical acquaintance,

---

may also be detected in the repeated emphasis upon (1) Paul's determined intention to go to Jerusalem (20.16, 22; 21.13); (2) the Holy Spirit's particular revelation of the trials which await Paul in the city (19.22-23; 21.11); and (3) the grief of Paul's friends over his departure and future destiny (20.36-38; 21.5, 12-13). Cf. Weiser, *Apostelgeschichte*, II, p. 588.

1. See A.J. Mattill, Jr, 'The Jesus–Paul Parallels and the Purpose of Luke–Acts: H.H. Evans Reconsidered', *NovT* 17 (1975), pp. 30-37; W. Radl, *Paulus und Jesus im lukanischen Doppelwerk: Untersuchungen zu Parallelmotiven im Lukasevangelium und in der Apostelgeschichte* (Europäische Hochschulscriften, ser. 23, vol. 49; Frankfurt: Lang, 1975), pp. 133-68; J. Neyrey, *The Passion according to Luke: A Redaction Study of Luke's Soteriology* (New York: Paulist Press, 1985), pp. 98-107; O'Toole, *Unity of Luke's Theology*, pp. 67-72. F. Bovon ('Le Saint-Esprit, l'Eglise et les relations humaines selon Actes 20,36–21.16', in Kremer [ed.], *Les Actes des Apôtres*, pp. 339-51) also suggests Luke's dependence in Acts 20.36–21.16 on conventional rhetorical patterns from classical Greek literature.

2. Harnack, *Acts*, pp. 186-94; *idem, Luke the Physician*, pp. 152-65; A.T. Robertson, *Luke the Historian in the Light of Research* (New York: Charles Scribner's Sons, 1920), p. 84. However, in supporting the view that the author of Acts personally encountered Philip the evangelist, we are not necessarily bound to follow Harnack in identifying this writer ('Luke') with Luke the physician.

but also as a literary character within Luke's unfolding drama of the early church's worldwide mission.

In comparing the portrait of Philip in Acts 21 with earlier images, we may be struck initially with an impression of Philip's present lowly status. Alongside his more dynamic and 'spiritual' pursuits on the mission field, Philip's vocation as a settled family man and home-owner who provides lodging for Paul may appear prosaic and insignificant. Are we now to envisage Philip sitting on the sidelines, so to speak, retired from front-line missionary duty? Is not Paul so much the center of attention at this stage in Luke's story that Philip appears as a mere 'bit player', just another member of the gallery cheering Paul onward to Jerusalem? Is our final encounter, then, with the Lukan Philip an essentially unmemorable one, even functioning retro-spectively to diminish Philip's previous successes?

Thus far in this study, I have investigated other facets of Luke's presentation which might be construed as demeaning Philip's reputa-tion. In each case, however, the conclusion has been reached that the role which Philip plays is in fact a vital and venerated one when viewed in the context of Luke's overall narrative. The possibility thus remains open that careful literary analysis might also lead to a more positive assessment of Philip's role as Paul's host.

2. *Philip's Role as Paul's Host*

In order to evaluate the status of Philip's domestic vocation in Acts 21, we must explore the social significance of hospitality for Luke and his world. Whatever our modern appraisals of the importance of hospitality in comparison with other ministries such as preaching, counseling or administration, these must not be allowed to inhibit or distort a candid investigation of Luke's perspective on hospitality in relation to the outlook of the wider first-century church.

a. *The Practice of Hospitality in the Early Church*
The great system of roads and highways throughout the Roman empire in an age of peace and order made for a very mobile society in the ancient world; and, naturally, the proliferation of travellers cre-ated a high demand for accommodation. Inns were available along the routes at regular intervals, but given their notoriety as brothels, they were normally not frequented by the upper classes or by any morally

scrupulous parties (such as the early Christians). The way around this dilemma was to secure lodging in the homes of personal friends or trusted members of some fraternity.[1]

Ever on the move, the apostle Paul often availed himself of the hospitality of Christian acquaintances. He told Philemon to prepare a guest room for his expected visit (Phlm 22). He anticipated wintering with the Corinthians so that they might 'speed him on his journey' (1 Cor. 16.5-7; cf. 2 Cor. 1.15-16). On the occasion of writing the first Corinthian letter, Paul apparently was living in Ephesus with Aquila and Priscilla (1 Cor. 16.9), and his correspondence to the Romans was drafted while staying with Gaius in Corinth (Rom. 16.23). The privilege of receiving hospitality was certainly not unique to Paul, however. As a rule, any itinerant missionary could rightfully expect room and board in exchange for services rendered (Mt. 10.5-14; Mk 6.7-13; Lk. 10.1-12; 2 and 3 John; *Did.* 11–13). But such provision was not restricted to travelling ministers. Caring Christians were even encouraged to open their homes to wayfaring strangers, never knowing when they might be treated to the company of an angel in disguise (Heb. 13.2).

In addition to hosting sojourners from outside the community, the early Christians were known for their consistent hospitality toward one another. Without church buildings, community life centered on individuals' homes (Rom. 16.5, 23; 1 Cor. 16.19; Col. 4.15; Phlm 2).[2] Although only the owners of the most spacious dwellings could serve as hosts for the larger congregational assemblies, every believer could use his or her residence, however humble, as a place of fellowship with other believers and a means of sheltering the local poor. The virtue of hospitality was a serious obligation incumbent upon every Christian seeking to fulfill the law of love (Rom. 12.9-13; 1 Pet. 4.8-9; Heb. 13.12).[3] It was particularly enjoined on behalf of destitute

---

1. Cf. A.J. Malherbe, *Social Aspects of Early Christianity* (Philadelphia: Fortress Press, 2nd edn, 1983), pp. 62-66; J. Stambaugh and D. Balch, *The Social World of the First Christians* (London: SPCK, 1986), pp. 37-38; L.T. Johnson, *The Writings of the New Testament: An Interpretation* (London: SCM Press, 1986), p. 27.

2. Cf. Stambaugh and Balch, *Social World*, pp. 138-40; G. Stählin, 'ξένος κτλ.', *TDNT*, V, p. 23; R. Banks, *Paul's Idea of Community: The Early House Churches in their Historical Setting* (Exeter: Paternoster Press, 1980).

3. Bishops and widows were singled out as having particular responsibilities for hospitality (1 Tim. 3.2; 5.10), but all believers were expected to participate in this duty as well. Cf. D.W. Riddle, 'Early Christian Hospitality: A Factor in the Gospel

widows and prisoners awaiting trial (Hermas, *Mand.* 8, 10; *Sim.*
9.27.2; Justin, *Apol.* 67.6), which proves most interesting in light of
Philip's former table-waiting assignment (directed especially to needy
widows) and current duty as host to one (Paul) facing imminent arrest
and imprisonment (cf. Acts 21.11-14).[1]

Obviously, the ministry of hospitality was widely practiced in the
early church and highly prized as a noble expression of Christian
charity. Nevertheless, certain problems related to hospitality did arise.
Conflicts among various house churches in a given locale could create
a situation in which members of one faction refused to host any representative from a rival group. Witness the obstinacy of Diotrophes
within the Johannine community (3 John 9–10).[2] Another difficulty
was the tendency for some to abuse the privilege of hospitality, such
as idle young widows prone to 'gadding about from house to
house. . . gossips and busybodies, saying what they should not say'
(1 Tim. 5.13).

The most acute dilemma, however, involving troublesome guests
pertained to roving prophets and missionaries whose influence over
their hosts could be quite considerable, both positively and negatively.
On the harmful side, they might gain entrance into gullible households
in order to peddle some dangerous doctrine. As the writer of 2 John
warned: 'Do not receive into the house or welcome anyone who comes
to you and does not bring this teaching [that Christ has come in the
flesh, v. 7]; for to welcome is to participate in the evil deeds of such a
person' (vv. 10-11; cf. 2 Tim. 3.6-9; *Did.* 11.1-2). While hosts were
being swept off their feet by deceptive, smooth-talking preachers, they
were often being parted from their money as well. Exploitation by
bogus travelling ministers was an all too common phenomenon in
ancient society (see e.g. Sir. 11.29, 34; Lucian *Pas. of Pereg.* 11-13;
Alex. the False Prophet 22-24). This is why the *Didache* stipulated
that a wandering prophet should be entertained for only two or three
days at most and then sent on his way with nothing but bread. If he

Transmission', *JBL* 57 (1983), pp. 141-54.

1. Note the parallel experiences of Paul and Ignatius as venerated Christian
ministers who, on the road to martyrdom, receive hospitality from loyal and loving
disciples; cf. Riddle, 'Early Christianity', pp. 142-44.

2. Cf. A.J. Malherbe, 'The Inhospitality of Diotrophes', in *God's Christ and his
People: Studies in Honour of Nils Alstrup Dahl* (ed. J. Jervell and W.A. Meeks;
Oslo: Universitetsforlaget, 1977), pp. 222-32.

solicited additional compensation, he was judged to be a 'false prophet' (*Did.* 11.3-6; 12.1-5).[1] The fraudulent tendencies of many itinerant ministers also accounts in large measure for Paul's frequent practice of self-support as a means of legitimating his apostleship (cf. 1 Thess. 2.1-12; 2 Thess. 3.7-9; 1 Cor. 9.1-18; 2 Cor. 11.7-15).[2]

b. *The Theme of Hospitality in Luke–Acts*
The ministry of hospitality receives special attention in Luke–Acts, appearing at both the beginning and end of the narrative (Lk. 1.40; 2.1-7; Acts 28.23, 30-31) and throughout the material related to Jesus and Paul in particular.[3] Generally speaking, Luke shares the early church's high evaluation of hospitality; more specifically, of course, he handles the subject in his own unique way.

1. *Hospitality in the Gospel of Luke.* More than any other Gospel, Luke presents Jesus as an itinerant prophet without family ties and a home base,[4] ever dependent on others' hospitality. Even his birth occurs during a journey in a makeshift location (Lk. 2.1-7). Throughout the course of his ministry, 'the Son of man has nowhere [permanent] to lay his head' (9.58). He is regularly entertained in the homes of his followers, such as tax collectors like Levi and Zacchaeus (5.27-32; 19.1-10) and women like Mary and Martha (10.38-42). On three occasions—which Luke alone reports—Jesus even dines in a Pharisee's home (7.36-50; 11.37-52; 14.1-24). After his resurrection, Jesus continues to appear in the role of a guest, hosted by Cleopas (and

---

1. Stählin ('ξένος', p. 23 n. 165) suggests that the early church's custom of requiring letters of introduction (cf. 2 Cor. 3.1; Rom. 16.1-2; Acts 18.27) arose because of the exploitative practices of unscrupulous travelling ministers.

2. Cf. G. Theissen, *Social Setting of Pauline Christianity: Essays on Corinth* (ed. and trans. J.H. Schütz; Philadelphia: Fortress Press, 1982), pp. 40-54; B. Holmberg, *Paul and Power: The Structure of Authority in the Primitive Church as Reflected in the Pauline Epistles* (Philadelphia: Fortress Press, 1980), pp. 86-93.

3. I am especially indebted in this section to Koenig, *New Testament Hospitality*, pp. 85-123; cf. also D. Juel, *Luke–Acts* (London: SCM Press, 1984), pp. 88-90; H.J. Cadbury, 'Lexical Notes on Luke–Acts. III. Luke's Interest in Lodging', *JBL* 45 (1926), pp. 305-22; Robinson, 'Place of the Emmaus Story', pp. 485-87.

4. Cf. Koenig: 'In contrast to Mark and Matthew, Luke allows Jesus no regular headquarters in Peter's house at Capernaum' (*New Testament Hospitality*, pp. 86-87).

partner) and the eleven disciples in the climactic scenes of the Gospel narrative (24.28-30, 36-43).

Not only does the Lukan Jesus personally play the part of a nomadic preacher sustained by the hospitality of grateful respondents, he also exhorts his emissaries, both the Twelve and the Seventy, to follow the same pattern (9.1-6; 10.1-12). However, while maintaining that 'the laborer deserves his wages', Jesus appears concerned that his disciples not abuse the privilege of support. They are not to roam from house to house in search of benefits; rather, they must settle in one place within a receptive village and be content to eat and drink whatever is set before them (10.7-8). The main order of business is not the missionary's sustenance but his obligation to proclaim the kingdom of God and heal the sick (9.1-2, 6; 10.9). A similar point is emphasized in the home of Mary and Martha when Jesus upholds the priority of listening to his word over the duty of serving him dinner (10.38-42).[1]

While Jesus clearly appears in Luke as a *guest* preacher reliant upon his hearers' hospitality, he also functions as a gracious *host* attendant to the needs of others. He is notorious among the Pharisees and scribes as a man who 'receives (προσδέχεται) sinners and eats with them' (15.1-2).[2] In the company of his disciples he takes on the character of 'one who serves' (22.27; cf. 12.35-37). When the Twelve recommend that the crowd which had flocked to hear Jesus be sent away to find their own food and lodging,[3] Jesus intervenes and miraculously provides a feast for the lot (9.10-17).[4] Several of Jesus' parables recounted only in Luke feature scenes of table-fellowship focusing on the duties of servants and hosts as well as the privileges of masters and guests (11.5-8; 15.11-32; 16.19-31; 17.7-10). The clearest example is the Parable of the Great Banquet (14.7-24) uttered at a dinner party in the home of a prominent Pharisee (14.1, 12). This story calls for humility on the part of guests and magnanimity on the part of hosts.

1. The contrast drawn here is between the minister's right to be served and his responsibility to minister the word, not between the relative values of table-service and proclamation in general (cf. discussion in Chapter 5 section 2b above).

2. δέχομαι and related compounds are frequently used in Luke–Acts in connection with hospitality: e.g. Lk. 9.5, 53; 10.8, 10, 38; 16.4, 9; 19.6; Acts 17.7; 21.17; 28.7, 30.

3. Only here and in Lk. 19.7 in the New Testament is καταλύω used intransitively in the sense of 'find lodging'/'be (someone's) guest'.

4. Note the link with 9.1-6 where the disciples are sent out and promised lodging. Here they are slow to provide for others what Jesus had authorized for them.

2. *Hospitality in Acts.* At the beginning of Acts the small band of disciples huddle together in a common dwelling (upper room, 1.13-14). As the Christian community expands, the custom of regular fellowship in members' homes starts to develop (2.46; 5.42; 12.12). When the missionary movement finally gets underway, propelled by the dispersion of the Jerusalem church, it is carried forward principally by itinerant evangelists who sojourn in the homes of converts and seekers. During Peter's coastal mission, for example, he lodges in the seaside home of Simon the tanner (10.5-6, 32) and is invited to Cornelius's residence to proclaim the gospel to the household assembled there (10.22-48). Above all, however, it is Paul who epitomizes the travelling missionary who avails himself of others' hospitality. Following his dramatic vision on the Damascus road, he is welcomed into Judas's home on Straight Street where he receives further instruction from Ananias (9.10-19). Throughout his journeys across the Mediterranean world, there arise people like Lydia (16.14-15, 40), the Philippian jailer (16.27-34), Jason (17.5-9), Aquila and Priscilla (18.2-3), Titius Justus (18.7), Mnason (21.16) and Publius (28.7-10)—all of whose main claim to fame is the fact that they accommodate Paul in their homes. While Philip's reputation is more broadly based, he nonetheless assumes a place of honor alongside these several hosts of the great missionary to the Gentiles.

The picture of Paul as a wandering preacher without roots and personal means of support does not, however, reflect the whole story in Acts. To an even greater extent than we found with Jesus, Paul also assumes a more 'residential' profile.[1] Though travelling extensively, he works from a stable home base at Antioch. And far from always flitting from one place to another, he settles down for relatively prolonged ministries in three places: Corinth (18 months, 18.11), Ephesus (3 years, 20.31) and Rome (2 years, 28.30). Interestingly, in each of these settings Paul's self-sufficiency is accentuated. At Corinth, he works alongside Aquila and Priscilla in their tent-making trade (18.3). In his final encounter with Ephesian elders, Paul takes great pains to remind them that, while he ministered 'from house to house', he also labored hard throughout his stay to supply his own needs and avoid the snare of covetousness (20.33-35). At Rome, even though a prisoner and thus patently entitled to the support of the local Christian

---

1. Koenig speaks of the 'residentialization' of Paul in Acts (*New Testament Hospitality*, p. 99).

community, Paul lives at his own expense in rented quarters and welcomes (ἀποδέχομαι) all inquirers (28.30-31; cf. v. 23). Thus, the Paul of Acts steers well clear of any charges of abusing his missionary calling financially and proves himself to be a generous host as well as a grateful guest. The situation is remarkably similar to that revealed in the Pauline letters.

3. *Conclusion.* In short, both Jesus and Paul in Luke's narrative combine within themselves the roles of itinerant guest and residential host. From such a presentation, set predominantly within a missionary context, we may reasonably conclude that part of Luke's purpose in treating the theme of hospitality was to sort out problematic relations which often developed between itinerant prophets and resident ministers, as evidenced, for example, in the Corinthian and Johannine letters and the *Didache*.[1]

Clearly, the wandering preachers dependent upon the hospitality of their hearers receive favorable treatment in Luke's story. Much of the material unique to Luke (L) as well as that shared with Matthew (Q) reflects the special concerns of a radical itinerant mission, including not only the need for accommodation, but also the requirement of rigorous integrity in financial matters. Dillon has suggested that these two blocks of material may be traced back to a common pool of tradition transmitted in wandering-charismatic circles.[2] In any case, even if Luke has received rather than created the bulk of his account of the roving ministry of Jesus and his followers, he has certainly made this tradition his own and fully endorsed its radical approach to mission.

Theissen's contention that Luke actually sets out to *attack* the leaders of the wandering-charismatic movement as 'false prophets' cannot be sustained by a balanced reading of the text. Theissen bases his opinion on (1) an extreme periodization of Lukan history in which the circumstances surrounding the life of Jesus are too sharply demarcated from conditions in Luke's own time; (2) an excessively restrictive view of the twelve apostles as the only legitimate missionaries in Luke's eyes; and (3) a misinterpretation of Lk. 22.35-36 as over-

---

1. On the conflicts in leadership styles between wandering charismatics and community organizers in earliest Christianity, see G. Theissen, *Sociology of Early Palestinian Christianity* (Philadelphia: Fortress Press, 1978), pp. 8-23; *Social Setting*, pp. 22-67.

2. Dillon, *From Eye-witnesses to Ministers of the Word*, pp. 227-49.

turning the original itinerant-charismatic model.[1] Concerning this last matter, Jesus' charge to his disciples suddenly to take along purse and bag is not a blanket repudiation of their former mendicant practice (cf. 10.4), but merely a policy appropriate to more drastic times. Among the provisions now required is also a sword (22.36), surely an indication that the threat of persecution is in the air. During more peaceful days the original plan of unencumbered travel would still commend itself.[2]

Granting that Luke does not discount the continuing validity of an itinerant-charismatic mission, it must still be admitted that much of his material is suited to the concerns of a relatively stable, well-to-do residential community,[3] even to the extent of showing a markedly domestic side to heroic figures such as Paul. In the final analysis, then, is there perhaps something to be said for Theissen's view that Luke tips the scales, if only slightly, to favor the resident minister and undercut the reputation of the travelling prophet? Such a stance might be warranted if we could detect any trace of a polemical tone to the material dealing with itinerant missionaries or any sign of resistance on the part of resident hosts to accommodate wayfaring preachers. Neither element, however, is transparent anywhere in Luke–Acts.[4] A better evaluation of the evidence appreciates that Luke gives due weight to both itinerant and resident ministers and typically portrays their interaction in positive terms. No doubt aware of the potential for tension between these two very different types of ministers, Luke advocates, as always, the need for cooperation and unity.

A similar interpretation has been put forward in much greater detail by J. Koenig, and his conclusions merit an extended hearing:

> But why should we call such a mission 'cooperative'? We do so because
> Luke, in managing his material, clearly makes special efforts to promote

---

1. G. Theissen, 'Wanderradikalismus, Literatursoziologische Aspekte der Überlieferung von Worten Jesu im Urchristentum', in *Studien zur Soziologie des Urchristentums* (WUNT, 19; Tübingen: Mohr [Paul Siebeck], 1979), p. 104.

2. Cf. R.J. Karris, 'Poor and Rich: The Lucan *Sitz im Leben*', in Talbert (ed.), *Perspectives on Luke–Acts*, pp. 115, 118-19.

3. Cf. Esler, *Community and Gospel*, pp. 183-87; Karris, 'Poor and Rich', pp. 116-25.

4. In Lk. 7.36-50 Simon proves to be a reluctant and less than gracious host to both Jesus and the sinful woman, but Simon, of course, appears in the story not as a typical disciple of Jesus but rather as a Pharisaic critic of Jesus' social habits.

harmonious relationships between itinerants and residents for the sake of their common work. While his main interest is in supporting and encouraging the prophetic ministry of residential believers. . . he does not simply forget about the contributions of the itinerants or declare their missionary efforts obsolete. Nor does he deny them an important share in the ongoing leadership of the church. Rather, what we find in Luke's two-volume work, particularly in Acts, is an attempt on his part to provide models for *flexibility with regard to ministerial roles.* Neither itinerants nor residents can define themselves too exclusively in terms of the activities they have come to regard as specific to their manner of life (guest, host, leader, servant, giver, receiver, minister of the word, minister of tables, etc.). It is the nature of God's Spirit always to challenge the self-images of believers so that the gospel may advance [emphasis added].[1]

c. *Philip's Hospitality to Paul in Acts 21*

In view of Luke's high esteem for the ministry of hospitality, we should not regard Philip's accommodation of Paul in Acts 21 as merely a trifling courtesy. The role of host is an honorable and indispensable one in Luke's narrative, numbering among its players both Jesus and Paul in addition to Philip and several others. By the same token, the juxtaposition of Philip's settled domestic vocation in Caesarea with his erstwhile evangelistic endeavors throughout Samaria and Judea should not be interpreted as disparaging Philip in any way. As a notable itinerant preacher and miracle-worker who becomes a local host for another travelling missionary, Philip strikingly exemplifies that 'flexibility with regard to ministerial roles' so integral to Lukan ecclesiology. This flexibility is very similar to that displayed by Philip as both table-servant and minister of the word in Acts 6–8. Moreover, the specific encounter between Philip the gracious host (and sometime wandering charismatic) and Paul the guest preacher (and sometime host)—far from subordinating the former to the latter or endorsing any division between them—serves in the larger context of Luke–Acts to illustrate a basic compatibility between the two individuals and the itinerant and residential types which they both represent.

The significance of this cooperative bond between Philip and Paul may be further apprehended against the backdrop of earlier depictions of relations between Paul and the Stephen–Philip circle in Acts. As noted above, the first encounter between these parties appears as a

---

1. Koenig, *New Testament Hospitality*, p. 107.

violent clash. Paul (Saul) emerges as a conspicuous collaborator in Stephen's lynching (Acts 7.58; 8.1a) and the chief instigator of the ensuing persecution which breaks out against Stephen's associates, including Philip (8.1-5; 9.1-2). However, immediately following the sketch of Paul's oppressive activities (in references framing the Philip stories) is the report of Paul's extraordinary conversion on the Damascus road. The way is thus paved for a dramatic reversal in relations with the Stephen–Philip group. The church at Antioch, founded by refugees from Paul's assault on Christians in Jerusalem, now benefits from Paul's instruction and becomes his missionary headquarters (11.19-26; 13.1-3). While questions arise among remaining Jewish Christians in Jerusalem concerning the validity of Paul's Gentile mission, communities in Samaria and Phoenicia—established by Philip and other fugitives from Jerusalem (cf. 11.19)—enthusiastically receive Paul and his report of Gentile conversions (15.3).

This pattern of reconciliation between Paul and the Stephen–Philip circle continues and climaxes in Acts 21–22. As ch. 22 opens, Paul finds himself in a defensive situation before hostile Jerusalem Jews similar to that faced earlier by Stephen, and in v. 20 he even explicitly commends 'Stephen your [the Lord's] witness' whom he had formerly persecuted. The previous chapter discloses that Paul's troubles in Jerusalem on this occasion had been fomented by Asian Jews distressed over his fraternization with Trophimus, an Ephesian Gentile who had accompanied Paul on his journey and allegedly been brought into the sacred temple precincts (21.27-35; cf. 20.4). In contrast, however, to this Jewish attack on Paul and his associates, ch. 21 also reports that certain Christian assemblies and individuals with ties to the original Stephen-circle welcome the Pauline travel party with open arms.[1] At Tyre in Phoenicia, the Christian community (founded by Stephen's sympathizers; cf. 11.19) hosts Paul and his companions for a week and sends them on their way to Jerusalem in a touching farewell scene (21.3-6). Philip himself then receives Paul and his friends into his home for several days. Along with Philip's four daughters, various additional members of the Caesarean church apparently gather at Philip's home and express their concern for

---

1. F.F. Bruce (*The Pauline Circle* [Exeter: Paternoster Press; Grand Rapids: Eerdmans, 1985], p. 98) regards Paul's seven travelling companions listed in Acts 20.4 as a mixed group of Jewish and Gentile Christians. In addition to Trophimus, the Gentiles are represented by Secundus and Gaius.

Paul's safety in Jerusalem (21.12).[1] A contingent of these Caesarean disciples even accompany Paul to Jerusalem and direct him to the home of Mnason where another joyous reception awaits (21.15-17). As an 'early disciple' (ἀρχαίῳ μαθητῇ) and native of Cyprus, Mnason may be linked both with Barnabas and with those 'Hellenists' who first proclaimed the gospel to Greeks in Antioch (cf. 4.36; 11.20).[2]

In summary, Philip's hospitality to Paul in Acts 21 represents part of a cluster of events demonstrating the prevailing unity between Paul and those Christians he had formerly persecuted. Harmony has replaced hostility. Paul, who had previously ravaged the church by (a) 'entering house after house. . . , (b) drag[ging] off men and women and (c) commit[ting] them to prison' (8.3), is now (a) gladly received in house after house (21.1-17), (b) accommodated by men and women like Philip and his four daughters (21.8-9) and (c) himself branded as a lawbreaker facing imprisonment (21.11-14). In the course of Luke's narrative, a thorough reversal has occurred in Paul's personal experience and relations with Philip and other associates of Stephen.

As Philip's gracious welcome of Paul in Caesarea stands in marked contrast to the Asian Jews' harsh treatment of Paul in Jerusalem, M. Hengel suggests that Acts 21 sets up a similar opposition between the respective receptions of Paul by Philip and James.

> the friendly reception of Paul and his companions when they arrive in Caesarea on the last journey, described in the 'we report' (21.8ff.). . . is clearly contrasted with the more reserved account of the reception by James and the elders in James's 'residence', where the advice, or rather command of James leads to the subsequent conflict in the temple (21.18ff.). . . Luke wants to use this background account to demonstrate that in contrast to the threatening situation in Jerusalem, his hero

---

1. οἱ ἐντόπιοι in Acts 21.12 is a New Testament *hapax* meaning 'the local residents' (BAGD, p. 269) or 'the local people' (J.P. Louw *et al.*, *Greek-English Lexicon of the New Testament Based on Semantic Domains* [2 vols.; New York: UBS, 1988], I, p. 131) and seems to refer to a wider group of Caesarean disciples than Philip's immediate family.

2. Cf. Bruce, *Pauline Circle*, p. 99; Dunn, *Unity and Diversity*, p. 256; G. Lüdemann, *Paulus, der Heidenapostel*. II. *Antipaulinismus im frühen Christentum* (FRLANT, 130; Göttingen: Vandenhoeck & Ruprecht, 1983), p. 91.

was *persona grata* to Philip and the Christians in Caesarea who accompanied him on his difficult journey to Jerusalem (21.16).[1]

While it is true that Paul's interaction with James and the Jerusalem elders appears somewhat more official and less intimate than his encounter with Philip and the Caesarean community, nevertheless, the antithesis between Philip and James is not as sharply drawn in Luke's narrative as Hengel avers. We should not suppose that Luke has suddenly abandoned his interest in portraying the unity of the early church. Despite James's 'more reserved' reception of Paul, there are clear signs in Acts 21 that no serious break in relations had occurred.

1. James and the elders still 'glorify God' when Paul reports his ministry among the Gentiles (21.19-20a).
2. The 'Apostolic Decree' is mentioned again (21.25), and though awkwardly cited as if Paul is hearing it for the first time, in the Lukan schema it surely recalls the momentous council of Acts 15 and the unity which prevailed there between Paul and the Jerusalem church.
3. The Jacobean party may show its suspicion of Paul by insisting on a public demonstration of his loyalty, but the fact remains that Paul complies with their wishes, thereby eliminating the grounds of dissension.
4. The trouble which erupts in the temple stems from the machinations of the *Jews from Asia*, not the Jewish Christians in Jerusalem,[2] and although the lack of intervention by James on Paul's behalf may raise some questions about how fully James embraced Paul, this silence in the narrative can scarcely suggest that James actually plotted with the Asians to entrap Paul.[3]
5. Agabus, the prophet from Judea who comes to Philip's home

---

1. Hengel, *Between Jesus and Paul*, p. 115.
2. J.T. Sanders greatly exaggerates the evidence of Acts 21 by claiming that the Jewish Christians in Jerusalem 'are involved in a "scheme" to get rid of Paul' and are 'little to be distinguished from non-Christian Jews. Both are hostile to Gentile Christianity . . . ' (*Jews*, p. 284). To be sure, the Jewish Christians within James's community are concerned about Paul's commitment to uphold the Mosaic law (21.20-22), but there is no indication that this concern leads them to participate with 'the Jews from Asia' in fomenting the violent uprising against Paul in the temple (21.27-29).
3. On James as 'the defender of Paul' in Acts, see Jervell, *Luke and the People of God*, pp. 185-207.

and warns Paul of impending Jewish hostility against him (Acts 21.10-11), represents a bridge figure in Acts (similar to Barnabas) uniting the settled Jerusalem church, the 'Hellenist' disciples scattered after Stephen's death and Paul (cf. 11.27-30).

In short, the juxtaposed receptions of Paul in Acts 21.8-26 by Philip and the Caesarean Christians, on the one hand, and James and the Jerusalem Christians, on the other hand, are more alike than dissimilar in their basic demonstration of support for Paul and his ministry.

3. *Philip the 'Evangelist' and Paul*

Throughout this study I have utilized conventional nomenclature in distinguishing Philip the 'evangelist' from Philip the 'apostle', one of Jesus' twelve disciples. The term εὐαγγελιστής, a cognate of εὐαγγελίζομαι and εὐαγγέλιον, is obviously an appropriate designation for the Philip in Acts 8, known for proclaiming the gospel to the Samaritans and Ethiopian eunuch. Of course, other missionaries in Luke–Acts also participate in 'evangelistic' activities, but Philip is the only character specifically labelled ὁ εὐαγγελιστής in the narrative, and that on only one occasion—in Acts 21.8. On the basis of this restricted usage, the possibility arises that εὐαγγελιστής has a more specialized meaning in relation to Philip than simply 'one who preaches the gospel'.

This possibility becomes more intriguing when we consider the wider distribution of εὐαγγελιστής in the New Testament. Apart from the lone Lukan reference, εὐαγγελιστής appears in only two other New Testament texts, Eph. 4.11 and 2 Tim. 4.5. Interestingly, both of these emerge in writings widely accepted as 'deutero-Pauline', due in part to their emphasis on more developed structures of ministry. Since Luke–Acts may also be classified as 'post-Pauline' literature, and since Philip is uniquely called 'the evangelist' in the context of a meeting with Paul, we should perhaps regard εὐαγγελιστής as something of a technical term in established Pauline circles. At any rate, a comparative analysis of the rare cases of εὐαγγελιστής in the New Testament, together with a look at selected patristic references, promises to shed important light on Philip's singular role in Luke's narrative as 'the evangelist' of the early church.

a. *Ephesians 4.11*

> The gifts he gave were that some would be apostles, some prophets, some
> evangelists, some pastors and teachers. . .

Here 'evangelists' are listed between two related pairs of gifted ministers. The 'apostles and prophets', though distinguished from each
other by μέν. . . δέ and the use of the definite article with each term,
are clearly linked together in the Ephesian letter (2.20; 3.5), and
'pastors and teachers', governed by a single article, can be taken to
denote two aspects of the same 'office' (pastor-teacher).[1] The gift of
'evangelist', then, standing alone in the middle of the series, would
seem to be defined in opposition to and in comparison with the two
flanking ministerial pairs.

Apostles and prophets are distinguished in Ephesians as foundational
pillars of the church (2.20) and special recipients of the Spirit's
immediate revelation of the mystery of Christ (3.3-5). They are
clearly servants of the church at large, the 'one body' of Christ (1.22-
23; 2.15-22; 4.4-6, 11-16). The precise identity of these apostles and
prophets is never disclosed, although one might assume that Jesus'
twelve disciples were among those in view. Whatever the total company, there is no doubt that Paul is ranked as an apostle and prophet
par excellence (3.1-12). Concerning their ministry, it is interesting
that Paul and his fellow apostles and prophets are presented as
conveyors of the Christian *gospel* of grace to all humankind (3.5-11;
εὐαγγέλιον, v. 6; εὐαγγελίζομαι, v. 8). They thus engage in
'evangelistic' functions but are still set apart from those explicitly
labelled as 'evangelists' in 4.11.

What can be inferred from this parallel-yet-distinct relationship
between apostles/prophets and evangelists in Ephesians? The most
cogent hypothesis conceives of evangelists as missionaries who proclaimed the gospel just like the apostles and prophets but who could
not, with Paul and the Twelve, lay claim to a direct commission from
Christ and to immediate revelation of the gospel by the Spirit. They
were second-generation preachers, from the perspective of Ephesians,

1. Cf. J. Gnilka, *Der Epheserbrief* (HTKNT, 10/2; Freiburg: Herder, 1971),
p. 211; R. Schnackenburg, *Der Brief an die Epheser* (EKKNT, 10; Zürich:
Benziger; Neukirchen–Vluyn: Neukirchener Verlag, 1982), pp. 182-85;
H. Merklein, *Das kirchliche Amt nach dem Epheserbrief* (SANT, 33; Munich:
Kösel, 1973), pp. 332-35, 345-47.

who differed from the apostles and prophets not in their essential function but only in the relative originality of their message. The apostles and prophets laid the foundation; the evangelists built upon it.[1]

There is no need in this arrangement to posit a strict line of apostolic succession or a clear-cut hierarchy subordinating evangelist to apostle.[2] These are notions tied to narrow conceptions of ecclesiastical office which go beyond the primarily functional understanding of evangelistic ministry. In the case of the Pauline circle, evangelists likely represented the many co-laborers of Paul who were indebted to the apostle for their initiation into the gospel, but who often conducted independent (although not necessarily competitive) missions.[3] Harnack's theory may well be right that evangelists were mentioned in Ephesians precisely because the community(ies) addressed in this letter was 'founded by non-apostolic missionaries [= evangelists], and not by Paul himself'.[4]

Relating the role of evangelist to that of pastor-teacher is more difficult, since Ephesians provides no elaboration on the latter's significance. Nevertheless, it is probably safe to assume that pastor-teachers in Ephesians, as elsewhere in the New Testament, represent

---

1. Commentators generally agree on this assessment. See, e.g., M. Barth, *Ephesians: Translation and Commentary on Chapters 4–6* (AB, 34A; Garden City, NY: Doubleday, 1974), p. 430; Schnackenburg, *Brief*, pp. 182-85; Gnilka, *Epheserbrief*, pp. 211-12; H. Schlier, *Der Brief an die Epheser: Ein Kommentar* (Düsseldorf: Patmos, 6th edn, 1968), p. 196; U. Becker, 'Gospel, Evangelize, Evangelist', *NIDNTT*, II, p. 114. Compare 1 Cor. 12.28 where a similar list of gifted ministers is provided *minus* 'evangelist'. In 1 Corinthians a less restrictive concept of apostles and prophets seems to be in view (cf. 4.9-13; 9.1-12; 14.1-5, 22-40). In the 'post-apostolic' period, however, apostles and prophets became more narrowly defined in Pauline circles, creating a need for a category of apostle-like ministers distinguished from the apostles. Hence Eph. 4.11 *adds* 'evangelists' to the list.

2. As suggested, for example, in Merklein, *Kirchliche Amt*, pp. 345-47.

3. Although not calling them 'evangelists' *per se*, Ellis acknowledges the presence within the wider Pauline circle of a number of ministers 'who, though in friendly association with the Apostle, for the most part work in relative independence of him' (*Prophecy and Hermeneutic*, p. 5).

4. A. Harnack, *The Mission and Expansion of Christianity in the First Three Centuries* (2 vols.; London: Williams & Norgate; New York: Putnam's Sons, 2nd edn, 1908), I, p. 321 n. 4; cf. Barth, *Ephesians (4–6)*, p. 438; Schlier, *Brief*, p. 196.

the local community leaders responsible for the continuing spiritual care and instruction of the 'flock' (cf. Acts 20.28; 1 Pet. 5.1-3). As residential ministers within established congregations, they would naturally have been distinguished from the more itinerant, church-planting evangelists. This does not eliminate, however, the possibility of continuing work for evangelists within the local community, since the need to add new converts remained a pressing concern for young congregations and since preaching the gospel was critical not only for generating community life, but for sustaining it as well.

b. *2 Timothy 4.5*

. . . do the work of an evangelist, carry out your ministry fully.

In this instance 'evangelist' points chiefly to the *act* (ἔργον) of proclaiming the gospel which Timothy must perform rather than to any official church position he might hold. However, while we might expect a variety of ministers to carry out such a duty, it is interesting to note that throughout the Pastorals no other local community leaders—bishops, deacons or elders—are exhorted to function as an evangelists nor is their work described in εὐαγγελίζομαι/εὐαγγέλιον terms (cf. 1 Tim. 3.1-12; 5.17-22; Tit. 1.5-9). In addition to Timothy, only the apostle Paul emerges explicitly as one entrusted with 'the glorious gospel' (1 Tim. 1.11; cf. 2 Tim. 1.8-11). A rather exclusive Pauline claim upon the gospel may even be detected in the reference to 'my gospel' (τὸ εὐαγγέλιόν μου) in 2 Tim. 2.8. Yet, however unique Paul appears in the Pastorals as the supreme 'herald (κῆρυξ) and . . . apostle . . . and teacher' (2 Tim. 1.11; cf. 1 Tim. 2.7), these letters also disclose that Paul had transmitted his gospel message and ministry to his beloved son in the faith, Timothy (1 Tim. 1.2, 18-20; 4.11-16; 6.20; 2 Tim. 1.2, 6-14; 2.1-26; 3.10–4.5). It would then seem that Timothy's role as 'evangelist' is that of an apostle-like preacher of the gospel. This is similar to the conception of 'evangelist' in Ephesians, only here the connecting link between apostle and evangelist appears stronger and more sharply defined,[1] and the principal

---

1. The Pastorals seem to reflect an ecclesiastical situation further on the road toward rigid institutionalization of ministry than Ephesians (cf. Dunn, *Unity and Diversity*, pp. 114-16, 351-52). Timothy, for example, is clearly subordinated to Paul; even so, Timothy's particular role as 'evangelist' is still conceived primarily in functional rather than 'official' terms.

scope of Timothy's work is more local or regional than universal.

In short, from the scanty New Testament evidence outside of Acts, the most balanced description of εὐαγγελιστής we can offer is that of a minister of the Christian gospel with close functional, but not necessarily 'official', ties to the foundational apostles—especially Paul (and probably the Twelve); like the apostles, the evangelists bore witness to Christ both on the mission field, resulting in the planting of new churches, and among established local congregations.[1] Along similar lines, L. Goppelt provides a succinct definition of εὐαγγελιστής: 'The name referred to a circle of men who, partly independent of the apostles and partly as their companions and fellow workers, had carried out the mission and the pastoral care of the churches'.[2]

c. Patristic Sources

Before dealing with the 'evangelist' tag applied specifically to Philip in Acts, it might be useful to supplement the rough sketch of εὐαγγελιστής in the New Testament with extrabiblical data. Unfortunately, secular sources supply no really illuminating parallels. In fact, the paucity of references to εὐαγγελιστής in ancient Greek literature has sparked the suggestion that the term was originally coined in Christian circles.[3] After the New Testament period, εὐαγγελιστής surfaces in the writings of the church fathers around the beginning of the third century as a technical title for the authors of the Gospels (τὰ εὐαγγέλια, Hippolytus, De Antichr. 56; Tertullian, Adv. Prax. 21.23). Such a usage could only arise at a time when the gospel began to be closely identified with certain authoritative books about Jesus' life and teaching. It is thus anachronistic to impose this later notion of 'evangelist' on the New Testament material, in which the gospel is still conceived of principally as oral proclamation.[4]

Coming to Eusebius's *Ecclesiastical History*, however, a work

---

1. Roloff (*Apostelgeschichte*, p. 310) and G. Strecker ('εὐαγγελίζω', *EWNT*, II, p. 176) stress the *local* dimension of an evangelist's ministry, and others focus chiefly on the *missionary* dimension. But it seems best not to demarcate these functions too sharply. Cf. G. Friedrich, 'εὐαγγελίζομαι, εὐαγγέλιον, κτλ.', *TDNT*, II, p. 737.

2. L. Goppelt, *Apostolic and Post-Apostolic Times* (London: A. & C. Black, 1970), p. 191.

3. Merklein, *Kirchliche Amt*, p. 347.

4. Cf. Friedrich, 'εὐαγγελίζομαι', pp. 735-36; contra D. Hadidian, '*tous de euangelistas* in Eph 4,11', *CBQ* 28 (1966), pp. 317-19.

composed in the fourth century but recounting events from an earlier period, we encounter uses of εὐαγγελιστής more in tune with the 'deutero-Pauline' conception. In discussing the 'shining lights' of the first half of the second century, Eusebius mentions the many evangelists, those 'pious disciples of great men' who 'built in every place upon the foundations of the churches laid by the apostles'. They were travelling missionaries who, like their apostolic predecessors, engaged in founding new communities and appointing local pastors before moving on to spread the gospel in other regions. Of particular interest in comparison with Philip's portrait in Acts 8 is Eusebius's profile of evangelists as those who displayed miraculous signs through the Spirit and inspired great crowds through their preaching to turn from false gods to the one true God (*Eccl. Hist.* 3.37).[1]

From the latter part of the second century, Eusebius recalls the exploits of a man named Pantaenus, an esteemed philosopher of the Alexandrian school who 'was appointed as a herald for the gospel of Christ' in India. In this missionary capacity Pantaenus functioned as an *evangelist*, furthering the work in India begun by the apostle Bartholomew who had left behind a copy of Matthew's Gospel. After completing his tour of duty, Pantaenus returned to Africa to take up the post of principal of the Alexandrian academy (*Eccl. Hist.* 5.10).[2]

d. *Acts 21.8*

It might be thought that Philip's designation as 'evangelist' simply reflects a traditional ('Hellenist'?) title taken over by Luke[3] or a natural label utilized by Luke to acknowledge Philip's reputation as a preacher of the gospel and to distinguish him from his apostolic namesake (cf. Lk. 6.14; Acts 1.13).[4] While either of these explanations is possible, as far as they go, they do not take into account the

---

1. Eusebius also refers to the evangelists as distributors of inspired written Gospels to their audiences, but not as the actual authors of those Gospels. Eusebius citations are from *The Ecclesiastical History* (2 vols.; ed. and trans. K. Lake; LCL; Cambridge, MA: Harvard University Press; London: Heinemann, 1926–32).

2. Like Philip in Acts, Pantaenus returned to a more settled ministry after his missionary tour.

3. Schmithals suggests that the title 'evangelist' in Acts 21.8 'kennzeichnet Philippus vermutlich als Missionar einer hellenistisch-jüdischen Gemeinde' (*Apostelgeschichte*, p. 192).

4. Cf. Giles, 'Is Luke an Exponent of "Early Protestantism"?', part 2, p. 15; Marshall, *Acts*, p. 339.

specialized understanding of εὐαγγελιστής in post-Pauline circles which may have influenced Luke's usage. As a matter of fact, the overall presentation of Philip's ministry in Acts conforms remarkably to the picture of an evangelist pieced together from Ephesians and the Pastorals and later corroborated by Eusebius. Philip functions as a gospel-proclaiming, miracle-working missionary in much the same way as the apostles Peter and Paul, although not being a direct recipient of Christ's personal revelation and commission, he himself is not called an apostle.[1] Philip's mission in Samaria and the coastal plain is initially conducted independently of the apostles, but, as we have seen, soon Peter comes along in the same territory to complement Philip's efforts. A strong continuity (although not a strict hierarchy) is established between Philip and the Twelve, precisely the relationship between evangelist and apostle which underlies the 'deutero-Pauline' writings.

A similar arrangement between Philip and Paul seems to be in view, centered on the city of Caesarea. Philip pioneers the preaching of the gospel in this place (Acts 8.40) and eventually settles down here and raises a family (21.8-9). It is Peter, of course, who first ministers in Caesarea after Philip (10.24-48), but later Paul also arrives on the scene, lodging in Philip's home and making contact with the Caesarean disciples (21.8-16). By identifying Philip as 'the evangelist' in this setting of Paul's visit, Luke may be subtly casting Philip in a role parallel to the evangelists of Eph. 4.11 and Timothy in the Pastorals. Philip may have preceded Paul in Caesarea, but his vocation as an evangelist insures that both he and the Caesarean church have solid ties to the Pauline mission. When Paul arrives in Caesarea in Acts 21, Philip may appear more as a resident minister than an itinerant missionary, but like Timothy, he may continue to 'do the work of an evangelist' and so complement Paul's own gospel ministry. In short, by dubbing Philip 'the evangelist', Luke not only characterizes the nature of Philip's activity, but in effect also incorporates Philip into the ranks of Paul's co-laborers. A unity is thus established between Philip and Paul in the common cause of heralding the gospel. In this

---

1. As is well known, it is questionable whether even Paul enjoys full 'apostolic' status alongside the Twelve in Luke's presentation, although in Acts 14.4, 14, the ἀπόστολος label is applied to him (and Barnabas). Nevertheless, by virtue of his encounter with the risen Christ, Paul does share with the Twelve one vital qualification of apostleship (cf. Acts 1.22) which Philip could not claim.

respect, Philip's unique identification in Acts 21.8 as 'evangelist' serves roughly the same purpose as Stephen's designation in 22.20 as 'witness', a title which otherwise Luke exclusively reserves for the Twelve and Paul.[1]

This opinion that the lone Lukan reference to εὐαγγελιστής should be coordinated with 'deutero-Pauline' usage is also supported by the larger narrative surrounding Acts 21.8. Of particular interest are the various other ministries mentioned in the account of Paul's journey to Jerusalem in 20.5–21.17. In the Miletus incident the leaders of the Ephesian church are characterized as elders (πρεσβύτεροι, 20.17), bishops (overseers, ἐπίσκοποι, 20.28) and pastors (ποιμαίνειν τὴν ἐκκλησίαν τοῦ θεοῦ, 20.28), and in the Philip scene we encounter Agabus the prophet (προφήτης) along with Philip's daughters 'who prophesied' (προφητεύουσαι) (21.9-10). Such a grouping of various types of ministry is unique in Acts. Elders and prophets appear elsewhere (11.27; 13.1; 14.23; 15.2, 4, 6, 22; 16.4; 21.18), but 20.28 represents the only reference to bishops and pastors. Significantly, however, this particular cluster of ministries is matched in Ephesians (prophet/pastor) and the Pastorals (bishops/elders), precisely those parts of the New Testament which contain the only other occurrences of εὐαγγελιστής. Therefore, we may reasonably surmise that Luke's report of the final Pauline journey to Jerusalem reflects a late first-century, post-Pauline ecclesiology.[2] This being the case, his use of εὐαγγελιστής may be interpreted as similar to that found in Ephesians and 2 Timothy.

---

1. N. Brox (*Zeuge und Märtyrer: Untersuchungen zur frühchristlichen Zeugnis-Terminologie* [SANT, 5; Munich: Kösel, 1961], pp. 64-66) notes the parallel between Philip's and Stephen's respective designations as evangelist and witness. He further suggests that Luke regards Philip as a witness as well, not in the technical sense reserved for eyewitnesses of the resurrection, but in the broader sense connected with the function of preaching.

2. I am not suggesting that all of Luke–Acts reflects this more developed ecclesiastical situation. Lukan ecclesiology is quite complex and cannot as a whole be simply equated with Ephesians and the Pastorals, which themselves are not identical. Parts of Luke–Acts strike one as more primitive and supportive of charismatic authority (e.g. Acts 6–8 discussed in previous chapters); others, like Acts 20–21 seem to reflect a later period. E. Schweizer wisely speaks of 'very diverse forms [of church order] standing side by side' in Luke's writing (*Church Order in the New Testament* [SBT, 32; London: SCM Press, 1961], p. 72); cf. also Dunn, *Unity and Diversity*, pp. 106-109, 352-58.

4. *Conclusion*

The final Philip scene in Acts 21.8-9, though brief, makes a vital contribution to Luke's overall *Philippusbild*. Philip's principal role in this scene is that of host to Paul and his companions on their way to Jerusalem. I have found no reason to doubt the historical basis of this encounter between Philip and Paul and I have even concluded that the author of Luke–Acts, as part of the 'we'-group attending Paul, also met Philip personally. Our main interest, however, has been in the element of hospitality interpreted against the backdrop of the wider Lukan narrative.

Few expressions of Christian service are as highly prized in Luke–Acts as the practice of hospitality, and Philip's participation in this duty may be regarded as an unmitigated commendation of his ministry. Moreover, far from being inconsistent with or inferior to his earlier activities of wonder-working and gospel-preaching, Philip's hospitality represents a complementary labor of love (similar to table-service), repeatedly promoted by Jesus himself in Luke's Gospel.

The dominant Lukan purpose behind Acts 21.8-9 which has come to light in this chapter has been the concern to establish a bond of unity and cooperation between Philip and Paul. This purpose can be detected from three angles:

1. Philip is depicted as a resident minister who extends hospitality to the itinerant Paul. The friction which often characterized relations between resident and itinerant ministers in early Christian communities is notably absent in Acts 21.
2. Philip's gracious reception of Paul in Acts 21 represents the crowning example of the reversal of hostilities between Paul and the Stephen–Philip circle since the former's conversion.
3. Philip is uniquely designated 'the evangelist' as a means of incorporating him into the Pauline network of missionaries, thus matching the pattern of the 'deutero-Pauline' letters.

Generally speaking, the hospitality motif and the 'evangelist' label serve to illustrate the unity between Philip and Paul in much the same way as the forerunner–culminator model brings together Philip and Peter in the Lukan schema.

Chapter 7

CONCLUSION

I have identified and examined numerous components of the portrait of Philip in Acts over the course of this study, and no attempt will be made here to reiterate all of my findings. But it should prove useful to take a final, panoramic look at this Lukan figure and highlight the most salient features of his characterization.

On the whole, we have found Philip to be a truly significant and positive figure within Luke's narrative. He does not, of course, enjoy the stature of Luke's heroic triumvirate—Jesus, Peter and Paul—but neither is he totally eclipsed by these men; he emerges as a notable character of substance and distinction in his own right. Still less should Philip be viewed as a figure whom Luke has consciously set out to belittle or 'put in his place'. I have consistently maintained that alleged failures (the 'apostasy' of Simon Magus), deficiencies (not imparting the Spirit to his converts) and inconsistencies (table service/ hospitality versus proclamation of the word) in Philip's ministry are in fact either commendable elements of his vocation or at least in no way damaging to his reputation when viewed from Luke's over-arching narrative perspective.

In more specific terms, the favorable depiction of Philip in Acts may be ascertained by focusing on three critical roles which Philip plays within the narrative.

1. *Philip the Pioneering Missionary*

It is commonplace to observe that the structure of Acts reflects the Lukan purpose to chart the gospel's extension beyond the borders of Jerusalem-based Judaism out to the ends of the earth (cf. Acts 1.8). It is also customary to credit Peter and Paul with the strategic advances in this missionary program. This study, however, while not denying the focus on Peter's and Paul's accomplishments, has argued that Philip also appears in Acts as a pioneering missionary. His evangelistic exploits, recounted in Acts 8, represent for Luke genuinely trail-blazing and barrier-breaking steps, not merely transitional and bridge-building efforts, in forwarding the global dissemination of the Christian message.

In Acts 1–7 the earliest Christian community is localized exclusively in Jerusalem and, from all indications, directs its ministry exclusively to resident or immigrant Jews within the city (cf. 2.5-11). It is only in Acts 8, in conjunction with the forced dispersion of some members of the Jerusalem church following Stephen's execution, that a Christian witness begins to be carried to outlying regions and outcast peoples. The *first* itinerant preacher featured in this mission story is Philip the evangelist.

In Acts 8.5-13 Philip preaches to and baptizes a throng of Samaritans in the city of Samaria. In terms of ethnic-religious status, Samaritans in Luke–Acts occupy something of a middle position between Jews and Gentiles, difficult to pin down precisely. But, in any event, Luke clearly assumes the problem of persisting conflict between Samaritans and Jews and thus presents a situation in which compassionate outreach to Samaritans by Jews or Jewish Christians stands out as a radical social gesture. The Lukan Jesus, in his actions (Lk. 9.51-56; 17.11-19), teachings (Lk. 10.25-37) and commands (Acts 1.8), sets the stage for such a ground-breaking project, but it is Philip in Acts 8 who brings the Samaritan mission to fruition. To be sure, Peter and John later complement this work, but we must not forget that Philip initiates the Samaritan 'crusade' by himself, while the apostles remain cloistered in Jerusalem (Acts 8.1). Moreover, we must recall that certain of the apostles originally exhibited the standard Jewish antipathy toward Samaritans, contrary to the spirit of Jesus' vocation (Lk. 9.54-56). Obviously, these hostilities had to be overcome before the apostles could sincerely accept Samaritans into the Christian community. Philip, however, requires no such transformation. Apart from the list of seven servants in 6.5, the first reference to Philip in Acts relates in notably matter-of-fact terms his commitment to taking the gospel outside of Jerusalem to the despised Samaritans: 'Philip went down to the city of Samaria, and proclaimed the messiah to them' (8.5).

The last episode in Acts 8 describes Philip's encounter with an

Ethiopian eunuch on a 'desert' road leading away from Jerusalem to the coastal plain (8.25-40). Once again the apostles are stationed at their home base in Jerusalem (8.25), while Philip embarks on a solitary mission outside the city's limits. On this occasion, Philip directs his witness to a 'God-fearing' Gentile from the 'ends of the earth' (Ethiopia) barred ('prevented', κωλύω) from full incorporation into the people of God on account of his physical 'defect' as a eunuch. We have seen that Luke regards this figure as a bona fide Gentile, standing in a similar relation to Judaism as the Roman centurion, Cornelius. Hence, the eunuch's conversion to the Christian faith and baptism at the hands of Philip marks the *first* breakthrough in the early church's Gentile mission reported in Acts. Peter's outreach to Cornelius (10.1–11.18) has a greater overall impact, but Philip's mission to the Ethiopian eunuch is still distinguished as the inaugural venture among the Gentiles. What is more, Philip takes this innovative step decisively and without complaint, despite the peculiar circumstances associated with it, whereas such a willing heart scarcely characterizes Peter's initial response to the challenge of embracing the 'unclean'.

In short, Philip the evangelist must be accorded his share of the spotlight as one who spearheads the initial thrust of the early church's expanding mission in Acts. In both Samaria and the coastal plain, Peter comes along to build upon and supplement Philip's work, particularly in the area of imparting the Spirit to new believers. But in this process we have discerned the contours of a more cooperative/mutual rather than competitive/hierarchical relationship between Philip and Peter in Luke's presentation. I have also suggested that Philip functions in this relationship as Peter's *forerunner*, modelled in part on the role of John the Baptist in relation to Jesus.

2. *Philip the Dynamic Prophet*

Building on several studies of Luke's use of biblical-prophetic models in casting his principal characters, I have explored various ways in which the portrait of Philip fits this pattern. Generally speaking, Philip's vocation as a Spirit-endowed preacher and miracle-worker, mighty in word and deed, recalls the dynamic ministry of many venerated prophets from Israel's history. More particularly, however, the Lukan Philip especially reflects the prototypes of Moses and Elijah/Elisha.

The demonstration of Philip's superior greatness as an authentic channel of divine power in direct contrast to Simon the magician, the self-styled 'Great Power of God' who had mesmerized the Samaritan nation, manifests Philip's role as a prophet like the great Moses who overwhelmed Egypt's finest magicians and liberated the people of God. Moreover, Philip's emergence in Acts as a Moses-type instrument of 'the finger of God' matches his ministry with that of Jesus, the ultimate 'prophet like Moses', in Luke's Gospel (cf. Lk. 11.20; Exod. 8.15 LXX).

A further link between Philip and Moses in Luke's presentation may be observed in conjunction with the 'rejected-prophet' motif. As Moses was initially spurned by his own Israelite kinsmen and forced to flee into a foreign land where he found God's presence (cf. Acts 7.23-35), so Philip launches his evangelistic mission in alien territory (Samaria; cf. Shechem reference, Acts 7.16) as a fugitive from the Jewish establishment in Jerusalem. Of course, this 'rejected-prophet-like-Moses' pattern also associates Philip with other characters in Luke–Acts, principally Jesus, Stephen, Peter and Paul.

We discovered Philip's reflection of the Elijah/Elisha model especially in his encounter with the Ethiopian eunuch. To rehearse only selected parallels, we noted that, like Elijah, Philip is supernaturally guided and even transported by the Spirit of God, and, like Elisha with Naaman, Philip is instrumental in incorporating a physically 'defective' foreign official into the community of God's people. Given this correspondence between Philip and both Elijah and Elisha in a social setting outside the boundaries of hostile Judaism, I suggested further that Philip's ministry in Acts 8 echoes in some measure Jesus' stark portrayal of the prophetic vocation in Lk. 4.24-27.

3. *Philip the Cooperative Servant*

Repeatedly we have seen Luke's well-known interest in unity and cooperation manifested in his portrait of Philip. As such, we have joined ranks with others who appreciate the significance of the *Philippusbild* for Lukan ecclesiology in general and the issue of Christian ecumenism in particular. I have reached somewhat distinctive conclusions, however—certainly in comparison with conventional 'early catholic' interpretations—regarding the precise role(s) which Philip plays in this unified church presented by Luke. The approach I have taken is clearly illustrated in conjunction with two important aspects of Philip's profile: (1) his various relations with other Lukan characters and (2) his various acts of Christian service.

Regarding the first matter, Philip emerges as one of the few secondary characters in Acts who interacts on some level with *both* of the early church's leading lights, Peter and Paul. Early in Acts, there are hints of underlying tension and even hostility between Philip and these two Lukan heroes. As a leading member of the branch of the Jerusalem church surrounding Stephen (the 'Hellenists'), Philip is, on the one hand, implicitly embroiled in conflict with Peter and his fellow-apostles over community administration (food-service) and, on the other hand, eventually driven from the city under the threat of Paul's persectuion (cf. 6.1-7; 8.1-5; 9.1-2). As the story ensues, however, these signs of discord between Philip, Peter and Paul disappear and are replaced by vivid pictures of harmony. Philip's missionary exploits (e.g. kingdom- and gospel-preaching, working signs and wonders, overwhelming magicians) match the activities of Peter and Paul at a number of points (we also noted important contacts between Philip's work and that of Jesus and Stephen), and his ministry in various locales serves to complement the endeavors of Peter and Paul, either by preparing the way for the gospel (Peter's forerunner in Samaria and the coastal plain) or by providing practical support (Paul's host in Caesarea). In each case we determined that Luke regards Philip more as an independent yet cooperative partner in ministry (co-laborer) than an inferior subordinate (underling).

Secondly, the variety of duties which Philip performs in Acts evinces a versatility with respect to ministerial roles which breaks down barriers between potentially competitive occupations. For example, Philip appears as both table-servant and minister of the word (as does the Lukan Jesus)—not as a means of undercutting Philip's missionary accomplishments by underscoring his more menial pursuits—but rather as a means of displaying the comparable value and compatible relation of diaconal and kerygmatic forms of service. Philip also appears as both an itinerant charismatic evangelist and a residential domestic host (as do Jesus and Paul in Luke–Acts), thus combining within himself two distinct and sometimes conflicting styles of leadership within earliest Christianity.

In short, Philip is a multi-dimensional, 'round' figure in Acts through whom socioreligious boundaries are crossed (pioneering missionary), scriptural links are established (dynamic prophet) and ministerial tensions are resolved (cooperative servant). The 'Philip-factor' thus represents an integral component of the Lukan equation.

BIBLIOGRAPHY

Achtemeier, P.J., 'The Lucan Perspective on the Miracles of Jesus: A Preliminary Sketch', in *Perspectives on Luke–Acts* (ed. C.H. Talbert; Edinburgh: T. & T. Clark, 1978), pp. 153-67.

Adler, N., *Taufe und Handauflegung: Eine exegetisch-theologische Untersuchung von Apg. 8,14-17* (NTAbh, 19.3; Münster: Aschendorff, 1951).

Alon, G., *Jews, Judaism and the Classical World: Studies in Jewish History in the Times of the Second Temple and Talmud* (Jerusalem: Magnes, 1977).

—*The Jews in their Land in the Talmudic Age (70–640 CE)*, I (trans. and ed. G. Levi; Jerusalem: Magnes, 1980).

Argyle, A.W., 'O. Cullmann's Theory Concerning κωλύειν', *ExpTim* 67 (1955–56), p. 17.

Aune, D.E., 'Magic in Early Christianity', *ANRW*, II.23.2, pp. 1507-1557.

—*The New Testament in its Literary Environment* (LEC, 8; Philadelphia: Westminster Press, 1987).

Bachmann, M., *Jerusalem und der Tempel: Die geographisch-theologischen Elemente in der lukanischen Sicht des jüdischen Kultzentrums* (BWANT, 109; Stuttgart: Kohlhammer, 1980).

Baer, H. von, *Der Heilige Geist in den Lukasschriften* (BWANT, 39; Stuttgart: Kohlhammer, 1926).

Bailey, J.A., *The Traditions Common to the Gospels of Luke and John* (NovTSup, 7; Leiden: Brill, 1963).

Bailey, K.E., *Poet and Peasant: A Literary Cultural Approach to the Parables in Luke* (Grand Rapids: Eerdmans, 1976).

Balsdon, J.P.V.D., *Romans and Aliens* (Chapel Hill: University of North Carolina Press, 1979).

Bammel, E., 'The Baptist in Early Christian Tradition', *NTS* 18 (1971–72), pp. 95-128.

Banks, R., *Paul's Idea of Community: The Early House Churches in their Historical Setting* (Exeter: Paternoster Press, 1980).

Barnett, P.W., 'The Jewish Sign Prophets—AD 40–70: Their Intentions and Origin', *NTS* 27 (1980–81), pp. 679-97.

Barrett, C.K., 'Apollos and the Twelve Disciples of Ephesus', in *The New Testament Age: Essays in Honor of Bo Reicke*, I (ed. W.C. Weinrich; Macon, GA: Mercer University Press, 1984), pp. 29-39.

—*Church, Ministry, and Sacraments in the New Testament* (Didsbury Lectures, 1983; Exeter: Paternoster Press, 1985).

—*The Holy Spirit and the Gospel Tradition* (London: SPCK, 1958).

—'Light on the Holy Spirit from Simon Magus (Acts 8.4-25)', in *Les Actes des Apôtres:*

Traditions, rédaction, théologie (ed. J. Kremer; BETL, 48; Paris-Gembloux: Duculot; Louvain: Louvain University Press, 1979), pp. 281-95.

—'Luke/Acts', in *It is Written: Scripture citing Scripture: Essays in Honour of Barnabas Lindars, SSF* (ed. D.A. Carson and H.G.M. Williamson; Cambridge: Cambridge University Press, 1988), pp. 231-44.

—*Luke the Historian in Recent Study* (London: Epworth, 1961).

—*New Testament Essays* (London: SPCK, 1972).

—'Old Testament History according to Stephen and Paul', in *Studien zum Text und zur Ethik des Neuen Testaments: Festschrift zum 80. Geburtstag von Heinrich Greeven* (ed. W. Schrage; Berlin: de Gruyter, 1986), pp. 57-69.

—'Paul Shipwrecked', in *Scripture: Meaning and Method: Essays Presented to Anthony Tyrrell Hanson for his Seventieth Birthday* (ed. B.P. Thompson; Hull: Hull University Press, 1987).

Barth, M., *Ephesians: Translation and Commentary on Chapters 4–6* (AB, 34A; Garden City, NY: Doubleday, 1974).

—*Die Taufe—ein Sakrament? Ein exegetischer Beitrag zum Gespräch über die kirchliche Taufe* (Zürich: Evangelischer, 1951).

Bauer, W., W.F. Arndt, F.W. Gingrich and F.W. Danker, *A Greek–English Lexicon of the New Testament and Other Early Christian Literature* (Chicago: University of Chicago Press, 2nd edn, 1979).

Bauernfeind, O., *Kommentar und Studien zur Apostelgeschichte* (WUNT, 22; Tübingen: Mohr [Paul Siebeck], 1980).

Baumbach, G., *Das Verständnis des Bösen in den synoptischen Evangelien* (Theologische Arbeiten, 19; Berlin: Evangelische, 1963).

Beasley-Murray, G.R., *Baptism in the New Testament* (Exeter: Paternoster Press, 1972).

—'Jesus and the Spirit', in *Mélanges bibliques en hommage au R.P. Béda Rigaux* (ed. A. Descamps and A. de Halleux; Gembloux: Duculot, 1970), pp. 463-78.

Becker, U., 'Gospel, Evangelize, Evangelist', *NIDNTT*, II, pp. 107-15.

Benko, S., *Pagan Rome and the Early Christians* (London: Batsford, 1985).

Benoit, P., 'L'enfance de Jean-Baptiste selon Luc 1', *NTS* 3 (1956–57), pp. 169-94.

—*The Passion and Resurrection of Jesus Christ* (London: Darton, Longman & Todd, 1969).

Bergmeier, R., 'Zur Frühdatierung samaritanischer Theologumena', *JSJ* 5 (1974), pp. 121-53.

—'Die Gestalt des Simon Magus in Act 8 und in der simonianischen Gnosis—Aporien einer Gesamtdeutung', *ZNW* 77 (1986), pp. 267-75.

—'Quellen vorchristlicher Gnosis?', in *Tradition und Glaube: Das frühe Christentum in seiner Umwelt* (ed. G. Jeremias, H.-W. Kuhn and H. Stegemann; Göttingen: Vandenhoeck & Ruprecht, 1971), pp. 200-20.

Best, E., 'Spirit-Baptism', *NovT* 4 (1960), pp. 236-43.

Betz, H.D., 'The Cleansing of the Ten Lepers (Luke 17.11-19)', *JBL* 90 (1971), pp. 314-28.

Bethge, H.-G., 'Die sogenannte "Brief des Petrus an Philippus"', *TLZ* 103 (1978), pp. 161-70.

Beyer, H., 'διακονέω, διακονία, διάκονος', *TDNT*, II, pp. 81-93.

Beyschlag, K., *Simon Magus und die christliche Gnosis* (WUNT, 16; Tübingen: Mohr [Paul Siebeck], 1974).

—'Zur Simon-Magus-Frage', *ZTK* 68 (1971), pp. 395-426.

Bietenhard, H., 'ὄνομα, ὀνομάζω, κτλ.', *TDNT*, V, pp. 242-83.

Bihler, J., *Die Stephanusgeschichte im Zusammenhang der Apostelgeschichte* (Munich: Hueber, 1963).

Bishop, E.F.F., 'Which Philip?', *ATR* (1946), pp. 154-59.

Black, M., 'The Parables as Allegory', *BJRL* 42 (1959–60), pp. 273-87.

Blackman, E.C., 'The Hellenists of Acts vi.1', *ExpTim* 48 (1936–37), pp. 524-25.

Blinzler, J., 'Die literarische Eigenart des sogenannten Reiseberichts im Lukas-Evangelium', in *Synoptische Studien* (ed. J. Schmid and A. Vögtle; Munich: Zink, 1953), pp. 20-52.

Blomberg, C.L., 'The Law in Luke–Acts', *JSNT* 22 (1984), pp. 53-80.

—'Midrash, Chiasmus, and the Outline of Luke's Central Section', in *Studies in Midrash and Historiography* (Gospel Perspectives, 3; ed. R.T. France and D. Wenham; Sheffield: JSOT Press, 1983), pp. 217-62.

Bock, D.L., *Proclamation from Prophecy and Pattern: Lucan Old Testament Christology* (JSNTSup, 12; Sheffield: JSOT Press, 1987).

Borgen, P., *Paul Preaches Circumcision and Pleases Men and Other Essays on Christian Origins* (Trondheim: TAPIR, 1983).

Bornhäuser, K., *Studien zur Apostelgeschichte* (Gütersloh: Bertelsmann, 1934).

Bouwman, G., 'Samaria im lukanischen Doppelwerk', in *Theologe aus dem Norden* (ed. A. Fuchs; Studien zum NT and Seiner Umwelt A/2; Linz, 1976), pp. 118-41.

Bovon, F., 'Les Actes de Philippe', *ANRW* II.25.6, pp. 4431-4527.

—*Luc le théologien: Vinqt-cinq ans de recherches (1950–1975)* (Neuchâtel: Delachaux & Niestlé, 1978).

—*Luke the Theologian: Thirty-Three Years of Research (1950–1983)* (PTMS, 12; Allison Park, PA: Pickwick Press, 1987).

—'Le Saint-Esprit, l'Eglise et les relations humaines selon Actes 20,36–21,16', in *Les Actes des Apôtres: Traditions, rédaction, théologie* (ed. J. Kremer; BETL, 48; Paris-Gembloux: Duculot; Louvain: Louvain University Press, 1979), pp. 339-58.

Bowman, J., *Samaritan Documents Relating to their History, Religion and Life* (Pittsburgh Original Texts and Translations, 2; Pittsburgh: Pickwick Press, 1977).

—*The Samaritan Problem: Studies in the Relationships of Samaritanism, Judaism, and Early Christianity* (PTMS, 4; Pittsburgh: Pickwick Press, 1975).

Brawley, R.L., *Luke–Acts and the Jews: Conflict, Apology, and Conciliation* (SBLMS, 33; Atlanta: Scholars Press, 1987).

Brodie, T.L., 'The Accusing and Stoning of Naboth (1 Kgs 21.8-13) as One Component of the Stephen Text (Acts 6.9-14; 7.58a)', *CBQ* (1983), pp. 417-32.

—'The Departure for Jerusalem (Luke 9,51-56) as a Rhetorical Imitation of Elijah's Departure for Jordan (2 Kgs 1,1–2.6)', *Bib* 70 (1989), pp. 96-109.

—'Greco-Roman Imitation of Texts as a Partial Guide to Luke's Use of Sources', in *Luke–Acts: New Perspectives from the Society of Biblical Literature Seminar* (ed. C.H. Talbert; New York: Crossroad, 1984), pp. 17-46.

—'Luke the Literary Interpreter: Luke–Acts as a Systematic Rewriting and Updating of the Elijah–Elisha Narrative' (dissertation, Pontifical University of St Thomas Aquinas, Rome, 1981).

—'Luke 7,36-50 as an Internalization of 2 Kings 4,1-37: A Study of Luke's Rhetorical Imitation', *Bib* 64 (1983), pp. 457-85.

—'Towards Unraveling Luke's Use of the Old Testament: Luke 7.11-17 as an *Imitatio* of 1 Kings 17.17-24', *NTS* 32 (1986), pp. 247-67.

—'Towards Unraveling the Rhetorical Sources in Acts: 2 Kgs 5 as One Component of Acts 8,9-40', *Bib* 67 (1986), pp. 41-67.

Brown, P., *The Body and Society: Men, Women and Sexual Renunciation in Early Christianity* (New York: Columbia University Press, 1988).

Brown, R.E., *The Birth of the Messiah* (London: Geoffrey Chapman, 1977).

—'Jesus and Elisha', *Perspective* 12 (1971), pp. 85-104.

Brown, R.E., K.P. Donfried and J. Reumann (eds.), *Peter in the New Testament: A Collaborative Assessment by Protestant and Roman Catholic Scholars* (London: Geoffrey Chapman, 1974).

Brown, S., *Apostasy and Perseverance in the Theology of Luke* (AnBib, 36; Rome: Pontifical Biblical Institute, 1969).

—' "Water-Baptism" and "Spirit-Baptism" in Luke–Acts', *ATR* 59 (1977), pp. 135-51.

Brox, N., *Zeuge und Märtyrer: Untersuchungen zur frühchristlichen Zeugnis-Terminologie* (SANT, 5; Munich: Kösel, 1961).

Bruce, F.F., *The Acts of the Apostles: The Greek Text with Introduction and Commentary* (Chicago: Inter-Varsity Press, 1952).

—*The Book of the Acts* (NICNT; Grand Rapids: Eerdmans, rev. edn, 1988).

—'The Holy Spirit in the Acts of the Apostles', *Int* 27 (1973), pp. 166-83.

—*New Testament History* (London: Pickering & Inglish, 1982).

—*The Pauline Circle* (Exeter: Paternoster Press, 1985).

—'Philip and the Ethiopian', *JSS* 34 (1989), pp. 377-86.

Bruners, W., *Die Reinigung der zehn Aussätzigen und die Heilung des Samariters Lk 17,11-19: Ein Beitrag zur lukanischen Interpretation der Reinigung von Aussätzigen* (FB, 23; Stuttgart: Katholisches Bibelwerk, 1977).

Büchsel, F., 'γενεά, γενεαλογία, γενεαλογέω, κτλ.', *TDNT*, II, pp. 662-65.

Bultmann, R., 'Zur Frage nach den Quellen der Apostelgeschichte', in *New Testament Essays: Studies in Memory of Thomas Walter Manson* (ed. A.J.B. Higgins; Manchester: Manchester University Press, 1959), pp. 68-80.

Burchard, C., 'Fußnoten zum neutestamentlichen Griechisch', *ZNW* 61 (1970), pp. 157-71.

Cadbury, H.J., *The Book of Acts in History* (London: A. & C. Black, 1955).

—'Four Features of Lucan Style', in *Studies in Luke–Acts: Essays Presented in Honor of Paul Schubert* (ed. L.E. Keck and J.L. Martyn; Nashville: Abingdon Press, 1966), pp. 87-102.

—'The Hellenists', in *The Beginnings of Christianity*. Part I. *The Acts of the Apostles*, V (ed. K. Lake and H.J. Cadbury; London: Macmillan, 1933), pp. 59-74.

—'Lexical Notes on Luke–Acts. III. Luke's Interest in Lodging', *JBL* 45 (1926), pp. 305-22.

—*The Making of Luke–Acts* (London: Macmillan, 1927).

—'Names for Christians and Christianity in Acts', in *The Beginnings of Christianity*. Part I. *The Acts of the Apostles*, V (ed. K. Lake and H.J. Cadbury; London: Macmillan, 1933), pp. 375-92.

—'The Titles of Jesus in Acts', in *The Beginnings of Christianity*. Part I. *The Acts of the Apostles*, V (ed. K. Lake and H.J. Cadbury; London: Macmillan, 1933), pp. 354-75.

—' "We" and "I" Passages in Luke–Acts', *NTS* 3 (1956–57), pp. 128-32.

Callaway, M., *Sing, O Barren One: A Study in Comparative Midrash* (SBLDS, 91; Atlanta: Scholars Press, 1986).

Caird, G.B., *The Gospel of St Luke* (Pelican NT Commentaries: Harmondsworth: Penguin Books, 1963).

Carroll, J.T., *Response to the End of History: Eschatology and Situation in Luke–Acts* (SBLDS, 92; Atlanta: Scholars Press, 1988).

Casey, R.P., 'Simon Magus', in *The Beginnings of Christianity*. Part I. *The Acts of the Apostles*, V (ed. K. Lake and H.J. Cadbury; London: Macmillan, 1933), pp. 151-63.

Chance, J.B., *Jerusalem, the Temple, and the New Age in Luke–Acts* (Macon, GA: Mercer University Press, 1988).

Charlesworth, J.H. (ed.), *The Old Testament Pseudepigrapha* (2 vols.; London: Darton, Longman & Todd, 1985).

Chilton, B., *Beginning New Testament Study* (London: SPCK, 1986).

Clarke, W.K.L., 'The Use of the Septuagint in Acts', in *The Beginnings of Christianity*. Part I. *The Acts of the Apostles*, II (ed. F.J. Foakes Jackson and K. Lake; London: Macmillan, 1922), pp. 66-105.

Coggins, R.J., 'The Samaritans and Acts', *NTS* 28 (1982), pp. 423-34.

—*Samaritans and Jews: The Origins of Samaritanism Reconsidered* (Growing Points in Theology; Oxford: Basil Blackwell, 1975).

Collins, J.J., *Between Athens and Jerusalem: Jewish Identity in the Hellenistic Diaspora* (New York: Crossroad, 1983).

—'The Epic of Theodotus and the Hellenism of the Hasmoneans', *HTR* 73 (1980), pp. 91-104.

—'A Symbol of Otherness: Circumcision and Salvation in the First Century', in *'To See Ourselves as Others See Us': Christians, Jews, 'Others' in Late Antiquity* (ed. J. Neusner and E.S. Frerichs; Chico, CA: Scholars Press, 1985), pp. 163-86.

Collins, M.F., 'The Hidden Vessels in Samaritan Traditions', *JSJ* 3 (1972), pp. 97-116.

Conzelmann, H., *Die Apostelgeschichte* (HNT; Tübingen: Mohr [Paul Siebeck], 2nd edn, 1972).

—'Luke's Place in the Development of Early Christianity', in *Studies in Luke–Acts: Essays Presented in Honor of Paul Schubert* (ed. L.E. Keck and J.L. Martyn; Nashville: Abingdon Press, 1966), pp. 298-316.

—*The Theology of Luke* (London: SCM Press, 2nd edn, 1982).

Coppens, J., 'L'imposition des mains dans les Actes des Apôtres', in *Les Actes des Apôtres: Traditions, rédaction, théologie* (ed. J. Kremer; BETL, 48; Paris-Gembloux: Duculot; Louvain: Louvain University Press, 1979), pp. 405-38.

Cosgrove, C.H., 'The Divine ΔΕΙ in Luke–Acts: Investigations into the Lukan Understanding of God's Providence', *NovT* 26 (1984), pp. 168-90.

Crocker, P.T., 'The City of Meroe', *BurH* 22 (1986), pp. 53-72.

Crockett, L.C., 'Luke 4.25-27 and Jewish–Gentile Relations in Luke–Acts', *JBL* 88 (1969), pp. 177-83.

Cross, F.M., Jr, 'Aspects of Samaritan and Jewish History in Later Persian and Hellenistic Times', *HTR* 59 (1966), pp. 201-11.

Crown, A.D. (ed.), *The Samaritans* (Tübingen: Mohr [Paul Siebeck], 1989).

Cullmann, O., *Baptism in the New Testament* (SBT; London: SCM Press, 1950).

—*The Christology of the New Testament* (London: SCM Press, 2nd edn, 1963).

—*The Johannine Circle* (London: SCM Press, 1976).

—'Von Jesus zum Stephanuskreis und zum Johannesevangelium', in *Jesus und Paulus: Festschrift für Werner Georg Kümmel zum 70. Geburtstag* (Göttingen: Vandenhoeck & Ruprecht, 1975), pp. 44-56.

Dahl, N.A., 'The Story of Abraham in Luke–Acts', in *Studies in Luke–Acts: Essays Presented in Honor of Paul Schubert* (ed. L.E. Keck and J.L. Martyn; London: SPCK, 1968), pp. 139-58.

Danby, H. (ed.), *The Mishnah* (Oxford: Clarendon Press, 1933).

Danker, F.W., *Jesus and the New Age according to St Luke: A Commentary on St Luke's Gospel* (Philadelphia: Fortress Press, rev. edn, 1988).

Daube, D., *The New Testament and Rabbinic Judaism* (Jordan Lectures, 1952; London: Athlone, 1956).

—'A Reform in Acts and its Models', in *Jews, Greeks and Christians: Religious Cultures in Late Antiquity: Essays in Honor of William David Davies* (ed. R. Hamerton-Kelly and R. Scroggs; Leiden: Brill, 1976), pp. 151-63.

—'Shame Culture in Luke', in *Paul and Paulinism: Essays in Honour of C.K. Barrett* (ed. M.D. Hooker and S.G. Wilson; London: SPCK, 1982), pp. 355-72.

Davies, W.D., *The Gospel and the Land: Early Christianity and Jewish Territorial Doctrine* (Berkeley: University of California Press, 1974).

Dawsey, J.M., *The Lukan Voice: Confusion and Irony in the Gospel of Luke* (Macon, GA: Mercer University Press, 1986).

Decock, P.B., 'The Understanding of Isaiah 53.7-8 in Acts 8.32-35', *Neot* 14 (1981), pp. 111-33.

Delling, G., 'Josephus und das Wunderbare', *NovT* 2 (1957–58), pp. 291-309.

—'μάγος, μαγεία, μαγεύω', *TDNT*, IV, pp. 356-59.

Derrett, J.D.M., *Law in the New Testament* (London: Darton, Longman & Todd, 1970).

—'Simon Magus (Acts 8.9-24)', *ZNW* 73 (1982), pp. 52-68.

—'The Son of Man Standing (Acts 7,55-56)', *Bibbia e Oriente* 30 (1988), pp. 71-84.

Dewar, L., *The Holy Spirit and Modern Thought* (New York: Harper, 1959).

Dexinger, F., 'Die frühesten samaritanischen Belege der Taheb-Vorstellung', *Kairos* ns 26 (1984), pp. 224-52.

—'Limits of Tolerance in Judaism: The Samaritan Example', in *Jewish and Christian Self-Definition*. II. *Aspects of Judaism in the Graeco-Roman Period* (ed. E.P. Sanders, A.I. Baumgarten and A. Mendelson; London: SCM Press, 1981), pp. 88-114.

—'Der "Prophet wie Moses" in Qumran und bei den Samaritanern', in *Mélanges bibliques et orientaux en l'honneur de M. Matthias Delcor* (ed. A. Caquot, S. Légasse and M. Tardieu; AOAT, 215; Neukirchen–Vluyn: Neukirchener Verlag, 1985), pp. 97-111.

—'Samaritan Eschatology', in *The Samaritans* (ed. A.D. Crown; Tübingen: Mohr [Paul Siebeck], 1989), pp. 266-92.

—'Der Taheb: Eine "messianischer" Heilsbringer der Samaritaner', *Kairos* ns 27 (1985), pp. 1-172.

Dibelius, M., *Studies in the Acts of the Apostles* (ed. H. Greeven; London: SCM Press, 1956).

Dietrich, W., *Das Petrusbild der lukanischen Schriften* (Stuttgart: Kohlhammer, 1972).

Dillon, R.J., 'Acts of the Apostles', in *The New Jerome Biblical Commentary* (ed. R.E. Brown, J.A. Fitzmyer and R.E. Murphy; Englewood Cliffs, NJ: Prentice-Hall, 1990), pp. 722-67.

—*From Eye-witnesses to Ministers of the Word: Tradition and Composition in Luke 24* (AnBib, 82; Rome: Biblical Institute, 1978).

—'Previewing Luke's Project from his Prologue (Luke 1.1-4)', *CBQ* 43 (1981), pp. 205-27.

Dinkler, E., 'Philippus und der ANHP AIΘIOΨ (Apg 8,26-40): Historische und geographische Bemerkungen zum Missionsablauf nach Lukas', in *Jesus und Paulus: Festschrift für Werner Georg Kümmel zum 70. Geburtstag* (Göttingen: Vandenhoeck & Ruprecht, 1975), pp. 85-95.

Diodorus of Sicily, *Works* (12 vols.; ed. C.H. Oldfather, C.L. Sherman, C.B. Welles, F.R. Walton and R.M. Greer; LCL; Cambridge, MA: Harvard University Press, 1933–67).

Doble, P., 'The Son of Man Saying in Stephen's Witnessing: Acts 6.8–8.2', *NTS* 31 (1985), pp. 68-84.

Domagalski, B., 'Waren die "Sieben" (Apg 6,1-7) Diakone?', *BZ* 26 (1982), pp. 21-34.

Dömer, M., *Das Heil Gottes: Studien zur Theologie des lukanischen Doppelwerkes* (BBB, 51; Bonn: Hanstein, 1978).

Drane, J.W., 'Simon the Samaritan and the Lucan Concept of Salvation History', *EvQ* 47 (1975), pp. 131-37.

Drury, J., *Tradition and Design in Luke's Gospel: A Study in Early Christian Historiography* (London: Darton, Longman & Todd, 1976).

Dubois, J.-D., 'La figure d'Elie dans la perspective lucanienne', *RHPR* 53 (1973), pp. 155-76.

Dunn, J.D.G., *Baptism in the Holy Spirit: A Re-examination of the New Testament Teaching on the Gift of the Spirit in Relation to Pentecostalism Today* (Philadelphia: Westminster Press, 1970).

—*Christology in the Making: An Inquiry into the Origins of the Doctrine of the Incarnation* (London: SCM Press, 1980).

—'The Incident at Antioch (Gal. 2.11-18)', *JSNT* 18 (1983), pp. 3-57.

—*Jesus and the Spirit: A Study of the Religious and Charismatic Experience of Jesus and the First Christians as Reflected in the New Testament* (London: SCM Press, 1975).

—'Spirit-and-Fire-Baptism', *NovT* 14 (1972), pp. 81-92.

—*Unity and Diversity in the New Testament: An Inquiry into the Character of Earliest Christianity* (London: SCM Press, 1977).

—' "They Believed Philip Preaching" (Acts 8.12): A Reply', *IBS* 1 (1979), pp. 177-83.

Dupont, J., 'The Meal at Emmaus', in *The Eucharist in the New Testament: A Symposium* (ed. J. Delorme *et al.*; London: Geoffrey Chapman, 1964), pp. 105-21.

—*Nouvelles études sur les Actes des Apôtres* (LD, 118; Paris: Cerf, 1984).

—'Les pèlerins d'Emmaüs (Luc, xxiv, 13-35)', in *Miscellanea Biblica B. Ubach* (Scripta et Documenta, 1; Montisserrati, 1953), pp. 349-74.

—*The Salvation of the Gentiles: Studies in the Acts of the Apostles* (New York: Paulist Press, 1979).

—*The Sources of Acts: The Present Position* (London: Darton, Longman & Todd, 1964).

—'La structure oratoire du discours d'Etienne (Actes 7)', *Bib* 66 (1985), pp. 153-67.

Edwards, O.C., Jr, 'The Exegesis of Acts 8.4-25 and its Implications for Confirmation and Glossolalia: A Review Article of Haenchen's Acts Commentary', *ATR* (Sup. Ser.) 2 (1973), pp. 100-12.

Ehrhardt, A., *The Acts of the Apostles* (Manchester: Manchester University Press, 1969).

Elderen, B. van, 'Another Look at the Parable of the Good Samaritan', in *Saved by Hope: Essays in Honor of Richard C. Oudersluys* (ed. J.I. Cook; Grand Rapids: Eerdmans, 1978), pp. 109-19.

Elliott, J.K., 'Jerusalem in Acts and the Gospels', *NTS* 23 (1976–77), pp. 462-69.

Ellis, E.E., *The Gospel of Luke* (NCB; London: Nelson, 1966).

—*Prophecy and Hermeneutic in Early Christianity: New Testament Essays* (WUNT, 18; Tübingen: Mohr [Paul Siebeck], 1978).

Enslin, M.S., 'Luke and the Samaritans', *HTR* 36 (1943), pp. 277-97.

—'Once Again, Luke and Paul', *ZNW* 61 (1970), pp. 253-71.

—'The Samaritan Ministry and Mission', *HUCA* 51 (1980), pp. 29-38.

Epp, E.J., *The Theological Tendency of Codex Bezae Cantabrigiensis in Acts* (SNTSMS, 3; Cambridge: Cambridge University Press, 1966).

Esler, P.F., *Community and Gospel in Luke–Acts: The Social and Political Motivations of Lucan Theology* (SNTSMS, 57; Cambridge: Cambridge University Press, 1987).

Ervin, H.M., *Conversion-Initiation and the Baptism in the Holy Spirit* (Peabody, MA: Hendrickson, 1985).

Eusebius, *The Ecclesiastical History* (2 vols.; ed. and trans. K. Lake; LCL; Cambridge, MA: Harvard University Press, 1926–32).

—*Preparation for the Gospel* (trans. E.H. Gifford; Oxford: Clarendon Press, 1903).

Evans, C.A., 'Luke's Use of the Elijah/Elisha Narratives and the Ethic of Election', *JBL* 106 (1987), pp. 75-83.

Evans, C.F., 'The Central Section of St Luke's Gospel', in *Studies in the Gospels: Essays in Memory of R.H. Lightfoot* (ed. D.E. Nineham; Oxford: Basil Blackwell, 1955).

—*Saint Luke* (TPI New Testament Commentaries; Philadelphia: TPI, 1990).

Evans, H., 'Barnabas the Bridge-Builder', *ExpTim* 89 (1977), pp. 248-50.

Farrer, A.M., 'The Ministry in the New Testament', in *The Apostolic Ministry: Essays on the History and the Doctrine of Episcopacy* (ed. K.E. Kirk; London: Hodder & Stoughton, new edn, 1957 [1946]), pp. 113-82.

Ferguson, E., 'The Hellenists in the Book of Acts', *ResQ* 12 (1969), pp. 159-80.

Filson, F.V., 'The Journey Motif in Luke–Acts', in *Apostolic History and the Gospel: Essays in Honour of F.F. Bruce* (ed. W. Gasque and R.P. Martin; Grand Rapids: Eerdmans, 1970), pp. 68-77.

Finn, T.M., 'The God-fearers Reconsidered', *CBQ* 47 (1985), pp. 75-84.

Fiorenza, E.S., *In Memory of Her: A Feminist Theological Reconstruction of Christian Origins* (London: SCM Press, 1983).

—'Miracles, Mission, and Apologetics: An Introduction', in *Aspects of Religious Propaganda in Judaism and Early Christianity* (ed. E.S. Fiorenza; Notre Dame, IN: University of Notre Dame Press, 1976), pp. 1-25.

Fitzmyer, J.A., *The Gospel according to Luke* (2 vols.; AB, 28; Garden City, NY: Doubleday, 1981, 1985).

—'Jewish Christianity in Acts in Light of the Qumran Scrolls', in *Studies in Luke–Acts: Essays Presented in Honor of Paul Schubert* (ed. L.E. Keck and J.L. Martyn; Nashville: Abingdon Press, 1966), pp. 233-57.

—' "Today you Shall Be with me in Paradise" (Luke 23.43)', in *Luke the Theologian: Aspects of his Teaching* (New York: Paulist Press, 1989), pp. 203-22.

Flender, H., *St Luke: Theologian of Redemptive History* (London: SCM Press, 1967).

Flusser, D., 'Lukas 9.51-56—Ein hebräisches Fragment', in *The New Testament Age: Essays in Honor of Bo Reicke*, I (ed. W.C. Weinrich; Macon, GA: Mercer University Press, 1984), pp. 165-79.

Foerster, W., 'πύθων', *TDNT*, VI, pp. 917-20.

Ford, J.M., *My Enemy is my Guest: Jesus and Violence in Luke* (Maryknoll, NY: Orbis, 1984).

—'Reconciliation and Forgiveness in Luke's Gospel', in *Political Issues in Luke–Acts* (ed. R.J. Cassidy and P.J. Scharper; Maryknoll, NY: Orbis, 1983), pp. 80-93.

Forster, E.M., *Aspects of the Novel* (ed. O. Stallybrass; Harmondsworth: Penguin Books, 1974).

Fossum, J.E., *The Name of God and the Angel of the Lord: Samaritan and Jewish Concepts of Intermediation and the Origin of Gnosticism* (WUNT, 36; Tübingen: Mohr [Paul Siebeck], 1985).

—'Samaritan Sects and Movements', in *The Samaritans* (ed. A.D. Crown; Tübingen: Mohr [Paul Siebeck], 1989), pp. 293-389.

Franklin, E., *Christ the Lord: A Study in the Purpose and Theology of Luke–Acts* (London: SPCK, 1975).

Freyne, S., *Galilee, Jesus and the Gospels: Literary Approaches and Historical Investigations* (Philadelphia: Fortress Press, 1988).

Friedrich, G., 'εὐαγγελίζομαι, εὐαγγέλιον, κτλ.', *TDNT*, II, pp. 707-37.

—'Die Gegner des Paulus im 2. Korintherbrief', in *Abraham unser Vater: Juden und Christen im Gespräch über die Bibel* (ed. O. Betz, M. Hengel and P. Schmidt; AGJU, 5; Leiden: Brill, 1963).

Funk, R., 'The Good Samaritan as Metaphor', *Semeia* 2 (1974), pp. 74-81.

Gaechter, P., *Petrus und seine Zeit: Neutestamentliche Studien* (Innsbruck: Tyrolia, 1958).

Gager, J., 'Jews, Gentiles, and Synagogues in the Book of Acts', *HTR* 79 (1986), pp. 91-99.

—*Moses in Greco-Roman Paganism* (SBLMS, 16; Nashville: Abingdon Press, 1972).

Garrett, S.R., *The Demise of the Devil: Magic and the Demonic in Luke's Writings* (Philadelphia: Fortress Press, 1989).

Gasque, W.W., *A History of the Interpretation of the Acts of the Apostles* (Peabody, MA: Hendrickson, 1989).

Gaster, M., *The Samaritans: Their History, Doctrines and Literature* (Schweich Lectures; London: Oxford University Press, 1925).

Gaston, L., *No Stone on Another: Studies in the Significance of the Fall of Jerusalem in the Synoptic Gospels* (NovTSup, 23; Leiden: Brill, 1970).

Gaventa, B.R., *From Darkness to Light: Aspects of Conversion in the New Testament* (OBT, 20; Philadelphia: Fortress Press, 1986).

George, A., *Etudes sur l'oeuvre de Luc* (Paris: Gabalda, 1978).

—'Le parallèle entre Jean-Baptiste et Jésus en Luc 1–2', in *Mélanges bibliques en hommage au R.P. Béda Rigaux* (ed. A. Descamps and A. de Halleux; Gembloux: Duculot, 1970), pp. 147-71.

Georgi, D., *Die Gegner des Paulus im 2. Korintherbrief: Studien zur religiösen Propaganda in der Spätantike* (WMANT, 11; Neukirchen–Vluyn; Neukirchener Verlag, 1964).

—*The Opponents of Paul in Second Corinthians* (Philadelphia: Fortress Press, 1986).

Gewalt, D., 'Der "Barmherzige Samariter" zu Lukas 10,25-37', *EvT* 38 (1978), pp. 403-17.

Giles, K., 'Is Luke an Exponent of "Early Protestantism"? Church Order in the Lukan Writings', Part 1, *EvQ* 54 (1982), pp. 193-205; Part 2, *EvQ* 55 (1983), pp. 3-20.

Glombitza, O., 'Zur Charakterisierung des Stephanus in Act 6 und 7', *ZNW* 53 (1962), pp. 238-44.

—'Der dankbare Samariter: Luk. xvii 11-19', *NovT* 11 (1969), pp. 241-46.

Gnilka, J., *Der Epheserbrief* (HTKNT, 10.2; Freiburg: Herder, 1971).

Goppelt, L., *Apostolic and Post-Apostolic Times* (London: A. & C. Black, 1970).

Goulder, M.D., *The Evangelists' Calendar: A Lectionary Explanation of the Development of Scripture* (London: SPCK, 1978).

—'A House Built on Sand', in *Alternative Approaches to New Testament Study* (ed. A.E. Harvey; London: SPCK, 1985), pp. 1-24.

—*Luke: A New Paradigm* (2 vols.; JSNTSup, 30; Sheffield: JSOT Press, 1989).

—*Type and History in Acts* (London: A. & C. Black, 1964).

Gourgues, M., 'Esprit des commencements et Esprit des prolongements dans les *Actes*: Note sur la "Pentecôste des Samaritains" (*Act*. VIII,5-25)', *RB* 93 (1986), pp. 376-85.

Gowler, D.B., 'Characterization in Luke: A Socio-Narratological Approach', *BTB* 19 (1989), pp. 57-62.

Grabbe, L.L., 'The Jannes/Jambres Tradition in Targum Pseudo-Jonathan and its Date', *JBL* 98 (1979), pp. 393-401.

Grant, F.C., *The Gospels: Their Origin and Growth* (London: Faber & Faber, 1957).

Grant, R.M., *Gnosticism and Early Christianity* (New York: Columbia University Press, 1959).

Grässer, E., 'Acta-Forschung seit 1960 (Fortsetzung)', *TRu* 42 (1977), pp. 1-68.

Grassi, J., 'Emmaus Revisited (Luke 24.13-35 and Acts 8.26-40)', *CBQ* 26 (1964), pp. 463-67.

Gray, L.H., 'Eunuch', *Encyclopaedia of Religion and Ethics*, V (ed. J. Hastings; New York: Charles Scribner's Sons, 1910–27), pp. 579-84.

Grayston, K., 'The Significance of the Word *Hand* in the New Testament', in *Mélanges bibliques en hommage au R.P. Béda Rigaux* (ed. A. Descamps and A. de Halleux; Gembloux: Duculot, 1970), pp. 479-87.

Grundmann, W., *Das Evangelium nach Lukas* (THKNT, 3; Berlin: Evangelische, 1971).

Haacker, K., 'Dibelius und Cornelius: Ein Beispiel formgeschichtlicher Überlieferungskritik', *BZ* (1980), pp. 234-51.

—'Samaritan, Samaria', *NIDNTT*, III, pp. 449-67.

Hadidian, D.Y., '*tous de evangelistas* in Eph 4,11', *CBQ* 28 (1966), pp. 317-19.

Haenchen, E., *The Acts of the Apostles: A Commentary* (Oxford: Basil Blackwell, 1971).

—'The Book of Acts as Source Material for the History of Early Christianity', in *Studies in Luke–Acts: Essays Presented in Honor of Paul Schubert* (ed. L.E. Keck and J.L. Martyn; Nashville: Abingdon Press, 1966), pp. 258-78.

—*Gott und Mensch: Gesammelte Aufsätze* (Tübingen: Mohr [Paul Siebeck], 1965).

—'Simon Magus in der Apostelgeschichte', in *Gnosis und Neues Testament* (ed. K.-W. Tröger; Studien aus Religionswissenschaft und Theologie; Berlin: Evangelische, 1973), pp. 267-79.

Hahn, F., 'Der gegenwärtige Stand der Erforschung der Apostelgeschichte: Kommentare und Aufsatzbände 1980–85', *TRev* 82 (1986), pp. 177-90.

—*Mission in the New Testament* (SBT, 7; London: SCM Press, 1965).

Hall, B.W., *Samaritan Religion from John Hyrcanus to Baba Rabba* (Studies in Judaica, 3; Sydney: Mandelbaum Trust, University of Sydney, 1987).

Hamerton-Kelly, R.G., 'A Note on Matthew XII.28 par. Luke XI.20', *NTS* 11 (1964–65), pp. 167-69.

Hamm, M.D., 'The Freeing of the Bent Woman and the Restoration of Israel: Luke 13.10-17 as Narrative Theology', *JSNT* 31 (1987), pp. 23-49.

Hanson, R.P.C., *The Acts in the Revised Standard Version* (New Clarendon Bible; Oxford: Clarendon Press, 1967).

Hardon, J.A., 'The Miracle Narratives in the Acts of the Apostles', *CBQ* 16 (1954), pp. 303-18.

Harnack, A., *The Acts of the Apostles* (CTL, 27; London: Williams & Norgate, 1909).

—*The Date of the Acts and the Synoptic Gospels* (CTL, 33; London: Williams & Norgate, 1911).

—*Luke the Physician: The Author of the Third Gospel and the Acts of the Apostles* (CTL, 20; London: Williams & Norgate, 1911).

—*The Mission and Expansion of Christianity in the First Three Centuries* (2 vols.; London: Williams & Norgate, 2nd edn, 1908).

Hengel, M., *Acts and the History of Earliest Christianity* (London: SCM Press, 1979); reprinted in Hengel, *Earliest Christianity* (London: SCM Press, 1986), pp. 1-146.

—*Between Jesus and Paul: Studies in the Earliest History of Christianity* (London: SCM Press, 1983).

—*Judaism and Hellenism: Studies in their Encounter in Palestine during the Early Hellenistic Period* (2 vols.; London: SCM Press, 1974).

—'Maria Magdalena und die Frauen als Zeugen', in *Abraham unser Vater: Juden und Christen im Gespräch über die Bibel* (ed. O. Betz, M. Hengel and P. Schmidt; Leiden: Brill, 1963), pp. 241-56.

Hennecke, E., and W. Schneemelcher (eds.), *New Testament Apocrypha* (2 vols.; ed. R.McL. Wilson; Philadelphia: Westminster Press, 1963–66).

Herodotus, *Works* (ed. and trans. A.D. Godley; LCL; Cambridge, MA: Harvard University Press, 1920–26).

Holmberg, B., *Paul and Power: The Structure of Authority in the Primitive Church as Reflected in the Pauline Epistles* (Philadelphia: Fortress Press, 1980).

Holtz, T., *Untersuchungen über die alttestamentlichen Zitate bei Lukas* (TU, 104; Berlin: Akademie, 1968).

Hooker, M.D., *Jesus and the Servant: The Influence of the Servant Concept of Deutero-Isaiah in the New Testament* (London: SPCK, 1959).

Horsley, R.A., ' "Like One of the Prophets of Old": Two Types of Popular Prophets at the Time of Jesus', *CBQ* 47 (1985), pp. 435-63.

—'Popular Prophetic Movements at the Time of Jesus: Their Principal Features and Social Origins', *JSNT* 26 (1986), pp. 3-27.

Horsley, R.A., and S. Hanson, *Bandits, Prophets, and Messiahs: Popular Movements in the Time of Jesus* (New Voices in Biblical Studies; Minneapolis, MN: Winston, 1985).

Hunter, H.D., *Spirit-Baptism: A Pentecostal Alternative* (Lanham, MD: University Press of America, 1983).

Isser, S.J., *The Dositheans: A Samaritan Sect in Late Antiquity* (SJLA, 17; Leiden: Brill, 1976).

—'Dositheus, Jesus, and a Moses Aretalogy', in *Christianity, Judaism and Other Greco-Roman Cults: Studies for Morton Smith at Sixty. Part 4. Other Greco-Roman Cults* (ed. J. Neusner; SJLA, 12; Leiden: Brill, 1975), pp. 167-90.

Jaeger, W., *Early Christianity and Greek Paideia* (Cambridge, MA: Belknap, 1961).

Jeremias, J., *Heiligengräber in Jesu Umwelt (Mt. 23.29; Lk. 11.47): Eine Untersuchung zur Volksreligion der Zeit Jesu* (Göttingen: Vandenhoeck & Ruprecht, 1958).

—'ΙΕΡΟΥΣΑΛΗΜ/ΙΕΡΟΣΟΛΥΜΑ', *ZNW* 65 (1974), pp. 273-76.

—*Jerusalem in the Time of Jesus: An Investigation into Economic and Social Conditions during the New Testament Period* (Philadelphia: Fortress Press, 1969).

—*Jesus' Promise to the Nations* (London: SCM Press, 1958).

—'Μωϋσῆς', *TDNT*, IV, pp. 848-73.

—'Σαμάρεια, Σαμαρίτης, Σαμαρῖτις', *TDNT*, VII, pp. 88-94.

—'Untersuchungen zum Quellenproblem der Apostelgeschichte', in *Abba: Studien zur neutestamentlichen Theologie und Zeitgeschichte* (Göttingen: Vandenhoeck & Ruprecht, 1966), pp. 238-55.

Jeremias, J., and W. Zimmerli, 'παῖς θεοῦ', *TDNT*, V, pp. 654-717.

Jervell, J., *Luke and the People of God: A New Look at Luke–Acts* (Minneapolis, MN: Augsburg, 1984).

Jewett, R., *A Chronology of Paul's Life* (Philadelphia: Fortress Press, 1979).

Johnson, A.M., Jr, 'Philip the Evangelist and the Gospel of John', *AbrN* 16 (1975–76), pp. 49-72.

Johnson, L.T., 'On Finding the Lukan Community: A Cautious Cautionary Essay', in *SBLSP, 1* (Missoula, MT: Scholars Press, 1979), pp. 87-100.

—*The Literary Function of Possessions in Luke–Acts* (SBLDS, 39; Missoula, MT: Scholars Press, 1977).

—*The Writings of the New Testament: An Interpretation* (London: SCM Press, 1986).

Jones, D.L., 'The Title *Christos* in Luke–Acts', *CBQ* 32 (1970), pp. 69-76.

—'The Title "Servant" in Luke–Acts', in *Luke–Acts: New Perspectives from the Society of Biblical Literature Seminar* (ed. C.H. Talbert; New York: Crossroad, 1984), pp. 148-65.

Josephus, *Works* (9 vols.; ed. and trans. H.StJ. Thackeray, R. Marcus, A. Wikgren and L.H. Feldman; LCL; Cambridge, MA: Harvard University Press, 1926–65).

Juel, D., *Luke–Acts* (London: SCM Press, 1984).

—*Messianic Exegesis: Christological Interpretation of the Old Testament in Early Christianity* (Philadelphia: Fortress Press, 1988).

Karris, R.J., *Luke: Artist and Theologian: Luke's Passion Account as Literature* (New York: Paulist Press, 1985).

—'Missionary Communities: A New Paradigm for the Study of Luke–Acts', *CBQ* 41 (1979), pp. 80-97.

—'Poor and Rich: The Lucan *Sitz im Leben*', in *Perspectives on Luke–Acts* (ed. C.H. Talbert; Edinburgh: T. & T. Clark, 1978), pp. 112-25.

Käsemann, E., *Essays on New Testament Themes* (London: SCM Press, 1964).

—*New Testament Questions of Today* (London: SCM Press, 1969).

Kee, H.C., *Good News to the Ends of the Earth: The Theology of Acts* (London: SCM Press, 1990).

—*Knowing the Truth: A Sociological Approach to New Testament Interpretation* (Minneapolis, MN: Fortress Press, 1989).

—*Medicine, Miracle and Magic in New Testament Times* (SNTSMS, 55; Cambridge: Cambridge University Press, 1986).

—*Miracle in the Early Christian World: A Study in Sociohistorical Method* (New Haven: Yale University Press, 1983).

Kilgallen, J., *The Stephen Speech: A Literary and Redactional Study of Acts 7.2-53* (AnBib, 67; Rome: Biblical Institute, 1976).

Kippenberg, H.G., *Garizim und Synagoge: Traditionsgeschichtliche Untersuchungen zur samaritanischen Religion der aramäische Periode* (Religionsgeschichtliche Versuche und Vorarbeiten, 30; Berlin: de Gruyter, 1971).

—'Ein Gebetbuch für den samaritanischen Synagogengottesdienst aus dem 2. Jhn. n. Chr', *ZDPV* 85 (1969), pp. 76-103.

Klein, G., 'Der Synkretismus als theologisches Problem in der ältesten christlichen Apologetik', *ZTK* 64 (1967), pp. 40-82.

Knibb, M.A., 'Martyrdom and Ascension of Isaiah', in *The Old Testament Pseudepigrapha*, II (ed. J.H. Charlesworth; London: Darton, Longman & Todd, 1985), pp. 143-76.

Knox, W.L., *The Acts of the Apostles* (Cambridge: Cambridge University Press, 1948).

Koch, D.-A., 'Geistbesitz, Geistverleihung und Wundermacht: Erwägungen zur Tradition und zur lukanischen Redaktion in Act 8.5-25', *ZNW* 77 (1986), pp. 64-82.

Kodell, J., 'Luke and the Children: The Beginning and End of the Great Interpolation (Luke 9.46-56; 18.9-23)', *CBQ* 49 (1987), pp. 415-29.

Koenig, J., *New Testament Hospitality: Partnership with Strangers as Promise and Mission* (OBT, 17; Philadelphia: Fortress Press, 1985).

Koester, H., *History, Culture, and Religion of the Hellenistic Age*. I. *Introduction to the New Testament* (Philadelphia: Fortress Press, 1982).

Koschorke, K., 'Eine gnostische Pfingstpredigt: Zur Auseinandersetzung zwischen gnostischem und kirchlichem Christentum am Beispiel der "Epistula Petri ad Philippum" (NHC VIII,2)', *ZTK* 74 (1977), pp. 323-43.

Kraabel, A.T., 'The Disappearance of the "God-fearers"', *Numen* 28 (1981), pp. 113-26.

—'Greeks, Jews, and Lutherans in the Middle Half of Acts', *HTR* 79 (1986), pp. 147-57.

—'Six Questionable Assumptions', *JJS* 33 (1982), pp. 445-64.

Kraeling, C.H., *John the Baptist* (New York: Charles Scribner's Sons, 1951).

Kränkl, E., *Jesus der Knecht Gottes: Die heilsgeschichtliche Stellung Jesu in den Reden der Apostelgeschichte* (Biblische Untersuchungen, 8; Regensburg: Pustet, 1972).

Kremer, J., *Die Osterevangelien: Geschichten um Geschichte* (Stuttgart: Katholisches Bibelwerk, 1977).

Krodel, G.A., *Acts* (Augsburg Commentary on the NT; Minneapolis, MN: Augsburg, 1986).

Kuhn, K.G., 'προσήλυτος', *TDNT*, VI, pp. 727-44.

Kurz, W.S., 'Narrative Approaches to Luke–Acts', *Bib* 68 (1987), pp. 195-200.

Lake, K., 'The Holy Spirit', in *The Beginnings of Christianity*. Part I. *The Acts of the Apostles*, V (ed. K. Lake and H.J. Cadbury; London: Macmillan, 1933), pp. 96-111.

—'Proselytes and God-fearers', in *The Beginnings of Christianity*. Part I. *The Acts of the Apostles*, V (ed. K. Lake and H.J. Cadbury; London: Macmillan, 1933).

Lake, K., and H.J. Cadbury, *The Beginnings of Christianity*. Part I. *The Acts of the Apostles*. IV. *English Translation and Commentary* (London: Macmillan, 1933).

Lampe, G.W.H., 'The Holy Spirit in the Writings of Luke', in *Studies in the Gospels* (ed. D.E. Nineham; Oxford: Clarendon Press, 1955), pp. 159-200.

—'Miracles and Early Christian Apologetic', in *Miracles: Cambridge Studies in their Philosophy and History* (ed. C.F.D. Moule; London: Mowbray, 1965), pp. 203-18.

—'Miracles in the Acts of the Apostles', in *Miracles: Cambridge Studies in their Philosophy and History* (ed. C.F.D. Moule; London: Mowbray, 1965), pp. 163-78.

—*The Seal of the Spirit: A Study in the Doctrine of Baptism and Confirmation in the New Testament and the Fathers* (London: SPCK, 2nd edn, 1967).

Larsson, E., 'Die Hellenisten und die Urgemeinde', *NTS* 33 (1987), pp. 205-25.

Laurentin, R., *Structure et théologie de Luc I–II* (EBib; Paris: Gabalda, 1957).

Leaney, A.R.C., *A Commentary on the Gospel according to St Luke* (BNTC; London: A. & C. Black, 1958).

Leivestad, R., 'ταπεινός-ταπεινόφρων', *NovT* 8 (1966), pp. 36-47.

Léon-Dufour, X., *Resurrection and the Message of Easter* (New York: Holt, Rinehart & Winston, 1975).

Levinsohn, S.H., *Textual Connections in Acts* (SBLMS, 31; Atlanta: Scholars Press, 1987).

Lienhard, J.T., 'Acts 6.1-6: A Redactional View', *CBQ* 37 (1975), pp. 228-36.

Lindijer, C.H., 'Two Creative Encounters in the Work of Luke: Luke xxiv 13-35 and Acts viii 26-40', in *Miscellanea Neotestamentica* (ed. T. Baarda, A.F.J. Klijn and W.C. van Unnik; NovTSup, 48; Leiden: Brill, 1978), pp. 77-85.

Lohse, E., 'Missionarisches Handeln Jesu nach dem Evangelium des Lukas', *TZ* 10 (1954), pp. 1-13.

—'Σιών, κτλ.', *TDNT*, VIII, pp. 292-338.

Longenecker, R.N., 'The Acts of the Apostles', in *The Expositor's Bible Commentary*, IX (ed. F.E. Gaebelein; Grand Rapids: Zondervan, 1981), pp. 207-573.

—*The Christology of Early Jewish Christianity* (London: SCM Press, 1970).

Löning, K., 'Lukas—Theologe der von Gott geführten Heilsgeschichte', in *Gestalt und Anspruch des Neuen Testaments* (ed. J. Schreiner and G. Dautzenberg; Würzburg: Echter Verlag, 1969), pp. 200-28.

—'Der Stephanuskreis und seine Mission', in *Die Anfänge des Christentums: Alte Welt und neue Hoffnung* (ed. J. Becker *et al.*; Stuttgart: Kohlhammer, 1987), pp. 80-101.

Lösch, S., 'Der Kämmerer der Königin Kandake (Apg. 8,27)', *TQ* 111 (1930), pp. 477-519.

Louw, J.P., E.A. Nida, R.B. Smith and K.A. Munson, *Greek-English Lexicon of the New Testament Based on Semantic Domains* (2 vols.; New York: UBS, 1988).

Lowy, S., *The Principles of Samaritan Bible Exegesis* (SPB, 28; Leiden: Brill, 1977).

Lucian, *Works* (8 vols.; ed. and trans. A.M. Harmon, K. Kilburn and M.D. MacLeod; LCL; Cambridge, MA: Harvard University Press; London: Heinemann, 1913–67).

Lüdemann, G., 'The Acts of the Apostles and the Beginnings of Simonian Gnosis', *NTS* 33 (1987), pp. 420-26.

—*Das frühe Christentum nach den Traditionen der Apostelgeschichte: Ein Kommentar* (Göttingen: Vandenhoeck & Ruprecht, 1987).

—*Paul: Apostle to the Gentiles: Studies in Chronology* (London: SCM Press, 1984).

—*Paulus, der Heidenapostel. II. Antipaulinismus im frühen Christentum* (FRLANT, 130; Göttingen: Vandenhoeck & Ruprecht, 1983).

—*Untersuchungen zur simonianischen Gnosis* (GTA, 1; Göttingen: Vandenhoeck & Ruprecht, 1975).

Lull, D.J., 'The Servant-Benefactor as a Model of Greatness (Luke 22:24-30)', *NovT* 28 (1986), pp. 289-305.

Luttikhuizen, G.P., 'The Letter of Peter to Philip and the New Testament', in *Nag Hammadi and Gnosis: Papers Read at the First International Congress of Coptology* (ed. R.McL. Wilson; NHS, 14; Leiden: Brill, 1978), pp. 96-102.

McCown, C.C., 'The Geography of Luke's Central Section', *JBL* 57 (1938), pp. 51-66.

—'Gospel Geography: Fiction, Fact, and Truth', *JBL* 60 (1941), pp. 1-25.

Macdonald, J., *Memar Marqah: The Teaching of Marqah* (2 vols.; BZAW, 84; Berlin: Töpelmann, 1963).

—*The Theology of the Samaritans* (NTL; London: SCM Press, 1964).

McEleney, N.J., 'Conversion, Circumcision and the Law', *NTS* 20 (1973–74), pp. 319-41.

MacLennan, R.S., and A.T. Kraabel, 'The God-Fearers—A Literary and Theological Invention', *BARev* (1986), pp. 46-53, 64.

MacRae, G., 'Miracle in *The Antiquities* of Josephus', in *Miracles: Cambridge Studies in their Philosophy and History* (ed. C.F.D. Moule; London: Mowbray, 1965).

Maddox, R., *The Purpose of Luke–Acts* (FRLANT, 126; Göttingen: Vandenhoeck & Ruprecht, 1982).

Malherbe, A.J., 'The Inhospitality of Diotrophes', in *God's Christ and his People: Studies in Honour of Nils Alstrup Dahl* (ed. J. Jervell and W.A. Meeks; Oslo: Universitetsforlaget, 1977), pp. 222-32.

—*Social Aspects of Early Christianity* (Philadelphia: Fortress Press, 2nd edn, 1983).

Malina, B., *The New Testament World: Insights from Cultural Anthropology* (Atlanta: John Knox, 1981).

Mann, C.S., ' "Hellenists" and "Hebrews" in Acts VI 1', in J. Munck, *The Acts of the Apostles* (rev. W.F. Albright and C.S. Mann; AB, 31; Garden City, NY: Doubleday, 1967).

Manson, T.W., *The Teaching of Jesus: Studies of its Form and Content* (Cambridge: Cambridge University Press, 1939).

Manson, W., *The Epistle to the Hebrews: An Historical and Theological Reconsideration* (Baird Lecture; London: Hodder & Stoughton, 1951).

—*The Gospel of Luke* (MNTC; London: Hodder & Stoughton, 1930).

Mare, W.H., 'Acts 7: Jewish or Samaritan in Character?', *WTJ* 34 (1971–72), pp. 1-21.

Marshall, I.H., *The Acts of the Apostles* (TNTC; Leicester: Inter-Varsity Press, 1980).

—*The Gospel of Luke: A Commentary on the Greek Text* (NIGTC; Exeter: Paternoster Press, 1978).

—*Kept by the Power of God: A Study of Perseverance and Falling Away* (London: Epworth, 1969).

—*Luke: Historian and Theologian* (Grand Rapids: Zondervan, 1970).

—'Palestinian and Hellenistic Christianity: Some Critical Comments', *NTS* 19 (1972–73), pp. 271-87.

Martin, C.J., 'A Chamberlain's Journey and the Challenge of Interpretation for Liberation', *Semeia* 47 (1989), pp. 105-35.

Martin, E.G., 'Eldad and Modad', in *The Old Testament Pseudepigrapha*, II (ed. J.H. Charlesworth; London: Darton, Longman & Todd, 1985), pp. 463-65.

Mattill, A.J., Jr, 'The Jesus–Paul Parallels and the Purpose of Luke–Acts: H.H. Evans Reconsidered', *NovT* 17 (1975), pp. 15-46.

Meeks, W.A., *The Prophet-King: Moses Traditions and the Johannine Christology* (NovTSup, 14; Leiden: Brill, 1967).

—'Simon Magus in Recent Research', *RelSRev* 3 (1977), pp. 137-42.

Meester, P. de, ' "Philippe et l'eunuque éthiopien" ou "Le baptême d'un pèlerin de Nube"?', *NRT* 103 (1981), pp. 360-74.

Ménard, J.E., *La Lettre de Pierre à Philippe: Texte établi et présente* (Bibliothèque Copte de Nag Hammadi; Section 'Textes' 1; Quebec: Laval University, 1977).

Merk, O., 'Das Reich Gottes in den lukanischen Schriften', in *Jesus und Paulus: Festschrift für Werner Georg Kümmel zum 70. Geburtstag* (Göttingen: Vandenhoeck & Ruprecht, 1975), pp. 201-20.

Merklein, H., *Das kirchliche Amt nach dem Epheserbrief* (SANT, 33; Munich: Kösel, 1973).

Metzger, B.M., 'Seventy or Seventy-two Disciples?', *NTS* 5 (1958–59), pp. 299-306.

—*A Textual Commentary on the Greek New Testament* (London: UBS, 1975).

Meyer, E., *Ursprung und Anfänge des Christentums* (3 vols.; Stuttgart: Cotta'sche, 1924).

Meyer, M.W., *The Letter of Peter to Philip: Text, Translation, and Commentary* (SBLDS, 53; Chico, CA: Scholars Press, 1981).

Meyer, M.W., and F. Wisse, 'The Letter of Peter to Philip (VIII,2)', in *The Nag Hammadi Library in English* (ed. J.M. Robinson; San Francisco: Harper & Row, 3rd edn, 1988), pp. 431-37.

Minear, P.S., *To Heal and to Reveal: The Prophetic Vocation according to Luke* (New York: Seabury, 1976).

—'Luke's Use of the Birth Stories', in *Studies in Luke–Acts: Essays Presented in Honor of Paul Schubert* (ed. L.E. Keck and J.L. Martyn; Nashville: Abingdon Press, 1966), pp. 111-30.

—'A Note on Luke 17:7-10', *JBL* 93 (1974), pp. 82-87.

Mínguez, D., 'Hechos 8.25-40: Análisis estructural del relato', *Bib* 57 (1976), pp. 168-91.

Miyoshi, M., *Der Anfang des Reiseberichts Lk 9.51–10.24: Eine redaktionsgeschichtliche Untersuchung* (AnBib, 60; Rome: Biblical Institute, 1974).

Moessner, D.P., ' "The Christ Must Suffer": New Light on the Jesus–Peter, Stephen, Paul Parallels in Luke–Acts', *NovT* 28 (1986), pp. 220-56.

—'The Ironic Fulfillment of Israel's Glory', in *Luke–Acts and the Jewish People: Eight Critical Perspectives* (ed. J.B. Tyson; Minneapolis, MN: Augsburg, 1988), pp. 35-50.

—'Jesus and the "Wilderness Generation": The Death of the Prophet like Moses according to Luke', in *SBLSP* (ed. K.H. Richards; Chico, CA: Scholars Press, 1982), pp. 319-40.

—*Lord of the Banquet: The Literary and Theological Significance of the Lukan Travel Narrative* (Minneapolis, MN: Fortress Press, 1989).

—'Luke 9:1-50: Luke's Preview of the Journey of the Prophet like Moses of Deuteronomy', *JBL* 102 (1983), pp. 575-605.

—'Paul and the Pattern of the Prophet like Moses in Acts', in *SBLSP* (ed. K.H. Richards; Chico, CA: Scholars Press, 1983), pp. 203-12.

Montgomery, J.A., *The Samaritans: The Earliest Jewish Sect: Their History, Theology and Literature* (New York: Ktav, 1968).

Moore, S.D., *Literary Criticism and the Gospels: The Theoretical Challenge* (New Haven: Yale University Press, 1989).

Morgenthaler, R., and C. Brown, 'Generation', *NIDNTT*, II, pp. 35-39.

Moule, C.F.D., 'The Christology of Acts', in *Studies in Luke–Acts: Essays Presented in Honor of Paul Schubert* (ed. L.E. Keck and J.L. Martyn; Nashville: Abingdon Press, 1966), pp. 159-85.

—'Once More, Who Were the Hellenists?', *ExpTim* 70 (1958–59), pp. 100-102.

—'The Vocabulary of Miracle', in *Miracles: Cambridge Studies in their Philosophy and History* (ed. C.F.D. Moule; London: Mowbray, 1965), pp. 235-38.

Moulton, J.H., *A Grammar of New Testament Greek*. I. *Prolegomena* (Edinburgh: T. & T. Clark, 3rd edn, 1908).

Moulton, J.H., and G. Milligan, *The Vocabulary of the Greek Testament* (London: Hodder & Stoughton, 1930).

Moxnes, H., *The Economy of the Kingdom: Social Conflicts and Economic Relations in Luke's Gospel* (OBT; Philadelphia: Fortress Press, 1988).

Muhlack, G., *Die Parallelen von Lukas-Evangelium und Apostelgeschichte* (Theologie und Wirklichkeit, 8; Frankfurt: Lang, 1979).

Munck, J., *The Acts of the Apostles* (rev. W.F. Albright and C.S. Mann; AB, 31; Garden City, NY: Doubleday, 1967).

Mussner, F., *Apostelgeschichte* (Neue Echter Bibel, 5; Würzburg: Echter Verlag, 1984).

Neil, W., *The Acts of the Apostles* (NCB; London: Oliphants, 1973).

Neirynck, F., 'The Miracle Stories in the Acts of the Apostles: An Introduction', in *Les Actes des Apôtres: Traditions, rédaction, théologie* (ed. J. Kremer; BETL, 48; Paris-Gembloux: Duculot; Louvain: Louvain University Press, 1979), pp. 169-213.

Neudorfer, H.-W., *Der Stephanuskreis in der Forschungsgeschichte seit F.C. Baur* (Giessen: Brunner, 1983).

New, S., 'The Name, Baptism, and the Laying on of Hands', in *The Beginnings of Christianity*. Part I. *The Acts of the Apostles*, V (ed. K. Lake and H.J. Cadbury; London: Macmillan, 1933), pp. 121-40.

Neyrey, J., *The Passion according to Luke: A Redaction Study of Luke's Soteriology* (New York: Paulist Press, 1985).

Nock, A.D., 'Paul and the Magus', in *The Beginnings of Christianity*. Part I. *The Acts of the Apostles*, V (ed. K. Lake and H.J. Cadbury; London: Macmillan, 1933), pp. 164-88.

Nolland, J., 'Proselytism or Politics in Horace *Satires* I,4,138-43?', *VC* 33 (1979), pp. 347-55.

Oliver, H.H., 'The Lucan Birth Stories and the Purpose of Luke–Acts', *NTS* 10 (1963–64), pp. 202-26.

O'Neill, J.C., *The Theology of Acts in its Historical Setting* (London: SPCK, 1961).

O'Reilly, L., *Word and Sign in the Acts of the Apostles: A Study in Lucan Theology* (Analecta Gregoriana, 243; Rome: Editrice Pontifica Università Gregoriana, 1987).

Origen, *Contra Celsum* (ed. and trans. H. Chadwick; Cambridge: Cambridge University Press, 1953).

O'Toole, R.F., 'Parallels between Jesus and his Disciples in Luke–Acts', *BZ* 27 (1983), pp. 195-212.

—'Parallels between Jesus and Moses', *BTB* 29 (1990), pp. 22-29.

—'Philip and the Ethiopian Eunuch (Acts VIII 25-40)', *JSNT* 17 (1983), pp. 23-34.

—*The Unity of Luke's Theology: An Analysis of Luke–Acts* (Good News Studies, 9; Wilmington, DE: Michael Glazier, 1984).

Oulton, J.E.L., 'The Holy Spirit, Baptism, and Laying on of Hands in Acts', *ExpTim* 66 (1954–55), pp. 236-40.

Overman, J.A., 'The God-Fearers: Some Neglected Factors', *JSNT* 32 (1988), pp. 17-26.

Owen, H.P., 'Stephen's Vision in Acts VII.55-56', *NTS* 1 (1955), pp. 224-26.

Paratt, J.K., 'The Rebaptism of the Ephesian Disciples', *ExpTim* 79 (1967–68), pp. 182-83.

Parsons, M.C., *The Departure of Jesus in Luke–Acts: The Ascension Narratives in Context* (JSNTSup, 21; Sheffield: JSOT Press, 1987).

Pauly, A.F., G. Wissowa *et al.* (eds.), 'Eunuchen', in *Real-Encyclopädie der klassischen Altertumswissenschaft*, sup. vol. III, cols. 449-55.

Pereira, F., *Ephesus: Climax of Universalism in Luke–Acts: A Redaction-Critical Study of Paul's Ephesian Ministry (Acts 18:23–20:1)* (Jesuit Theological Forum Studies, 1; Anand, India: Gujarat Sahitya Prakash, 1983).

Pervo, R.I., *Profit with Delight: The Literary Genre of the Acts of the Apostles* (Philadelphia: Fortress Press, 1987).

Pesch, R., *Die Apostelgeschichte* (2 vols.; EKKNT 5.1, 2; Zürich: Benziger, 1986).

—*Die Vision des Stephanus: Apg 7.55-56 im Rahmen der Apostelgeschichte* (SBS, 12; Stuttgart: Katholisches Bibelwerk, 1966).

Pesch, R., E. Gerhardt and F. Schilling, ' "Hellenisten" und "Hebräer": Zu Apg 9,29 und 6,1', *BZ* 23 (1979), pp. 87-92.

Petzke, G., 'εὐνοῦχος', *EWNT*, II, pp. 202-204.

Philo, *Works* (10 vols.; ed. and trans. F.H. Colson and G.H. Whitaker; LCL; Cambridge, MA: Harvard University Press; London: Heinemann, 1929–43).

Philostratus, *The Life of Apollonius of Tyana* (2 vols.; ed. and trans. F.C. Conybeare; LCL; Cambridge, MA: Harvard University Press; London: Heinemann, 1912).

Pietersma, A., and R.T. Lutz, 'Jannes and Jambres', in *The Old Testament Pseudepigrapha*, II (ed. J.H. Charlesworth; London: Darton, Longman & Todd, 1985), pp. 427-42.

Platz, H.H., 'Philip', *IDB*, III, pp. 784-85.

Plümacher, E., 'Acta-Forschung 1974–1982 (Fortsetzung und Schluss)', *TRu* 49 (1984), pp. 105-69.

—*Lukas als hellenistischer Schriftsteller: Studien zur Apostelgeschichte* (Göttingen: Vandenhoeck & Ruprecht, 1972).

—'Wirklichkeitserfahrung und Geschichtsschreibung bei Lukas: Erwägungen zu den Wir-Stücken der Apostelgeschichte', *ZNW* 69 (1977), pp. 2-22.

Plumptre, E.H., 'The Samaritan Element in the Gospels and Acts', *The Expositor* 7 (1878), pp. 22-40.

Porter, R.J., 'What Did Philip Say to the Eunuch?', *ExpTim* 100 (1988–89), pp. 54-55.

Potterie, I. de la, 'Les deux noms de Jérusalem dans les Actes de Apôtres', *Bib* 63 (1982), pp. 153-87.

Powell, M.A., *What Is Narrative Criticism?* (Minneapolis, MN: Fortress Press, 1990).

Preisker, H., 'Apollos und die Johannesjünger in Act 18.24–19.6', *ZNW* 30 (1931), pp. 301-304.

Pummer, R., 'Antisamaritanische Polemik in jüdischen Schriften aus der intertestament-arischen Zeit', *BZ* 26 (1982), pp. 224-42.

—'Genesis 34 in Jewish Writings of the Hellenistic and Roman Periods', *HTR* 75 (1982), pp. 177-88.

—'New Evidence for Samaritan Christianity?', *CBQ* 41 (1979), pp. 98-117.

—'The Present State of Samaritan Studies: I', *JSS* 21 (1976), pp. 39-61.

—'The Present State of Samaritan Studies: II', *JSS* 22 (1977), pp. 27-47.

—'The Samaritan Pentateuch and the New Testament', *NTS* 22 (1975–76), pp. 441-43.

—*The Samaritans* (Iconography of Religions, 23.5; Leiden: Brill, 1987).

Purvis, J.D., 'The Fourth Gospel and the Samaritans', *NovT* 17 (1975), pp. 161-98.

—*The Samaritan Pentateuch and the Origin of the Samaritan Sect* (HSM, 2; Cambridge, MA: Harvard University Press, 1968).

—'Samaritan Pentateuch', *IDBSup*, pp. 772-75.

—'The Samaritan Problem: A Case Study in Jewish Sectarianism in the Roman Era', in *Traditions in Transformation: Turning Points in Biblical Faith* (ed. B. Halpern and J.D. Levinson; Winona Lake, IN: Eisenbrauns, 1981), pp. 323-50.

—'The Samaritans and Judaism', in *Early Judaism and its Modern Interpreters* (ed. R.A. Kraft and G.W.E. Nickelsburg; Philadelphia: Fortress Press, 1986), pp. 81-98.

Quesnel, M., *Baptisés dans l'Esprit: Baptême et Esprit Saint dans les Actes des Apôtres* (LD, 120; Paris: Cerf, 1985).

Rackham, R.B., *The Acts of the Apostles* (London: Methuen, 1901).

Radl, W., *Paulus und Jesus im lukanischen Doppelwerk: Untersuchungen zu Parallelmotiven im Lukasevangelium und in der Apostelgeschichte* (Europäische Hochschulschriften, 23.49; Frankfurt: Lang, 1975).

Ramsay, W.M., *Luke the Physician and Other Studies in the History of Religion* (London: Hodder & Stoughton, 1908).

Reicke, B., 'Der barmherzige Samariter', in *Verborum Veritas: Festschrift für Gustav Stählin zum 70. Geburtstag* (ed. O. Böcher and K. Haacker; Wuppertal: Brockhaus, 1970), pp. 103-109.

—*Glaube und Leben der Urgemeinde: Bemerkungen zu Apg. 1-7* (ATANT, 32; Zürich: Zwingli, 1957).

—*The Roots of the Synoptic Gospels* (Philadelphia: Fortress Press, 1986).

—'Die Verkündigung des Täufers nach Lukas', in *Jesus in der Verkündigung der Kirche* (ed. A. Fuchs; Studien zum NT und seiner Umwelt A/1; Linz, 1976), pp. 50-61.

Remus, H., *Pagan-Christian Conflict over Miracle in the Second Century* (Patristic Monograph Series, 10; Cambridge, MA: Philadelphia Patristic Foundation, 1983).

Rengstorf, K., 'σημεῖον, σημαίνω, κτλ.', *TDNT*, VII, pp. 200-69.

Rese, M., *Alttestamentlich Motive in der Christologie des Lukas* (SNT, 1; Gütersloh: Gerd Mohn, 1969).

Reynolds, J., and R. Tannenbaum, *Jews and God-Fearers at Aphrodisias: Greek Inscriptions with Commentary* (Cambridge Philological Society, Sup. Vol. 12; Cambridge: Cambridge Philological Society, 1987).

Rhoads, D., and D. Michie, *Mark as Story: An Introduction to the Narrative of a Gospel* (Philadelphia: Fortress Press, 1982).

Richard, E., *Acts 6.1–8.4: The Author's Method of Composition* (SBLDS, 41; Missoula, MT: Scholars Press, 1978).

—'Acts 7: An Investigation of the Samaritan Evidence', *CBQ* 39 (1977), pp. 190-208.

—'Luke—Writer, Theologian, Historian: Research and Orientation of the 1970s', *BTB* 13 (1983), pp. 3-15.

—'The Polemical Character of the Joseph Episode in Acts 7', *JBL* 98 (1979), pp. 255-67.

Riddle, D.W., 'Early Christian Hospitality: A Factor in the Gospel Transmission', *JBL* 57 (1938), pp. 141-54.

Robbins, V.K., 'By Land and by Sea: The We-Passages and Ancient Sea Voyages', in *Perspectives on Luke–Acts* (ed. C.H. Talbert; Edinburgh: T. & T. Clark, 1978), pp. 215-42.

Robertson, A.T., *Luke the Historian in the Light of Research* (New York: Charles Scribner's Sons, 1920).

Robinson, B.P., 'The Place of the Emmaus Story in Luke–Acts', *NTS* 30 (1984), pp. 481-97.

Robinson, J.A.T., *Twelve New Testament Studies* (SBT, 34; London: SCM Press, 1962).

Rodd, C.S., 'Spirit or Finger', *ExpTim* 72 (1960–61), pp. 157-58.

Roloff, J., *Die Apostelgeschichte* (NTD, 5; Göttingen: Vandenhoeck & Ruprecht, 1981).

—*Apostolat-Verkündigung-Kirche: Ursprung, Inhalt und Funktion des kirchlichen Apostelamtes nach Paulus, Lukas und den Pastoralbriefen* (Gütersloh: Gerd Mohn, 1965).

—*Das Kerygma und der irdische Jesus: Historische Motive in den Jesus-Erzählungen der Evangelien* (Göttingen: Vandenhoeck & Ruprecht, 1970).

—'Die Paulus-Darstellung des Lukas: Ihre geschichtlichen Voraussetzungen und ihr theologisches Ziel', *EvT* 39 (1979), pp. 310-31.

Ross, J.M., 'The Rejected Words in Luke 9.54-56', *ExpTim* 84 (1972–73), pp. 85-88.

Rudolph, K., 'Simon—Magus oder Gnosticus? Zur Stand der Debatte', *TRu* 42 (1977), pp. 279-359.

Russell, E.A., ' "They Believed Philip Preaching" (Acts 8.12)', *IBS* 1 (1979), pp. 169-76.

Safrai, S., 'Pilgrimage to Jerusalem at the End of the Second Temple Period', in *Studies on the Jewish Background of the New Testament* (ed. O. Michel *et al.*; Assen: Van Gorcum, 1969), pp. 12-21.

—'Relations between the Diaspora and the Land of Israel', in *The Jewish People in the First Century*, I (ed. S. Safrai and M. Stern; Assen: Van Gorcum, 1974), pp. 184-215.

—*Die Wallfahrt im Zeitalter des Zweiten Tempels* (Forschungen zum jüdisch-christlichen Dialog, 3; Neukirchen–Vluyn: Neukirchener Verlag, 1981).

Saldarini, A.J., *Pharisees, Scribes and Sadducees in Palestinian Society: A Sociological Approach* (Wilmington, DE: Michael Glazier, 1988).

Sanders, E.P., *Jesus and Judaism* (London: SCM Press, 1985).

Sanders, J.A., 'The Ethic of Election in Luke's Great Banquet Parable', in *Essays in Old Testament Ethics (J. Philip Hyatt, In Memoriam)* (ed. J.L. Crenshaw and J.T. Willis; New York: Ktav, 1974), pp. 245-71.

—'From Isaiah 61 to Luke 4', in *Christianity, Judaism and Other Greco-Roman Cults: Studies for Morton Smith at Sixty*. Part 1. *New Testament* (ed. J. Neusner; SJLA, 12; Leiden: Brill, 1975), pp. 75-106.

—'Isaiah in Luke', *Int* 36 (1982), pp. 144-55.

Sanders, J.T., *The Jews in Luke–Acts* (London: SCM Press, 1987).

Scharlemann, M.H., *Stephen: A Singular Saint* (AnBib, 34; Rome: Pontifical Biblical Institute, 1968).

Schiffman, L., 'The Samaritans in Tannaitic Halakhah', *JQR* 75 (1985), pp. 323-50.

Schille, G., *Die Apostelgeschichte des Lukas* (THKNT, 5; Berlin: Evangelische, 1983).

Schlier, H., *Der Brief an die Epheser: Ein Kommentar* (Düsseldorf: Patmos, 6th edn, 1968).

Schmidt, K.L., 'διασπορά', *TDNT*, II, pp. 98-104.

Schmiedel, P.W., 'Philip, the Apostle, and Philip, the Evangelist', in *Encyclopaedia Biblica*, III (ed. T.K. Cheyne and J.S. Black; London: A. & C. Black, 1902), cols. 3697-3701.

Schmithals, W., *Die Apostelgeschichte des Lukas* (Zürich: Theologischer, 1982).

—*The Office of Apostle in the Early Church* (Nashville: Abingdon Press, 1969).

—*Paul and James* (SBT, 46; London: SCM Press, 1965).

Schnackenburg, R., *Der Brief an die Epheser* (EKKNT, 10; Zürich: Benziger, 1982).

—*God's Rule and Kingdom* (Freiburg: Herder, 1963).

Schneider, G., *Die Apostelgeschichte* (2 vols.; HTKNT, 5.1, 2; Freiburg: Herder, 1980–82).

—'Stephanus, die Hellenisten und Samaria', in *Les Actes des Apôtres: Traditions, rédaction, theologie* (ed. J. Kremer; BETL, 48; Paris-Gembloux: Duculot; Louvain: Louvain University Press, 1979).

Schneider, J., 'εὐνοῦχος, εὐνουχίζω', *TDNT*, II, pp. 765-68.

Schoedel, W.R., and B.J. Malina, 'Miracle or Magic?', *RelSRev* 12 (1986), pp. 31-39.

Schubert, P., 'The Structure and Significance of Luke 24', in *Neutestamentliche Studien für Rudolf Bultmann* (ed. W. Eltester; Berlin: Töpelmann, 1957), pp. 165-86.

Schürmann, H., *Das Lukasevangelium: Kommentar zu Kap. 1.1–9.50* (HTKNT, 3.1; Freiburg: Herder, 1969).

Schürer, E., *The History of the Jewish People in the Age of Jesus Christ (175 BC–AD. 135)* (3 vols.; rev. and ed. G. Vermes, F. Millar and M. Black; Edinburgh: T. & T. Clark, 1973–87).

Schwartz, D.R., 'The End of the ΓΗ (Acts 1:8): Beginning or End of the Christian Vision?', *JBL* 105 (1986), pp. 669-76.

Schweizer, E., 'Die Bekehrung des Apollos, Apg 18.24-26', in *Beiträge zur Theologie des Neuen Testaments: Neutestamentliche Aufsätze (1955–70)* (Zürich: Zwingli, 1970), pp. 71-79.

—*Church Order in the New Testament* (SBT, 32; London: SCM Press, 1961).

—'πνεῦμα, πνευματικός', *TDNT*, VI, pp. 332-451.

Scobie, C.H.H., *John the Baptist* (London: SCM Press, 1964).

—'The Origins and Development of Samaritan Christianity', *NTS* 19 (1972–73), pp. 390-414.

—'The Use of Material in the Speeches of Acts III and VII', *NTS* 25 (1978–79), pp. 399-421.

Scroggs, R., 'The Earliest Hellenistic Christianity', in *Religions in Antiquity: Essays in Memory of Erwin Ramsdell Goodenough* (ed. J. Neusner; Leiden: Brill, 1968), pp. 176-206.

Seccombe, D., 'Luke and Isaiah', *NTS* 27 (1980–81), pp. 252-59.

Sellin, G., 'Komposition, Quellen und Funktion des lukanischen Reiseberichts (Lk. ix 51–xix 28)', *NovT* 20 (1978), pp. 100-35.

Senior, D., and C. Stuhlmueller, *The Biblical Foundations for Mission* (London: SCM Press, 1983).

Sevenster, J.N., *Do You Know Greek? How Much Greek Could the First Jewish Christians Have Known?* (NovTSup, 19; Leiden: Brill, 1968).

Siegert, F., 'Gottesfürchtige und Sympathisanten', *JSJ* 4 (1973), pp. 109-64.

Simon, M., *St Stephen and the Hellenists in the Primitive Church* (Haskell Lectures, Oberlin College, 1952; London: Longmans, Green, 1958).

Skehan, P.W., 'Exodus in the Samaritan Recension from Qumran', *JBL* 74 (1955), pp. 182-87.

Sloan, R.B., Jr, *The Favorable Year of the Lord: A Study of Jubilary Theology in the Gospel of Luke* (Austin, TX: Schola, 1977).

Smalley, S.S., 'The Christology of Acts', *ExpTim* 73 (1961–62), pp. 358-62.

—'The Christology of Acts Again', in *Christ and Spirit in the New Testament: In Honour of Charles Francis Digby Moule* (ed. B. Lindars and S.S. Smalley; Cambridge: Cambridge University Press, 1973), pp. 79-93.

—'Spirit, Kingdom and Prayer in Luke–Acts', *NovT* 15 (1973), pp. 59-71.

Smith, D.E., 'Table Fellowship as a Literary Motif in the Gospel of Luke', *JBL* 106 (1987), pp. 613-38.

Smith, M., 'The Account of Simon Magus in Acts 8', in *H.A. Wolfson Jubilee Volume* (Jerusalem: American Academy for Jewish Research, 1965), pp. 735-49.

Smith, T.V., *Petrine Controversies in Early Christianity: Attitudes towards Peter in Christian Writings of the First Two Centuries* (WUNT, 15; Tübingen: Mohr [Paul Siebeck], 1985).

Snowden, F.M., Jr, *Before Color Prejudice: The Ancient View of Blacks* (Cambridge, MA: Harvard University Press, 1983).

—'Blacks, Early Christianity and', *IDBSup*, pp. 111-14.

—*Blacks in Antiquity: Ethiopians in the Greco-Roman Experience* (Cambridge, MA: Harvard University Press, 1970).

—'Ethiopians and the Graeco-Roman World', in *The African Diaspora* (ed. M.L. Kilson and R.I. Rotberg; Cambridge, MA: Harvard University Press, 1976).

Spencer, F.S., '2 Chronicles 28:5-15 and the Parable of the Good Samaritan', *WTJ* 46 (1984), pp. 317-49.

—Review of *The Narrative Unity of Luke–Acts: A Literary Interpretation*. I. *The Gospel according to Luke*, by R.C. Tannehill, *WTJ* 50 (1988), pp. 352-55.

—Review of *Luke–Acts and the Jews: Conflict, Apology, and Conciliation*, by R.L. Brawley, *WTJ* 52 (1990), pp. 156-58.

Spiro, A., 'Stephen's Samaritan Background', in J. Munck, *The Acts of the Apostles* (rev. W.F. Albright and C.S. Mann; AB, 31; Garden City, NY: Doubleday, 1967), pp. 285-300.

Stagg, F., *The Book of Acts: The Early Struggle for an Unhindered Gospel* (Nashville: Broadman, 1955).

Stählin, G., 'ἀποκόπτω', *TDNT*, III, pp. 852-55.

—*Die Apostelgeschichte* (NTD, 5; Göttingen: Vandenhoeck & Ruprecht, 1966).

—'Das Bild der Witwe: Ein Beitrag zur Bildersprache der Bibel und zum Phänomen der Personifikation in der Antike', *JAC* 17 (1974), pp. 5-20.

—'ξένος, κτλ.', *TDNT*, V, pp. 1-36.

Stambaugh, J., and D. Balch, *The Social World of the First Christians* (London: SPCK, 1986).

Stanton, G.N., *The Gospels and Jesus* (Oxford: Oxford University Press, 1989).

—*Jesus of Nazareth in New Testament Preaching* (SNTSMS, 27; Cambridge: Cambridge University Press, 1974).

—'Samaritan Incarnational Christology?', in *Incarnation and Myth: The Debate Continued* (ed. M. Goulder; London: SCM Press, 1979), pp. 243-46.

—'Stephen in Lucan Perspective', in *Studia Biblica 1978*. III. *Papers on Paul and Other New Testament Authors* (JSNTSup, 3; Sheffield: JSOT Press, 1980), pp. 345-60.

Steck, O.H., *Israel und das gewaltsame Geschick der Propheten: Untersuchungen zur Überlieferung des deuteronomistischen Geschichtsbildes im Alten Testament, Spätjudentum und Urchristentum* (WMANT, 23; Neukirchen–Vluyn: Neukirchener Verlag, 1967).

Stemberger, G., 'Die Stephanusrede (Apg 7) und die jüdische Tradition', in *Jesus in der Verkündigung der Kirche* (ed. A. Fuchs; Studien zum NT und seiner Umwelt A/1; Linz, 1976), pp. 154-76.

Stern, M., *Greek and Latin Authors on Jews and Judaism* (3 vols.; Jerusalem: Israel Academy of Sciences and Humanities, 1976–84).

Strack, H.L., and P. Billerbeck, *Kommentar zum Neuen Testament aus Talmud und Midrasch*, II (Munich: Beck, 1924).

Strecker, G., 'εὐαγγελίζω', *EWNT*, II, pp. 173-76.

Strobel, A., 'Armenpfleger "um des Friedens willen" (Zum Verständnis von Act 6.1-6)', *ZNW* 63 (1972), pp. 271-76.

Stronstad, R., *The Charismatic Theology of St Luke* (Peabody, MA: Hendrickson, 1984).

Sylva, D.D., 'Ierousalēm and Hierosoluma in Luke–Acts', *ZNW* 74 (1983), pp. 207-21.

—'The Meaning and Function of Acts 7:46-50', *JBL* 106 (1987), pp. 261-75.

Taeger, J.-W., *Der Mensch und sein Heil: Studien zum Bild des Menschen und zur Sicht der Bekehrung bei Lukas* (SNT, 14; Gütersloh: Gutersloher/Gerd Mohn, 1982).

Talbert, C., *Acts* (Knox Preaching Guides; Atlanta: John Knox, 1984).

—*Literary Patterns, Theological Themes and the Genre of Luke–Acts* (SBLMS, 20; Missoula, MT: Scholars Press, 1974).

—*Luke and the Gnostics: An Examination of the Lucan Purpose* (Nashville: Abingdon Press, 1966).

—(ed.), *Luke–Acts: New Perspectives from the Society of Biblical Literature Seminar* (New York: Crossroad, 1984).

—(ed.), *Perspectives on Luke–Acts* (Edinburgh: T. & T. Clark, 1978).

—*Reading Luke: A Literary and Theological Commentary on the Third Gospel* (New York: Crossroad, 1984).

—Review of *The Gospel according to Luke (X–XXIV)*, by J.A. Fitzmyer, *CBQ* 48 (1986), pp. 336-38.

—'Shifting Sands: The Recent Study of the Gospel of Luke', *Int* 30 (1976), pp. 381-95.

Tannehill, R.C., 'Israel in Luke–Acts: A Tragic Story', *JBL* 104 (1985), pp. 69-85.

—'The Mission of Jesus according to Luke IV 16-30', in *Jesus in Nazareth* (ed. W. Eltester; BZNW, 40; Berlin: de Gruyter, 1972), pp. 51-75.

—*The Narrative Unity of Luke–Acts: A Literary Interpretation* (2 vols.; Philadelphia: Fortress Press, 1986–90).

Tatum, W.B., 'The Epoch of Israel: Luke I–II and the Theological Plan of Luke–Acts', *NTS* 13 (1966–67), pp. 184-95.

Teeple, H.M., *The Mosaic Eschatological Prophet* (SBLMS, 10; Philadelphia: SBL, 1957).

Theissen, G., *The Social Setting of Pauline Christianity: Essays on Corinth* (ed. and trans. J.H. Schütz; Philadelphia: Fortress Press, 1982).

—*Sociology of Early Palestinian Christianity* (Philadelphia: Fortress Press, 1978).

—'Wanderradikalismus: Literatursoziologische Aspekte der Überlieferung von Worten Jesu im Urchristentum', in *Studien zur Soziologie des Urchristentums* (WUNT, 19; Tübingen: Mohr [Paul Siebeck], 1979), pp. 79-105.

Thomas, J., *Le mouvement baptiste en Palestine et Syrie (150 AV. J.C.–300 AD. J.-C.)* (Gembloux: Duculot, 1935).

Thornton, T.C.G., 'To the End of the Earth: Acts 1.8', *ExpTim* (1977–78), pp. 374-75.

Tiede, D.L., *Luke* (Augsburg Commentary on the NT; Minneapolis, MN: Augsburg, 1988).

—*Prophecy and History in Luke–Acts* (Philadelphia: Fortress Press, 1980).

Tov, E., 'Proto-Samaritan Texts and the Samaritan Pentateuch', in *The Samaritans* (ed. A.D. Crown; Tübingen: Mohr [Paul Siebeck], 1989), pp. 397-407.

Trebilco, P.R., 'Studies on Jewish Communities in Asia Minor' (unpublished PhD thesis, University of Durham, 1987).

Trocmé, E., *The Formation of the Gospel according to Mark* (London: SPCK, 1975).

—*Le 'Livre des Actes' et l'histoire* (Paris: Presses Universitaires de France, 1957).

Tuckett, C.M., *Reading the New Testament: Methods of Interpretation* (London: SPCK, 1987).

Turner, M.M.B., 'Jesus and the Spirit in Lucan Perspective', *TynBul* 32 (1981), pp. 3-42.

Tyson, J.B., 'Acts 6:1-7 and Dietary Regulations in Early Christianity', *PerRelSt* 10 (1983), pp. 145-61.

—*The Death of Jesus in Luke–Acts* (Columbia, SC: University of South Carolina Press, 1986).

—'The Gentile Mission and the Authority of Scripture in Acts', *NTS* 33 (1987), pp. 619-31.

Ullendorff, E., 'Candace (Acts VII.27) and the Queen of Sheba', *NTS* 2 (1955–56), pp. 53-56.

Unnik, W.C. van, 'Die Apostelgeschichte und die Häresien', in *Sparsa Collecta: The*

300   *The Portrait of Philip in Acts*

Collected Essays of W.C. van Unnik, Part 1 (NovTSup, 29; Leiden: Brill, 1973), pp. 402-409.

—'Der Befehl an Philippus', in *Sparsa Collecta: The Collected Essays of W.C. van Unnik*, Part 1 (NovTSup, 29; Leiden: Brill, 1973), pp. 328-29.

Vermes, G., *The Dead Sea Scrolls in English* (London: Penguin Books, 3rd edn, 1987).

Via, J., 'An Interpretation of Acts 7.35-37 from the Perspective of Major Themes in Luke–Acts', *PerRelSt* 6 (1979), pp. 190-207.

Völkel, M., 'Exegetische Erwägungen zum Verständnis des Begriffs ΚΑΘΕΞΗΣ im lukanischen Prolog', *NTS* 20 (1973–74), pp. 289-99.

—'Zur Deutung des "Reiches Gottes" bei Lukas', *ZNW* 65 (1974), pp. 57-70.

Waitz, H., 'Die Quelle der Philippusgeschichten in der Apostelgeschichte 8,5-40', *ZNW* 7 (1906), pp. 340-55.

Wall, R.W., ' "The Finger of God": Deuteronomy 9.10 and Luke 11.20', *NTS* 33 (1987), pp. 144-50.

—'Peter, "Son" of Jonah: The Conversion of Cornelius in the Context of Canon', *JSNT* 29 (1987), pp. 79-90.

Walter, N., 'Apostelgeschichte 6.1 und die Anfänge der Urgemeinde in Jerusalem', *NTS* 29 (1983), pp. 370-93.

Wanke, J., ' "... wie sie ihn beim Brotbrechen erkannten": Zur Auslegung der Emmauserzählung Lk 24,13-35', *BZ* 18 (1974), pp. 180-92.

Weiser, A., *Die Apostelgeschichte* (2 vols.; Ökumenischer Taschenbuchkommentar zum NT 5.1, 2; Gütersloh: Gerd Mohn, 1981–85).

Wengst, K., *Humility: Solidarity of the Humiliated* (Philadelphia: Fortress Press, 1988).

Wilcox, M., 'The "God-Fearers" in Acts—A Reconsideration', *JSNT* 13 (1981), pp. 102-22.

—*The Semitisms of Acts* (Oxford: Clarendon Press, 1965).

Wilkens, W., 'Wassertaufe und Geistempfang bei Lukas', *TZ* 23 (1967), pp. 26-47.

Williams, C.S.C., *A Commentary on the Acts of the Apostles* (BNTC; London: A. & C. Black, 1957).

Willimon, W.H., *Acts* (Interpretation; Atlanta: John Knox, 1988).

Wilson, R.McL., 'Simon and Gnostic Origins', in *Les Actes des Apôtres: Traditions, rédaction, théologie* (ed. J. Kremer; BETL, 48; Gembloux-Paris: Duculot; Louvain: Louvain University Press, 1979).

Wilson, S.G., *The Gentiles and the Gentile Mission in Luke–Acts* (SNTSMS, 23; Cambridge: Cambridge University Press, 1973).

—*Luke and the Law* (SNTSMS, 50; Cambridge: Cambridge University Press, 1983).

Wink, W., *John the Baptist in the Gospel Tradition* (SNTSMS, 7; Cambridge: Cambridge University Press, 1968).

Witherington, B., III, 'On the Road with Mary Magdalene, Joanna, Susanna, and Other Disciples—Luke 8.1-3', *ZNW* 79 (1979), pp. 243-48.

Wolter, M., 'Apollos und die ephesinischen Johannesjünger (Act 18.24–19.7)', *ZNW* 78 (1987), pp. 49-73.

Wright, G.E., 'The Samaritans at Shechem', *HTR* 55 (1962), pp. 357-66.

Yamauchi, E.M., *Pre-Christian Gnosticism: A Survey of the Proposed Evidences* (London: Tyndale, 1973).

Ziesler, J.A., 'Luke and the Pharisees', *NTS* 25 (1978–79), pp. 146-57.

—'The Name of Jesus in the Acts of the Apostles', *JSNT* 4 (1979), pp. 28-41.

INDEXES

INDEX OF REFERENCES

OLD TESTAMENT

PSEUDEPIGRAPHA AND EARLY CHRISTIAN WRITINGS